54

LONGLEY, C.

Chosen people: the big idea that shaped
England and America

70002344201   Hbk

Please return/renew this item by the last date shown

worcestershire
c o u n t y c o u n c i l
Cultural Services

Chosen People

Chosen People

the big idea that shaped England and America

Clifford Longley

Hodder & Stoughton
LONDON SYDNEY AUCKLAND

Typeset by Avon Dataset Ltd, Bidford-on-Avon, Warks

Printed and bound in Great Britain by
Clays Ltd, St Ives plc

Hodder & Stoughton Ltd
A Division of Hodder Headline Ltd
338 Euston Road
London NW1 3BH
www.madaboutbooks.com

Contents

Change – 'Morals without religion' – Princess Margaret and divorce – *Lady Chatterley* – *Honest to God* – anxieties of powers-that-be – end of social deference – role of social class

Foreword

We live in interesting times. This book was started before the World Trade Center attacks occurred in September 2001. Suddenly my quiet research into the nature of American identity and destiny seemed part of an acutely anxious conversation everyone was having. The British sense of involvement in American suffering, and its participation in the American 'war against terrorism', urgently highlighted Britain's general role *vis à vis* America, which is another key subject I was interested in.

My own sense of anguish was at first far too intense to allow me the necessary mental detachment to continue writing, not least because my wife comes from Manhattan and I know and love that great city. I had to stop for a while. What had been conceived as mainly a book about Anglo-American history had become a book about current affairs, indeed about what journalists were calling *the* news story of the decade and everyone else regarded as the single most dreadful catastrophe they had ever seen or heard of. Like millions of others, my wife and I had watched it as it happened, live on CNN.

What is America? Who are the English? My thesis is that the secret behind these mysteries lies in a view of themselves that the English, and later the Americans, had based on a powerful, transforming analogy between their own situation and that of the ancient Israelites. That is the origin of the term 'Chosen People'. It was not just that they had been specially selected by God. They had been specially selected with just the same purpose in mind for which God had selected (and then, pardon the phrase, deselected) the Jews. And that purpose was fundamental to the presence of the human race on this planet.

What continues to astonish me, once one starts to look with this perspective, is the extent to which these ideas drove forward a whole series of developments which were crucial to the direction of history:

the emergence of the nation-state and English isolation from Europe; the English Civil War that pitted Oliver Cromwell against Charles I; the overthrow of James II and the beguiling mythology of the Glorious Revolution; hatred of France and Spain; the early settlement of America; the separation of America from England in the Revolutionary War; the destruction of the native American 'Indians' by American expansion to the West; English profit from, and later opposition to, slavery; the American Civil War and the overthrow of slavery; the growth of the British Empire in India and Africa; the establishment in the Middle East of a 'homeland for the Jews'; Britain's involvement in the Crimean and then the First World War (and indeed the Second too); the American civil rights movement, political correctness, the collapse of apartheid – I could go on. If I did not extend my horizon to include Northern Ireland – the one place in the United Kingdom where ordinary people still believe in a type of 'Chosen People' theory – it is because I felt that to be part of a wider Scottish story, and my focus was England.

Northern Ireland aside, the book became almost the historical and theological equivalent of the scientific quest for a 'theory of everything'. It brings into the same arena Sir Isaac Newton and Martin Luther King, Field Marshal Douglas Haig and George Washington, George W. Bush and Thomas More, Adam and Eve and the European Union. The factual raw material for this theory is already well known, and some writers have brilliantly explored the parts they know best. But it is scattered among the specialists. Expertise has its drawbacks. Historians of the American Civil War do not know much about Henry VIII's breach with Rome; Calvinist theologians are not familiar with the East India Company's policy on the burning of widows; experts on the constitution of England or America do not know their way round Deuteronomy or Chronicles; researchers into anti-Semitism and the Holocaust see no connection between that and the American War of Independence. What ties all these things into the same bundle is the concept of a Chosen People. My only claim is that I know just enough about each of them to pull them together.

At first glance (at least to my modern eye) the concept sounds utterly outdated, or something confined to fundamentalist extremists. That is doubtless one reason why researchers have left it alone. Nor is it still fashionable to look in the direction of religion – Protestantism in particular – for explanations of anything. But this book inescapably concludes that the presence of this concept in England and America through the last few hundred years of their history proved absolutely decisive for the way that that history turned out, and the continued implicit presence – and sometimes no less significantly, absence – of that concept still reveals a great deal about the present state of these two extraordinary countries, including their motivations.

This book is not anti-religious, though it exposes the flaws in a certain version of Protestant Christianity – not so long ago, the only kind – that most modern Protestants would now regard as thoroughly obsolete. But it is not enough to say, 'Well, that was a mistake, let's forget about it' if the two nations still continue along the trajectory that was thus defined. If they want to know why they are the way they are, they have to look at their shared history. And they cannot do so through lenses that filter out the religion at the heart of it, just because 'people don't believe that any more'. So if this book helps us get in touch with our own past, in order to take better control of our own future, it will have served a purpose.

Clifford Longley
January 2002, England

1

Destiny Versus Identity

This book begins as it ends, with a series of questions about national identity, English and American. First, in historical order at least, come the English. Who are they? What is the point of Englishness? Is there too much of it about, or too little? Can a black person be English? Or is part of the definition racial? Can a Muslim be English? Or is part of the definition religious? To be English do you have to love England, or is it enough just to be born in England? Is part of the definition legal? Or is it a state of mind? And what has it to do with English history?

It is even more difficult asking similar questions about America. These are not the issues that most readily come to mind. The fact that there is no word 'Americanness' in regular use (the only example I have come across was self-consciously hyphenated: 'American-ness') should alert us immediately to the presence of basic differences. Few Americans would find the question 'What is the point of Americanness?' worth asking, nor 'Can a black person or Muslim be American?' For anyone to the left of outright racism, the answer has to be an automatic yes, no problem.

If we phrase the questions a little differently, however, substituting 'destiny' for 'identity', then we are at once faced with issues that Americans take very seriously and disagree about strongly. It is the English who start to have problems understanding the question. What is the destiny of England? What can that possibly mean? To be forever beaten by Australia at cricket? But destiny is what Americans debate endlessly: the true meaning or purpose of 'the American way', sometimes called Americanism, the American national creed or ideology. It is significant that I have never come across the equivalent words 'England-ism' or 'Englishism' (in the latter case, except with reference to the English language). Where a word is missing from the language, the chances are that that is because people feel they can make sense of their world without it. The opposite can also be true. When the world and their place in it start to make less sense, people may need to expand their language in order to expand the possibilities of thought. A little attention

1

to 'Americanness' and 'Englandism' might do wonders. This is a subject to which we shall return in the final chapter.

It is also striking that whereas there is seriously such a thing as an 'un-American activity' – for instance the allegedly pro-Communist behaviour investigated by the American Inquisition under Senator Joseph McCarthy in the early 1950s – it is hard to envisage what 'un-English' activity might consist of, and positively hilarious to think of a House of Commons committee solemnly investigating it. It is much more likely to lie in the area of bad manners than of bad politics, or some violation of the received rules of emotional self-control, the so-called 'English stiff upper-lip'. In this respect the description 'un-English' is not particularly negative. Agony aunts who think the English are in general too buttoned up and emotionally cool for their own good do not hesitate to urge them to be 'less English' in the expression of their feelings. A responsible American writer telling fellow Americans to be 'less American' is unthinkable.

It is potentially very useful for the English (whoever they are) to take America as a parallel but different society, and learn from the parallels and differences, and the causes thereof. It might even be useful to Americans to do this operation too – more useful, perhaps, than most Americans would at first realise. Some do. In his book *American Exceptionalism*, Seymour Lipset asserts, 'It is impossible to understand a country without seeing how it varies from others. Those who know only one country know no country.'[1] It is particularly necessary for his subject, of course, as the very term 'exceptional' implies some norm from which America has broken away. But our comparison of England and America may not serve his purpose, as there is, at least historically, also such as thing as 'English exceptionalism' even if it is not usually called that. Therefore England cannot provide the norm. And the two exceptionalisms are linked: exactly how, is the main subject of this book.

These two nations have common origins and, up to a point, a common history. The question how and why they became different might illuminate national character on both sides of the Atlantic. The exercise might give Americans even more reasons to be proud of their American distinctiveness. The English might learn useful questions to ask about their own destiny (other than on the cricket field!) and Americans about their identity. May an Englishman tentatively ask, for instance: is there really no problem about the identity of black Americans? From the outside, it would seem that there was. In the land of the free, what is it like to be forced to be an American, as the first slave forebears of black Americans were forced? Or to be descended from such an origin? Are there exceptions to American exceptionalism?

2

These issues were hardly different a hundred years ago. The celebrated black writer and political leader W. E. B. Du Bois said in 1903:

> It is a peculiar sensation, this double-consciousness, this sense of always looking at one's self through the eyes of others, of measuring one's soul by the tape of a world that looks on in amused contempt and pity. One ever feels his two-ness – an American, a Negro; two souls, two thoughts, two unreconciled strivings; two warring ideals in one dark body, whose dogged strength alone keeps it from being torn asunder.
>
> The history of the American Negro is the history of this strife – this longing to attain self-conscious manhood, to merge his double self into a better and truer self. He would not Africanize America, for America has too much to teach the world and Africa. He would not bleach his Negro blood in a flood of white Americanism, for he knows that Negro blood has a message for the world. He simply wishes to make it possible for a man to be both a Negro and an American . . .[2]

In both England and America women, too, have acquired a strong sense of having been excluded from the national identity-making processes of the past, to the extent that there are serious questions about whether they can own an identity they did not participate in forging. In England, furthermore, there are now several important communities whose background is not white Anglo-Saxon Protestant and who have not, despite living in England, come to regard themselves as fully English. The issue whether the very word 'English' refers to a race or a nation is unresolved, with some black people being prepared to use the word of themselves and some preferring the less specific term 'British'.

The 'white English' themselves, meanwhile, seem more willing in theory to accept the concept of 'black English' than they are in practice. Partly this is because of racism, but partly also the opposite – an honourable reluctance to press cultural integration into 'Englishness' harder or faster than black or Asian people would find acceptable. But Du Bois's sense of black alienation in America a hundred years ago is far from absent in England today. Sybil Phoenix, who was born in the British colony of Guyana and settled in England in 1956, is a Methodist who wrote of the painful ambiguities of black British identity in *Belonging to Britain*:

> It is fact that one is black and belongs to Britain. You belong – you know you belong. No one can take away that fact. You make your niche in it because you know you belong there. But it is not possible to be black and to feel that you belong to Britain. All the same, because of your humanness you go on working, praying and hoping that eventually there will be an acceptance.[3]

Yet there are white 'English' Catholics who would say that Sybil Phoenix already possesses the distinguishing mark of Englishness that, in the last four centuries, has really mattered – Protestantism – so she is already a candidate for Englishness, as historically defined, in a way they are not.

The English and the Americans (all races and colours) have much more in common than they have differences, though most of it is hidden below the surface. The stories they tell themselves about themselves are interlinked. Part of being American is in a sense 'not being English' but also 'once being English'. (That seems to apply even to those whose genetic ancestors were manifestly never English.) If nothing else, the English connection has a high heritage count. Part of being English is 'not being American', a bitter-sweet cocktail of snobbery, affection and envy. Even so, the English have more settled confidence about being English than the Americans have about being American. After all, the English tell themselves, it is we who once ruled an empire covering a quarter of the globe, and who thereby earned the right to wear the ultimate put-down laid-back top-dog T-shirt – 'Been There, Done That' – even if they can't be bothered to get it out of the laundry.

An American journalist living in Britain, Brenda Maddox, wrote in *The Guardian* shortly after the terrorist attacks on New York and Washington in 2001:

> One of the strongest lessons of my Massachusetts childhood was the purposefulness of the United States. All human history seemed to have been leading to the creation of God's Own Country, with liberty and justice for all ... It wasn't Fortress America; rather America the Beautiful, safe – protected by God and geography – 'from sea to shining sea'. When I came to live in Britain in the Kennedy era, I pontificated freely about the superiority of the American way. 'In my country ...' I began one day, when a well-spoken young man interrupted me to say, 'In my country we don't say "in my country".' The polite rebuke struck me with the force of revelation. There was an alternative to mindless patriotism. In a tolerant, mature, self-confident country it was not necessary to put your hand on your heart to say you loved it, or even to refer to it with possessive adjectives. Have you ever heard anyone say 'our Queen' or even 'our Prime Minister'?[4]

Tolerant, mature and self-confident is perhaps a little flattering a description for modern Britain, though the English habit of humorous and ironic self-deprecation, as long as it survives, is hardly a mark of insecurity. The English can only sing 'Land of Hope and Glory' with a blend of sentimentality and irony. Americans would regard the same approach to 'God Bless America' as impious and disloyal. Maybe for this reason the English can ask themselves more searching questions than Americans can. They have fewer sacred cows (and not just because of BSE or Foot and Mouth).

A geographical country is just an area on a map and the people in it. But a nation is an 'imagined community', an idea existing in the minds of its members. They inhabit and experience their country, which fertilises their imagination with memories of sights, sounds and smells. They absorb their identity through their individual senses as well as through their collective memories. To be English or American is to be a member of a particular society, a nation, a community of people with certain basic things in common (though what precisely those things are may be in dispute). If they are English or American, furthermore, then for nearly 500 years their relationship with their nation has dominated their religious imagination as well as all other kinds. That may be why these matters are so deeply felt. Being English or American belongs up there with 'God, the Universe and Everything'.

The concept of an 'imagined community' is one we owe to the American sociologist of government, Benedict Anderson. In his book indeed called *Imagined Communities* he argues that a nation exists in the imagination of its members because even in the smallest nation, no citizen can know all the other members of that nation, but nevertheless feels in communion with them:

> ... it is imagined as a community, because, regardless of the actual inequality and exploitation that may prevail in each, the nation is always conceived as a deep, horizontal comradeship. Ultimately it is this fraternity that makes it possible, over the past two centuries, for so many millions of people, not so much to kill, as willingly to die for such limited imaginings.[5]

Hence the citizen of such a nation shares an identity with other people he or she does not know but can imagine. He does not feel that communion with members of other nations who live beyond the finite boundaries of that nation (who are also not known but are also, to an extent, imaginable).

It is worth exploring more closely what that effort of the imagination entails. In the English case, the effort traditionally required is essentially an act of memory. The search for an answer to the question 'Who are we?' begins with asking, first, 'Who were we?' Unless we know who we were, the English would say to themselves, we do not know who we are. But in the American case, the effort of imagination is an act of will. The search for an answer to the question 'Who are we?' begins by asking 'Who do we want to be?'

Thus one answer takes us back in time, the other points forward. One is obviously the more dynamic, the other more passive. The future can be changed, the past cannot be (though how we remember it can). In the American case, the baseline is obviously the American Revolution and its immediate consequences for the American imagination. The Founding Fathers, in such documents as the Declaration of Independence, the Federalist Papers and the Constitution, as well as a vast deposit of lesser contemporary texts, were consciously asking themselves the question 'Who do we want to be?' The answer, breathtaking in its scope, was that they wanted to be 'God's Own Country': they wanted to be the perfect society. As Thomas Paine declared, 'We have it in our power to begin the world over again.'

They were 'imagining' America into existence by an act of will. And what they imagined was not a description of what existed then, not least because of the inherent injustice of slavery and of the Indian Question. What they imagined was an ideal, towards which America should grow. Pauline Maier, in *American Scripture*, describes the Declaration of Independence as 'a statement of values that more than any other expresses not why we separated from Britain, and not what we are or have been, but what we ought to be, an inscription of ideals that bind us as a people but have also been at the centre of some of the most divisive controversies in our history'.[6]

This is why the high principles professed by such men as George Washington and Thomas Jefferson, slave owners both, ought not to be dismissed as hypocritical or cynical but as their most sincere convictions. The American act of imagination was obviously not an act of memory, as no 'America' had existed – except as a disgruntled colony – before that time. In so far as the past came into that present and future, it was as a memory of an earlier act of will, that of the first New England settlers who had willed themselves to survive and endure.

But they had not defined themselves as who they had been before. They did not want to be who they had been before. Indeed, the New England Puritans did not want it so much that they had crossed the Atlantic in order to escape from it, in order to be something else. Prior to the rapid spread of the infection of revolutionary dreams from north to south in the mid-eighteenth century, the Virginian settlers had been among the most conservative. They had been much more interested in imagining their community into existence by the exercise of memory. They wanted to be like English gentry, and to do that they had to remember what the English gentry were. These two methods of imagining America were forcibly harmonised under the pressure of a British military invasion. But the tension remained, and the two tendencies collided again in the American Civil War when the act of will again triumphed over the act of memory. Nor can this be totally detached from the English Civil War of the previous century, when the right-wing Cavaliers pitted their act of memory – continuity, royalty, episcopacy, even fashion – against the left-wing Roundheads and their act of will, the building of a plain but perfect (Puritan, as in 'pure') society.

The explanations of these differences are not purely psychological or political, not confined to the here and now. They also reflect what people thought about their place in the world, and what their duty was to God and their neighbour. The contemporary English baseline is more difficult to discern. Perhaps for the modern generation of English people it still lives on in their collective memory of the period of the Second World War. Most acutely remembered of all is the year that 'England stood alone' – between the fall of France in June 1940 and the invasion of Russia in June 1941. Indeed, far from bringing comfort to the British, the initial success of the German army as it advanced towards Moscow only increased the British sense of vulnerable isolation. This was not really ended until the United States came into the war after having been attacked by the Japanese at the end of 1941.

So the sense of being the nation that had uniquely resisted and defied evil – personified in the Nazi machine – was a reference to a period of about eighteen months' duration. Strictly speaking, of course, Britain was not alone. The British Empire was also at war, whether it wanted to be or not – though by and large the evidence is that British-ruled areas of Asia regarded British colonial status as vastly preferable to Japanese hegemony. And the British Dominions – independent countries that had kept the Crown, like Australia, New Zealand, Canada and South Africa – were at war because they did want to be, out of ties of loyalty to the Mother Country. Notwithstanding this moral support – and only Canada was close enough to offer much practical help – for those eighteen months England was acutely conscious of the fact that all that separated it from the might of the German army was the twenty-one-mile moat of the English Channel. And thanks to the loss of tanks and artillery in the military debacle at Dunkirk, Britain had no effective field army with which to resist an invasion, had one occurred.

The English survived that experience not because of what they wanted to be, but because of their knowledge of who they had been. It was their history that gave them no alternative historical destiny than resistance, especially their history of resistance to European aggression. No historical fact was better known than that England had not been successfully invaded by a foreign army since 1066, as if the nearly 900 years that had elapsed provided a moat in the mental landscape even more formidable than the Straits of Dover. The second best known historical fact would have been the defeat of the Spanish Armada in 1588; the third, Nelson's victory over the French fleet (thereby avoiding the risk of a Napoleonic invasion) at Trafalgar in 1805. This was what stiffened the nation's sinews in 1940: it was about what England had been, and in the imagination of its citizens, still was. And it was enough. God had protected it because God wanted it to be again what it was before. But England was not fighting for a better world, unless that is understood simply to mean a world without Nazis. It was fighting to remain itself. Because of the resources of memory available to their imagination, the English were able to maintain their lonely defiance of the Nazis for more than a year in what was indeed an astonishingly brave episode in their long history.

The record of it is not especially to be found in any particular document, though Winston Churchill's wartime speeches are a marvellous collection of English patriotic rhetoric. One of his most famous passages will serve us as representative of the whole. This is how he concluded a speech to the House of Commons in mid-June 1940, launching, in the process, the immortal phrase 'The Battle of Britain':

> What General Weygand called the battle of France is over. I expect the Battle of Britain is about to begin. Upon this battle depends the survival of Christian civilisation. Upon it depends our own British life, and the long continuity of our institutions and our Empire. The whole fury and might of the enemy must soon be turned on us. Hitler knows that he will have to break us in this island or lose the war. If we can stand up to him, all Europe may be free and the life of the world may move forward into broad sunlit uplands. But if we fail, the whole world, including the United States, including all that we have known and cared for, will sink into the abyss of a new Dark Age made more sinister and perhaps more protracted by the lights of perverted science. Let us therefore brace ourselves to our duties, and so bear ourselves that, if the British Empire and its Commonwealth last for a thousand years, men will say: 'This was their finest hour'.[7]

This distinction, between America imagining itself into existence by believing in the future, England imagining itself into existence by remembering the past, has some overlap with the traditional division of political styles in both countries into two separate ideological camps, Whigs and Tories. Whigs believed in progress – that things were programmed to get better. For them, the best is yet to come. Tories believed in tradition. For them, the best is here now, or already past. There are Tories in America and Whigs in England, but these are the predominant styles: optimism versus nostalgia, restlessness versus inertia.

The English self-definition, the imagining of itself as a national community in Anderson's terminology, is to be found, *par excellence*, in the national celebration that occurred a few years after the end of the war, at the coronation of Queen Elizabeth II in 1953. It was definitive, frequently described in the newspapers as the start of a New Elizabethan Age (thus feasting off the glory of the earlier one). It was a renewal of an old imagination, not the imagining of something new. It was a less bold act of self-imagining than the American one, and at least superficially, it was much more an act of the religious imagination. That does not mean the American act of national imagining was unreligious, only that it did not take place in the course of a specifically Christian religious ceremony as the coronation did. In less obvious ways, the American act was more, not less, religious than the English one. At the heart of the American act of self-imagining was a willed belief in destiny, and however ill-defined, destiny demands faith. At the heart of the English act of self-imagining was continuity. Most of the time that demands nothing much more than stubborn inertia (though in 1940–41, it had also demanded supreme courage).

The significance of the 1953 coronation seen in this light is examined more fully in a later chapter. It will be sufficient for the moment to glance at a more contemporary equivalent, the swearing in and inaugural speech of President George W. Bush in January 2001. He used explicit religious references, yet it is notable that these passages of his speech caused no controversy. It is expected that American presidents should talk like that, whereas it would be inconceivable for a British prime minister to do so. In Britain, the right place for recognising the hand of God in the affairs of the nation would be a coronation service or something similar. Perhaps an American presidential inauguration has just a shade of a coronation about it. In his address, Mr Bush mused patriotically on America's place in the great scheme of things. He declared:

> Americans are generous and strong and decent, not because we believe in ourselves, but because we hold beliefs beyond ourselves. When this spirit of citizenship is missing, no government program can replace it. When this spirit is present, no wrong can stand against it.
>
> After the Declaration of Independence was signed, Virginia states-man John Page wrote to Thomas Jefferson: 'We know the race is not to the swift nor the battle to the strong. Do you not think an angel rides in the whirlwind and directs this storm?'
>
> Much time has passed since Jefferson arrived for his inauguration. The years and changes accumulate. But the themes of this day he would know: our nation's grand story of courage and its simple dream of dignity. We are not this story's author, who fills time and eternity with his purpose. Yet his purpose is achieved in our duty, and our duty is fulfilled in service to one another.

9

Never tiring, never yielding, never finishing, we renew that purpose today, to make our country more just and generous, to affirm the dignity of our lives and every life. This work continues. This story goes on. And an angel still rides in the whirlwind and directs this storm. God bless you all, and God bless America.

The argument of this book is that we are never going to reach the bottom of these issues of national identity and destiny until we delve into the religious dimension as well as the others, and give it its proper weight alongside them. We will find it has not been given its proper weight in the past – for a long time it was given too much, more recently (in reaction, no doubt), too little. But those who apply their modern minds to the past necessarily bring to bear a modern mindset, which it is the art of the historians to transcend. They do not always succeed.

Religion is a weightier ingredient in these national stories than most modern English people or Americans would expect it to be. It is also more unusual, more bizarre to modern tastes, and more dramatic in its effects. It is also intensely controversial, and the controversies are exceedingly interesting. This is no dry-as-dust excavation. This is a search for smoking guns. Those who like to throw blame around will have plenty of fun. The fact that modern readers no longer share the religious imagination of the sixteenth or eighteenth century does not mean those ideas are incomprehensible, just that they take a bit of getting used to. Indeed, we are likely to discover that we still share more of them than we might have expected.

In both the English and American case, the religious dimension has in the past answered questions about national identity and purpose that still have not been adequately answered in any other way. The English are actually ahead of the Americans in the search for alternative, non-religious, solutions, but it is not proving easy. They are still hung up on answers that they know do not serve them very well any more. Comparisons here are likely to be as helpful to Americans as to the English. For once, the English can show their American cousins a glimpse of their own possible future, and warn of mistakes to be avoided. The lesson may well be that once a nation like England or America stops believing in its destiny, the next problem it has to face is about its identity. Or that a nation which has a clear sense of destiny has no difficulty with its identity.

This division of emphasis – between English identity and American destiny – is reflected in the literature, especially historical writing. There has been a recent vogue in England for books asking 'Who are the English?' Two of the best, one from the liberal end of the intellectual spectrum and one from the conservative, were *The English*[8] by the television journalist Jeremy Paxman, and *England*[9] by the philosopher and newspaper journalist Roger Scruton. Paxman notices the poverty of English cultural rallying points, and remarks:

> No English person can look at the swearing of allegiance that takes place in American schools every day without feeling bewilderment: that sort of public declaration of patriotism seems, well, so naive. When an Irishman wears a shamrock on St Patrick's Day, the English look on with patronising indulgence: scarcely anyone sports a rose on St George's Day. This worldly wisdom soon elides into a general view that *any* public display of national pride is not merely unsophisticated but somehow morally reprehensible.[10]

He notes that George Orwell had stated even in 1948 that English intellectuals felt there was something slightly disgraceful about professing to being an Englishman, and they would no more stand for the national anthem than steal from a church poor box.

> No one stands for 'God Save the Queen' any more, and any cinema manager who tried to revive the custom of playing the national anthem would find the place empty before he'd reached the end of the first verse. At the time of Orwell's irritation, left wing disdain was cheap because the English didn't need to concern themselves with the symbols of their own identity: when you're top dog in the world's leading empire, you don't need to.

But Paxman neatly contradicts his own thesis. Americans, having replaced the English as top dog (if not imperially, at least militarily and politically), undoubtedly do still seem to need to concern themselves with the symbols of their identity, exactly as he has already drawn to our attention. What he fails to note is that the American concern with symbols – and the schoolchild's pledge of allegiance is surely that and more than that – is part of the continuous act of will by which Americans re-imagine America afresh every day. The English do not regularly re-imagine England, and therefore they have much less need of symbols to help them do so.

Paxman's condescension towards what he sees as American 'patriotic naivety' is akin to the popular English misunderstanding of the way Americans talk about themselves and their country. To an English ear, they seem immodest and boastful, and indifferent to the fact that the superiority they are claiming is likely to give offence to the legitimate national pride of other breeds. That is not the most favourable basis for warm friendships. But the American internal conversation about 'how good America is', tactless though it may seem when overheard by outsiders, is just another manifestation of America as an 'imagined community', imagining itself by an act of collective will. Americans are telling themselves again not so much who they are, but who they want to be. And they are teaching their children how to do that too. It almost suggests that, were they to stop imagining America into existence by a continuous act of will, America would cease to be.

This presence of an act of will at the core of American identity has important theological origins in Anglo-American Protestantism, as we shall see. For all its theoretical reliance on salvation by faith alone, in practice Protestantism did indeed demand an act of will, indeed an earnest and difficult one. Protestantism is not visible. It is an idea. To picture it demands an effort of the imagination, achieved by an act of will. In this it is clearly dissimilar to, say, Judaism or Roman Catholicism. They are tangible. To 'imagine' them requires only an uncomplicated act of memory, or just looking around. They are solid. Jews or Catholics do not have to will their religion into existence. Anglicanism stands somewhere between these two poles. Its act of memory requires a particular version of English history which is now widely held to be far from the whole truth. Its act of will is to bring into existence by a supreme effort of imagination a national church which stands in continuity with the ancient universal church of Christendom. This sense of striving, and with it a corresponding sense of insecurity – what if the striving is not enough? – is characteristically Protestant.

The English have no difficulty calling England itself into existence in their imagination by an act of memory, for the raw material for that act is all around them. (They are saved, perhaps, by the 'good work' of being English.) It has been estimated that not one single acre of the whole countryside of England is 'as nature originally intended it', for every tree in every wood and every hedge in every field is where it is and how it is, only through human intervention. Every detail of the English landscape, town and country, is the creation of past generations of Englishmen. England is a garden: there is no English wilderness. England is its own history. It follows that when England is uncomfortable with its memory, with its own history, it is uncomfortable with its identity. For the English, the act of 'imagining the nation' then becomes problematical.

Roger Scruton is the sort of intellectual who would not share Paxman's difficulty in standing up for the national anthem in his local cinema. He links English identity directly with monarchy. The English monarch, he writes in *England, an Elegy*,

> . . . is the light above politics, which shines down on the human bustle from a calmer and more exalted sphere. Not being elected by popular vote, the monarch cannot be understood as representing the interests

only of the present generation. He or she is born into the position, and also passes it on to a legally defined successor. The monarch is in a real sense the voice of history, and the very accidental way in which the office is acquired emphasises the grounds of the monarch's legitimacy, in the history of a place and culture . . .[11]

But the England he is writing about is passing away, and his book is an attempt at an epitaph, written in grief. In the official map of Europe issued by the European Commission in Brussels, claims Scruton, England is shown as a space but is not given its name.

Clearly the crisis of Englishness is highly relevant to various current political developments. One factor is external. How much closer should Great Britain get to the rest of the European Union? Should we share a currency with them? What are the objections to a European superstate? The question is asked in terms of Great Britain rather than England (a fact which Scruton's EU map unconsciously points to) because that is the modern political unit that might or might not move closer to or further away from the EU. But most of the debate about 'relations with Europe', between Euro-phile and Euro-phobe, is peculiar to England. It is rare to find a Welshman or Scot complaining that 'Europe' threatens his national identity. Indeed, if being 'closer to Europe' means being slightly less dominated by England, then Scots or Welsh nationalists actively welcome it.

And this growth of national consciousness in the other two 'nations' living on the island of Great Britain has caused the English to wonder if they ought to be developing a national consciousness themselves. Paxman addresses that positively; for Scruton, on the other hand, it is too late. A preoccupation with English identity has seemed to belong with a particular form of nationalism that was characteristic of the far right, mainly because it appeals to their racism and xenophobia; or it is of marketable value as a selling point in the eyes of the English Tourist Board, in which case it largely means red buses, thatched cottages and cream teas. Though his description of decline is probably correct, all Scruton has to offer is nostalgia and a romance of royalty.

American writing is much more concerned with the phenomenon of 'American exceptionalism', themes to do with Manifest Destiny and the origins of America in colonial settlement, revolution, and civil war. Commentators endlessly speculate about the fact that the end of the Cold War has left 'America the only super-state'. It was a concern that seemed to be made more bearable by a certain complacent satisfaction at America's good fortune, at least until the formula 'super-state equals super-target' emerged from the terrorist attacks of September 2001. What is America to do with its unique opportunities? Simply re-organise the world in its own interests, and when the world protests (perhaps violently), kick it about (even more violently)? Or is there a moral meaning to America's mission? Is it to be, say, a 'light unto the Gentiles'? There is no doubt that that still makes a strong appeal to the moralistic streak in the American national character: that it is morally good to be American, and the way to make others morally good is to make them resemble Americans too.

Which brings us back to the Puritans. It is obvious that an interest in American history cannot leave out religious history. Where all the writers seem to agree is that without religion there would have been no America to write about, and certainly no Americanism, no national creed, no Manifest Destiny, no exceptionalism. It is not surprising that there is a contemporary feel to most American writing about American religion. Even when the writer is concerned with the past, he or she is hardly less addressing the present and future. And that is not just because religion remains deeply rooted in the American way of life. In fact most of this writing is done by, and for the benefit of, the American academic community. It is a discourse within the intelligentsia. And in America (as in England) that is one of the most secular mental environments, where religion is least deeply rooted. But academics are still interested in it, if not so much how it is now, then how it was once.

But this is less of an English preoccupation. If investigating the state of the American soul 200 years ago is thought to illuminate the state of the American soul now – not just through similarities but also differences – this approach is not valued so highly in the intellectual life of the English. Scruton is unusual in stating:

> Without this religious dimension nations and countries do not emerge as clearly defined moral entities. Of course, there can be states without religion – the modern world is full of them . . . No student of English history can fail to see that religion was from the very first mingled with the sense of English history, and that the history of English religion and the history of England are in many epochs inseparable.[12]

But it is not a popular view. One of the reasons is that these arguments have in the past more often been produced not, as in this case, as objective descriptions of a cultural reality, but as a form of moralistic nagging by those with a vested interest in seeing the nation return to church-going. If one is told one cannot be patriotic without being religious, then one can either be both patriotic and religious or neither patriotic nor religious. The English, presented with the choice, have inclined towards the latter, even though those who presented the choice wanted them to choose the former.

Sometimes it seems as if there is almost a conspiracy to pretend the English never believed anything different from what they believe now, which tends, in any formal doctrinal or organisational sense, to be very little. But there are exceptions. The religious climate before and during the English Civil War still attracts good scholarship. And an outbreak of Reformation historical revisionism has compelled the rethinking – towards a less triumphalist version of the national story – of certain aspects of the received tradition of English sixteenth-century history. This has allowed discussions in books, magazines, newspapers and television of such once-taboo subjects as whether Shakespeare (voted 'Englishman of the Millennium' in an opinion poll) was or was not a Roman Catholic, with those who say he was being awarded the verdict on points, at least at this stage of the argument.

But while biographies of exotic or unusual historical individuals have continued to sell well, it is not fashionable for the authors to dwell on their religious thoughts and feelings. Indeed, there has grown up a general cultural bias in England of treating religious affiliations, past or present, as either too private or too marginal a consideration to be worth much attention. One example of this phenomenon is the novelist George Eliot (Mary Ann Evans). In his *Theology in the Fiction of George Eliot*, Peter C. Hodgson writes:

> The conventional wisdom about George Eliot is that, after her exposure to higher criticism and German theology, she abandoned the fervent evangelical faith of her youth and became a disciple of the 'religion of humanity'. Thereafter, it is thought, she lost interest in religion and turned to the exploration of other subjects in her novels ... Recent critical studies of George Eliot virtually ignore her engagement with religious issues or find various deconstructive devices to explain it away.[13]

On the contrary, as he demonstrates, she had an endless fascination with and deep sympathy for religious ideas, implicit in her novels and explicit in many of her letters. It may not be irrelevant that Hodgson is an American, a theology professor at Vanderbilt University in Nashville, Tennessee, and most of the studies he is referring to are from English sources. On the whole, English professors of English do not knock around much in the company of English professors of theology.

When Roy Hattersley, former deputy leader of the Labour party and now a Labour peer and newspaper columnist, drew attention in 2001 to the presence of Roman Catholics in the leadership positions in British politics, there was some surprise that he thought it worth mentioning.[14] He had pointed out that it was quite possible that by the time of the next

British general election, all three major political parties in Britain might be headed by Roman Catholics. That would have been unthinkable fifty years ago. Charles Kennedy, leader of the Liberal Democrats, was already one, as was Iain Duncan Smith, at that time standing for the leadership of the Tories (which he went on to win). And Tony Blair was well known to have a Catholic wife and four Catholic children, with whom he went regularly to Sunday Mass. He had also been seen several times in Westminster Cathedral on his own, leading to speculation that he might convert. He used regularly to accompany his wife to the altar for Holy Communion, until this practice – against Catholic rules, but not uncommon among Anglicans married to Catholics – was stopped at the request of Cardinal Basil Hume. Hattersley made it clear he was not himself a Catholic, but he did not disclose the curious twist that his father had been a well-known Catholic priest in Sheffield before the Second World War, and left the ministry to marry Hattersley's mother.

So little stir did his article cause that his fellow *Guardian* columnist Michael White also claimed to be the first to notice the same thing, three months later. He wrote, 'Less than a generation ago, having 2.5 Catholics at the head of our three great parties would have been unthinkable, such was the grip, still powerful but less often spoken, of Britain's Protestant heritage upon all the higher nooks and crannies of the establishment.'[15]

Once again there was no appetite in the press for stirring up religious controversy, which some may take as a sign of the public's maturity, others of apathy and ignorance. And this disinclination to notice the presence of religion in public life even when it is obvious was similarly displayed during Margaret Thatcher's time as Prime Minister. At one point she had six practising Jews in her Cabinet (a quarter of the whole). It was virtually unmentionable, even though it was not difficult to notice a certain affinity between the policies she was pursuing and the pro-business ethic of the British Jewish community. According to Graham Turner, writing in the *Daily Telegraph*,[16] the Queen once asked Robert Runcie, then Archbishop of Canterbury, whether he regarded Mrs Thatcher as a religious woman, to which he is alleged to have replied: 'I think she is more of a Hebrew than a Christian.'

But she was a strange exception. Not only does the modern mind not believe, but it is very hard for the modern mind to imagine anyone else believing. So whenever a historical individual says his motives for doing something are religious, many modern historians and journalists will look for every conceivable alternative explanation – power, fame, money, fear, emotional disturbance, even lunacy – rather than take him at his word. An typical example of this would be the 1999 standard edition *Encyclopaedia Britannica* entry on witchcraft. Nowhere does it address the possibility that people might have believed in witches because their religious belief system told them witches existed. Witchcraft is condemned in the Old Testament, by the medieval church, and by Protestant reformers in the sixteenth century. If this is not in itself an adequate explanation of a widespread belief in witches, further exploration might have been useful into the history of religious ideas, to see why public concern about the dangers of witchcraft seemed to rise in Europe when it did, just before the Reformation. But the *Encyclopaedia Britannica* takes a purely anthropological line:

> Beliefs in witchcraft in the generic sense are conspicuous in most small-scale communities (e.g. in preliterate cultures), where interaction is based upon personal relationships that tend to be lifelong and difficult to break. In such societies belief in witches makes it possible for misfortunes to be explained in terms of disturbed social relationships; and the threat either of being accused of witchcraft or of being attacked by witches may well be a source of social control, making people more circumspect about their conduct toward others . . . Beliefs in witchcraft provide the mystical medium in which deep-lying structural conflicts, especially those not susceptible to rational adjustment by social intervention and arbitration, may be expressed and in some measure discharged. The inherent disharmonies in the social system are thus cloaked under an insistence that there is harmony in the values of the society, and the surface disturbances that they cause are attributed to the wickedness of individuals.[17]

In other words it cannot be the case that people believe in witches simply because their religious beliefs tell them witches exist. Or in reverse, even if their religious beliefs told them witches existed, they would automatically know such beliefs were not true unless there were in place the necessary 'inherent disharmonies in the social system' such as 'personal relationships which are difficult to break'. How so?

American reticence about emphasising the influence of religion has additional origins. If one detects in the standard academic approach a desire to be restrained, it comes largely from a refusal to hand over ownership of America's past to doctrinaire and fundamentalist religious movements, who are only too keen to capture it. The unspoken fear seems to be that to concede too readily that George Washington or Thomas Jefferson, say, were religiously minded in their time might hand too much ammunition to those who are religiously minded today. They have their own agendas. They will gladly cry 'George Washington was one of us, therefore do what we say!' even though the secret of his religious mind was, in reality, no more than that he was a creature of his age. He was probably as religious as his peers, and as private about it. In his introduction to the Everyman edition of the *Book of Common Prayer* of the Church of England,[18] Diarmaid MacCulloch estimates that two thirds of those who signed the Declaration of Independence as well as two thirds of those who signed the American Constitution were Episcopalians (i.e. American Anglicans) 'whose devotional life had been formed by the 1662 Book of Common Prayer'. And, he might well have added, whose sense of the right use of the English language had also been so formed, alongside frequent recourse to the Authorised Version (which Americans call the King James Version) of the Bible.

Washington and Jefferson, along with James Madison, Benjamin Franklin and John Adams and various others, are usually described as Deists, and assumed on the basis of that to be religiously indifferent if not even actively hostile to religion, children of the Enlightenment and heirs of Voltaire.

The notion is deep-rooted that the America that emerged from the war with Britain and then the making of a new republic was secular. But as historians have gradually become more interested in sources than in theories, another view is slowly gaining ground. There was a lot of religion in America in the late eighteenth century. Culture and language were saturated by it. As J. C. D. Clark writes in *The Language of Liberty*, one of the most significant and influential books marking this change among historians:

Many studies of politics in Britain and America in the late eighteenth century have been premised on a view of the Enlightenment as a process of secularisation embracing as a necessary unity aristocratic scepticism, bourgeois materialism and proletarian emancipation from patriarchal social relations. Yet each of these component parts have been challenged separately, and finally the ensemble itself is progressively questioned... The elite's support for religion in the form of the established church was strong, and periodically reasserted in political crises from the Restoration through the Revolution of 1688 to the French Revolutionary challenge of the 1790s and beyond. The middle ranks of society markedly failed to develop a group consciousness, whether as a commercial bourgeois or a middle class, and their attachment to church or Dissent was even more evident than that of the elite. Finally, if rates of church attendance did decline among the populace after 1689, it is now clear that this cannot easily or simply be interpreted as emancipation into a new social order. Patriarchal forms were undoubtedly modified, but the structures of authority and order still engaged with a mental world very different from that of nineteenth-century utilitarianism. The writing conventionally assigned to the Enlightenment in England, far from being secular, was suffused with theological and ecclesiastical argument, and heterodoxy was not a high road to secularisation . . .[19]

In some circles upholding 'the Deism of the Founding Fathers' has simply become a synonym for 'Keep your right-wing Republican hands off the First Amendment.' It is assumed, not without evidence, that part of the hidden agenda of new-right Republicanism is to bring about the redesignation of America as a 'Christian society', contrary to the separation of church and state the amendment promised, through such devices as tax funding for church welfare groups and by allowing prayers in public-sector schools. Even more reactionary hidden agendas, for instance to do with making life uncomfortable for homosexuals, are assumed to lurk in the background. To recruit the Founding Fathers as being in favour of religion, or even more so of holding a religious view of American identity, is regarded as a most effective way of tipping the argument in favour of this notion of 'Christian America'. And it needs to be noted that the term 'Christian' in this context has been hijacked by fundamentalists to refer only to themselves.

Not that all scepticism about the religiosity of the Founding Fathers has come from the anti-religious camp. The Jesuit Joseph Koterski of Fordham University, writing about Jefferson's beliefs in the American Catholic magazine *Crisis*, warned his readers:

> It is also well to remember that Jefferson and many of his colleagues, including Benjamin Franklin, George Washington, and Thomas Paine, were all Deists, not Christians.
>
> The God of Deism is a First Cause who has created the world and instituted its immutable and universal laws. But the Deist insistence on conceiving of this God as an absentee landlord intentionally precludes any hint of divine immanence or divine intervention into history. Many of the Enlightenment philosophers who took Deism to heart were quite critical even of the possibility of divine revelation, let alone of Christianity's claims about the necessity of such revelation.
>
> While the open atheism of strict Deism as championed by Voltaire made little headway in America, a softer theistic form of Deism tended to thrive on this soil. In the course of time this theistic Deism took firm root among the American intelligentsia of the colonial period, who regarded secularised Christianity as the natural religion to which any intelligent person would subscribe. Like Jefferson's famous cut-and-paste Bible, this sort of Deism rejected the supernatural elements of Christianity but kept an important place for Christian morality and always presented a sincerely religious tone . . .[20]

The rejection of the 'supernatural elements of religion', without which, to someone of Koterski's mind, religion was not really religion at all, was what Jefferson and his ilk would have regarded as rejection of the superstitious elements of religion. That in fact means the rejection of miracles, as in Jefferson's carefully edited unmiraculous version of the New Testament. What Koterski does not notice is that the God of Jefferson's universe was just as much an interventionist as a miracle-performing God would have been, but whose interventions were through the invisible hand of Providence. Indeed, Providence being everywhere while miracles by definition are rarities, such a God is even more of an interventionist.

Nor does rejection of miracles preclude a different sort of supernaturalism. For this debate draws attention to a unique feature of American political culture: the sacralisation of the American Constitution and Declaration of Independence, and the deification in historical memory of the men responsible for them. They have become what in religious terms would be called shrines, sacraments and saints; their images are icons. The founders may have been life-sized when they were alive, but in the American imagination they have grown to the dimensions of Mount Rushmore's famous statues. The original copies of the documents themselves are guarded in a solemn national shrine in Washington, for all the world as if they were the Tablets from Mount Sinai contained in the Ark of the Covenant of the Israelites. Indeed, in the religion of Americanism, that is precisely what they are.

Similar national shrines exist elsewhere, such as St Paul's Chapel in New York near to the World Trade Center site destroyed by terrorists in September 2001. Mayor Rudi Giuliani chose St Paul's for his farewell address as mayor in December 2001, a speech which, coming from a practising Catholic, is all the more notable for its adoption of something very close to the Protestant notion of a Chosen People. This American God is certainly an interventionist God, but through Providence not through miracles.

> All that matters is that you embrace America and understand its ideals
> and what it's all about. Abraham Lincoln used to say that the test
> of your Americanism was not your family tree; the test of your
> Americanism was how much you believed in America. Because we're
> like a religion really. A secular religion. We believe in ideas and ideals.
> We're not one race, we're many; we're not one ethnic group, we're
> everyone; we're not one language, we're all of these people . . .
>   The reason I chose this chapel is because this chapel is thrice-
> hallowed ground. This is a place of really special importance to people
> who have a feeling and a sense and an emotion and an understanding

of patriotism. This is hallowed by the fact that it was consecrated as a house of God in 1766. That's a long time ago. And in 1789, in April of 1789 George Washington came and after he was inaugurated as the first president of our republic he prayed right here in this church, which makes it very sacred ground to people who feel what America is all about.

But then it was consecrated one more time, in 2001 on September 11. This church existed for many years in the shadow of the twin towers. And on September 11 when the twin towers were viciously attacked and came crashing to the ground in the worst attack on America, destroyed buildings all around, did damage as far away as City Hall all the way south in the southern part of Battery Park City and covered this whole area with debris, body parts and in many, many ways damaged buildings, this chapel remained not only not destroyed, not a single window was broken, not a single thing hurt. And I think there's some very, very special significance in that. The place where George Washington prayed when he first became President of the United States stood strong, powerful, untouched, undaunted, by the attacks of these people who hate what we stand for. Because what we stand for is so much stronger than they are.

So this chapel stands for our values. And it's a very important place. And I hope you return here often to reflect on what it means to be an American and a New Yorker.[21]

This is manifestly a claim that faith in America is exactly like faith in a religion (or indeed *is* faith in a religion), and that America stands under God's special protection. This is a style of public piety that has long since passed out of favour in Britain. Mayor Giuliani's address can be contrasted with the strikingly similar subject of the Queen's Christmas address, broadcast only two days before the mayor's speech; similar subject, but quite different approach. (The other connection between them is that she had recently announced that Giuliani was to be awarded an honorary knighthood, a singular British honour for an American whose duties required no particular attention to British interests.) She showed great reticence with regard to divine Providence or special protection, offering no hint of England as special or chosen. In the American, Giuliani, sense, it is clear there is no longer any claim to a 'civic' or 'secular' religion in England. She said:

As so often in our lives at times of tragedy – just as on occasions of celebration and thanksgiving – we look to the Church to bring us together as a nation or as a community in commemoration and tribute. It is to the Church that we turn to give meaning to these moments of intense human experience through prayer, symbol and ceremony.

In these circumstances so many of us, whatever our religion, need our faith more than ever to sustain and guide us. Every one of us needs to believe in the value of all that is good and honest; we need to let this belief drive and influence our actions.

All the major faiths tell us to give support and hope to others in distress. We in this country have tried to bring comfort to all those who were bereaved, or who suffered loss or injury in September's tragic events through those moving services at St Paul's and more recently at Westminster Abbey.

On these occasions and during the countless other acts of worship during this past year, we came together as a community – of relations, friends and neighbours – to draw strength in troubled times from those around us. [The St Paul's she was referring to was of course the cathedral in London, not the chapel in New York where Giuliani was speaking.]

Is this secular or 'civic' American religion a substitute for Christianity? The evidence shows that it was grafted on to Christianity as received, not adopted in opposition to it. Biblical symbols were employed, consciously and subconsciously, to confirm in the minds of the post-Revolutionary Protestant Americans that the Breach with Britain was what God had ordained. It was all part of the Divine Plan, the same plan that had enabled the ancient Israelites to escape from Pharaoh under Moses. As Thomas Paine proclaimed in his massively influential tract *Common Sense*:

No man was a warmer wisher for reconciliation than myself, before the fatal nineteenth of April 1775, but the moment the event of the day was made known, I rejected the hardened, sullen tempered Pharaoh of England for ever, and disdain the wretch, that with the pretended title of Father of His People can unfeelingly hear of their slaughter and composedly sleep with their blood upon his soul. [19 April was the British attack at Lexington, usually regarded as the opening engagement of the war.]

The Manuscript Division of the Library of Congress holds papers relating to the proposal in 1776 for a new Great Seal for the United States, which shows the extent to which Benjamin Franklin and Jefferson himself – usually cited as among the most secular of the Founding Fathers – conceived of the American Revolution in biblical terms. On 4 July 1776, Independence Day itself, Congress appointed Franklin, Jefferson and John Adams 'to bring in a device for a seal for the United States of America'. Franklin's proposal adapted the biblical story of the Parting of the Red Sea. Jefferson first recommended the 'Children of Israel in the Wilderness, led by a Cloud by Day, and a Pillar of Fire by night . . .' He then embraced Franklin's proposal and rewrote it. Jefferson's revision of Franklin's proposal was presented by the committee to Congress on 20 August, but, as it happens, not proceeded with. In view of Jefferson's anti-miraculous views, it is remarkable that the image he chose was unambiguously miraculous, whereas Franklin's, as will be discussed later, could refer merely to an intervention to save the Israelites by means of Providence (as he would have been well aware of various non-miraculous explanations of the parting of the sea, such as the effect of wind and tide).

By all accounts the fashion for Deism among the educated élites of England and America did not last long. A religious revival had already swept the English-speaking world, and no doubt its excesses gave the élites a taste for a rather supercilious view of popular enthusiasms. There was a lull in the level of religious excitement after the so-called First Great Awakening – a lull more or less coinciding with the revolutionary period – before the Second Awakening, which deepened the American commitment to Evangelical Protestantism outside those areas, like New England, which had never lost their ardour. It was then that Anglicanism surrendered most of the ground it had held up to the Revolution. (Many Anglican clergymen were Tory, and had decamped to Canada.) The religious character of England and America, which had always been different in emphasis, began to be different in kind. American élites may have flirted briefly with Deism, but abstract philosophising is not, and never was, an American taste. Alexis de Tocqueville, who toured America in the 1830s, observed in *Democracy in America*, 'I think that in no country in the civilised world is less attention paid to philosophy than in the United States. The Americans have no philosophical school of their own; and they care very little for the schools into which Europe is divided, the very names of which are scarcely known to them.'[22]

The Deism of the late eighteenth century is often treated in America as a forerunner of modern secularism, agnosticism, even atheism. It is commonly identified with 'the values of the Enlightenment', which were taken up in the new secular religion of Freemasonry to which many of the Founding Fathers belonged. It would be truer to say, taking English experience into account here too, that Deism had many descendants of which the most recognisable is probably not secular agnosticism but Liberal Protestantism (in Anglicanism especially). It was this branch of mainstream Christianity which was most open to the findings of critical biblical scholarship that were beginning to emerge from Germany by the mid-nineteenth century, not least the grounds that that scholarship gave for discounting stories of miracles. It was this branch of Christianity that had least difficulty with the work of Charles Darwin, as it was only too ready to agree that the accounts of the Creation in Genesis were myths.

23

Like Deism, liberal theology tends towards Unitarianism because it is uncomfortable with the doctrine that Jesus was the incarnate Son of God. The kind of religion Liberals most deplore are Roman Catholicism, because of its dogma, its miracles and its confidence; and Conservative Evangelicalism (otherwise known as Protestant Fundamentalism), because of its confidence, its reliance on the Bible, and its insistence on 'a leap of faith' or a personal experience of salvation, which seems contrary to rational principles. One thing we may be certain of is that those American Founding Fathers who were called Deists, with however much or little justification, would have stood four square with these Liberal Protestants in what they most disliked.

'Soft' Deist or not, George Washington had a strong belief in Providence: that God's unseen hand directs the affairs of men towards their advantage. In his first inaugural address as President he said as much and more:

> It would be peculiarly improper to omit in this first official act my fervent supplications to that Almighty Being who rules over the universe, who presides in the councils of nations, and whose providential aids can supply every human defect, that His benediction may consecrate to the liberties and happiness of the people of the United States a Government instituted by themselves for these essential purposes, and may enable every instrument employed in its administration to execute with success the functions allotted to his charge. In tendering this homage to the Great Author of every public and private good, I assure my self that it expresses your sentiments not less than my own, nor those of my fellow-citizens at large less than either. No people can be bound to acknowledge and adore the Invisible Hand which conducts the affairs of men more than those of the United States. Every step by which they have advanced to the character of an independent nation seems to have been distinguished by some token of providential agency; and in the important revolution just accomplished in the system of their united government the tranquil deliberations and voluntary consent of so many distinct communities from which the event has resulted can not be compared with the means by which most governments have been established without some return of pious gratitude, along with an humble anticipation of the future blessings which the past seem to presage.

Providence did not smile on Britain's defeated General Cornwallis, of course. Those whom Providence favours feel they have been chosen to be touched by the hand of destiny. Those whom Providence does not favour have not been so touched. Washington does not shirk from avowing his belief in God, nor that God is a friend of America. If he was a Deist, it is a very theistic sort of Deism. His God is an interventionist

God, albeit – like the God of the Old Testament – a one-sided intervention.

But neither Providence nor Destiny are strictly compatible with the purer forms of Deism, which accepts the action of a Creator at the beginning of time but considers him (her? it?) to have withdrawn thereafter, as a watchmaker winds up a watch and then leaves it to tick. A Deist, strictly speaking, cannot believe in American destiny, Manifest or otherwise. Destiny implies that events are not purely random but gradually (and occasionally suddenly) take up a pattern, as a result of which progress is made towards an advantageous end. However lightly hinted at, Washington plainly saw that Destiny, like Providence, always implies the presence of an invisible guiding hand.

Nevertheless the mindset that went with Deism may have had an incalculable influence on the shaping of the American project that Washington and the other Founding Fathers were engaged in. His colleague and successor as President (and Deist), John Adams, wrote in his *Thoughts on Government* in 1776 that a republic was by definition 'an empire of laws, and not of men'. (The US Supreme Court later refined this into 'a government of laws, not of men'.) The Deist ideal – a universe made by a divine watchmaker and left to tick – is also a system that obeys rules. There is no need for the divine watchmaker to move the hands second by second to keep pace with the time, because they move by themselves in accordance with those rules. Similarly Adams's conception of a republic is of a constitutional system that has such well-constructed laws that endless minute-by-minute intervention by those in authority is not necessary: the state ticks by itself. The direction of the movement forwards is still that dictated by Providence's 'invisible guiding hand'. The Deists were all believers in Progress. The Deist idea of a republic is in principle, therefore, inclined towards 'small government', meaning a state that intervenes as little as possible. Progress is left to happen more or less by itself. The theories of Adam Smith, just surfacing at the time in question, neatly filled out the theory. In his *The Wealth of Nations* (1776) he declared that in an entirely free economy, each citizen, through seeking his own gain, would be 'led by an invisible hand to promote an end which was not part of his intention', namely the prosperity of society. And such beliefs have been characteristic of the American philosophy of government since independence.

Progress, of course, was part of the faith of any eighteenth-century Whig gentleman. Alistair Mason, in his entry in Deism in the *Oxford Companion to Christian Thought*,[23] describes Deists as 'more at home in coffee house than in churches, a world of good-humoured discussion and common sense, sharply aware of the evils of religious intolerance'. While Christian writers used the term of writers they disliked, many so-called Deists shunned the name. 'Deism has been a useful sparring partner for Protestant Christianity, but standing alone as one of the world's monotheist religions it is a shadowy creature.'

There is a little more to it than that. In disbelieving in miracles in particular, Deists were following David Hume's injunction that they were 'impossible'. In the sceptical world-view of eighteenth-century educated Englishmen and Americans, miracles were part of superstition, and superstition – as used in the writings of John Locke, for instance – was a code word for Roman Catholicism. To an educated liberal Protestant, Catholicism was veritably steeped in miracles, not just in the Bible but in all the miraculous appearances of saints and the Blessed Virgin, miraculous statues, miraculous cures – and above all the supposed 'miracle', as it were, of Transubstantiation during the Mass (when in Catholic doctrine bread and wine 'become' the body and blood of Christ). It is no coincidence that Deism appears simultaneously with the European Enlightenment, whose heartland was in Catholic Europe and whose particular hatred was the superstitious belief in miracles. It was by the manipulation of such wonders, Enlightenment philosophers like Voltaire argued, that the priests retained their power over the people. How the coffee houses and dinner tables of London and Washington must have shuddered at the thought!

Possibly the idea that 'miracles equal Roman Catholicism' explains another more enduring influence attributed to Deism – its effect on Conservative Evangelicals (who were later to be called Fundamentalists; and until the latter part of the nineteenth century the term Conservative would have been redundant, as 'Liberal' Evangelicalism is a relatively late phenomenon). They abhorred Deism, or what they thought Deism was. The fact that Deists disputed the literal truth of the Bible gave Fundamentalists a reason for repudiating all biblical criticism, even when it came with good Christian credentials. But while antagonistic to Deism, or what they thought Deism was, they did actually incorporate its bias against the miraculous into their own belief system.

In *Fundamentalism*,[24] James Barr lists many instances in Conservative Evangelical literature when natural explanations are offered for seemingly miraculous events. In the *New Bible Commentary Revived*,[25] for instance, the manna given by God to the Children of Israel to feed them in the desert was a natural substance; the crossing of the Red Sea fleeing from the Egyptians was made possible by a strong east wind dividing the waters; nine plagues with which God afflicted Egypt were natural phenomena with everyday explanations, such as flooding of the Nile to cause an explosion of micro-organisms called flagellates which would make the water look blood-red. And so on. God's intervention was limited to ensuring that these natural events occurred at times and places convenient to the biblical narrative. They were providential. And faith in providential intervention, rather than a belief in literal (Roman Catholic-style) miracles, was a distinguishing mark of Anglo-Saxon Protestantism from the beginning.

Providence was actually more powerful than miracles. Instead of being very rare and confined to specific events, as in the Catholic case, the concept of a benign Providence covered almost everything. Every lucky break became divine intervention. Did the wind drive the Spanish galleons on to the rocks in 1588? That was Providence. Did the original Puritan settlers survive the first winter? That was Providence. Did the New Model Army vanquish the King's forces? That was Providence. Did Washington's bedraggled army live through its ordeal in Valley Forge? That too was Providence. In the theology of Providence, God only intervenes in this way on the side of the just and righteous. Or to reverse the equation, God is on the side of the winners and so 'might is right'. These beliefs are important constituents not just of a Fundamentalist view of the world. They would not have been repudiated by the so-called Deists of late-eighteenth-century America, who were quite convinced the God they did not quite believe in was on America's side. Which is of course a very English way of looking at it. Being the Chosen People, and having Providence on your side, were all part of the same thing.

The lively controversy in the United States about the religious beliefs of the Founding Fathers is in reality not about historical truth for its own sake, but about a battle to control the American collective memory, in order to control the way the future of America is to be imagined. Anyone who wants a taste of this cultural warfare need only log on to one of the numerous American websites devoted to one side or the other of this raging dispute. Every pro-religious utterance of someone like Jefferson is marshalled on one site, every anti-religious utterance on another. It is hard to image the English getting anything like as excited about the religious beliefs, say, of the Duke of Wellington. But he was probably just as publicly pious and privately sceptical as the American statesmen round whom battle continues. That is how such men were, and to a large extent, still are. If the Anglo-Saxon brand of Protestantism, as someone once said, tends to be marked by doctrinal dilution, that does not protect it from ferocious partisanship.

The settled verdict of professional historians appears now to be that the average American of the revolutionary period, including the average American legislator, was a pretty religious sort of person, at least as far as the surface face of religion was concerned. Just how deep was what we would nowadays call his spirituality may be open to further debate. But these were generally pious times: piety was expected. The compilers of a Library of Congress exhibition in 1998 based on surviving official and unofficial texts of the period concluded from the evidence on display:

> The Continental-Confederation Congress, a legislative body that governed the United States from 1774 to 1789, contained an extra-ordinary number of deeply religious men. The amount of energy that Congress invested in encouraging the practice of religion in the new nation exceeded that expended by any subsequent American national government. Although the Articles of Confederation did not officially authorise Congress to concern itself with religion, the citizenry did not object to such activities. This lack of objection suggests that both the legislators and the public considered it appropriate for the national government to promote a nondenominational, nonpolemical Christianity.
>
> Congress appointed chaplains for itself and the armed forces, sponsored the publication of a Bible, imposed Christian morality on the armed forces, and granted public lands to promote Christianity among the Indians. National days of thanksgiving and of 'humiliation, fasting, and prayer' were proclaimed by Congress at least twice a year throughout the war. Congress was guided by 'covenant theology', a Reformation doctrine especially dear to New England Puritans, which held that God bound himself in an agreement with a nation and its people. This agreement stipulated that they 'should be prosperous or afflicted, according as their general Obedience or Disobedience thereto appears'. Wars and revolutions were, accordingly, considered afflictions, as divine punishments for sin, from which a nation could rescue itself by repentance and reformation.
>
> The first national government of the United States, was convinced that the 'public prosperity' of a society depended on the vitality of its religion. Nothing less than a 'spirit of universal reformation among all ranks and degrees of our citizens', Congress declared to the American people, would 'make us a holy, so that we may be a happy, people'.[26]

In the opening of *American Exceptionalism*[27] Seymour Lipset deals with a related objection to the emphasis of religious factors in discussing the special character of American destiny (and by analogy, English identity), namely that they may have been important once but they are not any more.

> Some who criticise an emphasis on American exceptionalism as a way of understanding current and future events have questioned the insistence that historical factors linked to the settlement of the colonies and the ideology of the founders continue to influence American behaviour and values . . . [The ideology he is referring to is of course Puritanism]. Max Weber[28] dealt with this topic in an interesting and insightful way . . . He suggested that history operates to determine the

future the way a game in which the dice become loaded does. According to Weber, by conceiving of a nation's history starting as a game in which the dice are not loaded at the beginning, but then becomes biased in the direction of each past outcome, one has an analogue of the way in which culture is formed. Each time the dice come up with a given number, the probability of rolling that number again increases.

Weber's most influential work, *The Protestant Ethic and the Spirit of Capitalism*,[29] was derived from his noticing in late nineteenth- and early twentieth-century Germany that it was in the most Calvinist parts of the country that capitalism was most successful. He observed that Calvinism (which in England and America was better known as Puritanism) influenced the personalities of its adherents, by imposing on them painful spiritual and emotional burdens, above all a fear of damnation. Hard work and the denial of rest or pleasure, the two marks of the 'Protestant ethic', offered relief from those burdens. The capital assets that accrued were regarded as a mark of God's approval and hence were a sign that perhaps damnation had after all been avoided. Where Calvinism was dominant, this philosophy shaped the culture of the whole society. Those brought up in that culture were psychologically shaped by it whether they consciously accepted Calvin's specific religious doctrines or not. Once dice are loaded, they stay loaded, only becoming more so. He could well have been speaking of himself: a sceptic in religious matters, he had a Calvinist father. Even if there are no longer any actual believing Calvinists in it at all, a culture shaped by Calvinism will be both industrious and suspicious of pleasure, simultaneously greedy and guilty. The reader can judge for himself to what extent this describes either England or America in the present day.

Calvinists were indeed biblical Fundamentalists in the full sense of the term. Religion was about the whole of life, and the Bible was their only authority in matters of religion. The religious map that was unfolded before them by the ideas of John Calvin (1509–64), the most radical of the major Protestant Reformers of the sixteenth century, was complex, tortuous and somewhat threatening. The demands made on Christians were stressful. To know what God wanted of one, it was necessary to search the Bible minutely and worry endlessly over the meaning of every passage. The parallel Protestant movement started by Martin Luther (1483–1546) was no less Bible-focused. It also made stressful demands. Both of them agreed that humanity received its message of salvation directly from the pages of the Word of God rather than through the medium of priests and the Church. Both agreed that humanity itself was inherently depraved and wicked, incapable, without God's help, of any good act. Protestant Christianity brought the Bible to the centre of

Christian attention, greatly facilitated by the fact that the relatively new industry of printing had at last made possible the production of books on a large scale. One could almost say that the Reformation had to wait for printing to be invented, before it could happen. Without a readily available copy of the vernacular Bible, reliance on the wisdom and guidance of the clergy was more or less inevitable.

The Catholic Church had always fed the faithful the contents of the Bible through the filter of its own official interpretation. The theory was that fullness of the Christian faith was contained in the Church's official teaching; the Bible was a companion to that, for the purpose of illustrating, illuminating and edifying. It was not regarded as the primary source of doctrine, though it was an accepted principle that no church teaching should contradict the New Testament. It was the Church itself which had decided, in the fourth century, which texts belonged in the official version, or canon, and which did not. The *Encyclopaedia of Theology*[30] describes the conclusion of a long process of debate and decision as follows:

> In 367, Athanasius designated the 27 books of the New Testament, in addition to the books of the Old Testament, as together comprising a firmly established canon ('Let no one add anything or take anything away from them . . .'). In the second chapter of the Decree of Gelasius, going back to the Synod of Rome in 382, the canon of the 27 writings of the New Testament was defined, and this was confirmed at the latest in 405 by a letter of Pope Innocent I as well as by the African synods of Hippo Regius (393) and Carthage (297, 419). After the fifth century no new decrees on the canon are found . . .

To that extent it is not unfair to speak of the Bible as the Church's creation. It was the church authorities, in the decisions listed above, which had rejected some texts for inclusion and accepted others, according to whether they agreed with or contradicted the orthodoxy of the day. An a priori appeal to 'the Bible' as a superior source of doctrine by which the Church itself could be judged was, prior to 367, simply not logical. This difficulty resurfaced in the sixteenth century, when the chief Protestant reformers assessed afresh the 'canon', as the list of books regarded as authentically scriptural is called, and threw out several books (as 'apocrypha') that were not part of the original Hebrew canon as defined by the Jewish authorities, but which the Catholic and Eastern Orthodox churches had accepted a thousand years earlier. Partly that was because the reformers did not like the doctrines the rejected books seemed to imply.

After the sixteenth-century Reformation, Protestants who were antagonistic to the Catholic Church accused it of distorting the meaning of the biblical text so as not to compromise the content of Catholic teaching. That was why, they claimed, the Church had been so reluctant to allow open access to the Bible and had opposed the publication of English translations. There is undoubtedly some truth in that. But an impartial and objective interpretation of the Bible is no more possible than an impartial and objective interpretation of Shakespeare's plays. Even with the most honourable intentions, the same text can be made to mean different things. And so those parts of the Bible which the Catholic Church had given only marginal importance to, would now be taken seriously as God's Word and their meaning pondered afresh. This was especially significant in those Old Testament stories which the Church had interpreted as prophesying and foreshadowing the coming of Christ and the Church's own existence thereafter.

Protestants did not feel they had to accept that interpretation, even if they knew of it. They could look at those passages afresh: each person was entitled to interpret the Bible in his or her own way. A good Protestant could definitely not accept the interpretation of certain Old Testament passages which the Catholic Church had regarded as anticipating God's concern for the welfare of itself. On the contrary, they found quite different prophecies (mainly in the New Testament) concerning the Catholic Church: that it was the agent of Satan which had to be fought and defeated before the end of time. Nevertheless the common Protestant charge that the medieval Church had hidden the text of Scripture from the people because it plainly compromised the Church's teaching is more a polemical than a historical judgment. There are areas where the exact meaning of Scripture was hotly disputed between the Protestant reformers and Catholic counter-reformers. But none where it would have been plain to any casual reader – had he been allowed access to the text – that the Church had gone wrong. Judging church teaching by Scripture is a much more difficult exercise than that. There are several texts whose most obvious meaning seems to be the one traditionally favoured by Protestants, but others which lean more towards a Catholic interpretation.

What the Reformers claimed to have found in the Bible was a much simplified form of Christianity, which, shorn of the pious accretions of centuries, had a strong and fresh appeal. Many of the obligations of faith loaded upon the people by church doctrine were either absent altogether or only hinted at in Scripture. While traditional teaching said there were seven sacraments, biblical evidence pointed conclusively only to two. If the Church was the authentic interpreter of Christianity, a reliable guide to true doctrine, then none of this mattered. If the Bible was the only true guide, on the other hand, then the Church stood accused of distorting the Gospel to suit its own purposes. For instance such church practices as confining the laity to Holy Communion in only one kind, wine, seemed plain contrary to the Word of God. Whereas popular morality in the Middle Ages depended on such devices as memorising lists of vices and virtues, Reformed Biblical Christianity offered the stark and simple phrases of the Ten Commandments. Whereas Catholic Christianity in the Middle Ages had relied strongly on rituals, images and visual aids, the Protestant Christianity which succeeded it relied very largely on texts.

If nothing else, this was a major incentive to the spread of literacy – though for a long time there was bias in favour of teaching the ordinary people to read but not to write. The underlying fear of the Protestants, especially the Puritans in England and America in the first half of the seventeenth century, was that the Old Religion would be reimposed on them by authority of the state, and they would be prohibited from worshipping under the tenets of their new form of Christianity. As the Old Religion was not just wrong but the gateway to hell itself, in their view, the threat was a deadly one. Memory of the persecutions of Protestants under Mary Tudor halfway through the previous century were kept very much alive by regular reading of Foxe's *Book of Martyrs*, the one book, apart from the Bible, which it was said could be found in every church and every household in the kingdom. It may have been more a brilliant work of propaganda than an accurate piece of history, but those who read it took it literally. That, plus vivid (and somewhat exaggerated) reports of the oppression of Protestants under the Spanish Inquisition, convinced generations of English and American Protestants that Roman Catholicism was the cruel and despotic antithesis of everything they held dear.

With hindsight, it appears that where the two sides differed most in their attitude to the Bible was in their understanding of the relevance of the Old Testament to later events. It consists largely of a chronological narrative of the history of the Israelites, the People of God, a nation or tribe, or group of tribes, which had stayed more or less together as a visible society through all their various trials and tribulations. The Church believed itself to have become the People of God in turn, but the analogy with the Israelites was far from perfect. The Church was not a nation nor a visible society concentrated in one place. It was a religious community, spread out, existing across all the nations of the known world. As the Church was not a nation it did not do the things nations do, such as maintain armies, fight wars or conquer territory, as ancient Israel had done. Its combat was spiritual. If it wanted the other kind, for instance to liberate the Holy Lands from the Saracen, it had to call on Catholic princes to fight for it. But Protestants saw the Old Testament more literally. For them New Israel was as much a nation as ancient Israel had been. Whereas the medieval Church had spiritualised the message of the Old Testament, treating most of it as complex metaphor or allegory, Protestants took it much more literally, and more politically.

Thus the great narratives of the Old Testament have always figured strongly in Protestantism. Some historians have suggested that, lacking a long history of their own, Americans were all the happier to adopt the history of the ancient Israelites as a substitute. Before that, the early English Protestants could well have found a similar advantage. Treating the history of the Israelites as a sort of English pre-history distracted attention from that other pre-history closer to hand, the history of England as a Catholic country (of which Puritans, if they thought about it at all, were either in denial about or ashamed). When Prime Minister David Lloyd George headed the British government that issued the Balfour Declaration in 1917, promising the Jews a national homeland in the Middle East, he remarked that he probably knew more about the kings of Israel than the kings of England. That would have reflected a very common state of mind among his contemporaries, especially those like him – he was raised a Welsh Baptist, with a lifelong liking for Welsh hymns – who had not been to Oxford or Cambridge to study the classics.

2

New Jerusalem

A sophisticated visitor from Mars who wandered into Westminster Abbey on Tuesday 2 June 1953 would have quickly realised that a great public ceremony was about to take place. There was to be a coronation. With due solemnity, a new sovereign was about to be sworn in, enthroned, crowned, paid homage to, and then publicly acclaimed. A few more seconds' inspection would have revealed to our Martian spaceman that what was about to start was a religious service, though the preliminary parade outside was almost exclusively military. The ceremony had a great deal more to do with God – with making promises to him, being faithful to him, praying to him, thanking him – than with politics. The senior ministers present and in the spotlight were religious ministers: government ministers were buried somewhere in the watching crowd, with virtually no role in the ceremonial. Was this, perhaps, a theocracy?

The Martian could easily have jumped to another misleading conclusion: that the nation whose monarch was being ceremonially crowned and anointed was called Israel, and its capital city Jerusalem. For the service began with a prayer from ancient Israel's own official book of Scriptures, when the choir sang from the opening of Psalm 122:

> I was glad when they said unto me: We will go into the house of the Lord. Our feet shall stand in thy gates: O Jerusalem. Jerusalem is built as a city: that is at unity in itself. O pray for the peace of Jerusalem: they shall prosper that love thee. Peace be within thy walls: and plenteousness within thy palaces.

This ambiguity between London-England and Jerusalem-Israel returned at several points in the ceremony. It is true the coronation service of Queen Elizabeth II required her to take an oath of office, the start of which, at least, was four square in the real world of London, England. In the opening two clauses of the oath she vowed, first, that she would wisely govern the countries under her jurisdiction. At that time these included the remaining parts of the British Empire (including much of Africa), the old English-speaking dominions of Canada, Australia and New Zealand and such newly independent ex-colonies as Pakistan, South Africa and Ceylon as well as Great Britain and Northern Ireland (but not Israel, neither ancient nor modern; nor India, which though part of the British Commonwealth since its independence from Britain in 1947, was a republic). Secondly, she swore that she would dispense justice mercifully. All the judges in all the courts in all those lands sat in the name of the Crown, and she was, so to speak, swearing this on behalf of every one of them. They in turn took an oath of allegiance to her. Thus does mercy become part of the common law.

Then contemporary reality departed and kingly mysticism descended again. The remaining four clauses – by far the greater part of the oath-taking by which she sealed her commitments as monarch – obliged her to defend and advance the interests of the state religion of one part, albeit the chief part, of those many territories: England. Something important was being said about its unique religious character, something that could best be understood in the light of the metaphorical (or metaphysical) references to Israel already given. But something in code, that also required a good grasp of the history of religious conflict in England over the last five centuries.

Administering the oath, the Archbishop of Canterbury, Dr Geoffrey Fisher, formally asked her: 'Will you to the utmost of your power maintain the Laws of God and the true profession of the Gospel? Will you to the utmost of your power maintain in the United Kingdom the Protestant Reformed Religion established by law? Will you maintain and preserve inviolably the settlement of the Church of England, and the doctrine, worship, discipline, and government thereof, as by law established in England? And will you preserve unto the bishops and clergy of England, and to the churches there committed to their charge, all such rights and privileges, as by law do or shall appertain to them or any of them?' And she replied, hand on the Bible: 'All this I promise to do.'

The Queen would have been well aware that the Archbishop of Canterbury who had taken her Protestant oath and who was to anoint and crown her, Geoffrey Fisher, was appointed to his present post by her father, George VI. She would also have been aware that despite the words on the page, neither she nor he could do any of the things she had just sworn to do. The reality of political power rested elsewhere – in the hands of Parliament and the politicians who were mere onlookers at the ceremony. Indeed, it was not in fact George VI but his first minister at the time, Winston Churchill, who decided that Dr Fisher was the right man to succeed to the post of Archbishop of Canterbury and Primate of

All England after the death of the previous holder, William Temple, in 1944.

Nevertheless, she was swearing to a public avowal that she, as sovereign, was responsible for the religious and spiritual welfare of the people of England – just as the great king Solomon had been for the people of Israel – as well as their temporal and material welfare. And yet her direct ability to influence the spiritual and religious welfare of the people was marginal. In practice she could do little more than set a good example. In constitutional theory, the Queen acts only on the advice of her ministers. Would her coronation oath entitle her to refuse to appoint as Prime Minister someone who belonged to the Roman Catholic faith? It would not. If he recommended someone to be a new Archbishop of Canterbury that she thought unreliable on matters of doctrine, could she refuse under her oath to make the appointment on such grounds? She could not. In 1829 King George IV was forced by his ministers, much against his will and his interpretation of his coronation oath, to agree to Catholic Emancipation (directly against the wishes of the bishops of the Church of England). The precedent quickly became part of English constitutional law. Of course a sovereign might have a conscience, but did not have the right to refuse to approve legislation that went against that conscience. If he or she felt strongly enough, the only course open would be abdication.

To the confusion of Martian visitors, things at a coronation service are indeed not what they seem. The residual anti-Catholic elements in the ritual would have been regarded by those taking part as little more than symbolic. Nevertheless, the service was clearly a fundamental constitutional event in the life of the nation. Yet the world in which coronation services take place is a world of metaphor and illusion. Nor is this accidental. As discussed in the first chapter, the English 'imagine their community' (to use Benedict Anderson's useful expression) by an act of memory. They tend to answer the question 'Who are we?' by asking, in turn, 'Who were we?' A coronation is the supreme example of that process in action. In so far as it is not a satisfactory answer – and just how unsatisfactory is something we shall explore further – that is because the English are trying to draw water from a dried-up well.

A coronation service is a world where large things are stated boldly but, almost as in a dream, they mean something quite different. 'Israel' in such a context does not mean Israel, the modern nation. It is a way of designating England as exceptional and unique, with a special relationship to the Israel of the Old Testament, for which the technical term is a 'typological' relationship (the meaning of which is explored more fully in the next chapter). And it is this which makes sense of the otherwise baffling fact that in so far as England has an institutional enemy, then according to the coronation ceremony understood as an act of remembering history – remembering with a purpose – that enemy is the Roman Catholic Church. And the underlying reason is also typological. The Catholic Church, more or less throughout its existence, has claimed to be the New Israel itself. If the Catholic Church is, then England plainly is not. The primary symbolic function of these anti-Catholic elements in the English constitution is to preserve England's unique status as the successor Chosen People of God to the Old Testament's Chosen People. Both the Roman Catholic claim and the Jewish claim to that title are set aside. In both cases, the English constitution is what is called 'supersessionist' (defined more fully in a later chapter). But this is not racism or religious bigotry. The belief that neither Judaism nor Roman Catholicism are true religions is, needless to say, one a perfectly reasonable and civilised person may hold. Holding those religions in contempt, however, may well lead to racism or bigotry.

Above all, this Old Testament typology applies to the part of the service called the anointing. It was here that the link between London in 1953 and Jerusalem some 3000 years previously was most conspicuous, most misleading – and most revealing. Anointing with oil is the ancient and unmistakable sign of priesthood and kingship. It was used that way in ancient Egypt, and the Hebrew tribes that lodged there before the event known as the Exodus would have picked up this Pharaonic ritual symbolism for themselves. King Solomon, who ruled Israel within a few hundred years of the Exodus, would have been among those ancient kings who were anointed with oil as a seal on their kingship.

The words of the 1953 coronation service were explicit on this point. As Dr Fisher placed a smear of oil on the skin of the Queen, he recited, first, 'Be thy Hands anointed with holy oil'; then 'Be thy Breast anointed with holy oil', and finally 'Be thy Head anointed with holy oil: as kings, priests, and prophets were anointed.' Then he intoned: 'And as Solomon was anointed king by Zadok the priest and Nathan the prophet, so be thou anointed, blessed, and consecrated Queen over the Peoples, whom the Lord thy God hath given thee to rule and govern . . .'

And these words were echoed in the anthem *Zadok the Priest*, adapted from the Authorised Version 1 Kings 1:39,40 in a setting by George Frederick Handel, which was sung at Elizabeth II's coronation as it had been sung at her father's: 'Zadok the priest and Nathan the prophet anointed Solomon king; and all the people rejoiced and said God save the king, Long live the king, May the king live for ever. Amen.'

Linda Colley, in *Britons, Forging the Nations, 1707–1837*, argues that in the eighteenth century one of the most powerful transmitters of the idea of Britain as New Israel was by the use of music:

From the moment he settled in London, George Frederick Handel flattered his new surroundings, and especially his patrons at court, by inserting into his music regular comparisons between events in British history and the endeavours of the prophets and heroes of the Old Testament. The anthem he composed for George II's coronation in 1727, which has been played at every subsequent coronation, is a case in point ... But it was in his oratorios that he exploited the parallel between Britain and Israel to the full. *Esther, Deborah, Athalia, Judas Maccabaeus* (which was composed in honour of the Duke of Cumberland's victory over the Jacobites at Culloden), *Joshua, Susannah, Jephtha,* and self-evidently *Israel in Egypt* all have as their theme the deliverance of Israel from danger by leaders inspired by God. The moral Handel wanted his listeners to draw was an obvious one. In Great Britain, second and better Israel, a violent and uncertain past was to be redeemed by the new and stoutly Protestant Hanoverian Dynasty, resulting in an age of unparalleled abundance.[1]

The phrase 'God save the king' or 'God save King ...' is used elsewhere in the Old Testament at the proclamation of kings of Israel. Thus, from 1 Samuel 10:24: 'And Samuel said to all the people, See ye him whom the Lord hath chosen, that there is none like him among all the people? And all the people shouted, and said, God save the King.' And when the National Anthem, otherwise known since the death of George VI as 'God Save the Queen', was sung by the congregation – and indeed the whole nation – at the conclusion of the coronation, the Queen processed to the great west door of the Abbey, wearing the crown of England and bearing the orb and sceptre which are the ancient symbols of her office. (The sceptre is a regular symbol of kingship in the Old Testament.) The national anthem, too, dates from the Hanoverian era, when, as Linda Colley demonstrates, the linkage between the kings and queens of England and the kings of Israel was brought to the fore for ideological reasons.

Just as Solomon would have been obliged to rule according to the manner set down in the Pentateuch, the Hebrew Bible's first five books, so Queen Elizabeth was handed a copy of the Christian Bible, which opens with those same five books, the books of the Law of Moses. 'To keep your Majesty ever mindful of the Law and the Gospel of God as the Rule for the whole life and government of Christian Princes,' the Archbishop told her 'we present you with this Book, the most valuable thing that this world affords.' Then the Moderator of the General Assembly of the Church of Scotland, sharing the conduct of the service with the Archbishop, intoned: 'Here is Wisdom; this is the Royal Law; these are the lively Oracles of God.'

Yet once more, the words and the reality do not quite match. No one expected the Queen to insist that her subjects should observe every detail of Mosaic law. What was being underlined here was an aspect of national identity, not a source of legislation for Parliament. And the aspect in question was not just that the English nation was a Christian nation. That would be a reductionist point. What was being emphasised again was that in the way it related itself to God, England could be compared to ancient Israel, the English to the Israelites.

Virtually all nation-states in the modern world, with the conspicuous exception of Britain, define the fundamental common purposes and mutual duties of the rulers and the ruled by means of a written constitution. The American Constitution's pre-eminent document is the Declaration of Independence promulgated by Congress on 4 July 1776, which proclaims the famous words:

> We hold these truths to be self-evident, that all men are created equal, that they are endowed by their Creator with certain unalienable rights, that among these are life, liberty and the pursuit of happiness; that to secure these rights, governments are instituted among men, deriving their just powers from the consent of the governed; that whenever any form of government becomes destructive of these ends, it is the right of the people to alter or to abolish it, and to institute new government . . .

Other states have other declarations of fundamental principle in their own written constitutions, though none quite so fine. Great Britain, which has overseen the independence of a great variety of nations not all of whom had to wrest it so painfully at the point of a musket, has seen that they were all equipped with written constitutions before casting off from the mother country. But Great Britain itself has no written constitution, no ringing declaration of truths that are held to be self-evident. It has, instead, a coronation. It is in that service that the British constitution offers its only clear statement of the duties of a crowned ruler, though these duties have to be carried out by elected ministers.

As the Sword of State was blessed, ready to be passed to the Queen by the archbishop and other dignitaries, he intoned:

> Hear our prayers, O Lord, we beseech thee,
> and so direct and support thy servant Queen Elizabeth,
> that she may not bear the Sword in vain;
> but may use it as the minister of God
> for the terror and punishment of evildoers,
> and for the protection and encouragement of those that do well,
> through Jesus Christ our Lord. Amen.

As he passed the sword to her, and while she held it, he went on:

Receive this kingly Sword,
brought now from the Altar of God,
and delivered to you by the hands of us
the Bishops and servants of God, though unworthy.
With this sword do justice,
stop the growth of iniquity,
protect the holy Church of God,
help and defend widows and orphans,
restore the things that are gone to decay,
maintain the things that are restored,
punish and reform what is amiss,
and confirm what is in good order:
that doing these things you may be glorious in all virtue;
and so faithfully serve our Lord Jesus Christ in this life,
that you may reign for ever with him
in the life which is to come. Amen.

The monarch personifies the Crown; and the Crown represents all the visible and invisible moral qualities with which the English wish to be endowed. What those qualities are is established in a solemn state ceremony, and that which opened the reign of Queen Elizabeth II was the event on 2 June 1953 which our puzzled Martian visitor stumbled upon.

What were those moral qualities, beyond the outline above? The questions cannot easily be answered simply by reference to the Bible. The answer is carefully encoded into the coronation service itself. Most people in Britain in the 1950s would probably have been content to say that the core values of their society were Christian – the more inclusive phrase 'Judaeo-Christian' was not yet in fashion – but they would have meant Christianity as it was understood by the consensus at the time in the Anglican church. Anglican leaders of that period would probably have insisted that there was no real difference between the ethos of their church and the teaching of the Bible, but they would of course be wrong – as Anglican leaders of fifty years later, or for that matter fifty years earlier, would have been the first to insist. It is one of the advantages of an unwritten constitution that the 'things a nation holds self-evident' can change with time and circumstances. The coronation of 1953, almost identical in form to the coronation of Edward VII in 1902, said something very different about the nation and its values.

The Anglican ethic that existed in 1953 – the national ethic, one could still call it – was of relatively recent origin. William Temple, Dr Fisher's brief predecessor at Canterbury after a far longer period as Archbishop of York, was largely responsible for producing a theory of the responsibility of the state towards its citizens that was much more activist and interventionist – and more left-wing – than his predecessors would have favoured. He and his generation had lived through both the First World War and the Great Depression. The Church of England, he decided, could not stand aside from the suffering of the ordinary people of England. In particular, he contributed to the ideas that became translated into the post-war Welfare State, a term he invented. He held a famous wartime 'Malvern Conference' – at Malvern in Worcestershire in 1941 – at which notable people were invited to discuss together privately how to build a better world after the Second World War was won. One result was his *Christianity and Social Order* of 1942 (which sold 140,000 copies), and *The Church Looks Forward* (1944).

Though son of an earlier Archbishop of Canterbury and himself a former public school headmaster, Temple had belonged to the Labour party (1918–25) and was president of the Workers' Educational Association. The British Council of Churches and the World Council of Churches owe their formation largely to his initiatives, and his influence brought the churches to support the Education Act of 1944, which introduced the principle of free education for everyone, paid for by the state. Temple's theological position has been described as a Hegelian Idealism, in favour of close links between church and state and of churchmen making pronouncements on social and economic problems of the day. His remedies for social ills were top-down state paternalism. His objection to capitalism was more from romantic pre-industrialism – he equated commercial competition to 'selfishness' – than socialism. As befitted the kindly English gentleman he was, the very personification of the cult of the well-meaning amateur, he had little grasp of economics or any real understanding of industry. But his achievement was to make the kind of Britain that was emerging in 1953 (eight years after his untimely death) look like the very model of an ideal Christian society. In his history of Christian Socialism in Britain, Alan Wilkinson writes: 'It is vital to realise that Temple was not an isolated social prophet, but one who articulated and did much to consolidate the social consensus. Temple was much too much an insider, too much a product of powerful institutions in church and state, ever to be a radical prophet against them.'[2]

Part of Temple's legacy was the conviction that radical social prophecy was no longer necessary, having been made redundant by the Welfare State. The wide range of postwar economic and social reforms introduced by the Labour party in 1945 had been largely adopted by the Conservative party which returned to power in 1951, even those which it had bitterly opposed as they went through Parliament. Harold Macmillan, Tory Prime Minister in the later 1950s, described this consensus (to which he belonged) as 'paternalistic socialism'. The Beveridge Report of 1942 had promised a post-war society in which 'want' – in modern terms, poverty in all its manifestations – had been banished by the actions of government. Under his scheme, all classes of people were to be covered by compulsory insurance against all classes of misfortune. Though progressive for its time, a sample of its insight into social trends may be gleaned from this extract: 'In the next thirty years housewives as mothers have vital work to do in ensuring the adequate continuance of the British race and of British ideals in the world.' This aspiration would have been just as acceptable ten years later. If William Beveridge supplied the blueprint for the post-war Welfare State, it was certainly William Temple – a friend of Beveridge from Oxford days – who provided the theological blessing to go with it. Fisher, it may be said, was somewhat less enthusiastic. But he did not undermine what Temple had achieved.

Temple was one of the father figures of the so-called post-war consensus in Britain, which was not significantly challenged until Margaret Thatcher succeeded Edward Heath – a great Temple devotee – as Tory leader in 1975. Very firmly in the centre of it sat the Church of England, the 'post-war consensus at prayer'. As a political event, the coronation was a celebration of this happy and harmonious state. As Browning would have said, God was in his heaven and all was right with the world. The 1950s were truly the post-war high-water mark of Anglican England.

Correlli Barnett, in his four-part series *Pride and Fall*, describes this sense of a new world being built in post-war Britain, as Britain herself resumed her great power status, by the sarcastic label 'New Jerusalem'.[3] It was a name the Church of England would have been familiar with (without the sarcasm), as well as the Labour party and the wartime architects of the Welfare State. That was indeed how they saw what they were doing. They thought it was affordable, indeed, it was their entitlement. Having fought the good fight against Hitler, they were on the threshold of the Promised Land. Barnett, on the other hand, says the verdict of history is that it was the waste of a unique opportunity to rebuild the national economy. He writes:

> It was ... the British people at large who shared responsibility with their politicians for all the colossal overloads and overstrains that pursuit of this fantasy imposed on Britain between the end of the Second World War and the final self-deluding absurdity of the Suez adventure.[4] Yet it was they who no less shared responsibility for that second great cause of postwar economic overload, 'New Jerusalem'. For they had demanded, and the politicians had promised, that there be fulfilled without delay the wartime prospectus of state welfare from crib to

coffin, 'free' health care, 'full employment', and an ideal home for every family.

Though Archbishop of Canterbury for only a short, if momentous period, Temple had dominated Anglican mainstream thinking since before the First World War. He presided over a Commission on Doctrine that met in the inter-war years and gradually gave up the attempt to carve out a distinctive Anglican theology. Its report, published in 1938, established if not what Anglicans believe, at least how they believed it. Temple came to reject the idea of precise and certain dogma, an approach which was to become almost standard in the Church of England after him. He preferred to have on board all those who wanted to be called Christian, rather than test them with theological definitions which could only exclude the hesitant. John Kent says of him:

> Temple set out to give a coherent view of the relationship between Christianity and philosophy, and he did so by taking as central to our understanding of the universe the idea of Purpose. He argued that such a universal Purpose could not exist without the active presence of a real Will, which lay behind the world. Purposeful action, moreover, must (or so it seemed to Temple) be personal, and this in turn suggested that the 'creative purpose' behind the world must also be Personal. In this way Temple built up the idea of a Governing Will, or personal 'god'.[5]

One needs to be wary of the term 'personal God', because it is easily confused, thanks to modern marketing, with the altogether different notion of a self-made God, or one designed to suit one's particular 'personal' needs or inclinations (as in a typical savings bank promotion of 'a personal loan for your personal circumstances'). A regular question asked by pollsters researching into religious belief is 'Do you believe in a personal God?' (To which one researcher recorded the reply, 'No, just the ordinary one.') But, to the puzzlement of such surveyors of public opinion, the number saying Yes is consistently far lower than the number claiming that they prayed regularly.

However, the meaning of a 'personal God' in Temple's theology (and in the pollster's question) is really no different from 'Do you believe in a God who can hear your prayers?' Personal God in this context means a God one can relate to and communicate with. Temple (and modern pollsters) are using 'personal' in that sense, not in the sense of 'designed to your own specification'. In other words the unexpected reply – 'No, just the ordinary one' – was the right one. Those who said No to the personal God question were trying to be orthodox, distinguishing themselves from a New Age or Post-Modernist notion of 'you have your god and I have mine'. Ironically, Temple's eschewing of doctrinal standards for membership of the Church of England might indeed have laid the foundations for the post-modern 'your God/my God' approach to 'personal' faith in the modern marketing sense.

His wanting to define the membership of the established church as all-embracingly as possible was typical of Temple's optimism. Fittingly, the mood of the country at the time of the coronation in 1953 was upbeat. The name of the new Queen, Elizabeth, was an immediate reminder of an earlier Queen of that name, Good Queen Bess of popular memory. The war was eight years over, and the nation had a strong sense that it was a good fight well fought, in a righteous cause. The years immediately afterwards had been hard ones, but by 1953 conditions were easing, rationing had largely ended, goods were returning to the shops, bomb damage was ceasing to scar the urban landscape. The Welfare State was beginning to make it look as if the harsh conditions of the 1930s would never return. Major industries had been taken into public ownership, and at that point it was still imagined that that would quickly bring an end to trade union militancy. The National Health Service – providing free medical treatment for everyone – was a prime symbol of this new, unified, caring Britain. It seemed that a fresh compact between rulers and ruled had been forged in the post-war years, with the state far more involved in the everyday details of people's lives. And it was a Christian and compassionate state, one which made it its business to play Good Samaritan to any citizen in need.

Omens of national success were popular in the press that coronation summer, such as the British expedition that climbed to the summit of Everest for the first time. In fact the mountaineers who made it to the top were a New Zealander, Sir Edmund Hillary, and a Nepalese guide, Sherpa Tenzing Norgay; but this did not seem to matter. And the coronation itself was overflowing with glamour and romance: the new Queen was young and beautiful, her husband was dashingly handsome (and a bit of a war hero), and they were loving parents of a growing family. The Church of England needed no encouragement to portray them as an exemplary Christian family, a model the whole country should admire and aspire to imitate (if not in lifestyle, at least in domestic virtue). This image of an almost unbelievably happy family life at Buckingham Palace became something like the core message of the coronation service itself. See how well good sensible moderate Anglican Christianity works when you give it a chance, it said. The message was repeated in a thousand sermons.

Needless to say, what actually went on inside the royal household was kept well hidden from public view, largely because the press accepted almost without question the custom of deference and respect. What the public got was more mythology than fact – but no doubt it preferred things that way. One of the purposes of a coronation is to invest the royal personages with a mystique that sets them apart from ordinary human beings. Although it is not necessarily Christian – much the same mystique would have surrounded the Japanese Emperor and members of his royal family – the flavour of this sense of specialness was decidedly religious. The 'mystical reverence, the religious adherence' which Walter Bagehot[6] said were 'essential to a true monarchy' were very much intact.

Possessors of this mystical quality of royalty, above all the royal personage who actually wore the Crown, were different, larger than life, more honest, more intelligent, more beautiful, more privileged. They were beyond criticism. All the apparatus of church and state was deployed to keep it that way. This too was part of the Anglican ethos at the start of the 1950s: this too was contained in the message the coronation was intended to convey. It added extra sweetness to the English sense of being a special nation, uniquely blessed by God.

Continuity was also part of the message. It said that this was an ancient nation, many of whose traditions went back a thousand years or more. The custom of placing a crown on the head of the king or queen, as the supreme mark of sovereignty, can be traced back to the first Roman Emperors after Constantine made the Empire officially Christian in AD 313. Herbert Thurston, writing in the *Catholic Encyclopaedia*,[7] cites Valentinian (364) and his son Gratian (367) as both having been crowned on becoming Emperor:

> Patriarch Anatolius in 450 crowned Marcian and by that act originated a ceremony which became of the greatest possible significance in the later conception of kingship. At first there seems to have been no idea of lending any religious character to this investiture; and the selection of the patriarch may possibly have been due simply to the desire to preclude jealousy and to avoid giving offence to more powerful claimants of the honour. But already in 473, when Leo II was crowned in the lifetime of his grandfather, we find the Patriarch Acacius not only figuring in the ceremony but reciting a prayer before the imposition of the diadem. If it was Leo's grandfather and not Acacius who actually imposed it, that is only on account of the accepted rule, that the reigning emperor in his lifetime is alone the fount of honour whenever he chooses to commit any portion of his authority to colleague or consort. Following close upon the first intervention of the patriarch, the ecclesiastical element in the coronation ceremonial rapidly develops. At the election of Anastasius (491) the patriarch is present at the assembly of the senate and notables when they make their formal choice, and the book of the Holy Gospels is exposed in their midst . . . The coronation does not take place in a sacred building, but an oath is taken

by the emperor to govern justly and another written oath is exacted of him by the patriarch that he will keep the Faith entire and introduce no novelty into the Church . . . Then after the emperor had donned a portion of the regalia, the patriarch made a prayer, and the *Kyrie eleison* (possibly an ektene or litany) being said, put upon his sovereign the imperial chlamys and the jewelled crown. The acclamations also which accompany and follow the emperor's speech with its promises of the usual largess, are pronouncedly religious in character; for example 'God will preserve a Christian Emperor!'

Thurston found evidence of both crowning and anointing with oil in coronation rituals in use before the Norman Conquest. The form settled into more or less its modern form, minus pre-Reformation elements which were thought to be too Roman Catholic in style, at the coronation of Edward II in 1307. The rite became known as the *Liber Regalis*. 'It may be said even at the present day to form the substance of the ritual by which the monarchs of Great Britain are crowned,' states Thurston.

When Dr Fisher as Archbishop of Canterbury presided over the coronation of Queen Elizabeth in 1953, therefore, the precedent for his involvement was approximately 1500 years old. As he placed the crown on her head, he said later, he felt the whole nation hold its breath. The coronation that year was the first major public ceremony to be televised nationally in Great Britain, and it was apparent from the national mood that all those watching on flickering black and white television screens were as much part of the action as those in Westminster Abbey. Newspapers advised their readers to stand for the National Anthem, for instance, even in their own homes.

The status being conferred on the Queen in that sacred action sealed the holy bonds between ruler and ruled, and therefore said something both mysterious and profound about the identity of the nation itself. But it was not a contract between Queen and People. It was a covenant between Queen and God. The covenant was sealed by an act of state, rather than by an act by the state church on behalf of the state. The whole nation, whether members of the Church of England or some other religious group or none at all, was implicated. The nation was acting as its own church, and was perfectly entitled to alter the ceremonial if it wanted to. In a sense, it did not matter who placed the crown on the royal head. But not altering the ceremonial was the very point, for it symbolised how ancient the monarchy was, and how continuous. The fact that the exact meaning of various details of the ceremony were lost in the mists of time was no disadvantage, even if they rendered those moments incomprehensible to those watching or taking part. It was sufficient that Edward II had done them in 1307. Commentators positively wallowed in the obscurity of such coronation objects as the Bracelets of Sincerity and Wisdom, the Robe Royal with the Stole Royal, the Sceptre with the Cross and the Rod with the Dove, and the Ring of Kingly Dignity, whose reception by the Queen went with the archbishop's prayer: 'As you are this day consecrated to be our Head and Prince, so may you continue steadfastly as the Defender of Christ's Religion; that being rich in faith and blessed in all good works, you may reign with him who is the King of Kings, to whom be the glory for ever and ever. Amen.'

Archaic language adds to mystery, and mysteriousness is a godly quality. The crowned Queen emerged from Westminster Abbey into the light, a radiant and godly personage. Though it may not have had that language for it, the nation felt she had undergone a sacramental change – not one of the two sacraments recognised by her own church, nor even the seven recognised by Rome, but another invented English sacrament that made her holy, and through her the whole nation was sanctified. The tradition for this predates the English Reformation, as Shakespeare recalls in *Richard II*: 'Not all the water of the rough rude sea can wash the balm off from an anointed king.' Ernst Kantorowicz, in his *The King's Two Bodies: A Study in Mediaeval Political Theology*,[8] describes this as the theory that the monarch has two selves, a divine self and a natural self (echoing the Creed's description of Christ as True God and True Man), and in the former capacity she is a representative of Christ, in whose name she wields political power.

The last time this sense of the divination of queenship had been so manifest was in the reign of her namesake, Elizabeth Tudor. This added to the illusion that a second Elizabethan Age had just begun, in which Britain (England especially) would return to the greatness that was God's special blessing for it.

With kingly continuity went aristocracy and social hierarchy. In *England, An Elegy*, Roger Scruton describes how this stabilising influence worked:

> Monarchy and the hereditary peerage were both ways in which past and future acquired a voice in present politics. The hereditary peerage, as traditionally understood, caused political office to go hand in hand with enhanced social status, and with a title attached directly or indirectly to a piece of England . . . The Upper Chamber of Parliament therefore consisted largely of people whose interests were not short-term interests of a living human being but the long-term interests of a territory. First among such interests is a deep-seated desire for social and political continuity. A privilege enjoyed by inheritance can be safeguarded only if the social and political arrangements which confer

it are maintained. Inevitably, therefore, a hereditary Upper House will see itself as guardian or trustee of a social and political legacy, and to that extent a brake on the democratic process.[9]

It may be impossible to imagine a royalty without an aristocracy of some sort, but the British aristocracy was in a class of its own. It was the solid pyramid at whose head royalty stood. It was the source of the company of courtiers with which royalty surrounded itself. It was the gene pool of new blood, when eligible royals needed wives or husbands. Collectively, it constituted the House of Lords, which gave it direct political power. And the aristocracy, together with the Church of England, supplied most of the *dramatis personae* for that day's performance.

Furthermore the British aristocracy is traditionally associated with the Conservative party, whose aristocratic leader, Winston Churchill (born at Blenheim Palace), had returned to the scene of his wartime triumphs, 10 Downing Street, two years before. He said in a post-election broadcast that he felt there was 'a growing sense of the need to put Britain back in her proper place, which burns in the hearts of men far beyond the ranks of any political organisation'.

The loss of the election in 1945 to a reformist, not to say radical, Labour party, had led the Tories into a fundamental reappraisal of their policies and enabled them to present themselves in 1950 and 1951 on an entirely new platform, largely made up of clothes borrowed from Labour. The smaller Liberal party, positioned half way between Tories and Labour, refused an offer of seats in Cabinet, but the offer itself was a measure of the consensus. (Even so, the Conservatives won a majority of seats in Parliament without gaining a majority of the popular vote.) This consensual and unifying approach to government by the Conservatives took its inspiration from Disraeli's mid-nineteenth-century account of 'One Nation' Toryism, designed to heal the split between rich and poor. It is also entirely consistent with the aristocratic doctrine of *noblesse oblige*, the duty of the well-born to be honourable and generous to their social inferiors.

The aristocracy is the old feudal government of Britain on modern ermine; the Conservative party the channel through which it kept a hand on the national tiller. So the 'natural party of government', led by the world's leading statesman, Churchill, was in charge of the nation's fortunes at the unfolding of the New Elizabethan Age (as newspapers were not at all shy about calling it). Churchill himself received the premier royal honour (better than a peerage), being made a Knight of the Garter (KG) that year. The fact that the great majority of peers were Tory meant that the Upper House of Parliament had a permanent Tory majority, but in 1953, to all but a few, that seemed the natural order of things.

The flirtation of a former Archbishop of Canterbury with the Labour party has already been noted. But it was the fate of the Tories (the American phrase Manifest Destiny captures the flavour of it) through two centuries to be the natural party of throne and altar, Church and Crown. And the great majority of Anglican churchmen went along with it. In this way, therefore, one of the messages of the 1953 coronation was counter-revolutionary. It said that the egalitarian socialist radicalism, even republicanism, urged by those on the left of the Labour party was not the English way; that the Labour party had only briefly borrowed the reins of government in the years since the war, part of the way the nation periodically chastised the Conservatives for falling out of date; and that they had now bucked up, so the party of patriotism could be duly restored to its rightful place in the political sun in time for the coronation. Throne and altar the Tories stood for, but also the view that each man had his station (women scarcely counted in the hierarchy of birth and class), and ought to know it.

The relationship between royalty, aristocracy, the Tory party and the English class structure was fairly plain to see, though it made the English uneasy. It was necessary to show that it served some higher purpose. The clergy of the Church of England overwhelmingly went to public (i.e. independent fee-paying) schools and to Oxford or Cambridge, and would have justified the relationship between the classes in England as a matrix of mutual dependency and responsibility, for the benefit of all. The idea that there should not be social classes at all would have been quite alien to them. So the coronation was a celebration of class, but an English class structure of shared obligations and common purposes (and hence, reconcilable with Christian principles). Hadn't that been the lesson of the recent war, when British officers, overwhelmingly middle or upper class, led NCOs and other ranks, overwhelmingly their social as well as military subordinates, to a glorious victory?

Class was a potent symbol at the coronation. The principal actors in the drama were either senior members of the aristocracy or senior prelates in the Church of England. By convention, for each rank of prelate there was an equivalent rank in the nobility, so that diocesan bishops were usually addressed as 'My Lord', the proper form of address for a baron, and archbishops as 'Your Grace', the proper form for a duke. Between prelates and peers, therefore, there was no real social distinction. At the stage in the coronation proceedings when participants were to pay homage to the newly crowned Queen, the order of precedence was according to strict rank in the social pecking order.

The first to pay homage was the Archbishop of Canterbury. It would be a mistake, however, to regard this as a symbol that in the English constitution the spiritual power was subservient to the temporal (which is called the Erastian theory of church-state relations). It is rather the case that, in the person of the monarch, the spiritual and the temporal power came together. Neither in church nor state was there any higher authority than the Crown. Herbert Thurston, in his article in the *Catholic Encyclopaedia* already referred to, demonstrated the powerful influence that coronations of Holy Roman Emperors (or Kings of Rome as they were sometimes styled) had had in the development of coronation services throughout pre-medieval Europe. When conducted in Rome, a feature of the service was the Emperor's homage to, and his swearing of fealty to, the Pope. The apparent reversal of these roles in the modern English coronation service – the archbishop's swearing fealty to the Queen – makes most sense if the monarch is seen as having replaced the Pope, which, since the time of Henry VIII, was indeed the constitutional theory.

So Dr Fisher knelt before the Queen and placed his hands between hers while saying the words of fealty, a promise to serve her faithfully and truly. This was repeated by the remaining bishops of the Church of England, who knelt in their stalls. The same action was performed by the Duke of Edinburgh, the Queen's husband, who promised to be 'your liege man of life and limb, and of earthly worship . . .' The relationships being forged here were essentially feudal – the duty of an inferior in social rank to offer the protection of his arms to one who was his superior. (This was still the nation of Henry V!) Prince Philip was followed by the two other adult male members of the Royal Family present, the Dukes of Gloucester and Kent, and they in turn by a long queue of dukes, marquesses, earls, viscounts, and barons. (The Duke of Windsor, the Queen's uncle and former King Edward VIII, was still in disgrace and had not been invited.) When the homage was ended – no commoners took part – martial drums were beaten and a fanfare of trumpets blown, and the entire congregation let out a manly shout of 'God save Queen Elizabeth! Long live Queen Elizabeth! May the Queen live for ever!' as ordained in the order of service.

Apart from the change of gender, these were exactly the words of the anthem by Handel that the choir had sung earlier, adapted from 1 Kings 1:39 (following the anointing of King Solomon): 'God save the king, Long live the king, May the king live for ever.' In fact the subliminal reference was cleverer even than that, for the literal text of the Authorised Version at this point had, like the Abbey service, trumpets as well: 'And Zadok the priest took an horn of oil out of the tabernacle, and anointed Solomon. And they blew the trumpet; and all the people said, God save king Solomon.'

What a visitor from Mars might find strange about all this is that it seems to have something to do with England's typological identification with ancient Israel but nothing at all to do with the rest of the territory the Queen was being crowned to reign over. What did all these references to King Solomon, Zadok the priest and so on have to do with the people of Ceylon, say, or Britain's West Indian colonies? What were the Catholics of Canada or Muslims of Pakistan supposed to make of them? Why should *their* Queen have to swear her special protection to just one religion of just one part of all these many territories? Why should they care about some ancient quarrel with the Catholic Church? In fact Sri Lanka (formerly Ceylon) opted to become a republic in 1972; Pakistan in 1956; South Africa in 1961. Many others followed, especially Britain's other former African colonies (not one of which has kept the Queen). Britain's former Caribbean colonies remain dominions (with the Queen as head of state) as does Canada, though French-speaking Canada has long been restless for autonomy. In Australia and New Zealand republicanism is a live issue, though more so in the former than the latter. It is easy to conclude, therefore, that far from welding the countries of the British Commonwealth and Empire closer together, the coronation was either divisive and alienating or a supreme irrelevance except as a splendid spectacle of pomp and pageantry. It was about the English having a private conversation with themselves, in terms incomprehensible to everyone else.

In fact there was a connection, and a very profound one. Though it must have been in the minds of many English people as they watched the coronation, it was nowhere stated out loud. The link between all these nations represented in various ways at Westminster Abbey that day in 1953 was that somewhere in their past they had all been either settled by, or conquered by, that nation called Great Britain of which England made up four-fifths. And the driving force in that great campaign of conquest and settlement was precisely the English belief that their nation had been singled out by God for a unique role in world history. The role of this chosen nation, inheritor of the mission of ancient Israel, was to spread English civilisation – Protestant civilisation – to the four quarters of the globe. Those who resisted were resisting the will of God, and could be swept aside or, if necessary, eliminated. The coronation was a celebration of that extraordinary history, and it gave the English nation immense quiet satisfaction. The early 1950s were far too soon for liberal guilt about colonialism to diminish the Englishman's pride at an empire on which the sun still did not set, even in 1953. It was something to give thanks for to the Englishman's God. It was He who had made it possible.

The result of decoding the coronation service of 1953 is to lay bare a rich deposit of history, mythology and theology. At the core of this ideology (there is no other name for it) is the idea of chosenness, a covenant based on a typological relationship to the history recorded in the Old Testament. The assumption was that English history would happen on parallel lines to ancient Israelite history, so that what was true of the latter would also be, in some sense, true of the former. The parallels would not always be obvious. Interpretations would differ. But by and large, if England was unfaithful to God, God would chastise it by sending defeat and misfortune; if England was faithful, God would reward it with victory, peace and prosperity. Provided the covenant was intact, at times of great danger God would intervene. The gale that drove the Spanish Armada on to the rocks in 1588 was known as the 'Protestant wind'. Nor was such confidence absent from more secular times. The archetypal story of this Protestant road to salvation – told of an individual but applicable just as easily to the whole country – was *The Pilgrim's Progress* by John Bunyan. Christian, the hero, struggles towards the heavenly city with a heavy burden on his back, surviving a terrifying encounter at one point with two ugly giants, Pagan and Pope. This book was the third in a Protestant trinity consisting of the Authorised Version of the Bible, and Foxe's *Book of Martyrs*, which defined what it was to be a Protestant Englishman. As Linda Colley writes, it was by this means that the lesson was learnt that suffering and recurrent exposure to danger were a sign of grace, and if met with fortitude, were the prelude to victory under God:

> This way of making sense of adversity, and of comforting themselves in the face of it, would persist subliminally into the twentieth century. During the First World War, British soldiers in the trenches regularly turned to *The Pilgrim's Progress*, some even comparing themselves to Christian himself . . . Identifying themselves with Christian was clearly also a way of steeling themselves against danger and suffering, and a way too of reassuring themselves that their cause was just. Britons drew on the selfsame Protestant culture during the Second World War. When the Germans drove the British expeditionary army back through France in 1940, for instance, and the survivors were rescued in only a haphazard and partial fashion by flotillas of brave civilian boats, this near-fiasco was speedily converted by the British themselves into an auspicious deliverance. Instinctively and under pressure, they incorporated this event with the Protestant interpretation of their history, and drew the customary moral: civil exertions among miscellaneous and humble Britons had, under Providence, won out against a powerful and malignant enemy.[10]

And of course God had arranged for the sea to be calm, those four vital days. Had a storm blown up, no such escape would have been possible.

On the whole the British, the English especially, have been shy about trumpeting this special relationship with God, more so than the Americans, certainly. At first sight there was much 'typical English understatement' in the coronation service of 1953. It was bad form to boast, or declare too explicitly that 'the English are best'. (The British comedy team Flanders and Swann had a gently satirical hit – their song of Patriotic Prejudice – whose chorus began 'The English, the English, the English are best . . .') This deep conviction of national specialness was almost too precious to parade. It was only hinted at, never quite declared. That does not mean it was not widely shared. There are always some things people do not feel the need to say, especially when they are already implicit in familiar national institutions such as the monarchy or the established church.

A taste of the 1940–60 English mindset can be gleaned from an influential essay, 'The Idea of an Christian Society' written by T. S. Eliot, who during his lifetime was thought of not only as the leading poet of the age but as an important social commentator. (He addressed Temple's 1941 Malvern Conference on the subject of Christian education, for instance.) More or less taking for granted the desirability of a Christian society, as distinct from a secular or pagan one, Eliot had written:

> But a positive culture must have a positive set of values, and the dissentients must remain marginal, tending to make only marginal contributions . . . If the idea of a Christian society be grasped and accepted, then it can only be realised, in England, through the Church of England . . . I have maintained that the idea of Christian society implies, for me, the existence of one church that shall aim at comprehending the whole nation. Unless it has this aim, we relapse into that conflict between citizenship and church-membership, between public and private morality, which today makes moral life so difficult for everyone . . . [By 'comprehending' he means including or embracing.][11]

Half a century after the coronation the British have become accustomed to treating church ceremonial as an exercise in poetic licence. Couples who do not believe in God, or who have no intention of remaining married much longer than they feel like it, regularly go up to the altars of the nation's churches to plight their troth before the Almighty 'until death do us part'. Many of them still have their children baptised – 'christened' is still the more fashionable expression – while meaning hardly a word of the promises they are required to make. If they know anything of the 1953 coronation service they are likely to assume that those who actually took part in it did so in the same spirit of solemn but insincere play-acting. They would be wrong. The erosion of ceremonial language had begun, but the Church of England was still held in high respect, not to be monkeyed with. Its public services were assumed to mean what it said they meant.

If mental adjustments were required to understand them, it was only the adjustment from realistic language to symbolic language and from the decoding of ritual acts. That still represented a valid kind of truth. This approach to the meaning of church ritual was later to be endorsed in a report by the Doctrine Commission of the Church of England in 1981, which explicitly stated it was trying to establish what had long been the Anglican way with these things: 'Those beliefs that take possession of people's minds by implication and insinuation have greater persuasive power than direct assertion . . . The more profound and basic the doctrine, the more likely it is to be preserved in the myths, symbols, rituals and behaviour-patterns of the believing community, rather than being placarded explicitly in formal propositions.'[12]

So if the coronation oaths were two parts about the civil administration of a Commonwealth and Empire of some 400 million people, and four parts about maintaining the privileges of the Church of England, then that merely showed how important the Church of England was. And if indeed it was true, as William Temple had written in 1941,[13] that the Church of England was the one unique religious institution in the world that had got Christianity right while all the rest had got it wrong, and if getting Christianity right made the difference between souls going to heaven when they died or going to hell, then the Church of England was indeed a national asset – a global asset – of unsurpassed significance and eternal value. It was what the English had most to be proud of and thankful for. It was at the core of their national covenant with God. Pledges of wise civil administration and of justice and mercy in the courts paled into insignificance by comparison.

The Church of England itself was later to inch towards another kind of treatment of its own ceremonial, repeating the words 'as if' they were true without being fully and finally convinced of it. The fact that earlier generations of Anglicans had taken their formal words and actions to be literally true was of evidential value, but not binding. Since 1975, those entering Holy Orders in the Church of England are required to swear not to the Thirty-nine Articles or anything like them, but merely to 'declare my belief in the faith which is revealed in the Holy Scripture and set forth in the Catholic creeds, and to which the historic formularies of the Church of England bear witness . . .' As was plain from the debates in the General Synod when the new Canon was being drafted, this declaration describes not a new way of consenting to the doctrine of the Church of England, but the way doctrine was already being regarded. It was understood that they were bringing the rules into line with what already actually happened. As to the Thirty-nine Articles themselves, one of the objectives was to cure the 'flippant' way they were being treated. It is clear that the custom of the clergy uttering solemn words on public occasions that they privately did not agree with was already very widespread.

But that was not the mood of church and state in 1953. The coronation service meant what it said it meant. The unsustainability of what it said it meant was later to become a powerful factor in undermining public confidence in official religion, all of which came to be regarded, little by little, as allegorical, mythical, pious posturing – or just plain untrue. And that is the trouble with an unwritten constitution. It can unravel. No English person really believes in everything the coronation stood for: many now believe in none of it. Every American believes in everything the American constitution stands for.

There is one further dimension of the coronation service that would not have been immediately obvious to an outside observer. The coronation oath sworn by the Queen contained the hint of an unspecified threat. Why would she have to promise to use 'the utmost of her power' to preserve the privileges of the Church of England, unless someone else, unnamed, was trying to rob it of them? There is no clue here to the nature of the threat except perhaps in the words 'Protestant Reformed'. And then the threat becomes a little clearer. It is an anti-Protestant threat, in other words a Roman Catholic threat – 'Pope' of John Bunyan's famous fable.

This hint of a Catholic threat becomes even more obvious if one considers the past history of coronation oaths in England. The oath sworn by Queen Elizabeth in Westminster Abbey to uphold the Protestant religion was one of two required by English constitutional law. On her accession to the throne following the death of her father King George VI, she had also been required to swear before Parliament: 'I do solemnly and sincerely in the presence of God, profess, testify and declare that I am a faithful Protestant, and that I will, according to the true intent of the enactments to secure the Protestant Succession to the Throne of my realm, uphold and maintain such enactments to the best of my power.'

This was the form of words laid down by Parliament since 1910, when they were revised at the insistence of George V who had just succeeded to the throne at the death of Edward VII. He considered the oath sworn by his father in 1902 to be offensive to the British Empire's many Roman Catholic subjects – not surprisingly, as the words of the pre-1910 oath are an object lesson in just how offensive it is possible to be. There had been indignant complaints about the unrevised words of the oath from Catholic Ireland, and from Australia, with its large Irish Catholic population, and Canada, with its large French Catholic population, as well as various attempts at amendment in the House of Commons. So the 1953 form of oath was a compromise.

The 'Royal Declaration' that Queen Elizabeth might have had to swear before Parliament, and that Edward VII, Victoria and all monarchs back to William and Mary in 1689 did actually swear, was as follows:

> I, N, by the grace of God King (or Queen) of England, Scotland and Ireland, Defender of the Faith, do solemnly and sincerely in the presence of God, profess, testify, and declare, that I do believe that in the Sacrament of the Lord's Supper there is not any Transubstantiation of the elements of bread and wine into the Body and Blood of Christ at or after the consecration thereof by any person whatsoever: and that the invocation or adoration of the Virgin Mary or any other Saint, and the Sacrifice of the Mass, as they are now used in the Church of Rome, are superstitious and idolatrous. And I do solemnly in the presence of God profess, testify, and declare that I do make this declaration, and every part thereof, in the plain and ordinary sense of the words read unto me, as they are commonly understood by English Protestants, without any such dispensation from any person or authority or person whatsoever, or without thinking that I am or can be acquitted before God or man, or absolved of this declaration or any part thereof, although the Pope, or any other person or persons, or power whatsoever, should dispense with or annul the same or declare that it was null and void from the beginning.

The doctrines to be denied were characteristic doctrines of the Roman Catholic Church which the Church of England rejected, so it was intentional that faithful Roman Catholics could not take the oath. Article 22 of the Thirty-nine Articles of Religion of the Church of England declared: 'The Romish Doctrine concerning Purgatory, Pardons, Worshipping, and Adoration, as well of Images as of Reliques, and also invocation of Saints, is a fond thing vainly invented, and grounded upon no warranty of Scripture, but rather repugnant to the Word of God.' Article 28 stated: 'Transubstantiation (or the change of the substance of Bread and Wine) in the Supper of the Lord, cannot be proved by Holy Writ; but it is repugnant to the plain words of Scripture, overthroweth the nature of a Sacrament, and hath given occasion to many superstitions.' And Article 31 denounced 'the sacrifices of Masses, in the which it was commonly said that the Priest did offer Christ for the quick and the dead, to have remission of pain or guilt' and labelled them 'blasphemous fables, and dangerous deceits'. Since 1865, Church of England clergy had had to declare that the doctrine in the Articles was 'agreeable to the Word of God', which was understood as falling short of swearing that the doctrine was agreeable to themselves, which they were previously required to do. (After 1975 the Form of Assent to the Thirty-nine Articles became much vaguer.)

The requirement to take a coronation oath is laid down in the Act of Settlement of 1701. This also declares that any person who 'shall or may take or inherit the Crown . . . and is, are or shall be reconciled to, or shall hold communion with, the See or Church of Rome, or shall profess the popish religion, or shall marry a papist . . .' shall be treated as legally dead for purposes of the succession, and passed over so that the Crown passes to the next in line (provided they are not similarly disqualified). The Act also decrees that 'whosoever shall hereafter come to the possession of this Crown, shall join in communion with the Church of England, as by law established'.

That this extraordinary public oath was required of the British sovereign was rather ironic. By 1910 no other subject was required to take it. That was the reverse of the case when these words were first introduced, under what was known as the Test Act – a generic term for a series of anti-Catholic laws, some applicable to Britain, some to Ireland, some to the colonies. At first, an anti-Catholic oath was required of subjects, but not of the sovereign. Taking it was a condition of ordination to holy orders in the Church of England, of entry to the universities of Oxford and Cambridge, of having a commission in the army or Royal Navy, of being sworn as a member of the judiciary or as a magistrate, or of becoming a Member of Parliament.

The Test Act's most extreme oath dated from 1678. That was the year of the alleged unmasking by one Titus Oates of a supposed plot by various Catholics, including Jesuits, to kill King Charles II and install the Duke of York (later James II, England's last Catholic king) in his place. Before the authorities realised that Oates had made it all up, some thirty-five Catholics had been executed for treason, the final victim, in 1681, being the Catholic Archbishop of Armagh, Oliver Plunkett, now canonised as a martyr. He was the last Catholic to die 'for the faith' in England (though he was tried for treason, a non-denominational offence). Titus Oates was disgraced, imprisoned, fined and flogged, but came back into favour after the fall of James II, and given a state pension.

There were anti-Catholic loyalty oaths before 1678, one of which insisted the swearer should deny that the Pope could depose an English sovereign (which arose from the papal excommunication and attempted deposition of Elizabeth I in 1570). There was even an earlier simpler seventeenth-century oath denying the Catholic doctrine of Transubstantiation, which caused the Duke of York to resign as Lord High Admiral. But paradoxically while he was prevented by law from serving his brother the king, he was not prevented by the same law from becoming king himself. One of the major projects of his short reign, and one of the major reasons he was deposed by Parliament in 1688, was his desire to abolish or at least modify the Test Act (which he had actually suspended in New York when it was for a while under his direct administration as Duke of York. He even appointed a Catholic governor and other officials.).

Already some Catholics had attempted to neutralise the force of the earlier form by arguing that it did not mean what it seemed to mean. Hence the strange reference in the 1678 version to 'the plain and ordinary sense of the words read unto me, as they are commonly understood by English Protestants'. Nor, despite the insinuation in the language, did Catholics believe that the Pope could dispense people from an oath, once taken. The English Parliament was perhaps thinking of itself. It did claim the power to dispense from oaths, and abrogated the oath of loyalty to James II after he was driven into exile in 1688. Eight bishops of the Church of England, most of whom had opposed the religious policies of James II, refused to renounce the allegiance to him they had sworn on oath, and lost their jobs. Some 400 other Anglican clergy were also among these 'nonjurors'.

The Test Act was finally repealed in 1829, though rumours that the government intended to repeal it was one of the factors that led to the Gordon Riots in London in 1780. Indeed, the actual repeal of the Test Act as it applied to Canada was a contributory cause of the American Revolutionary War. A military invasion of Canada, including a brief siege of the capital, Quebec, was one of the first but also one of the least successful adventures of the new republic's military forces.

The Quebec Act of 1774 was designed to deal with major questions that had arisen during the attempt to make the French colony of Canada a province of the British Empire in North America. Among these questions were whether an assembly could be summoned when nearly all the inhabitants of the province of Quebec, being Roman Catholics, would, because of the Test Acts, be ineligible to be representatives; whether the practice of the Roman Catholic religion should be allowed to continue, and on what conditions; and whether French or English law was to be used in the courts of justice.

The Act, declaring it inexpedient to call an assembly, put the power to legislate in the hands of the governor and his council. But the practice of the Roman Catholic religion was allowed, and the church was authorised to continue to collect the tithe. The Test Act was waived and an oath of allegiance substituted so as to allow Roman Catholics to hold office. This led to fears in the American colonies that the Quebec Act might see the revival of French rule, France being perceived at that time as an enemy (rather than, as later in the war against Britain, a powerful friend).

But the *Encyclopaedia Britannica*, from which this summary of the episode is taken, is being too tactfully political. It fails to mention the substantial influence of pure anti-Catholic sentiment behind the invasion of Canada. For instance the Continental Congress, meeting in September 1774, expressed its outrage to the British public 'that a British Parliament should ever consent to establish in that country [i.e. Quebec] a religion that has deluged your island in blood'. Clearly members of the Congress were familiar with the persecution of Protestants in the sixteenth century under 'Bloody' Mary I, as luridly told in Foxe's *Book of Martyrs*, and they took it for granted the British would be too. The *Pennsylvania Packet* newspaper said never before had there been 'such a bare faced attempt against the success of the Protestant religion'. Pope Day, 5 November (Guy Fawkes Day to the English), was celebrated with particular fury in 1774. Within a few years, however, Washington was to forbid his army to mark the Day, not least for fear of upsetting America's new-found Catholic friends, the French.

So the expedition to Canada was fuelled by much the same Protestant rage as would cause the London mob to run riot five years later, burning and looting every property owned by Catholics that they could find throughout the city. The rioters immediate target was the Catholic Relief Act of 1778, which removed some of the legal penalties of practising the Catholic faith. It did not go as far as the Quebec Act and repeal the Test Act, though Lord Gordon, leader of the riot, liked to suggest that was next on the list. Charles Dickens's novel *Barnaby Rudge* gives a vivid account of the mayhem. But neither the invasion of Canada nor the London riot brought any credit to its leaders. Lord Gordon was arrested, tried and acquitted, but later died in prison on an unrelated matter; Benedict Arnold, the senior military commander to survive the Canadian campaign, later betrayed his side to the British and is branded a traitor to this day.

The American aggression against Canadian soil put paid to any possibility that most Canadians might want to join their southern neighbours in rebellion against the Crown (though some of the more Protestant Canadians did move south when the war against Britain was over). Nor were oaths for the suppression of Catholicism to be in favour in North America much longer. Perhaps the fact that Catholics from France had fought on the American side had had an effect on national opinion. Article VI of the Constitution of the United States, in force from 1789, laid down that 'no religious test shall ever be required as qualification to any office or public trust under the United States'. The use of the word 'test' is obviously significant. A similar provision is written into the constitutions of most American states.

Ray Raphael, in *The American Revolution, a People's History*, is commendably frank about the bigotry behind the Canada expedition.

Hoping to revive the patriotic fervour, American military leaders decided to grasp the initiative by striking where the British were weak. In retrospect it is hard to see how the invasion of a foreign colony related to the fight against tyranny at home, but Yankees steeped in the Protestant faith had little trouble drumming up the motivation to invade the stronghold of Catholicism on their northern border. Britain had recently placed all the lands west of the Appalachians under Canadian control, while simultaneously granting official recognition to the Catholic Church in Quebec. American Protestants of all denominations, from Yankee Congregationalists to Southern Anglicans, noted the obvious parallels between the political tyranny of the British monarch and the religious tyranny of the Catholic pope: in each case, an authoritarian ruler was interfering with the freedom of individuals to live or worship as they pleased. The expedition into Canada, a continental cleansing in the name of political and religious liberty, promised to dethrone two tyrants at once. Here was the greatest Pope's Day riot of them all – and not only effigies would be burned this time. One army chaplain spoke for many when he wrote in his diary: 'Had pleasing views of the glorious day of universal peace and spread of the Gospel through this vast extended country, which has been for ages the dwelling of Satan, and reign of Antichrist.'[14]

In the light of this, it is less surprising that before the coronation in 1902 and again in 1910, the Canadian government had been pressing hard for a revision of the Royal Declaration which had to be made by the British sovereign (who was also head of state in Canada) at the start of his or her reign. Canadian legislators had been freed from having to swear such an outlandish anti-Catholic declaration in 1774, and indeed had had to fight off an American invasion the main purpose of which, undoubtedly, was to reimpose it at the point of a freedom-loving Massachusetts bayonet. That this has not been a popular theme among American historians is remarked upon by Kevin Phillips in his *The Cousins' Wars*: 'To many eighteenth century Britons and British colonials, Roman Catholicism was a Pope-led conspiracy on behalf of idolatrous religion and autocratic, tyrannical government . . . British historians have pursued this religious insistence with much more candour than their American colleagues, but both countries have been affected.'[15]

In his *The Language of Liberty* the historian J. C. D. Clark has called the 'virulence and power of popular American Anti-Catholicism' the 'suppressed theme of [American] colonial history'.[16] Raphael's *History* confirms rather than confounds this, for as well as being written after Phillips's comment, it is something of an anti-history, a revisionist look at received American historical assumptions.

Phillips credits the British with being more honest about this aspect of their past. It is true that all vestiges of anti-Catholicism have been removed from the public ritual aspects of the United States constitution, and the inauguration of a new President, if not purely secular, is at least a tamely non-denomination occasion. This has not yet been done in the equivalent British ritual, the coronation service. But American ceremonial tends to mean what it says. British ceremonial no longer does.

It should not be assumed that the deliberate intention of those taking part in a coronation service was to isolate or alienate any actual live Roman Catholics, any more than that was the intention of people who celebrated Guy Fawkes Day every 5 November. Indeed, the Master of Ceremonies at Westminster Abbey on 2 June 1953 – as at the coronation of the Queen's father, King George VI in 1937 – was by tradition the Earl Marshal of England, an office held by the premier non-royal nobleman of the kingdom, the sixteenth Duke of Norfolk. And Norfolk was a staunch Roman Catholic, as were his ancestors – one of them, Philip Howard, was later to be canonised by the Pope as a Catholic martyr of the sixteenth century.[17] As explained more fully in other chapters, the real function of anti-Catholicism in English constitutional theory since the Reformation was to protect the religious and political identity of the English nation-state. Roman Catholicism undermines the theological basis for that identity. Naturally, this 'institutional' anti-Catholicism was helped by personal prejudice against individual Catholics. It was easier to persuade the population that Catholicism was discredited if those who practised that faith were seen to be (whether they actually were or not) feckless, immoral or treacherous.

A serious objection to this way of decoding the coronation may be anticipated. It is that, notwithstanding the symbolism, those taking part would not have had the slightest time for any anti-Catholic sentiments and would have regarded the oaths upholding the Church of England as quaint, and on the whole empty, relics of a time long past (much as if the Queen had had to swear to uphold the Beefeaters at the Tower of London). Hence the English national identity manifested so confidently at the coronation did not need to define itself by opposition to some other religious system (Catholicism or whatever). That would have given Catholicism (or whatever) far more importance in the English scheme of things than it actually had.

As a sociological observation, that objection has some weight. The actual state of Roman Catholicism in England in the 1950s was indeed largely irrelevant to the national self-understanding. It had its own agenda, which impinged on the rest of the nation only when there was a clash of interests. As I wrote in *The Worlock Archive*, the English Catholic Church in 1953 under the leadership of Cardinal Bernard Griffin was, for perfectly good social and historical reasons, highly insular. It kept itself to itself. Indeed, the exclusively Anglican coronation service of that year might have been designed to keep it that way. It defined the nation in a way that left Catholics feeling if not shut out altogether then at least left at the margins. But in no way did English Catholics wish to challenge the Anglican ascendancy. They preferred to mind their own business.

> What was lacking was a sense of responsibility for the whole of society rather than the relatively small part of it that was Catholic. Unconscious and unstated was an image of the British nation as a foreign country, not so much because it wasn't Irish – Griffin was indeed an Englishman – but because, to Catholics of Griffin's generation, it was still distinctly Protestant. Catholics felt excluded from the national discourse. These were not just unecumenical times, but actively anti-ecumenical. It was an 'us-and-them' world. 'They' made the decisions, had the power. 'We' had to defend our interests or have them snatched away.[18]

So the answer to this objection is actually quite simple. It has nothing to do with the actual Catholic Church present in England at that time, a largely Irish body which thought it wise to mind its own business. It did not buy into the English national ideology. Whereas those taking part in the coronation service undoubtedly felt there was something inexpressibly special about being English. They got this sense from a coronation service which had revisited the roots of English identity and declared them to be religious, and in so doing rehearsed and affirmed again the grounds for believing England was a uniquely favoured nation. 'Religious' in this context does not just mean 'Anglican'. It also plainly means 'not Roman Catholic'. A Protestant is someone who protests. The protest is at Roman Catholicism: but in principle, not the community led by Cardinal Griffin, which was, so to speak, neither here nor there.

Like 99 per cent of his fellow citizens, he was not a member of the British Establishment, that exclusive group of people who dominated public life and operated within a shared system of values which they took for granted as self-evident. The coronation was an event participation in which was confined to the élite of the Establishment. Indeed, in so far as it signalled 'ownership' of the state and its institutions, this group was limited to the monarchy, the aristocracy and the English National Church – also called, appropriately, the Established Church. In 1953 the rules of this English Establishment had a lot to do with a system of social ranking, or class, which was understood almost instinctively by the English of that generation. Thus the 'Crowning Glory' (as the newspapers called it) which cheered the nation on the morning of the coronation – news from

Nepal that a British expedition had become the first to conquer Everest – was later commemorated by the award to Edmund Hillary of a knighthood (a KBE – Knight of the British Empire) and to Tenzing Norgay of a George Medal. Apart from the anomaly that the GM is more usually awarded for gallantry, not achievement, it is somewhat below a knighthood in status. To the English mindset of 1953 the disparity between the award to Hillary (white New Zealander and an amateur mountaineer) and Tenzing (a Nepalese/Indian employed as a sherpa) seemed natural. Certainly it went unremarked. Sir John Hunt (also knighted) who led the expedition later said he felt it was a bold modern departure from the customs of the British Empire to admit someone like Tenzing into the mountaineering team at all. Even so, he was not invited to share a tent with the white men.

3

A Succession of Covenants

We can no longer take for granted familiarity with the Bible, Old Testament or New. Queen Victoria may have described it as the world's most priceless treasure. It is still an incomparable piece of English literature, 'full', as someone once said about Shakespeare 'of quotations'.[1] Parts of it have passed into the general language – from 'Let no man put asunder' to 'Thou shalt not . . .' (almost anything). But for the rest – though even more in England than in America – public ignorance reigns unchallenged. A professor of English Literature at a leading English university decided he was making so little progress teaching his students about the poetry of Milton that he had to organise a crash course in the Bible for them. To their generation it was literally a closed book.

Yet this is a work with more direct influence on English and American history than any other. Though one sympathises with the professor's exasperation, to study the Bible purely as a literary source, and even that only in order to make better sense of Milton, is a strange order of priorities.

Christopher Hill, in his definitive study *The English Bible and the Seventeenth Century Revolution*,[2] says the Bible 'played a large part in moulding English nationalism, in asserting the supremacy of the English language in a society which from the eleventh to the fourteen century had been dominated by French speaking Normans'. In authorising the publication of an English version of the Bible, Henry VIII 'had been mainly concerned to secure England's political independence from the papacy'. Thus it was a crucial part of the struggle to establish the world's first totally self-contained nation-state.

In the English revolutions of the seventeenth century all sides appealed to the Bible for support. Hill asserts that by the end of the eighteenth, in contrast, it was no longer regarded as the source of all truth: the Enlightenment virtually ignored it. But that judgment runs rather against the evidence. The Bible was perhaps no longer a total explanation of everything, as it had been previously. But it was still a major influence in politics, not least because of its hold on the public imagination.

So when he writes 'it was no longer the revolutionists' handbook' – referring to the Bible's influence over Cromwell and the Puritans a century before – his point is true only on one side of the Atlantic, and even then only up to a point. As Linda Colley shows convincingly in her ground-breaking book *Britons*,[3] Bible-based religion was at the centre of the Protestant ideology of Britishness which was used to keep the Jacobites at bay for the greater part of the eighteenth century. Whether its function was revolutionary or counter-revolutionary depends whose side one was on. The Jacobites were the followers of the deposed Stuart and Catholic king James II and his Catholic offspring, turfed out by what the supporters of William and Mary called the Glorious Revolution. They used the Bible to support their revolution, therefore; but once they were in power, it was the Jacobites who in turn became the revolutionaries, and the Bible was then used against them. On the other side, the use of the Bible against the Glorious Revolution did not greatly interest the Jacobites as such, though it did receive much attention from the Non-Jurors (Protestant clergy who remained faithful to their oath to the Stuart king).

And the Bible was indeed the revolutionists' handbook in the American colonies as the breach with Britain widened to breaking point. Nowhere is this better demonstrated than in the meeting of the First Continental Congress, which was convened in September 1774 as war with England grew imminent. As news of the British bombardment of Boston reached Philadelphia, an Episcopalian (Anglican) pastor, the Reverend Jacob Duche, was called upon to lead the assembly in prayer. He was not of the Puritan persuasion – indeed, that was partly why New England delegate Sam Adams proposed him for the task, as a symbol of unity at a unique time of crisis. But the text he chose to read, and the words he said after it, can unambiguously be seen as recruiting the Bible to America's side in the coming struggle. He is putting America into the place of Israel, and invoking God's defence of Israel in ancient times as the reason for him to defend America now. As delegates bowed their heads and Virginian delegate George Washington was seen to kneel, Duche selected from the Psalms the 35th, which begins:

Plead my cause, O Lord, with them that strive with me: fight against them that fight against me. Take hold of shield and buckler, and stand up for mine help. Draw out also the spear, and stop the way against them that persecute me: say unto my soul, I am thy salvation. Let them be confounded and put to shame that seek after my soul: let them be turned back and brought to confusion that devise my hurt. Let them be as chaff before the wind: and let the angel of the Lord chase them. Let their way be dark and slippery: and let the angel of the Lord persecute them . . .

(This is the reference to 'angels in the wind' which George W. Bush alluded to in his inaugural address quoted previously.) And it ends with a reminder that the chosen of God are rewarded not just with victory over their enemies but with prosperity; but in return they have to remain faithful:

Keep not silence: O Lord, be not far from me. Stir up thyself, and awake to my judgment, even unto my cause, my God and my Lord. Judge me, O Lord my God, according to thy righteousness; and let them not rejoice over me. Let them not say in their hearts, Ah, so would we have it: let them not say, We have swallowed him up. Let them be ashamed and brought to confusion together that rejoice at mine hurt: let them be clothed with shame and dishonour that magnify themselves against me. Let them shout for joy, and be glad, that favour my righteous cause: yea, let them say continually, Let the Lord be magnified, which hath pleasure in the prosperity of his servant. And my tongue shall speak of thy righteousness and of thy praise all the day long.

While Puritans would already have been familiar with the preaching device of putting New England in the place of Israel, the many Episcopalians present would have been more familiar with the traditional liturgical custom (adapted from the medieval Catholic practice) of seeing the Church of England – or England in its spiritual aspect – as standing in Israel's shoes. It was at the opening of the Continental Congress in 1774, and by this reading and the prayer that followed, that America formally introduced itself into those shoes, thereby both expelling England from them and enlarging the Puritan claim to them to embrace the entire thirteen colonies. It was, *par excellence*, the act that founded America upon a specific understanding of God's purposes. Henceforth the Chosen People were to be not the Jews, not the Catholics, not the English, and not just the New Englanders, but all Americans. Henceforth 'being an American', like being a Jew or being a Christian, was to possess a distinct religious status as one of the elect.

In the following two centuries, there has survived a sense that entry into American citizenship was like the initiation ceremony of a religious movement, just as baptism was the process of initiation into membership of the Christian church. It changed the fundamental character of the individual concerned, who was henceforth regarded as indelibly special in a way he or she was not before. (The technical theological description in the case of baptism is that it bestows once for all a 'sacramental character' on the individual, who is thereby inwardly changed.) Applicants for American citizenship are given a course on what membership of their new status requires of them, examined on it – 'catechised' would be an appropriate word – and then sworn into American citizenship at a ritual swearing of allegiance to the Flag. It is best understood as part of the ongoing process by which Americans 'imagine' their community into existence by an act of will (see chapter one), which now begins to look more like an act of faith. Furthermore, each adult immigrant who becomes an American does so by an act of will, which is also an act of submission of the will. He or she chooses no longer to be what he or she was before: he or she chooses instead to submit to whatever is involved in 'being an American'.

One may suspect that very many Americans would recognise as correct the idealised portrait of an America written by the 'poet of America', Walt Whitman, in his introduction to the 1855 edition of his collection *Leaves of Grass*. What non-Americans need to remember is that this is a description of how things ought to be, not, despite Whitman's use of a direct voice, how things actually were. He is, in other words, imagining 'an American' into existence.

> The United States themselves are essentially the greatest poem ... The genius of the United States is not best or most in its executives or legislatures, not in its ambassadors or authors or colleges or churches or parlors, nor even in its newspapers or inventors ... but always most in the common people. Their manners, speech, dress, friendships – the freshness and candor of their physiognomy – the picturesque looseness of their carriage ... their deathless attachment to freedom – their aversion to anything indecorous or soft or mean – the practical acknowledgement of the citizens of one state by the citizens of all other states – the fierceness of their roused resentment – their curiosity and welcome of novelty – their self-esteem and wonderful sympathy – their susceptibility to a slight – the air they have of persons who never knew how it felt to stand in the presence of superiors – the fluency of their speech – their delight in music, the sure symptom of manly tenderness and native elegance of soul ... their good temper and openhandedness – the terrible significance of their elections – the President's taking off his hat to them not they to him – these too are unrhymed poetry.

There are similarities and significant differences here with St Paul's famous tribute to Christian charity in 1 Corinthians 13:4–8, which is somewhat at odds with Whitman's approval of 'roused resentment' and 'susceptibility to slight':

Love is patient and kind. Love envies no-one, is never boastful, never conceited, never rude; love is never selfish, never quick to take offence. Love keeps no score of wrongs, takes no pleasure in the sins of others, but delights in the truth. There is nothing love cannot face; there is no limit to its faith, its hope, its endurance. Love will never come to an end.[4]

Despite such differences of outcome, the resemblance between the process of initiation into American citizenship and the Christian sacrament of initiation is strong. It also has points in common with the process by which a convert is admitted into Judaism. This parallel is borne out by the habitual way Americans in general and government officials in particular have of speaking of fellow Americans as a people set apart from the rest of humanity. They may not be conscious of it, but this is not how the rest of the world's nationalities think or speak about their own. An Englishman who goes to live in France, even taking French citizenship and speaking French, will never be anything other than an Englishman in his own eyes and the eyes of his French neighbours. He cannot will himself not to be an Englishman. He is what his memory tells him he is. Nor is this held against him. And a Frenchman living in England would not stop being French.

This is one answer to those who argue that, however America saw itself in the late seventeenth or eighteenth century, it has long since lost any sense of itself as a religious entity. Do Americans still think of themselves as, in some sense, having a 'destiny' that is not entirely of their own devising? And do Americans think of their fellow Americans as somehow metaphysically or ontologically different from the rest of humanity? The reply has to be Yes, and both these marks of identification appear to have been greatly strengthened by events on and since the terrorist attacks of September 2001. This sense of destiny and sense of specialness go to make up what modern commentators call 'American exceptionalism' (as in two recent books of that name, by Seymour Martin Lipset[5] and Deborah L. Madsen[6]). American exceptionalism is but eighteenth-century chosenness ('election' is the less familiar word, and in this context does not mean the ballot box) dressed in modern clothes. Calling it a religion, as if America were eligible for membership of the World Council of Churches, is obviously a category mistake. Calling it a religion in the sense that Islam is a religion is, however, much nearer the mark. The Great Smokescreen behind which this essentially religious view of America has been hidden is the First Amendment, the Separation of Church and State, which will be considered in more detail later.

The British take it to the opposite extreme – applicants meeting the residence and other qualifications for 'naturalisation', as it is termed, receive a curt letter from the Home Office telling them that they are now entitled to apply for a passport. Americans who receive British citizenship – usually in the form of 'dual citizenship' that does not require them to surrender their American rights – are universally struck by the extreme contrast. Meanwhile the British are beginning to think that as well as a residence requirement, a language requirement would also be helpful to good community relations. But there is no inclination to turn British naturalisation into a crypto-sacrament, as in America.

Oddly, this rival spiritual status does not have seemed to have disturbed any of the guardians of religious orthodoxy in America, neither Catholic nor Protestant nor Jewish nor Muslim. Perhaps blinded by the constitution theory of the separation of church and state, they did not notice that America itself had become a quasi-religious entity. As for questioning whether the treatment of the American flag as sacred amounted to idolatry, Americans would regard it as sacrilege even to mention the possibility (which perhaps proves the point).

As if to confirm this designation, the Rev. Mr Duche followed his reading of the defiant Psalm 35 with a prayer, in which the words pronouncing Americans henceforth to be 'Thy people' were by no means the least significant. It was by this act of dedication that Congress submitted the nation it was soon to create to God's will, in return for his protection – the classic biblical formula for a divine covenant. Duche prayed:

> O Lord our Heavenly Father, high and mighty King of Kings and Lord of Lords, who doest from Thy throne behold all the dwellers on earth, and reignest with power supreme and uncontrolled over all kingdoms, empires and governments; look down in mercy we beseech Thee, on these American States, who have fled to Thee from the rod of the oppressor, and thrown themselves on Thy gracious protection, desiring to be henceforth dependent only on Thee; to Thee they have appealed for the righteousness of their cause; to Thee do they now look up for that countenance and support which Thou alone canst give; take them, therefore, Heavenly Father, under thy nurturing care; give them wisdom in council . . . Be Thou present, O God of wisdom, and direct the councils of this honourable assembly; enable them to settle things on the best and surest foundation, that the scene of blood may be speedily closed, that order, harmony, and peace, may be effectually restored; and truth and justice, religion and piety, prevail and flourish among Thy people.

The Congress was deeply moved. John Adams later wrote to his wife: 'I never saw a greater effect upon an audience. It seemed as if heaven had ordained that psalm to be read on that morning . . .'

It is no coincidence that the more historically aware of the rising breed of American patriots regarded Cromwell's rebellion against the King very much as a precedent for their own. The example they followed was not just based in his actions, but also his grounds for them. The Puritan Roundheads' argument that a Christian people had the right to free itself from the oppression of a tyrant was firmly rooted in biblical, especially Old Testament, principles. It was the theme of thousands of pre-Revolutionary sermons across the thirteen colonies. Indeed, the English Civil War and subsequent Glorious Revolution – whereby both Charles I and his son James II were overthrown, the former by execution and the latter by exile – became an almost universal model for European and American revolutionaries. As Bridget Hill notes in *The Republican Virago*, her study of the life of Catharine Macaulay, favourite British historian of Thomas Jefferson among others:

> It was not only English radicals that drew analogies – whether or not mistakenly – between present politics and those of the pre-Civil War period. As the crisis in relations with the American colonies worsened many Sons of Liberty were interpreting government policy towards the colonists in terms of the 17th century English experience. In her interpretation of the early stages of the French Revolution in 17th century English terms, Catharine Macaulay was far from alone. Many revolutionaries in the 1790s concerned with the legitimacy of removing, and possibly executing, a king looked back to 17th century England. Burke's condemnation of the French revolutionaries, as indeed the many answers, including Catharine Macaulay's, that condemnation provoked, hinged on different interpretations of the achievements of the Glorious Revolution of 1688. For those contemplating revolutionary change what more natural than to examine and draw lessons from an earlier revolution – and one sufficiently distant to allow for a relatively dispassionate analysis? For the French as for the American revolutionaries there were parallels to be drawn and lessons to be learnt from the events of the previous century in England. Knowledge of those events relied on an understanding of 17th century English history. Catharine Macaulay's *History* played no small part in providing the basis of such understanding.[7]

While the precedent of the English Civil War is plainly helpful to the American Patriots' case, they were more tentative about the relevance of the events of 1688. For it was the regime installed in place of James II which soon logically led to the Hanoverian succession, and gave legitimacy to George III. The American Revolutionaries were more interested in arguments which undermined King George's legitimacy than any which upheld it.

One is tempted to ask whether Christopher Hill, distinguished English historian of the Cromwellian period, is understating the influence of the Bible on eighteenth-century revolutionary politics in his own work in order to throw into sharper relief the implication to the contrary in the work of the distinguished English historian Bridget Hill. It is a pleasing thought – they are, after all, husband and wife, and each of them thanks the other generously for help in revising their books. Whether through the gallantry of the husband or not, the wife wins the argument. If the Bible was a decisive shaper of revolution in the seventeenth century, and seventeenth-century revolution was a decisive shaper of revolution in the eighteenth, then the Bible was indirectly decisive in the eighteenth as well. Perhaps no longer the revolutionists' handbook in the French case. But still one in America.

Macaulay, says Bridget Hill, was an admirer of the American preacher Jonathan Edwards, whose famous hellfire sermons were at the very core of the Evangelical 'Great Awakening' in the mid-eighteenth century. As we shall see when we examine one of them more closely later in this chapter, he was steeped in a biblical view of the world and convinced of America's special role in God's plan of salvation. 'Behind Edwards' ideas also there lurked a millennialism, a belief that the Awakening fore-shadowed a "time when all nations and countries shall be full of light and knowledge",' says Bridget Hill. She also reports that historians are increasingly seeing Edwards' 'new spirit of defiant individualism' as 'playing a central part in preparing America for the revolution'. But as Hill is also at pains to show, Catharine Macaulay herself was a consider-able influence on American revolutionary thought. And her outlook too was strongly biblical, tending even to a modified form of Calvinism though not quite orthodox in terms of eighteenth-century Anglicanism.

A biblical view of world history is inescapably a belief in Providence. The fortunes of the ancient Israelites are constantly shaped by the unseen hand of God, for good or ill. Many found in the combination of Old and New Testaments a justification for believing that God's work was leading up to a culminating event, a religious Millennium (rather different from the literal kind that was universally celebrated in the year 2000). That idea too had a powerful influence in America. Many of the Founding Fathers read and appreciated Catharine Macaulay. Benjamin Franklin praised her *History*; Jefferson listed it as a 'preferred authority', purchased all eight volumes, and had them installed in the library of the University of Virginia. John Adams viewed it 'with much admiration'. She was the historian who George Washington knew best. Josiah Quincy and Benjamin Rush were familiar with her work.

All of which highlights the significance of her own views on Providence, which must have been very influential in these circles.

Indeed, in seeking to unscramble the origins of the whole American way of thought, Catharine Macaulay must deserve much more credit than she has been given. It is a little surprising that the doyen of American historians of this period, Bernard Baylin, does not rate her significance more highly. In his *The Ideological Origins of the American Revolution*[8] he says only that 'The republican historian Catharine Macaulay, whose *History of England* has aptly been called "an imaginative work in praise of republican principles under the title of a *History of England*" was also an important intellectual figure of this generation of colonists . . .' but not as important as some others he names. What discourages admiration of Macaulay among contemporary historians is undoubtedly her dubious synthesis of pre-Norman Conquest mythology and her tendency to blame everything on the Normans, who allegedly laid waste some sort of Anglo-Saxon paradise. It was an unsound theory, though Thomas Jefferson, among others, accepted it. It is not her historical accuracy we are concerned with here, however, but her influence, especially on her American contemporaries. Her views on Providence and the coming millennium are therefore worth attending to, as they, the principal actors in this drama, certainly attended to them. Are they biblical? She would certainly have said so. Bridget Hill describes them as follows:

> Catharine Macaulay saw the 'events of human life' as 'but a series of benevolent providences.' Not always was the 'omnipotent will' seen behind them, but when it was seen 'declaring itself in favour of the future perfection and happiness of the moral world', little wonder if men were transported by 'hope and gratitude'. It was this, she wrote in 1790, that Burke failed to understand in men's reactions to the French Revolution. She questioned whether he had 'heard of any millennium' except 'that fanciful one that is supposed to exist in the kingdom of the saints.' The view that the 'doctrine of post-millennialism was central to Macaulay's religious beliefs' is a valid one . . . Catharine Macaulay envisaged the nature of the millennium as 'a period of time when the iron sceptre of arbitrary sway shall be broken; when righteousness shall prevail over the whole earth, and a correct system of equity take place in the conduct of man'. It was towards such a millennium that all improvement in men and society tended. This was God's plan for the world, but by co-operating with it men 'had the power to affect the course of history'.[9]

The charge that Burke only believed in 'a fanciful millennium' that existed in the 'kingdom of the saints' may well have been a barbed reference to Burke's alleged Roman Catholic sympathies, a highly damaging innuendo. Good Protestants, she seemed to be saying, believed in the millennium as a coming possibility, indeed a likelihood, in the real world. The breaking of the 'iron sceptre of arbitrary sway' would also have been heard by her contemporary listeners as meaning, in apocalyptic terms, the final overthrow of Anti-Christ (in other words, the Pope).

In Macaulay's blend of non-popery, republicanism and millennialism it is hard to imagine a more explicit statement of what lay behind Manifest Destiny and the American dream. At the outset, Manifest Destiny had a distinct anti-Catholic colour to it. One of its first tasks was to 'liberate' areas of southern North America living under a Spanish, i.e. Catholic, yoke. Macaulay was never as popular in England, where she was involved on behalf of John Wilkes, the pre-eminent English rake and radical of his time. He was not to everybody's taste and neither was she, though the American colonists made a hero out of him.

But her role establishes that religious ideology, appealing to the Bible for general support, was still a vibrant force in political affairs in the eighteenth century. Indeed, so deep was the influence of the English Bible from the sixteenth onwards, it is incredible to suppose that its influence could somehow be switched off in subsequent centuries. By the end of the sixteenth century, writes Christopher Hill, the Bible in English:

> was the property of all the literate laity, and radical Protestant preachers made a point of trying to extend knowledge of it to all levels of society. By the seventeenth century the Bible was accepted as central to all spheres of intellectual life: it was not merely a 'religious' book in our narrow modern sense of the word religious. Church and State in Tudor England were one; the Bible was, or should be, the foundation of all aspects of English culture. On this principle most Protestants were agreed. If we do not grasp this we shall fall into the anachronistic trap of speaking of 'a more religious age' than our own. In many senses it was a less religious age than ours.[10]

Some rehearsal of the salient points of Old Testament mythology will be necessary if we are to understand its full influence. It was not read simply for its history. It was also prophecy. The Old Testament narrative describes patterns of human behaviour which have since been repeated again and again. Hence they provide biblical parallels which can illuminate contemporary cases. They describe God's dealings with ancient individuals and societies when they went morally astray. They still go astray today, and God may be presumed to be consistent in his responses. Hence biblical stories can be used to predict outcomes. They are not, like Shakespeare's plays, merely illustrations of human nature and human situations. To say of someone that they are like Hamlet is to describe them as indecisive and conscience-torn. But a mere metaphor does not tell them how to resolve their difficulties. In this Protestant way of reading the Bible, however, to describe someone as being like Moses, Joshua or Solomon, is to point to a path that has been trodden before with an implied invitation to follow in those footsteps again. The technical term for this particular use of biblical allegory or metaphor is 'typology'. Moses, in this terminology, is a 'type', prefiguring Christ. It is also possible for other individuals to be a type, in this sense, in relation to Moses. This is not how the word 'type' is commonly used, and to avoid further confusion this specialised use of 'type' will be avoided as far as possible. It is defined in the *Oxford English Dictionary*[11] as 'a person, object or event in Old Testament history, prefiguring some person or thing revealed in the new dispensation'. The word 'prefiguring' means something more profound than 'symbolising' or 'representing'. Nor does the OED definition adequately describe Protestant typology.

The narrative of the Old Testament slowly reveals one continuing relationship from its inception: Israel's relationship with its God. As it unfolds, it gradually becomes clear that it is the key not just to God's relationship with the Jews but to his relationship with the whole of humanity for all time. The Jewish God is the universal God. In this understanding, God develops his relationship with humanity through what are called covenants, solemn agreements or contracts which have divine sanction. The most critical covenant is that which awards Israel its status as the Chosen People of God. Much of the unfolding story describes the working out of the terms of that covenant, especially what happens when the covenant is breached. In Jewish thought, both in the ancient world and in modern times, the covenant is unbreakable. God is always faithful to his promises, even if the Jews are not faithful to theirs. In the event of them not being faithful, he chastises them as a stern but loving father would a recalcitrant child. Providence intervenes to inflict poverty, tyranny, defeat in war, captivity, even exile.

These various corrective blows from the hand of God are suffered without understanding, until a prophet appears to point out what has gone wrong and what the people must do to regain God's favour. Invariably, they must return to the practice of the Law, above all the Ten Commandments. And of all the Commandments, that whose violation incurs the greatest divine wrath is not theft or murder, but idolatry. The God of the Old Testament is a jealous God. And there is a good reason. The idea of a jealous God serves as a protective for the ideal of monotheism: that there is one God, alone. If one accepts the biblical chronology as putting Patriarch Abraham (usually put at around the eighteenth century BCE) before Pharaoh Akhenaten (usually put at around the fourteenth century BCE), then the Jews were the first people in history to have such an idea. It was quite contrary to the *zeitgeist*. Ancient peoples took it for granted that the world was full of gods. Backsliding from monotheism to polytheism was easy. The road in the other direction was rough and uphill.

This is the true meaning of chosenness. It does not necessarily mean that the Chosen People are under God's special protection and care, for it can also mean that he has a special way of neglecting or reproaching them. At times, Jewish theologians have suggested, God 'withdraws', when the protection of Providence, for whatever ineffable reason, is temporarily suspended. Even then, chosenness means that they are under his special attention. There has been Jewish speculation, for instance, that God's 'withdrawal' of his protection from the Chosen People during the Nazi Holocaust, in which six million Jews died, was the means to the end of the restoration of the Jews to Israel. Uncomfortable though the thought may be – except perhaps for the most ardent of religious Zionists – it is more acceptable to Jewish thinkers than the proposition that the Holocaust was some sort of chastisement for wrongdoing. It may be noted in passing that the rules governing the interventions of Providence in human affairs do not always follow the rules of earthly morality. It appears that though God may be the author of moral law, he is not himself bound by it.

But Jews certainly are. Chosenness means that they are under a special duty to watch their step; they have extra obligations; they can expect to receive extra punishment if they transgress. And the purpose of their chosenness, far from being for their own advantage, is simply so that they can point to God's goodness and above all to his oneness. They are chosen in order to be special witnesses to monotheism. This is why idolatry – worshipping false gods, refusing to worship the One God – is the worst betrayal.

Rabbi Louis Jacobs, in his encyclopaedia *The Jewish Religion*, comments that some Jewish scholars have regarded Jewish chosenness as indicating that the Jews have a particular divine spark or genius for religion, compared with others. The sense of chosenness may have emerged at a time when the Israelites were the only monotheists, surrounded by pantheistic pagans. They had been chosen by God to believe in him. He adds:

> The average Jew takes pride in his conviction that he belongs to a people with a special role to play in God's world. Rarely has such pride gone beyond the harmless boasting most people engage in with regard to the particular group to which they belong, their nation, their religion, their country, even their club or football team. And virtually all Jewish teachers stress that the choice of the Jews is not for

privilege but for service. In the best Jewish thought, the election of Israel is by God and for God and for the fulfilment of his plan for all mankind.[12]

Similarly a former Chief Rabbi of Great Britain, (Lord) Dr Immanuel Jakobovits, is quoted as saying, in *Lord Jakobovits in Conversation*:

> Only to the degree that we possess values that are based on Judaism, values that contribute something to the world as a whole, is there justification ... for our continued existence ... The mission of the people of Israel is to function as a signpost for the whole world. We may possibly have tired of the realisation of this vision, but without it, what purpose is there in our continuing as Jews?[13]

He felt that non-Jews were beginning to see the point of Jewishness in these terms too, a perhaps optimistic view of how the rest of the world sees modern Israel – whose creation, in his view, was brought about by an act of divine Providence.

Traditionally, the fundamental difference between the Christian and Jewish understandings of the covenant occurs in connection with Jesus. Either, as Christians believed, the Jews breached the covenant finally and irrevocably by their failure to recognise their Messiah when he came, at which point God, so to speak, gave up on them; or the Jews remained steadfast to the covenant by refusing to be seduced from it by false claims for the Messiah-hood of Jesus. In the former case, Christians assumed the covenant had been continued or renewed, but henceforth it was to be with them, not with the Jews, who therefore ceased to be 'chosen'. So the titles of the two major sections of the Christian Bible, the Old Testament and the New Testament, should more logically be titled the Old Covenant and the New Covenant.

Rabbi Norman Solomon of Oxford, in an unpublished paper given at a Jewish-Christian conference in the United States in 2001, showed the parallels and contradictions between Jewish and Christian teaching contained in the rival theories of Jochanan Nappacha, a leading third-century Jewish Palestinian teacher, and the church father Origen who lived in Caesarea.

> Both commented on the biblical Song of Songs; both interpreted it as allegory. For Origen, it stands for God, or Christ and his 'bride,' the Church; for Jochanan, it is an allegory of the love between God and his people Israel. Reuven Kimelman (1980) has analysed their comments and found five consistent differences between them, corresponding to five major issues that divided Christians and Jews:

1. Origen writes of a covenant mediated by Moses between God and Israel; that is, an indirect contact between the two, contrasted with the direct presence of Christ. Jochanan, on the other hand, refers to the Covenant as negotiated by Moses, hence received by Israel direct from God, as 'the kisses of his mouth' (Song of Songs 1:2). Jochanan emphasises the closeness and love between God and Israel, whereas Origen sets a distance between them.
2. According to Origen, the Hebrew scripture was 'completed', or 'superseded', by the New Testament. According to Jochanan, scripture is 'completed' by the Oral Torah.
3. To Origen, Christ is the central figure, replacing Abraham and completing the reversal of Adam's sin. To Jochanan, Abraham remains in place and Torah is the 'antidote' to sin.
4. To Origen, Jerusalem is a symbol, a 'heavenly city'. To Jochanan, the earthly Jerusalem retains its status as the link between Heaven and Earth, the place where God's presence will again be manifest.
5. Origen sees the sufferings of Israel as the proof of its repudiation by God; Jochanan accepts the suffering as the loving chastisement and discipline of a forgiving father.

Hence in the Christian tradition the Old Covenant heralds, foreshadows and prophesies the New. Once the Old Covenant is made void, the New replaces – supersedes – it.

This has recently become known as the theory of 'supersessionism' (or 'replacement theory'). It has received a great deal of attention in the last few years as Christian and Jewish scholars have worked together to come to grips with the reasons for their 2000-year history of antagonism.

Rabbi Solomon's own solution (in the address already referred to) was for both Jews and Christians to regard talk of a 'covenant' as a poetic metaphor, not as a hard-edged objective (metaphysical) fact. If it is an 'object', only one group can possess it, and they are bound to quarrel over its ownership. As a metaphor it simply describes a relationship in an illuminating way: it does not impose any obligations, nor promise anything in return. The difficulty is that while this might soften the Christian claim to a covenant with God to the point where it no longer threatens the Jewish claim, it also dilutes the Jewish claim to the point where Jewish identity might seem to be undermined. If everyone can choose to imagine themselves to be in a covenantal relationship with God, the concept is emptied of meaning. (Needless to say, the 'covenant relationship' that Protestantism became interested in was the hard-edged kind, one that imposed duties and bestowed privileges on Protestant nation-states. Mere poetic metaphor would not have interested Oliver Cromwell nor the Continental Congress.)

What has given urgency to that task, in the aftermath of the Nazi

Holocaust, is the need to understand the rise of anti-Semitism in order to avoid its happening again. Although Christian anti-Semitism is in theory non-racial and it might be more technically correct to call it anti-Judaism, a racial element has never been far from the surface. It is hard to separate race from religion in this case. The explanation may be that the Jews do not speak of themselves as simply a religion, but as a religious people whose line continues down the generations largely by inheritance. A Jew is anyone born of a Jewish mother. This quickly shades into the modern notion of a race, though until modern times it was contradicted by the Christian assumption that any Jew who was baptised became a Christian. At that point, as far as the church is concerned, he or she was no longer to be regarded as a Jew. A contemporary Christian view would be much less categorical. In modern times both an Anglican Bishop of Birmingham, Hugh Montefiore, and a Catholic Archbishop of Paris, Cardinal Jean-Marie Lustiger, were converts to Christianity from Judaism, and both unambiguously described themselves as Jewish. It would be true to say, however, that the Jewish response to this claim is a little reserved. Though courtesy would forbid them saying so publicly, a Jew who becomes a Christian is still seen privately as some sort of a traitor.

Christian anti-Judaism and anti-Semitism had poisoned the soil of Europe for hundreds of years, eventually making it ripe for the deadly phenomenon of Nazism in the twentieth century. Christian scholars are now agreed that the Christian religion's disparagement of the Jews goes back to Christianity's origins, when the theory of supersessionism (though not the term) first appeared. They are not agreed whether that means the theory has to be abandoned, or what else to do about it. Thus Cardinal Walter Kasper, president of the Vatican Commission for Religious Relations with the Jews, told the meeting addressed by Solomon (quoted above) that the doctrine of the covenant was 'the central issue of the Jewish-Christian dialogue'. He said the relationship between the 'old covenant' of Judaism and the 'new covenant' of Christianity was 'so complex that it cannot be reduced to a concise formula'.

Jewish scholars are similarly engaged. They are not agreed whether a supersessionist theory must necessarily lead to anti-Semitism, or whether it is possible to maintain the theory while still treating Jews decently and respecting their religious beliefs. At the very least, however, crude supersessionism needs modification.

It is a new word in the language of theology and inter-faith relations. At a conference organised jointly by the Vatican and the Reformed Synagogues of Great Britain in London in 2000, learned scholars could not even agree how to spell it. Some wrote it as 'supercessionism' with a c. Neither Louis Jacobs's *The Jewish Religion, a Companion*, nor Adrian Hastings's *The Oxford Companion to Christian Thought*, nor Cross's and

Livingstone's *The Oxford Dictionary of the Christian Church* gives it an entry under either spelling. Nor is supersessionism recognised by the *Oxford English Dictionary* (though supersession is, used non-theologically).

The most emphatic, authoritative and dramatic Christian repudiation of supersessionism – affirming that the Jews were still 'chosen', even if the church was also correct to describe itself as 'chosen' too – came during the visit of Pope John Paul II to Israel in 2000. He went to the Western Wall in Jerusalem, the only surviving remnant of Solomon's Temple, and prayed as a pious Jew would pray, at Judaism's most sacred place. And following the custom of Jews who pray at the Western Wall, he inserted a paper carrying his personal prayer into a niche in the wall. He was, so to speak, borrowing one of their lines of communication with God. That was an unambiguous demonstration that he believed the traditional channels of grace and prayer between the Jews and God were still effective. This was made even plainer when the text of his prayer was published later that day. It was written in English and on a letter headed with the crest of the Holy See; at the bottom was his signature, Johannes Paulus II, and the date. And it was the most important prayer he could have uttered on such an occasion. It was a plea for forgiveness for the great sins committed by Christians against Jews. It said:

> God of our fathers, you chose Abraham and his descendants to bring your Name to the Nations. We are deeply saddened by the behaviour of those who in the course of history have caused these children of yours to suffer, and asking Your forgiveness we wish to commit ourselves to genuine brotherhood with the people of the Covenant.

Supersessionism is a difficult theory to maintain when the Pope himself has declared the Jews to be 'the people of the covenant'. It is true he did not speak for all Christians, and most Protestants would still maintain at least some milder variety of supersessionism to explain the exact relationship between Judaism and Christianity. But the days are finally gone when the Christian belief that the Jews failed to recognise Jesus Christ as their Saviour can readily be turned into the belief that the Jews were cursed and rejected by God as a consequence, and hence were fair game for every kind of insult.

The implications have by no means been fully explored. At the least, authoritative Christian texts have to be looked at again. In some cases they have to be treated as deliberate misrepresentations. As the New Testament tells it, both the ordinary Jews of Jerusalem and the Jewish religious authorities had a hand in Jesus's death. The latter found him guilty of blasphemy, and had him handed over to the Roman occupiers for punishment (and the usual form of death penalty in such cases was by crucifixion). When given the chance to save him, the Jewish mob instead brayed for his death, shouting, according to one account, 'His blood be on our heads, and on our children' (Matthew 27:25).

They probably said nothing of the sort, for the principle of collective or inherited guilt was contrary to Jewish ethics: Deuteronomy 24:16 – 'The fathers shall not be put to death for the children, neither shall the children be put to death for the fathers.' But what matters is that they were recorded as having said it, and countless Christian congregations since then have taken it at face value (though the idea that children could be held responsible for the crimes of their fathers is also contrary to Christian ethics). The traditional word for this accusation is 'deicide' – killing God. Not surprisingly, considering that it commemorates the day Jesus was crucified, Good Friday was the day throughout eastern and central Europe when sensible Jews stayed at home and kept their children in, right up to the outbreak of the Second World War. The fact that such precautions were no longer seen after the war is not because Christians had become tolerant, but because virtually all the Jews were dead. And the vast majority of those who carried out the orders for the killings were, at least by education and background, Christians. Such is the horrible legacy of the 'teaching of contempt', which many Jewish (and some Christian) scholars see as a logical consequence of Christian supersessionism.

Traces of it still lingered in Christian liturgy even until the 1960s and 1970s. Then the Catholic Church revised its implicitly anti-Semitic (and overtly anti-Judaic) bidding prayers for Good Friday, which in the Tridentine rite of Mass had required the priest to say the prayer '*Oremus et pro perfidis Judaeis . . .*', followed by '*Omnipotens sempiterne Deus, qui etiam judaicam perfidiam . . .*' This translates as:

> Let us pray also for the unbelieving Jews, that our God and Lord will remove the veil from their hearts, so that they too may acknowledge our Lord Jesus Christ . . . Almighty eternal God, who dost not withhold thy mercy even from Jewish unbelief, heed the prayers we offer for the blindness of that people, that they may acknowledge the light of thy truth, which is Christ, and be delivered from their darkness . . .[14]

It is notable that the modern translator balked at translating *perfidis* and *perfidiam* with the traditional word 'perfidious', with its implications of betrayal and hence of deicide. Even so, 'unbelieving Jews' is harsh. The Anglican *Book of Common Prayer* Collect for Good Friday took a softer tone at this point, but not much:

> O Merciful God, who hast made all men, and hatest nothing that thou hast made, nor wouldest the death of a sinner, but rather that he should

be converted and live; have mercy upon all Jews, Turks, Infidels and Hereticks [sic], and take from them all ignorance, hardness of heart, and contempt of thy word, and so fetch them home, blessed Lord, to thy flock, that they may be saved among the remnants of the true Israelites, and be made one fold under one shepherd, Jesus Christ our Lord...[15]

The presence of Turks and Infidels in this mixture is a little anomalous, as the reference to 'remnants of the true Israelites' aims the thrust of the prayer squarely at the Jews alone.

Events soon after the death of Jesus – the destruction of the Temple by the Romans in AD 70, and the dispersal (diaspora) of the Jewish population to other parts of the known world – were incorporated into Christian mythology (though not into official doctrine) as proofs of God's repudiation of the Jews. It was in this climate that much of the New Testament was written, including passages that indicated a high degree of hostility. This is especially true of the Gospel of John, where Jesus is reported to have said (John 8:42–5):

If God were your Father, ye would love me: for I proceeded forth and came from God; neither came I of myself, but he sent me. Why do ye not understand my speech? Even because ye cannot hear my word. Ye are of your father the devil, and the lusts of your father ye will do. He was a murderer from the beginning, and abode not in the truth, because there is no truth in him. When he speaketh a lie, he speaketh of his own: for he is a liar, and the father of it. And because I tell you the truth, ye believe me not.

Relations between the two faiths had already broken down, with Christian preachers like Stephen being persecuted by Jewish agents like Saul (who was later to become St Paul the Apostle). Although Christianity had an appeal to Gentiles, the first converts outside Israel were largely Jews, often Hebrew slaves serving Roman masters. The argument that God had closed the book on Judaism but had started again with Christianity was a compelling one with those exiled Jews, and early Christian apologists used it tellingly. The clearest New Testament statement of 'replacement theology' (supersessionism) is to be found in the Letter to the Hebrews, whose authorship is uncertain (though tradition recognises it as influenced by Paul even if not written by him). Christ, it says,

is the mediator of a better covenant, which was established upon better promises. For if that first covenant had been faultless, then should no place have been sought for the second. For finding fault with them, he saith, Behold, the days come, saith the Lord, when I will make a new covenant with the house of Israel and with the house of Judah: Not according to the covenant that I made with their fathers in the day when I took them by the hand to lead them out of the land of Egypt; because they continued not in my covenant, and I regarded them not, saith the Lord. For this is the covenant that I will make with the house of Israel after those days, saith the Lord; I will put my laws into their mind, and write them in their hearts: and I will be to them a God, and they shall be to me a people: And they shall not teach every man his neighbour, and every man his brother, saying, Know the Lord: for all shall know me, from the least to the greatest. For I will be merciful to their unrighteousness, and their sins and their iniquities will I remember no more. In that he saith, A new covenant, he hath made the first old. Now that which decayeth and waxeth old is ready to vanish away. (Hebrews 8:6–13)

What this establishes is not just the replacement of one covenant by another, the Abrahamic/Mosaic covenant by the covenant made in Christ, but the displacement and replacement of the Jewish people – the 'House of Israel and the House of Judah' – by another Israel, another Judah, using the same name. And that 'people' with whom the new covenant was made, the New Israel and new Judah, was the church. So the narrative of the Old Testament is reinterpreted as taking its meaning from what it led up to, the coming of Christ.

The Exodus of the Israelites from Egypt is a powerful typological metaphor for Easter. Thus as God rescued his 'first' people from actual bondage under the leadership of Moses, so Christ, the new Moses, leads God's 'second' people from the spiritual bondage of sin.

However, as so often in the Bible, one interpretation has to be offset by another. St Paul may or may not have been the author of the letter to the Hebrews, but he is much more likely to have been the author of the letter to the Romans (11:25–9) which argues in the opposite sense: '. . . blindness in part is happened to Israel, until the fullness of the Gentiles be come in. And so all Israel shall be saved . . . As concerning the gospel, they are enemies for your sakes: but as touching the election, they are beloved for the fathers' sakes. For the gifts and calling of God are without repentance.'

For once the translation in the Authorised Version, despite its elegance, is too opaque to convey the full meaning, for which we need something clearer, if more prosaic, like the *Jerusalem Bible* translation:

One section of Israel has become blind, but this will last only until the whole pagan world has entered, and after this the rest of Israel will be saved as well . . . The Jews are enemies of God only with regard to the Good News, and enemies only for your sake; but as the chosen people they are still loved by God, loved for the sake of their ancestors. God never takes back his gifts or revokes his choices.[16] [Here 'entered' appears to mean 'received into the Church'.]

Indeed, the logic of Israel's covenant with God throughout the Old Testament is that the Jews might have rebelled and disobeyed repeatedly – so often in fact that one Jewish scholar has called the Bible an 'anti-Semitic book' – but God always kept his end of the bargain. Failure to recognise the Messiah may be a further act of infidelity – St Paul clearly seems to believe this – but, as ever, God remains faithful despite this.

It was on the basis of this reading of Scripture that the Second Vatican Council condemned Christian anti-Semitism in 1965, in its decree *Nostra Aetate*.

[The Church] professes that all who believe in Christ – Abraham's sons according to faith – are included in the same Patriarch's call, and likewise that the salvation of the Church is mysteriously foreshadowed by the chosen people's exodus from the land of bondage . . .

As Holy Scripture testifies, Jerusalem did not recognise the time of her visitation, nor did the Jews, in large number, accept the Gospel; indeed not a few opposed its spreading. Nevertheless God holds the Jews most dear for the sake of their Fathers; He does not repent of the gifts He makes or of the calls He issues – such is the witness of the Apostle . . . Since the spiritual patrimony common to Christians and Jews is thus so great, this Sacred Synod wants to foster and recommend that mutual understanding and respect which is the fruit, above all, of biblical and theological studies as well as fraternal dialogues . . .

True, the Jewish authorities and those who followed their lead pressed for the death of Christ; still, what happened in His passion cannot be charged against all the Jews, without distinction, then alive, nor against the Jews of today. Although the Church is the new People of God, the Jews should not be presented as rejected or accursed by God, as if this followed from the Holy Scriptures.[17]

Expressions like 'People of God' and 'Peculiar people' are used several times in the Old Testament to refer to the Israelites. The definitive New Testament ascription of this title to the Christian church is contained in 1 Peter 2:9–10:

But ye are a chosen generation, a royal priesthood, an holy nation, a peculiar people; that ye should shew forth the praises of him who hath called you out of darkness into his marvellous light; Which in time past were not a people, but are now the People of God: which had not obtained mercy, but now have obtained mercy.

The better that readers of St Peter's first epistle knew their Scriptures, the better they would understand that the word 'peculiar' was a distinctive description of the Jewish people that was being deliberately reassigned to the Christians. (The word translated thus in the Authorised Version is sometimes interpreted differently by later translators, the better to express the concept that the 'peculiarity' of the 'people' is that they belong specially to God. But those with whom we are mainly concerned would all have encountered it in this way.) They would have found it in Exodus 19:5–6 –

> Now therefore, if ye will obey my voice indeed, and keep my covenant, then ye shall be a peculiar treasure unto me above all people: for all the earth is mine: And ye shall be unto me a kingdom of priests, and an holy nation. These are the words which thou shalt speak unto the children of Israel.'

in Deuteronomy 14:2 –

> For thou art an holy people unto the Lord thy God, and the Lord hath chosen thee to be a peculiar people unto himself, above all the nations that are upon the earth.

in Deuteronomy 26:18–19 –

> And the Lord hath avouched thee this day to be his peculiar people, as he hath promised thee, and that thou shouldest keep all his commandments; And to make thee high above all nations which he hath made, in praise, and in name, and in honour; and that thou mayest be an holy people unto the Lord thy God, as he hath spoken.

and in Psalm 135:4 –

> For the Lord hath chosen Jacob unto himself, and Israel for his peculiar treasure.

St Peter's appropriation of the phrase 'peculiar people' is also made in St Paul's letter to Titus, the leader of the Christians in Crete, which again only comes to life in the light of those Old Testament references.

> For the grace of God that bringeth salvation hath appeared to all men, teaching us that, denying ungodliness and worldly lusts, we should live soberly, righteously, and godly, in this present world; looking for that blessed hope, and the glorious appearing of the great God and our Saviour Jesus Christ; Who gave himself for us, that he might redeem us from all iniquity, and purify unto himself a peculiar people, zealous of good works. (Titus 2:11–14)

Nostra Aetate's reference to the Exodus foreshadowing 'the salvation of the Church' is a typical piece of contemporary Catholic typology. It imagines the Church to be a visible community, like the Israelite masses fleeing from Egypt; and as they were saved *en masse*, so to speak, so that is the type of salvation available to and through the Church. To be saved, you had to be a Catholic.

It was this doctrine in medieval Christianity which presented all sorts of difficulties to the first Protestant Reformers. They rejected the Catholic Church not just as wrong but as evil. They searched the Bible for an alternative way of salvation. If membership of the Catholic Church was not the way a Christian participated in Christ's saving action, then where was the 'saving community' the Bible speaks of, the real People of God, to be found? Was it, perhaps, invisible? Was it the community of all true Christians gathered in one place? Or was it, indeed, the newly emergent Protestant nation-state? Was it, in fact, England?

For those looking for an ideology to buttress the nation-state, that was a tempting solution. They went for it. In the case of England, moreover, the Reformation began with King Henry VIII's repudiation of papal authority and the substitution of himself as supreme ruler of the church. As Thomas More reminded him, in theory this made the King of England head of the Catholic Church; and by the same theory the church ruled by the Pope (to which More died faithful) could no longer truly be called by that name, at least in England. There was no room in anybody's theology for two True Catholic Churches, side by side or one on top of the other. The Nicene Creed spoke only of 'One Holy Catholic and Apostolic Church'. If one body was it, then the other body wasn't. Thus was it possible to root the English Protestant nation-state in a Catholic theology of the church? That made the idea very powerful and enduring. How the English authorities overcame the fairly obvious historical objections to this novel conception – objections made by More himself – we shall deal with later.

Jewish use of typology in interpretation had always been more individually figurative than Catholic or even Protestant use. It more often referred to individuals than to communities, for the good reason that the Jewish community was in its own eyes a unique type, not a metaphor for something else. Some group typology was still possible by relating later Jewish communities to earlier ones. For instance, the Jewish Passover meal is a typological re-presentation of the Exodus.

More often the typology was for purposes of edification and moral example. To take the story in Genesis chapter 18 of Abraham offering food and drink to strangers who visited him in his tent: what was important was not the precise detail of the hospitality that Abraham offered, but that he did so at all. The good example was what counted.

Rabbi Louis Jacobs in his *Companion to the Jewish Religion,* describes Abraham in Jewish teaching as a prototype:

> He is the seeker after truth, the philosopher who calmly discovered God by the application of his reasoning powers even before God addressed him directly . . . On the other hand he represents the lovable man (Kierkegaard's 'knight of faith') who trusts his God unquestioningly and follows him whenever he calls. In the old Jewish tale a man says that he does not want his son necessarily to become a famous scholar or saint but 'simply a Jew like our father Abraham'. Another of Abraham's traits is his hospitality. The Rabbinic Midrash imagines Abraham's tent as having openings on all four sides so that anyone seeking help could enter immediately from whichever direction he came . . . Abraham is depicted as one who does not retreat from the worship of God no matter how severe the temptation. Curiously enough, none of the Talmudic Rabbis has the name Abraham, perhaps because every Jew has to strive to become another Abraham.[18]

These uses of Scripture are examples of typology – in the Jewish case, of using Abraham as an ideal 'type' of men; in the Protestant and Catholic cases, of using episodes from Jewish history as historical precursors of the life of the Church. The Catholic Church and its eastern Orthodox cousins introduced into their liturgy and daily prayers constant reference to themselves as an Israel, a Jerusalem, a People of God, a Chosen People, and routinely mentioned the great prophets of Israel as prophets of the Church. The Canon of the Tridentine Mass, in use from the sixteenth century (Council of Trent, 1545–63) until the 1970s, has the priest offering the 'pure holy and unblemished' sacrifice of Christ's Body and Blood with the prayer *Supra quae propitio*: 'Deign to regard them with a favourable and gracious countenance, and to accept them as it pleased thee to accept the offerings of thy servant Abel the Just, and the sacrifice of our father Abraham, and that which thy great priest Melchisedech sacrificed to thee, a holy offering, a victim without blemish.'

The resonances with Old Testament parallels are deep and various, but are often merely alluded to rather than spelt out. Thus Abraham (Genesis 21) sacrifices a ram in place of his son Isaac, Abel 'the Just' (Genesis 4) offers a 'firstling' lamb to God in thanksgiving for the harvest, before Cain killed him, and Melchisedek (Genesis 14:18–20) meets Abraham and gives him bread and wine (which Catholic theologians took to be a precursor of the Eucharist). Even more significant is the implied reference to Exodus, where God ordered each Israelite to kill and eat an 'unblemished lamb' in preparation for their departure from bondage in Egypt. (Christians would have been thoroughly familiar with the idea of Christ as the 'Lamb of God' from John 1:29 – 'The next day John seeth Jesus coming unto him, and saith, Behold the Lamb of God, which taketh away the sin of the world . . .')

> And the Lord spake unto Moses and Aaron in the land of Egypt saying, This month shall be unto you the beginning of months: it shall be the first month of the year to you. Speak ye unto all the congregation of Israel, saying, In the tenth day of this month they shall take to them every man a lamb, according to the house of their fathers, a lamb for an house: And if the household be too little for the lamb, let him and his neighbour next unto his house take it according to the number of the souls; every man according to his eating shall make your count for the lamb. Your lamb shall be without blemish, a male of the first year: ye shall take it out from the sheep, or from the goats: And ye shall keep it up until the fourteenth day of the same month: and the whole assembly of the congregation of Israel shall kill it in the evening. And they shall take of the blood, and strike it on the two side posts and on the upper door post of the houses, wherein they shall eat it. And they shall eat the flesh in that night, roast with fire, and unleavened bread; and with bitter herbs they shall eat it. (Exodus 12:1–8)

The implication is that the sacrifice of the Mass (which also involves, in the act of Communion, eating the sacrificed offering) recreates the sacrifice of the Israelites. As noted above, the liberation this time is from slavery to sin, not slavery to the Egyptians.

What is implicit in such references – that the old (Jewish) order has ceased, and a new (Christian) one substituted – is much more clearly stated in St John's famous apocalyptic vision in the Book of Revelation (21:1–3):

> And I saw a new heaven and a new earth: for the first heaven and the first earth were passed away; and there was no more sea. And I John saw the holy city, new Jerusalem, coming down from God out of heaven, prepared as a bride adorned for her husband. And I heard a great voice out of heaven saying, Behold, the tabernacle of God is with men, and he will dwell with them, and they shall be his people, and God himself shall be with them, and be their God.

This journey into Catholic and Orthodox self-understanding, touching on the painful question of supersessionism and its link to anti-Semitism, is necessary if we are to understand what happened next: the development of a distinct Protestant supersessionism focused on the emerging English nation-state. The Jews had been unfaithful to their covenant, and been superseded by the early Church. But the Catholics had also proved unfaithful to their covenant, probably at about the time the papacy emerged, post-Constantine, as a new Roman Imperium. (The exact date at which the universal Church became unfaithful is not agreed by the early Protestant Reformers, as putting it too early could damage some of the causes they believed in. They were all agreed, at least, that it had become unfaithful by the Middle Ages.)

And so it was presumed that the Catholics too were repudiated by God. They stood, in relation to Protestants, as Jews had stood in relation to Catholics. In fact it is not difficult to see a further sequence: the English in turn proved unfaithful to their covenant, and so God made a new covenant with America. Black American Christians would eventually take it a stage further still – white America had failed, and so the covenant had passed on again. (See the analysis of Martin Luther King's 'I have a dream' speech in a later chapter.) It is also no coincidence that the spleen and vitriol that the Catholic Church began to use in its treatment of the Jews is mirrored in the spleen and vitriol with which the first Protestants treated Catholics. It suggests that part of the hidden logic of supersessionism is a desire on the part of the successors to punish, degrade and desecrate those who are being superseded. For if God has repudiated his people, he must have had a very good reason. Alternatively, if Jews are not unworthy of God's blessing, then perhaps the claims of the Catholic Church to have superseded them are open to question; if Catholics are not unworthy of God's blessing, then perhaps the similar claims of Protestants are open to question.

It is not far-fetched to see another example of this necessary supersessionist denigration in the way the first Americans thought about the English (or British, as by then they were). It was necessary to believe in a British tyrannical conspiracy against freedom far in excess of what the evidence would have supported, in order to justify rebellion (and in terms of 'chosenness', to justify supersession). As R. F. Foster remarks in another context[19] (quoting from Ernest Renan): 'Creating a nation involves getting one's history wrong.' In fact as free societies, late eighteenth-century England and America were about equal, and neither of them was a paragon of civil liberty in twenty-first-century terms. Indeed, England was some way ahead of America over the abolition of slavery. Lord Chief Justice Mansfield ruled in 1772 that James Somerset, a fugitive slave from Virginia brought into British waters, could not be forcibly returned to the colonies by his master, thus indicating that the absolute ownership of one person by another was not recognised in English law. Sir William Blackstone, the eighteenth century's leading authority on the English common law (later much relied on in American law schools), said in his 1765 Oxford lecture:

The idea and practice of this political or civil liberty flourish in their highest vigour in these kingdoms, where it falls little short of perfection, and can only be lost or destroyed by the folly or demerits of its owner: the legislature, and of course the laws of England, being peculiarly adapted to the preservation of this inestimable blessing even in the meanest subject. Very different from the modern constitutions of other states, on the continent of Europe, and from the genius of the imperial law; which in general are calculated to vest an arbitrary and despotic power of controlling the actions of the subject in the prince, or in a few grandees. And this spirit of liberty is so deeply implanted in our constitution, and rooted even in our very soil, that a slave or a Negro, the moment he lands in England, falls under the protection of the laws, and with regard to all natural rights becomes instantly a freeman.

What enflamed the American colonists' imagination in the years just before the Revolution was the conviction that, despite keeping up appearances as freedom-loving, the English had hatched a conspiracy to take away American freedom altogether, and the quarrels over stamp and import duty were a foretaste of much worse to come. Bernard Baylin quotes as representative of this mood the resolution of a Boston Town meeting in 1770 which declared that 'A series of occurrences, many recent events ... afford great reason to believe that a deep-laid and desperate plan of imperial despotism has been laid, and partly executed, for the extinction of civil liberty ...' While giving considerable weight to these suspicions of conspiracy in the fomenting of rebellion, he finds no evidence of any such conspiracy itself. He writes:

> The colonists believed they saw emerging from the welter of events during the decade after the Stamp Act a pattern whose meaning was unmistakable ... They saw about them with increasing clarity, not merely mistaken or even evil policies violating the principles upon which freedom rested, but what appeared to be evidence of nothing less than a deliberate assault launched surreptitiously by plotters against liberty both in England and America. The danger to America, it was believed, was in fact only the small immediately visible part of the greater whole whose ultimate manifestation would be the destruction of the English constitution, with all the right and privileges embedded in it.[20]

As noted in the previous chapter, one important clue to British intentions was soon to be found in the relaxation of the Test Act in Canada in 1774. Not only was it Britain's aim to enslave the colonists under a tyrannical king: they were to be enslaved by a tyrannical religion (Catholicism) as well. (Needless to say this judgment was not based on any experience of conditions in Quebec.) It was not so much the actual imposition of tyranny that sparked rebellion, though such measures as the suspension of trial by jury certainly seemed a foretaste of worse to come, as the declaration by Parliament in 1766 that it had the right to do so if it wanted to. In an 'Act for the better securing the dependency of His Majesty's Dominions in America upon the Crown and Parliament of Great Britain', it was declared that the British Parliament 'had, hath and of right ought to have full power and authority to make laws and statutes of sufficient force and vitality to bind the colonies and people of America . . . in all cases whatsoever'. It was as if the English doctrine of the totally sovereign nation-state, first proclaimed by Henry VIII, had ultimately produced a theory of Parliamentary government that was, in its very essence, tyrannical. If the English nation-state can do everything, even vary or invent its own religion if it wants to, or execute or dethrone a king, then Parliament's powers are indeed inherently unlimited.

Later on, Baylin notes:

> How to qualify, undermine, or reinterpret this tenet of English political theory was the central problem that confronted the leaders of the American cause; and there is no more fascinating spectacle in the history of American political thought than the efforts that were made – starting in the struggle with England over the extent of Parliament's power and continuing with the debates on the ratification of the Federal Constitution – to come to terms with this problem.[21]

What the English knew from familiarity, which the Americans at a distance did not, was that the theory of unrestrained Parliamentary sovereignty was just a theory. What stopped politicians with a majority behind them from pushing the theory to absurd or tyrannical limits was the human drama of politics conducted according to the Parliamentary system. The chambers of the House of Commons and House of Lords were relatively small and often crowded and noisy. Politicians expounding their policies had to stand looking in the eyes of their sworn opponents seated opposite facing them only a few feet away – jeering, shouting, waving, mocking – two sword lengths, in fact, in the case of the Commons (and no politician was allowed to cross the safety line which defined that no man's land). To face down those in front of him, he had to carry with him those behind him, his own side.

But their support was not unconditional. A fanatical or just unpopular political leader would soon find them melting away. Even silence behind him, instead of the usual voluble support, was a dangerous sign. It has happened time and time again, and indeed was to happen to Lord North's administration as his supporters lost confidence in his pursuit of the American war. He was eventually undermined by the deadly

Parliamentary crossfire of opponents likes Charles Fox and Edmund Burke. Thus was tyranny held in check. But 3000 miles away and more, these human constraints on the theory of unlimited sovereignty did not look sufficiently substantial. In any event, the colonists were conspiracy-minded.

Even the sensible proposal to appoint bishops to the Church of England in America – without them, all Anglican clergy had to cross the sea to be ordained – was regarded as an attempt to extend the English pattern of prelacy, which to American Protestants more than hinted at popery by the back door. Presbyterians in particular saw the idea of American bishops as a real danger to their interests. John Adams was quickly complaining that the conjunction of 'temporal and spiritual tyranny' was 'calamitous to human liberty', citing the philosopher David Hume for the view that 'in all the ages of the world priests have been enemies of liberty'. Thus, remarks Baylin, 'fear of the imposition of an Anglican episcopate brought into focus a cluster of ideas, attitudes and responses alive with century-old Popish-Stuart-Jacobite associations which would enter directly into the revolutionary controversy . . .'[22] So it was not actual tyranny the colonists rebelled against, but the threat or fear of one. As the Declaration of Independence itself declared, 'The history of the present King of Great Britain is a history of repeated injuries and usurpations, all having in direct object the establishment of an absolute Tyranny over these States.'

So the threat of tyranny was itself tyrannical, which has a certain logic to it. And did not the Bible give manifest examples where kings who became tyrants may be overthrown?

The role of the Church of England in all this is a curious one. On the one hand, as has already been noted, a considerable majority of those who signed the Declaration of Independence were at least nominal members of the Church of England. Clergy of that church in America, called Episcopalians, had been prominent on both sides of the pre-revolutionary fervour. But since the beginning of the eighteenth century, if not longer, the Church of England was notable for retaining in its membership some of its own most outspoken critics. Indeed, part of the religious settlement that went with the Restoration of Charles II was the concept of comprehensiveness, which meant that the Church would retain within its walls those who fundamentally disagreed with each other on matters they regarded as vital. The successors of the Roundheads coalesced into what became the Low Church party, and of the Cavaliers into the High Church party.

A 'High' view of the Church emphasised its sacramental activities and its supernatural status as an institution that was divinely created; a 'Low' view of the Church saw it as not much more than a convenient conglomeration of like-minded Christians. To be High was to be more 'Catholic', and not to mind too much about superficial resemblances between itself and the Roman Catholic Church (which of course it nevertheless looked down upon); to be Low was to be distrustful of the Highs precisely for that reason. In the nineteenth century the Lows generally became (Protestant) Evangelicals, the Highs became Anglo-Catholics (or sometimes 'Tractarians'); and each side had its own missionary societies and its own theological colleges. The term 'Anglo-Catholic' indicates the view that the Church of England is part of a wider 'Catholic Church', of which the Roman Catholic Church, though wrong in some of its doctrines, is also part. Both in England and in America the tradition grew up that some Anglican (in the US, Episcopalian) dioceses would always be occupied by High Church bishops, and some always by Low Church ones.

There was no love lost between High and Low, and the division had (and still has in the twenty-first century) a great deal to do with attitudes to Rome. The highest High Church Anglican priests are easily mistaken for Roman Catholic priests, as are their church buildings. The lowest of the Low Anglicans, on the other hand, opt for an almost Puritan reserve, both in the clothes they wear and the way they furnish and run their churches and ceremonies. The (Anglican) Church of Ireland, which was traditionally as Low as it was possible to get, banned not just crucifixes (the cross with the figure of Christ on it) but plain crosses (with no figure) as late as the 1960s, on the grounds that even a plain cross – in England, almost a Low Church trade mark – was too 'Roman'.

It is perhaps no surprise, given that the antecedent groups to the High and Low Church parties had fought a bitter civil war in England in the seventeenth century, that they were still heartily distrustful of each other on both sides of the Atlantic, in the eighteenth. Indeed, some of the surviving cultural, social and religious prejudices of the two groups were to draw America into its own civil war in the century that followed.

In his preface to his *The Cousins' Wars*, Kevin Phillips says that the underlying conflict between the two sides which erupted in ferocious wars, first in England, then between them, and finally in America, leads to his formulating the thesis:

> that from the seventeenth century, the English speaking people on both continents defined themselves by wars that upheld, at least for a while, a guiding political culture of a Low Church, Calvinistic Protestantism, commercially adept, militarily expansionist, and highly convinced, in Old World, New World or both, that it represented a chosen people and a manifest destiny. In the full three-century context, Cavaliers, aristocrats and bishops pretty much lost out and Puritans, Yankees, self-

made entrepreneurs, Anglo-Saxon nationalists and expansionists had the edge, especially in America.[23]

Phillips partly agrees with other historians who have postulated a sequence of 'three Puritanisms' on both sides of the Atlantic. The first peaked in the middle of the seventeenth century with the English Civil War and the victory of Cromwell; the second peaked in New England just before the American Revolution and was an important factor in the causes of it; and the third appeared similarly, just before the American Civil War.

> The idea is intriguing because it helps differentiate the revivals in these three cultures – invariably reform-minded, communitarian, and commercial as well as strictly religious – from the impacts of the revivals and great awakenings in the American south (and some would add the seventeenth and eighteenth century north of England) which were more emotional and less tied to middle-class reform or commercial values. The three cousins' wars, in many ways, overlap the three Puritanisms, although this book will leave the theology to others.

Puritanism, as will be discussed later, is a form of Christianity which places great emphasis on the Old Testament, draws parallels from it to the present, and thus sees strong analogies between the Puritan community and Israelites of the Bible, both Chosen People. Within Protestantism it has had to contend, from time to time, with various non-Calvinist forms of Christianity, both within Anglicanism and in separate denominations such as the Methodists. Those, mainly Evangelical, placed greater emphasis on the New Testament, and made more of the discontinuity than the continuity between the two sections of the Bible. The revivals and great awakenings that Phillips speaks of were Evangelical, and focused on the effort to convert people to Christianity (or to greater 'enthusiasm' if they were Christian already) by emotional preaching designed to arouse their fear of damnation and their need of spiritual consolation. Puritanism was always much cooler than that. So the theological distinction Phillips hints at lies in the area of Old Testament versus New Testament, predestination versus free will, or Arminianism versus Calvinism (explored more fully in a later chapter). In Anglo-Saxon cultural history, Puritanism is more likely to be associated with the advance of science (Sir Isaac Newton) or the industrial revolution (Adam Smith), and Evangelicalism with social reform (Wilberforce, Shaftesbury). There is no doubt that Puritanism was the more radical and subversive, and goes deeper into the soul. There can be no doubt, either, that the Cavaliers had more fun.

But the rise and fall of Puritanism in Britain had a slightly different rhythm to it, being associated first with the rise of political economy (*laissez-faire* capitalism) in the first half of the nineteenth century and then with the great industrial expansion of the second half. North America was about half a century behind this cycle, though when it did industrialise it eventually overtook Britain as the world's leading industrial power. The impact of industrialisation in Britain was drastic, leading to the rapid expansion of towns accompanied by vast population movements from the countryside, together with poverty, crime, decline in health and housing standards, industrial militancy and agitation for political reform. Britain was a country under unprecedented social stress. Religion was used to manage that stress. Methodism is very often credited with saving England from revolution in the nineteenth century, but Methodism is also credited with the rise of the trade unions and the Labour party. (Methodist meetings were often the first taste of democracy and equality the working class had ever experienced.)

Phillips also fails to draw attention to one major difference between the English and the Americans at the time of the war between them: that the Americans were at the time far more 'religious' in every sense of the word. English religion in the eighteenth century was going through the doldrums. Perhaps over-tired with the religious upheavals of the past two centuries, the people were content by and large to let matters drift, and the church drifted with them. One effect of the restoration of the monarchy was to entrench power over the church in the hands of the 'squire' class. These were small to medium local country gentry who farmed and hunted and married off their daughters. They had servants in the house and hands on the land, and the local parson was a useful agent in maintaining law and order and social and moral conformism. Many squires, as well as being local magistrates, could also 'own the living' of the local parish church – through a system called patronage, they had the right to nominate who the next incumbent of that living should be, though once appointed, the incumbent minister enjoyed what was called 'parson's freehold' – secure tenure of his office, and reliable income. The man who owned the living was also responsible for the church's upkeep, so it was sometimes an expensive privilege.

The landed squires – the squirearchy, as they became known – had provided the backbone of the so-called Cavalier Parliament that was convened after the return of Charles II, and it was they who drew the line at the toleration of Roman Catholics when the Duke of York, later James II, proposed it. Toleration of dissent – Protestant sects and denominations that had broken away from the Anglicans – was much easier for them. But the religion of the eighteenth century gradually grew torpid, and when Charles and John Wesley tried to stir things up with their national preaching campaigns, both parson and squire resented the threat to their peace. This was an unlikely base for an English episcopal conspiracy to overthrow the liberties of the American colonists; once the final (1745) Jacobite rebellion was out of the way, the favourite English bourgeois emotion was complacency and quiet self-satisfaction. The way to deal with religion was not to make too much fuss about it.

But that was not the impression given on the other side of the Atlantic. The English had a plan, the colonists believed, to bring all subjects of the Crown into the community of the official church. The Society for the Propagation of the Gospel, ostensibly set up to preach Christianity to the Indians, was suspected of being a fifth column aimed at pulling Presbyterians and sundry other Nonconformists into the arms of the church – which meant into the web of priestcraft, episcopacy and the smell of popery. Having no bishops of their own, it was easier to exaggerate how effective they could be. Indeed, at exactly this time and had the colonists but known it, the English bishops were giving a convincing demonstration of the exact opposite of the religious fervour they were presumed to feel. They were presiding over a religious slump, and did not have much clue what to do about it, nor did they much care. Being a superior sort of landed gentry was far more agreeable. This misreading of episcopal designs on American religious freedom was a fairly classic example of projection – the Puritans of New England assumed that English Anglicans were zealots, not being able to imagine someone less excited by religious ideas than they were. Large parts of the population, being Anglican anyway, were not taken in – 'not easily convinced', as Baylin puts it,[24] 'that liberty was being threatened by a plot of Churchmen'.

Nevertheless, especially in New England, the legitimate desire of Anglicans to have their own bishops fostered suspicion that far worse was intended. Why the fear of bishops became so easily exaggerated is worth exploring further. There is in fact a remarkable parallel between the pre-Revolutionary American fear of the arrival of English bishops in 1770 and the Victorian English fear of the arrival of Catholic bishops in 1850, and some of the more extravagant rhetoric of protest is virtually interchangeable between the two cases. On learning that the Pope proposed to appoint Catholic bishops in England, *The Times* of London led the public uproar with a leading article which denounced 'one of the grossest acts of folly and impertinence which the Court of Rome has ventured to commit since the Crown and people of England threw off its yoke . . .'

There is obviously 'something about a bishop', but perhaps only before he arrives. In both cases the eventual outcome, when the bishops in question came and eventually settled down, was vastly more timid than the expectation. No trace of tyranny was to be found. But in each case a bishop represented a church which made, implicitly or explicitly, a rival claim to be the Chosen People which was felt to threaten the community already believing it possessed that title. An Anglican bishop represented an English claim *vis à vis* the American claim; a Catholic bishop represented a Roman claim *vis à vis* the English one. Baylin remarks that 'fear of the imposition of an Anglican episcopacy thus brought into focus a cluster of ideas, attitudes and responses alive with centuries-old Popish-Stuart-Jacobite associations that would enter directly into the Revolutionary controversy . . .' It stimulated among highly articulate leaders of public opinion 'a general sense that they lived in a con-spiratorial world in which what the highest officials professed was not what they in fact intended, and that their words marked a malevolent design'.

In the perception of the New Englanders, John Adams in particular, bishops were bad *per se*, whether Anglican or Catholic. Adams, first Vice President and second President of the United States, was a major influence prior to the break with England. He did not have available to him any examples of episcopacy entirely void of political or secular power, for instance like modern Methodist bishops in the United States. Thus the bishops he knew about always came tied to larger systems, to the English Crown and His Majesty's Government, or to Rome and the Vatican. That was why they were dangerous.

Adams had in mind a study by Viscount Molesworth of the suppression of democracy in Denmark a century before: Molesworth's *An Account of Denmark* was required reading in pre-Revolutionary America. Comments Baylin:

> Fear of the conjunction of civil and ecclesiastical tyrannies was central to John Adams's understanding of American history as well as of the Revolutionary crisis. It had been, he wrote, 'a hatred, a dread, a horror, of the infernal confederacy before described, that projected, conducted and accomplished the settlement of America', and it was this same confederacy that confronted Americans in 1765: 'There seems to be a direct and formal design on foot to enslave all America. This, however, must be done by degrees. The first step that is intended seems to be an entire subversion of the whole system of our fathers by the introduction of the canon and feudal law into America.'
>
> Popery, the conjunction of the Church of Rome with aggressive civil authority, was felt to be the greatest threat, the classic threat; but popery was only a special case, though the superlative one, of the more general phenomenon. 'It has been a great mistake,' Molesworth had pointed out, to think that 'the popish religion is the only one of all the Christian sects proper to introduce and establish slavery in a nation

insomuch as that popery and slavery have been thought inseparable . . .
It is not popery as such but the doctrine of blind obedience, in what
religion soever it be found, that is the destruction of the liberty and
consequently of all the happiness of any nation.'[25]

The notion that the Church of England demanded blind obedience
from its members was patently absurd. And the Catholicism that Adams
was writing about is the ghastly caricature of it in Foxe's *Book of Martyrs*
of 200 years before, not the contemporary culture of, say, the Vienna of
Haydn, Mozart and Beethoven.

This was the recent emotional background against which the Founders
of America had to consider the issues of church and state. The tradition
they inherited was one that did not reject the principle of establishment
– that one religion in particular should be singled out for special subsidy,
status and protection, in return for a degree of control over its affairs by
state power. The colony of Virginia had established the Church of
England on this basis; Massachusetts and others had established Congregationalism; for a while Maryland even gave special protection to the
Roman Catholic faith though that was soon brought to an end. Behind
the fear of English bishops was a fear that the English Crown proposed
to aim for uniformity in these matters, with the Church of England
established throughout the thirteen colonies and with bishops in all the
major cities.

Such a church would be answerable not in America but in London,
but that did not seem to be the primary worry. It was the disestablished
religions, those that felt disadvantaged by their experience of another
rival church being established, that most vocally resisted the idea that
the fledgling United States of America might have its own official
religion. In other words they did not trust their fellow Protestants. Thus,
to take one example, the Baptists of Connecticut so resented the
establishment in that state of the Congregationalists that they wrote to
Thomas Jefferson, when he was president, to praise the First Amendment
(the separation of church and state). They received from him a reply that
has become a classic constitutional text:

> Believing with you that religion is a matter which lies solely between
> man and his God; that he owes account to none other for his faith or his
> worship; that the legislative powers of the government reach actions
> only, and not opinions, I contemplate with sovereign reverence that act
> of the whole American people which declared that their legislature
> should 'make no law respecting an establishment of religion, or
> prohibiting the free exercise thereof,' thus building a wall of separation
> between church and state.

Jefferson meant the church as a particular institution: there is no evidence that Congress had wished to banish religion as such. The first two Presidents, Washington and Adams, had proclaimed national days of fasting and abstinence – which, frankly, should have been the job of a church to proclaim, not a federal government. Far from 'separation', such actions pointed towards the opposite: the complete fusion of spiritual and temporal leadership in one office (as in England, as it happened). There were other early examples: the issuing of Bibles to the troops of the Revolutionary Army, the reciting of prayers before meetings of Congress, and the holding of church services in federal buildings. If the United States of America came to birth believing itself to be the People of God, the Chosen People, it is difficult to see it at the same time as a totally secular entity. The 'separation of church and state' actually facilitates this merging into one of the religious and political character of the new nation, for it means there is no rival institution within the household of the state, making alternative claims.

The issue of establishment was not so much one of secular principle but was mainly practical – if a church was to be established, which was it to be? Some parts of the thirteen colonies were heavily influenced by Scottish Presbyterianism, some by the Congregationalism that had developed from the Puritan 'independent' churches of the seventeenth century; Baptists were growing everywhere; German Lutherans had claims in one place, Quakers in another, Dutch Calvinists elsewhere; most states had strong Anglican connections, though this was not the careful comprehensive balance between High and Low which was developing in England. (American Episcopalianism began Low and stayed Low, though its leanings as time went by were towards liberal Protestantism rather than Calvinism, which was in any case an over-subscribed opinion.) There was no one version of Christianity that Anglican Virginia and Puritan Massachusetts were likely to agree on. Hence there was no great opposition when amendments to the constitution were proposed that prohibited the federal government from establishing any one church as an official church. But that did not stop individual states from establishing their own – or rather, continuing a pre-Revolutionary establishment. Massachusetts did not disestablish its Congregationalist Church until 1833, and the precedent suggests the First Amendment – which binds the federal but not state legislatures – would not prevent it re-establishing one again in the supremely unlikely event of it ever wanting to.

The idea of an established church was not so alien even to radical political thinkers of the eighteenth century – it was the concept of a totally secular state which was hard to grasp. What happened concerning church and state in America in that century was of course a continuation of the politics of church and state from the seventeenth century, which in turn dated back to the real start of the Reformation in England, Henry VIII's break with Rome in 1532.

His seizure of power over the church immediately posed the question: once the state controlled the church, what sort of church should it be? Jefferson's answer – that it was none of the state's business – was a very long time arriving. Henry VIII made it entirely his business, and killed those who stood in his way.

4

Hope, History and Hatred

Protestant typology, where our attention rests for now, used the Old Testament in an original manner. It was figurative in the Jewish way, in that personalities from the Old Testament were recruited to serve as new Protestant icons – Oliver Cromwell or George Washington (or even Henry VIII) as Moses leading God's chosen ones out of bondage to the Promised Land, for instance. The Puritans in both old and New England had raided the *dramatis personae* of the Old Testament for new names for their children, to avoid having to use saints' names (too medieval, too Catholic). They wanted their children to be endowed with the virtues of the characters they chose. Another way of achieving that was simply to name the child after the virtue, and cut out the middle-man – a popular Puritan naming device. Thus were added to the naming lexicon (mainly for girls) such names as Prudence, Faith, Grace, Felicity, Verity, Constance, and Joy.

But more particularly, they also raided the anecdotage of the Old Testament – the smaller stories of which the bigger ones are made up – to find parallels for their own experiences, not only to extract the moral lessons but also to predict the future. They firmly believed that the Bible was primarily about them, and not primarily about the ancient tribes of Palestine. It was not history. It was contemporary narrative and prophecy, but in a figurative or allegorical form that needed a great effort of understanding. This is a quite different way of regarding the Bible from the modern one, even among conservative Protestants, which puts the Bible back into history and regards resemblances between then and now as more or less accidental. In seventeenth-century New England, as in seventeenth-century East Anglia, Israel was the true name of the place where they lived, and they were the Israelites. No wonder they gave each other Israelite names.

A good illustration of this extraordinary Protestant thought process is the start of the most famous of all American sermons, that entitled 'Sinners in the Hands of an Angry God' preached at Enfield, Connecticut in 1741 by Jonathan Edwards (1703–58) (who, as already noted, was much admired by Catharine Macaulay). He was one of the chief preachers who stirred up the Great Awakening, the pre-Revolutionary revival of Evangelical religion and millenarian expectations in New England and elsewhere in the New World. (A similar revival was happening at about this time in England.) Edwards preached on the biblical text 'Their foot shall slide in due time' (Deuteronomy 32:35), which conjures up homely mental images of winter farmyards and muddy footpaths:

> In this verse is threatened the vengeance of God on the wicked unbelieving Israelites, who were God's visible people, and who lived under the means of grace; but who, notwithstanding all God's wonderful works towards them, remained void of counsel, having no understanding in them. Under all the cultivations of heaven, they brought forth bitter and poisonous fruit; as in the two verses next preceding the text. The expression I have chosen for my text, Their foot shall slide in due time, seems to imply the following doings, relating to the punishment and destruction to which these wicked Israelites were exposed . . .
> It implies, that they were always exposed to sudden unexpected destruction. As he that walks in slippery places is every moment liable to fall, he cannot foresee one moment whether he shall stand or fall the next; and when he does fall, he falls at once without warning: Which is also expressed in Psalm 73:18, 19. 'Surely thou didst set them in slippery places; thou castedst them down into destruction: How are they brought into desolation as in a moment!'
> Another thing implied is, that they are liable to fall of themselves, without being thrown down by the hand of another; as he that stands or walks on slippery ground needs nothing but his own weight to throw him down.
> That the reason why they are not fallen already, and do not fall now, is only that God's appointed time is not come. For it is said, that when that due time, or appointed time comes, their foot shall slide. Then they shall be left to fall, as they are inclined by their own weight. God will not hold them up in these slippery places any longer, but will let them go; and then at that very instant, they shall fall into destruction; as he that stands on such slippery declining ground, on the edge of a pit, he cannot stand alone, when he is let go he immediately falls and is lost.[1]

The terrifying lesson which Edwards gradually drew out of his long series of Old Testament examples was that his hearers deserved everlasting punishment, and only God's loving mercy prevented the direst justice from being instantly done. However the Old Testament examples he quoted also indicated, or so he argued, that he who accepted God's grace in time was saved. Thus the Old Testament pointed both to the problem and to its solution. As God had dealt with the old Israelites in the millennium before Christ, so he would deal with eighteenth-century Americans, the new Israelites. When Old Testament Scripture records God as addressing the Israelites reproachfully as 'you' or 'thou', Protestant typology translates that as addressing the congregation here and now and the community it represents. The congregation was required to say to itself: 'The "you" of the Old Testament is the "us" of now.'

Another forceful use of Protestant typology occurs in this later passage in Edwards's sermon:

> When the great and angry God hath risen up and executed his awful vengeance on the poor sinner, and the wretch is actually suffering the infinite weight and power of his indignation, then will God call upon the whole universe to behold that awful majesty and mighty power that is to be seen in it. Isaiah 33:12–14. 'And the people shall be as the burnings of lime, as thorns cut up shall they be burnt in the fire. Hear ye that are far off, what I have done; and ye that are near, acknowledge my might. The sinners in Zion are afraid; fearfulness hath surprised the hypocrites,' etc.
>
> Thus it will be with you that are in an unconverted state, if you continue in it; the infinite might, and majesty, and terribleness of the omnipotent God shall be magnified upon you, in the ineffable strength of your torments. You shall be tormented in the presence of the holy angels, and in the presence of the Lamb; and when you shall be in this state of suffering, the glorious inhabitants of heaven shall go forth and look on the awful spectacle, that they may see what the wrath and fierceness of the Almighty is; and when they have seen it, they will fall down and adore that great power and majesty. Isaiah 66:23–24. 'And it shall come to pass, that from one new moon to another, and from one sabbath to another, shall all flesh come to worship before me, saith the Lord. And they shall go forth and look upon the carcasses of the men that have transgressed against me; for their worm shall not die, neither shall their fire be quenched, and they shall be an abhorring unto all flesh.' It is everlasting wrath. It would be dreadful to suffer this fierceness and wrath of Almighty God one moment; but you must suffer it to all eternity. There will be no end to this exquisite horrible misery . . . [and so on].

Having whipped up his audience with the imminent prospect of almost certain hellfire – this kind of sermon was known as the 'preaching of terror' – Edwards threw them the final lifeline:

> Now undoubtedly it is, as it was in the days of John the Baptist, the axe is in an extraordinary manner laid at the root of the trees, that every

tree which brings not forth good fruit, may be hewn down and cast into the fire. Therefore, let every one that is out of Christ, now awake and fly from the wrath to come. The wrath of Almighty God is now undoubtedly hanging over a great part of this congregation: Let every one fly out of Sodom: 'Haste and escape for your lives, look not behind you, escape to the mountain, lest you be consumed'. [By 'out of Christ' he means in an unjustified state, unsaved.]

It was assumed that God was content to repeat himself. Hence if a situation occurred in everyday life that was analogous to a situation described in the Old Testament – the sinful city of Sodom, for instance – God would see to it that the outcome was similar too. As God destroyed Sodom, so he would destroy sinful cities today. What applied under one covenant would apply under its successor. If the people of New Israel had paused at the waters of some equivalent to the Red Sea, their pursuers hot behind them, God would again intervene (by a strong east wind, perhaps) to lead them across and destroy their enemies. And the application of Old Testament parallels was much more personal, reflecting the Protestant emphasis on God choosing ('electing') individuals rather than (or as well as) whole communities. This tension between individual election and communal election was a continuing feature of forms of Protestantism derived from Calvinism (proving important, for instance, not only in the story of Massachusetts Puritanism but also in the philosophy of Oliver Cromwell). Usually preachers did not try to resolve it, but switched confusingly from one form of language to the other. It heightened the uncertainty, and hence the peril, which was part of their message.

If the Israelites were in trouble with God because of unfaithfulness to their covenant, so were Christians in trouble for their unfaithfulness likewise. And just as this was true of the Israelites in general as well as individual Israelites in particular, so it was true both in general and in particular of Christians. One could be unfaithful, or the whole crowd of them could be.

Thus Protestant typology taught them that the Providence in which they mightily believed was not arbitrary or capricious. It followed biblical principles and patterns that could be sought after and discovered. The Bible was therefore a very important everyday companion, for it could unlock all sorts of secrets, and charting the way ahead was not the least of them. In an extremely precarious world, and preachers like Edwards were at pains to make it sound nothing less, it was the one staff that could safely be leant upon. No wonder daily Bible reading was regarded as such a necessity.

It is a matter of some surprise that many comprehensive works of

Christian scholarship fail completely to notice the significance of this form of Protestant typology, treating typology itself as an archaic practice that died out more or less with the Reformation. Thus the *Oxford Dictionary of the Christian Church*[2] limits its entry under 'types' to fifteen lines, defining them as

> In theology, the foreshadowings of the Christian dispensation in the events and person of the Old Testament. Just as Jesus Christ himself could refer to Jonah as a symbol of his Resurrection, so St Paul found in the Israelites' crossing of the Red Sea the 'type' of baptism, while to the author of *Hebrews* Melchisedek was the foreshadowing of Christ. A Christian 'type' differs from an allegory in that the historical reference is not lost sight of ... Typology, with an increasingly allegorical emphasis, was much employed in the early Church ...

No mention here of Protestant typology, perhaps because, notwithstanding its enormous influence, it is now regarded as intellectually discredited. Protestant typology is modern Protestantism's guilty secret. In fact a Protestantism with a biblical typology of this sort, and a Protestantism without it, are so different that they could almost be regarded as separate belief systems. All they have in common is that one evolved into the other. When we say the Anglo-Americans of the seventeenth or eighteenth centuries were Protestants, we are in danger of assuming their beliefs were akin to those of modern Protestants. In fact the state of mind was entirely different. The nearest contemporary approach to it would be something like that of the Church of Jesus Christ of the Latter Day Saints (Mormons), which still applies a fundamentalist version of typology in the seventeenth- or eighteenth-century style. In some examples of Mormon literature even such modern characters as Winston Churchill are regarded as prefigured in the Bible; and the Anglo-American nation is still definitively chosen. Nevertheless, while mainstream modern Protestantism as represented by the major non-Anglican and non-Catholic traditions in Britain and America no longer makes a straightforward equation between nation-states and chosen people, the residual influence of previous thinking that way is still powerful. As we shall note, a President Reagan or Bush can easily evoke such ideas. Nor were they far from the thoughts of the British in recent years.

Andrew Louth's entry on typology in the *Oxford Companion to Christian Thought*[3] points out that typology was a routine method for Rabbinical teachers. They treated the Torah (the first five books of the Bible) as 'an authoritative source for guidance about how to live a life pleasing to God within the covenant'. Christian typology plundered the Hebrew

Scriptures not just for proof texts of the Christian revelation, but to show how the coming of Christ had always been foreshadowed – even by Jewish writers who did not realise that that was what they were doing. Thus the story of the fall of Adam and Eve foreshadowed the reversal of the fall through the redeeming work of Christ, the second Adam (Mary being the second Eve); the story of Moses bringing the people of Israel out of Egypt foreshadowed Christ's redemption of the human race, with the crossing of the Red Sea prefiguring Christian baptism; the Song of Songs came to be seen as celebrating the mystical relationship between Christ and the Church; and so on.

Under the influence of the Early Fathers of the Church (a title usually limited to the first five centuries AD), typology became part of a systematic approach to the understanding of Scripture. According to Louth, Origen saw two layers of meaning in Scripture, a literal one and an allegorical one:

> This dual meaning was elaborated by later thinkers, who discerned different layers within the deeper meaning, into a fourfold meaning of Scripture, which became the norm in the Western Middle Ages. These four meanings were (1) the literal or historical (2) the allegorical (which usually meant the Christian meaning, doctrinal or sacramental) (3) the moral, or tropological, concerned with Christian conduct and (4) the anagogical (from the Greek, *anagoge*, ascent) concerned with the destiny of the Christian life . . .
>
> This approach to Scripture foundered in the west, partly on the striving after scientific rigour, estranged from the Christian life, found in scholasticism, and finally of the polemic born of the Reformation . . . This traditional approach to Scripture was rendered still more remote by the Enlightenment and the rise of the historical-critical method as the only way of interpreting texts, including the text of the Bible, reducing the meaning of the text to what the original writer intended.

The polemical post-Reformation form of typology to which he refers became popular from the middle of the sixteenth century, assisted by such works as Foxe's *Book of Martyrs*. Thus the enemies of England would be enemies of freedom, the Bible and God: idolatrous, superstitious, cruel, tyrannical, and above all *foreign*, just like the enemies of ancient Israel – the Pharaohs of Egypt, the Babylonian kings, and so on. Indeed, it was not necessary to go out and inspect the enemy to see whether it actually had these qualities. The parallel with ancient Israel answered the question in the affirmative. They were bound to have them, because the Good Book said so. But no matter how many times it is claimed that the Bible is on the side of freedom, that does not make it true. The word 'freedom' itself occurs once in the Old Testament and once in the New, and neither time in the sense being referred to here. It comes nearest to using the idea in this political sense in Isaiah 58:6–7, where the prophet explains why he was fasting:

> Is not this the fast that I have chosen? to loose the bands of wickedness, to undo the heavy burdens, and to let the oppressed go free, and that ye break every yoke? Is it not to deal thy bread to the hungry, and that thou bring the poor that are cast out to thy house? when thou seest the naked, that thou cover him; and that thou hide not thyself from thine own flesh?

What in fact was happening was that Roman Catholicism, being the national arch-enemy during the period that a distinct English sense of identity was being laid down, was being defined, a priori, as idolatrous, superstitious, cruel, tyrannical and of course foreign (or at least agents of foreign powers) without any need to refer to actual evidence. It was one of those things which 'everybody knew'. Indeed, the typology of the New Testament, largely based on the Book of Revelation, provided a further crop of choice epithets for this arch-enemy: Anti-Christ, the Beast, Man of Sin, Whore of Babylon, Scarlet Woman. So the enemy is a master of disguise, clever, seductive, a habitual liar, schemer and conspirator. If the enemy does not appear to be a schemer and conspirator, that is merely part of the deception. And the Book of Revelation explains how these Satanic forces will be overthrown in a final climactic battle, at a place called Armageddon. It is perhaps not surprising that ecumenically-minded modern scholars of all persuasions dismiss this as mere bigotry, not worthy of serious theological reflection. In doing so, however, they are minimising the role of one of the key formative influences of Anglo-Saxon culture over the last few centuries.

It is worth noting in passing, furthermore, that many of the qualities attributed by Protestants to Catholics, not least a tendency to engage in sinister conspiracies, are strikingly similar to the qualities once attributed by Catholics to Jews. One form of supersessionism mirrors another. Once Catholics regarded themselves as successors to the Jews as God's Chosen People, the Jews fell foul of the principle that 'he that is not with me is against me' (Matthew 12:30). They were deemed enemies of the 'Chosen People', whether they saw themselves that way or not. They were presumed to act that way. Logically, to be an enemy of God's work was to be in league with the devil. That is exactly how medieval Catholics saw Jews, and how post-medieval Protestants saw Catholics. Following the expulsion of the Jews from England in AD 1290, after bizarre allegations of ritual child murder (the so-called Blood Libels), death awaited any Jew who crept back. After the Reformation, the practice of

Catholicism became a serious crime in England and the penalty for being a Catholic priest was the ultimately horrific punishment of hanging, drawing and quartering. English Protestants were less interested in their supersession of the Jewish covenant for the good reason that there were no Jews in the kingdom: in Protestant countries with Jews, such as Germany, Protestant anti-Jewish invective was often extraordinarily virulent. Martin Luther, who had at first expected the Jews to join his new brand of Christianity, later addressed the public authorities in Germany with advice on how to treat them:

> First to set fire to their synagogues or schools and to bury and cover with dirt whatever will not burn, so that no man will ever again see a stone or cinder of them . . .
> Second, I advise that their houses also be razed and destroyed. For they pursue in them the same aims as in their synagogues. Instead they might be lodged under a roof or in a barn, like the gypsies. This will bring home to them that they are not masters in our country, as they boast, but that they are living in exile and in captivity, as they incessantly wail and lament about us before God.
> Third, I advise that all their prayer books and Talmudic writings, in which such idolatry, lies, cursing and blasphemy are taught, be taken from them.
> Fourth, I advise that their rabbis be forbidden to teach henceforth on pain of loss of life and limb . . .[4]

In such a climate, almost any calumny is likely to be believed no matter how strongly the evidence contradicts it. Furthermore the displaced group, no longer 'chosen', is presumed by the successor group to be intent on conspiring to undermine it. Thus the endless supposed Catholic conspiracies of the seventeenth and eighteenth centuries, credited to some degree both in England and in America, are a match for the notorious (and entirely fabricated) Protocols of the Elders of Zion which emerged before the First World War inside Tsarist Russia. The medieval Blood Libels were an earlier example. There is an echo of these conspiracy theories in the way many American colonists begun to suspect the motives of the British, prior to the Revolution. Many commentators have remarked on the similarities between anti-Semitism and anti-Popery, both of which were normal features of Anglo-Saxon consciousness until relatively recently. What these prejudices also had in common was that otherwise ordinary decent people seemed to hold them, yet were quite unaware that they did so. In so far as they would admit to dislike of Catholics or Jews, they would claim their attitude was rational and justified by the evidence. Anglophobia in America may therefore be seen as a supersessionist parallel to anti-Semitism in Christianity and anti-Catholicism in Protestantism. It is a human tendency to think the worst of those who have been displaced or superseded.

Nor is this purely theoretical. It can have profound implications on the mindset of those making national policy. There are significant examples of this even in recent history such as the 1956 Suez crisis, which will be examined more closely in a later chapter in the context of England in the 1950s. It was in 1956 that America, whose own empire of military and financial dominance was expanding globally, came very close to repudiating Britain's right to be a colonial power. In doing this it was being entirely true to the logic of supersessionism.

Typology has never really been absent from Christian liturgy, though until recent times it was not thought to be a particularly interesting subject for study. But efforts to eradicate all sources of anti-Semitism from Christian thinking have prompted re-examination of past assumptions, a process which is far from complete.

A study of modern attitudes towards Israel and the Jews, undertaken among members of the Church of England, showed supersessionism was still widespread.[5] The majority view was that scriptural promises and prophecies about the land of Israel were fulfilled in the person of Jesus Christ (that is to say, completed and hence no longer valid); a strong minority opinion was that the return of the Jews to Israel was the completion of biblical prophecy. This view relied, the report's authors said, on a 'literal exegesis of selected biblical texts', which 'many would argue takes little account either of recent scholarship or of contemporary political realities in the Middle East'. Both views are supersessionist, in that they imply the replacement of the Jewish covenant with a Christian one. The belief that the return of the Jews is in accordance with prophecy is not, as it might seem, a view friendly to the Jews. For the rest of the prophecy, as discussed in a later chapter, indicates the forthcoming conversion of Jews to Christianity, thereby meeting one of the conditions necessary for the Second Coming of Christ. It is, in other words, highly typological. The survival and prevalence of such beliefs among ordinary members of the Church of England clearly took the compilers of the survey somewhat by surprise. They had expected such opinions to be confined to extreme fundamentalist sects in America. Even there it is likely to be much more widespread than that, and may well be a constituent factor behind America's long-term support for the state of Israel.

However the Church of England has given far less attention to the Christian-Jewish supersessionist issue than the Catholic Church has done. It has not so far, for instance, overhauled its liturgy to ensure the eradication of anything that might give a new foothold to anti-Semitism. Renewed modern interest in typological questions has had other explanations. As Andrew Louth notes,[6] the liturgical revival in modern mainstream Christianity has reawakened interest in the subject not least because of a modern preference for poetic or allegorical routes to the knowledge of God over categorical factual statements. Attempts to tie down the truths of religion in the form of propositions are much less appealing to the imagination than the use of prose narrative, poetic metaphor or figurative allegories. It is also relevant that in the Catholic Church, renewed emphasis on the community of the faithful as the 'People of God' was a powerful force for liberalisation at the time of the Second Vatican Council (1962–65). It became an argument in favour of collective responsibility ('collegiality'), of giving greater weight to the laity, and it provided an alternative, more horizontal, way of looking at the Church, in place of the strictly hierarchical (or vertical) one.

What Louth and other writers on typology do not refer to at all is the persistence of typology in the Protestant exposition of Scripture, especially when given a high level of political significance. There are plenty of contemporary examples. When President Ronald Reagan addressed the British House of Commons in 1982, those with a sharp ear for biblical typology would have caught his reference to an 'Evil Empire' – the part of the world ruled by the Soviets – as a parallel to the corrupt and cruel Neo-Babylonian Empire which had taken the Jews into captivity in 587 BC. The fact that the Jews were only released when the empire was eventually conquered by King Cyrus of Persia, referred to in Isaiah as 'the Lord's anointed', frightened some well-informed commentators into thinking that Reagan saw himself as having a similar destiny. Those without an ear for biblical typology might have found themselves on the brink of World War III before they realised it.

An even more celebrated use of typology by Ronald Reagan was his reference to America as a 'shining city on a hill', which is a typological use of Matthew 5:14. It was by no means unique to him: in his farewell presidential address he gave its source not as the Bible but as the seventeenth-century New England Puritan settler John Winthrop. In a sense this is double typology: borrowing from Winthrop who was in turn borrowing from the New Testament. Or even triple: Jesus's words referred to in Matthew are themselves typological, for his hearers would have understood instantly that he was alluding to Mount Zion, the hill on which the city of Jerusalem was founded by King David a thousand years before. In Jewish literature Zion is synonymous with the Jewish homeland, longed for by exiles from a distance. In Christian literature it becomes spiritualised into the capital city of the Kingdom of Heaven, in other words no place actually on earth (except, in the eyes of a John Winthrop or a Ronald Reagan, when it is identified with America).

The context of Matthew 5:14 provides the clue. It is the Sermon on the Mount, Jesus's exposition of a radical new ethic for the coming mystical Kingdom. Reagan may not have known this, though it is more likely than not that he did. Winthrop most certainly did. The phrase 'city on a hill', in the King James Bible version that Reagan would have been familiar with, is, like most typological references, no mere metaphor serving merely to describe something. It is a metaphor-with-a-message. It says what is, but also what ought to be. In the full passage, it also becomes apparent where Winthrop got the adjective 'shining' from:

> And he opened his mouth, and taught them, saying, Blessed are the poor in spirit: for theirs is the kingdom of heaven. Blessed are they that mourn: for they shall be comforted. Blessed are the meek: for they shall inherit the earth. Blessed are they which do hunger and thirst after righteousness: for they shall be filled. Blessed are the merciful: for they shall obtain mercy. Blessed are the pure in heart: for they shall see God. Blessed are the peacemakers: for they shall be called the children of God. Blessed are they which are persecuted for righteousness' sake: for theirs is the kingdom of heaven. Blessed are ye, when men shall revile you, and persecute you, and shall say all manner of evil against you falsely, for my sake. Rejoice, and be exceeding glad: for great is your reward in heaven: for so persecuted they the prophets which were before you. Ye are the salt of the earth: but if the salt have lost his savour, wherewith shall it be salted? It is thenceforth good for nothing, but to be cast out, and to be trodden under foot of men. Ye are the light of the world. A city that is set on an hill can not be hid. Neither do men light a candle, and put it under a bushel, but on a candlestick; and it giveth light unto all that are in the house. Let your light so shine before men, that they may see your good works, and glorify your Father which is in heaven. (Matthew 5:2–17)

After devoting most of his address to praising the American way of life, especially the American love of freedom, Reagan described how he used to watch the dawn from a particular window in the White House:

> The past few days when I've been at that window upstairs, I've thought a bit of the 'shining city upon a hill'. The phrase comes from John Winthrop, who wrote it to describe the America he imagined. What he imagined was important because he was an early Pilgrim, an early freedom man. He journeyed here on what today we'd call a little wooden boat; and like the other Pilgrims, he was looking for a home that would be free. I've spoken of the shining city all my political life, but I don't know if I ever quite communicated what I saw when I said it. But in my mind it was a tall, proud city built on rocks stronger than oceans, windswept, God-blessed, and teeming with people of all kinds living in harmony and peace; a city with free ports that hummed with commerce

and creativity. And if there had to be city walls, the walls had doors and the doors were open to anyone with the will and the heart to get here. That's how I saw it, and see it still.

And how stands the city on this winter night? More prosperous, more secure, and happier than it was eight years ago. But more than that: After 200 years, two centuries, she still stands strong and true on the granite ridge, and her glow has held steady no matter what storm. And she's still a beacon, still a magnet for all who must have freedom, for all the pilgrims from all the lost places who are hurtling through the darkness, toward home.

It is a little ironic of course that the society founded by Reagan's 'freedom-loving man' John Winthrop was as totalitarian as any. His idea of political freedom was a narrow one. In religious matters it did not exist. He could not abide critics of his administration as governor of the colony of Massachusetts. When Anne Hutchinson, a mere woman, gained control of his Boston church in 1636 and endeavoured to convert the whole colony to a new religious position, Winthrop denounced her for blasphemy. He secured her banishment, and later, her formal excommunication. Her life at risk, she fled to Rhode Island. The *Encyclopaedia Britannica* reports that 'Winthrop sanctimoniously noted her tragic misfortunes – her deformed stillborn baby and her murder by Indians – as proof of God's judgment against heretics.'

As has constantly happened in Anglo-American political theory, most notably in connection with the so-called Glorious Revolution of 1688, the words 'freedom' and 'liberty' were almost synonymous with anti-Catholicism, which was held to stand at the opposite pole as a representation of total oppression. Whether this was factual or not is another matter: it was believed largely because Protestant biblical typology, especially from the Book of Revelation, said it must be so. Did not Foxe's *Book of Martyrs* prove the point? (In fact Foxe was also driven by the a priori logic of typology, and viewed the evidence of Catholic tyranny under Mary exclusively in that light. Lost on him, for instance, was the restraining influence of Catholic Spain over Mary's religious zealotry. It did not fit the theory.)

The sense of the word 'freedom' New England Puritans were really interested in was the escape from the allegedly Romanising tendencies of the English church, which were thought to threaten the freedom of people like themselves to follow the full Protestant message of John Calvin. They were the persecuted who Jesus had said were blessed. They failed to see themselves as persecutors. As to how Romanising the ecclesiastical regimes of James I and Charles I actually were is a discussion for another day: sufficient to say Roman Catholicism was rigorously outlawed in England, as in Massachusetts, and being a Roman priest was a capital crime. (The *Dictionary of Christian Biography*[7] records that between 1535 and 1680 some 357 English and Welsh Roman Catholics were put to death for their beliefs.) Presumably this, for men of Winthrop's temper, did not go far enough. He lived at a time when the great threat to Protestant England was seen to come not just from overt Catholics (who were lucky to be alive) but from secret papists. These were the so-called church papists who outwardly conformed to the established church but were presumed secretly to conspire against it. English official institutions were thought by the Puritans to be riddled with them. The presumed influence of such people (which historians now think was vastly exaggerated) was a major factor leading to the Civil War against Charles I, and to the overthrow of James II.

The political use of Protestant typology, as in Reagan's speeches and many others, is surprisingly overlooked in Adrian Hastings's own study of religion and national identity, *The Construction of Nationhood*.[8] He notes the designation of America as 'a city set on a hill', and also the way, at the time of the American revolution, George Washington was hailed as the new Moses and Britain as another Egypt, which are both typological references. But he does not relate these to any larger picture.

As seems to be common with modern scholars, the crucial fact that he misses is the way Protestants were so steeped in Scripture from regular, often daily, Bible study that it moulded their consciousness and provided an all-pervasive background to every other thought they had. Nor was this only true of the eighteenth century and before. For many English and American Protestant Christians up at least until the Second World War, the Bible supplied the lens through which the rest of the world was viewed. It is not surprising that Lloyd George was more familiar with the kings of Israel than the kings of England. He had been brought up in a biblical Protestant culture which regarded the history of ancient Israel as Britain's – New Israel's – own history.

If English theologians like Hastings missed the point, however, American historians did not. Deborah Madsen, in her book *American Exceptionalism*,[9] follows Sacvan Bercovitch's *The Puritan Origins of the American Self*[10] in describing

> the imperative under which Puritan believers laboured as they sought to identify themselves and the progress of their souls towards salvation with the promises and models represented in the Bible. In Bercovitch's estimation, the importance of typology for individual believers lay in its power to create identifications across time and so permit individual Puritans to identify with key events in God's providential history.

Individuals – and nations. The application of the designation 'Chosen People' to the English and later to the Americans had a particular origin in these Protestant, especially Puritan, ways of looking at the Bible. But it had two other origins, one of which – the desire of politicians in the eighteenth century to weld the three nations of Great Britain into a single Protestant entity in order to buttress the Hanoverian dynasty and turn people against the Catholic Jacobites – has already been explored, largely with reference to the work of Linda Colley.[11] But its roots reached right back to the moment of creation of the original English nation-state, namely Henry VIII's break with Rome over the matter of his divorce. And this is a relatively unexplored area.

For centuries afterwards the received view of Christianity in English history prior to the Reformation was of a corrupt and spiritually barren church, superstitious, ignorant and priest-ridden, that the people could not wait to get rid of. It was not difficult to suspect that this view had a high level of propaganda, but only in the last decade or so has it been possible to get a clearer picture. Scholars of the period are now more or less agreed that Eamon Duffy's work *The Stripping of the Altars*, based on his excavation of authentic pre-Reformation documents, shows an image of popular religion in the high Middle Ages that is closer to the truth. And it contradicts that received view in almost every respect. Duffy concludes:

> Late medieval Catholicism exerted an enormously strong, diverse and vigorous hold over the imagination and loyalty of the people right up to the very moment of Reformation. Traditional religion had about it no particular marks of exhaustion and decay; indeed in a whole host of ways, from the multiplication of vernacular religious books to adaptations within the national and regional cult of saints, it was showing itself well able to meet new needs and new conditions . . . When all is said and done, the Reformation was a violent disruption, not the natural fulfilment, of what was vigorous in late medieval piety and religious practice.[12]

It was in other words a real revolution, a sharp break with the past, but one disguised as something else, something continuous with the past. The imagining of the national community (in Benedict Anderson's sense) had still to be an act of memory, but the memory had to be altered – in effect, falsified. Physical evidence that sustained the old memory had to be removed. That meant the monasteries, which, more even than the cathedrals and parish churches, were the backbone of medieval Christian England. Monastic orders were far more difficult for the king to control, and he foresaw deep-seated opposition to his Reformation from that quarter unless they were abolished.

114

Medieval Europe was not a Europe of what we would nowadays call nation-states. Nor was it one entire nation-state, ruled from one capital. Though history offers examples of nation-states – ancient Israel as one of them – as a model based on a political theory of national sovereignty it did not exist before Henry VIII invented it (and his daughter Elizabeth I improved on it).

The sovereignty of the kingdoms of medieval Christian Europe had been partial; not only did they exist in a loose confederation of royal dynasties which often intermarried, but they lived under the influence of another kind of supremacy, that of the Roman Catholic Church, in all matters pertaining to faith and morals. Civil law – made by kings – co-existed with canon law – made by popes – which often took precedence. Appeals to Rome were possible, though the great distances involved and difficulty of travel (including, from northern Europe, crossing the Alps) made these uncommon. The pope also had jurisdiction as a kind of supreme magistrate, who could in extreme cases even depose kings. Excommunication and interdiction (prohibiting the celebration of the sacraments) were weapons to be feared, as Henry II demonstrated.

These relationships sometimes boiled over into open conflict. Medieval kings of England, for example, had tried to rein in papal jurisdiction on a number of occasions. Henry I nearly succeeded. Henry II had the Archbishop of Canterbury, Thomas à Becket, murdered because he supported the independence of the church from state interference, and had resisted Henry II's desire to emulate his grand-father in these matters. The papacy, in turn, often played politics with its power, giving or withholding dispensations for royal marriage, for instance, in accordance with the direction of the political wind and who was in or out of favour: Spain, France, England, the Holy Roman Emperor, and so on. But it was not utterly corrupt: reform movements were regular features of the Roman ecclesiastical landscape. The political power of the papacy was sometimes abused, but it was more often used with integrity.

Nor was the medieval idea of kingship secular. In the theology of the time, all political authority came from God; and the duty to obey the laws of the state was a religious duty. But the one thing the king was not allowed to do was to declare himself pope, supplanting the Bishop of Rome in that role and taking full jurisdiction over church as well as state. Not only is that what Henry VIII did, but he set out, with help from the political genius of Thomas Cromwell, to pretend that England had always been free of papal control. The examples of Henry I and II did not serve them well, not least because both were really Frenchmen who continued to rule part of France as well as England, and because Henry II's defiance of the church, which culminated in the killing of Becket in 1170, ended in his submission to Pope Alexander III and their reconciliation after a series of humiliating penances, including being publicly scourged. One of Henry VIII's most significant moves was to have the shrine and tomb of Thomas à Becket at Canterbury – one of the most celebrated objects of pilgrimage in Europe – destroyed, and the saint's remains, even the bones, burnt and scattered. Becket was a symbol of the independence of the church from the state, and the fact that after his death he instantly became one of the most popular saints in England or indeed all Europe may indicate that the public regarded that principle as a safeguard against absolute monarchical tyranny. After Henry VIII, with no independent church to contend with, English kings and queens became among the most absolute monarchs the world had ever seen. Certainly the institutions of the state that ought to have protected the citizen, the courts and Parliament, became mere instruments of that absolutism.

As Thomas More was to find. His statement after his conviction for treason in 1535 – he had refused to acknowledge Henry's divorce from Catherine of Aragon or the king's claim to supremacy over the church – is useful not least because of what it reveals about what Englishmen had until then taken for granted. William Roper, More's son-in-law, quotes More's rebuttal of the indictment in his *Life of Sir Thomas More*:

'Forasmuch as, my Lord' (quoth he), 'this indictment is grounded upon an Act of Parliament directly repugnant to the laws of God and Holy Church, the supreme government of which, or of any part thereof, may no temporal prince presume by any law to take upon him as rightfully belonging to the See of Rome, a spiritual pre-eminence by the mouth of our Saviour himself, personally present upon the earth, to St Peter and his successors, bishops of the same see, by special prerogative, granted, it is therefore in law amongst Christian men insufficient to charge any Christian.' And for proof thereof like as amongst divers other reasons and authorities he declared That this Realm, being but one member and small part of the Church, might not make a particular law dischargeable with the general law of Christ's holy Catholic Church, no more than the City of London, being but one poor member in respect of the whole Realm, might make a law against an Act of Parliament to bind the whole Realm unto; so further showed he, that it was contrary both to the laws and statutes of this land, yet unrepealed, as they might evidently perceive in Magna charta, *Quod Ecclesia Anglicana libera sit et habeat omnia jura sua integra, et libertates suas illaesas*, and contrary to that sacred oath which the King's Highness himself, and every other Christian prince always at their coronations received, alleging moreover, that no more might this Realm of England refuse obedience to the See of Rome, than might the child refuse obedience to his natural father', and so on.

This vigorous reposte did indeed cause the judges trying More to hesitate in passing judgment; but they, like More, were subject to the king's will in this matter on pain of death. Thomas Cromwell must have realised the power of such arguments, for he inserted into the main Acts which brought the church under Crown control a historical preamble which denied the very facts on which More had based his plea. The rewriting of English history by statute would hardly have been necessary had these already been things 'every schoolboy knows'. As Edwin Jones writes in *The English Nation*:

> . . . a false view of the English past was created deliberately by government in the sixteenth century, so as to fabricate an erroneous collective memory for the English people. This national memory became so deeply embedded in the mind of most English people that it became part of English folklore and one of the most powerful assumptions of thought operating on the outlook and behaviour of the English people for over four centuries. It represents one of the earliest and most successful attempts by a national state to shape the thinking of its own people. The techniques involved in this mass deception are themselves very intriguing. Only very recently have we been shown in detail how a new national and political theology, with obedience to the king – representing 'God's Word' – at its centre, was borrowed for political purposes and then used as government propaganda by Thomas Cromwell. Similarly, a new view of the whole English past, based on this same political theology, was created by the Henrician government to justify the revolution which we call the Reformation.[13]

The political theology he referred to was that version of Protestantism associated with the name of William Tyndale, who, in his *The Obedience of a Christian Man* published in 1527, had put forward the view that obedience to the word of God demanded obedience to the king. Cromwell's deliberate distortion of history was designed to suggest that such views were normal and traditional, not brand new. The same conclusion is drawn by Norman Davies, in his groundbreaking study *The Isles*:

> Until recently, little attention has been paid to the thoroughgoing ideological system which Thomas Cromwell invented in order to lubricate his legislative programme. Since few doctrinal novelties were introduced at this stage, it was long assumed that little had changed in the realm of ideas. Yet close examination of the Reformation statutes shows that each was prefaced by a preamble containing radical theological and historical postulates. Cromwell was not content to create a new legal framework for Church and State. He took great care to present theoretical arguments to justify the changes.[14]

Thus the preamble to the Act in Restraint of Appeals (1533), which effectively cut the English clergy off from the protection of canon law by depriving them of the right to appeal to Rome, began by referring to 'old authentic histories and chronicles' (without saying what they were)

> where . . . it is manifestly declared and expressed that this realm of England is an empire, and hath been accepted in the world, governed by one extreme head and king having the dignity and royal estate of imperial crown of the same, unto whom a body politic, compact of all sorts and degrees of people, divided in terms and by names of spirituality and temporality, be bounded and ought to bear, next to God, natural and humble obedience.

Cromwell, says Davies, was 'claiming to uphold a historic right whereby England has supposedly always been completely independent of all extraneous authority. He was denying the validity of the status which everyone in England had accepted for more than a thousand years.'

The Act for Ecclesiastical Appointments of the following year 'adopted a parallel fiction by claiming that the king's sole right to appoint bishops and archbishops was a practice "as of old time has been accustomed" '. And the Act of Supremacy, also of that year, went further still, declaring:

> Albeit the king's majesty justly and rightfully is and ought to be the supreme head of the Church of England, and so is recognised . . . be it enacted that the king, or our sovereign Lord, his heirs and successors . . . shall be taken, accepted and reputed the only Supreme Head on earth of the Church of England, called *Anglicana Ecclesia*.

The use of the phrase *Anglicana Ecclesia* in the statute is clearly no coincidence. It suggests that the church of which Henry was head was the same body that Magna Charta had declared 'shall be free' in the passage quoted by Thomas More that same year in his defence against the charge of treason. Thus it was a claim to historical continuity between the medieval church and Henry's church. The implication was that whatever freedom that Magna Charta had guaranteed for the church, it was not freedom from interference by the king: what other kind of freedom there was, was not clear. The recent historical context of Magna Charta was the crisis in church-state relations which led to the murder of Becket, forty-five years earlier. It is plain the barons at Runnymede (and Archbishop Langton) were trying to make sure King John did not repeat what Henry II had tried.

Anglicana Ecclesia can be translated as either 'the Church of England', which is how Henry wanted it to sound, or as 'the English Church', meaning the English part of the universal church, which is what More said the phrase in Magna Charta meant. The case made by Davies and Edwin Jones, previously quoted, is that More's interpretation was the one his contemporaries would have understood, which is in line with what we now know about church history in England up to that time. Whereas Cromwell's interpretation was a novelty, indeed a deliberate invention.

The rewriting of history, states Davies, is nowhere more evident than in the preamble to the Act of Appeals:

> . . . the king, his most noble progenitors, and the nobility and commons of this said realm, at divers and sundry parliaments as well in the time of King Edward I, Edward III, Richard II, Henry IV and other noble kings of this realm made sundry ordinances, laws, statutes and provisions for the entire and sure conservation of the prerogatives, liberties and pre-eminences of the said imperial crown of this realm, and of the jurisdiction spiritual and temporal of the same, to keep it from the annoyance as well of the See of Rome as from the authority of other foreign potentates, attempting the diminution or violation thereof, as often, and from time to time, as any such annoyance or attempt to be known or espied.

In order to show that Henry VIII was doing nothing new, Cromwell was prepared to revise the whole long story of Anglo-papal relations, says Davies. 'The hostility to "foreign powers" and "foreign potentates" is manifest in the language used. All non-English jurisdictions are described as "usurpations", "depredations", and "annoyances". English authority is the emanation of liberty. All foreign authority is "despicable", "tyranny", "subjugation", "bondage".' And this from a king who had less than six years previously appealed to the Pope for the dissolution of his marriage to Catherine – including giving evidence about it to a papal legate, Cardinal Campeggio, sitting at Blackfriars; whose Chancellor Wolsey was also called Cardinal (a title only Popes may bestow); and a king who proudly bore the title Defender of the Faith that the Pope had awarded him for his Defence of the Seven Sacraments against Lutheranism.

Notwithstanding any of that, this newly spun 'national history' was supported by what Davies calls 'a new and terrifying definition of treason'. Any deviation from the religious norms now laid down by law, as well as any denial that the king had the power to make that law, would henceforth be punished as high treason, for which the normal punishment was hanging, drawing and quartering (but mere decapitation for a nobleman). Erastianism – the doctrine that the secular ruler stands above the church – was henceforth to be the national ideology. In terms of ecclesiastical organisation, Henry VIII did not transfer the powers previously held by the Pope to the Church of England as such; he transferred them to himself. His Reformation was not so much towards a Catholicism without the pope as towards a Catholicism with himself as pope.

The skeleton of that structure still exists today. The modern Church of England, unlike all other parts of the Anglican Communion, lacks the final say over its own affairs in precisely those areas that were reserved to the papacy in the Middle Ages and transferred to the Crown and Parliament under Henry by the Reformation statutes of the 1530s: the appointment of bishops, and the determination of worship and doctrine. In both respects the state has by now shrunk its powers to the absolute minimum. Nevertheless Parliamentary approval was required for the Church of England's decision to ordain women as priests in 1992, and approval of the Prime Minister (acting on behalf of the Crown) is still necessary before any diocesan bishop can be appointed. (He usually has two nominations to choose from.) Despite Cromwell's pretence that they had always belonged to the Crown, these powers that Henry transferred to himself were once papal powers. They had never belonged to the church in England as of right; nor do they, even today.

Jones explains how this rewriting of history shaped English self-consciousness for generations to come:

> It is because of this deliberately conceived misunderstanding of their history that the English were to forget that they were Europeans. They were to become increasingly nationalistic and insular in outlook, despite the acquisition of a great empire overseas. They developed other qualities which were inspired by this view of their past, including a sense of specialness, self-sufficiency, superiority and separation from all other peoples of the world. This false memory influenced their psychology and their outlook on the world.[15]

But this psychological factor is not a complete explanation. As the last chapter describes, the Catholic Church up to the time of Henry VIII had taken over from the Jews the status of the People of God, becoming, in the words of 1 Peter 2:9, 'a chosen generation, a royal priesthood, an holy nation, a peculiar people'.

That described the church in theory, but where was the church to be found in practice? It had to be somewhere, if not in one place then in another. Until Henry, the answer (as far as the Latin, Western part of Christendom was concerned) was the institution centred on Rome. Henry's claim to head the church automatically meant that these words, if they no longer applied to Rome, must now apply to the Church of England. Henceforth the Church of England, not Rome, was 'an holy nation, a peculiar people'. But this was not now a separate institution from the Henrician state, as the medieval church, being part of the universal church, had been a separate institution. It was more what we would nowadays recognise as a 'ministry for religious affairs' – a department of government. That government was headed by the king. The temporal and the spiritual aspects of kingly power were two sides of the same coin. England was both church and state, and in both capacities it was 'an holy nation, a peculiar people'.

Thus, England (and England alone, for all intents and purposes) stood in the place of the Jews of the Old Testament and the Christians of the New, as an instrument not just for the king's purposes but for God's. Like the Hebrews of the Old Testament, this was a Chosen People defined both religiously and nationally. The boundaries of the one were the boundaries of the other: and citizenship of Israel, old or new, meant automatic membership of the People of God. England had acquired a Manifest Destiny. It had a unique role to play in God's master plan for salvation of mankind. The version of Christianity it professed was uniquely true – must be, otherwise God was party to a deception – and those bodies or churches which disagreed with it were wrong (or worse, in the hands of the devil).

But this was a conservative tradition, still Catholic in style, which reflected Henry's own religious tastes. This conservative position survived in the movement within the Church of England later known as Anglo-Catholicism. Its central claim was that all the essentials of Catholic Christianity were preserved intact within Anglicanism, and ought to be recognised as such by Rome and other national churches. In other words what prevented a reconciliation with Rome was Rome's insistence on an inflated view of papal jurisdiction. But Anglo-Catholicism has always been ready to concede that Rome should hold a 'primacy of honour' among the churches, something like the orthodox notion of 'first among equals', so the blame for disunity lay at Rome's door for overstating the papal claims for supremacy. The Church of England was 'the ancient Catholic Church of this nation'. If that formula proved indigestible to the more Protestant kind of Anglican, then the claim was adjusted to say that it was both 'Catholic and Reformed' – though the reality both at the outset and over the subsequent centuries was that part of the Church of England was much more Catholic than Reformed, and part of the Church of England was much more Reformed than Catholic (in other words several versions of Anglican Christianity existed side by side within the one Anglican ecclesiastical structure).

Henry's and Cromwell's conservative rendering of the heritage of Anglicanism did not go unchallenged for long. The Reformation they had affected turned out to be only the first bite of what was to prove a long meal. Largely this was due to a coincidence of timing: that Henry's impatience with the church's objection to his divorce and remarriage occurred just as the real Protestant Reformation was gathering pace on the Continent, particularly in Germany, France, Holland and Switzerland. (To a Protestant believer in Providence, of course, such coincidences were by God's design.) The passing of the royal succession from Henry to Edward VI swung the politics of English religion sharply to the left. Radical Protestants, some of whom were soon to be driven into exile in Lutheran Germany and Calvinist Switzerland by the ferocious anti-Protestant persecution of Mary Tudor, took their objections to the Roman version of Christianity much further than the Henrician quarrel over papal jurisdiction.

This development was to have far-reaching consequences. It set up a tension at the heart of the English Reformation between two conflicting models. One was conservative and the other radical, one monarchical and episcopal, the other republican, egalitarian, and in matters of church organisation, more in keeping with a 'bottom-up' theory of church authority as in Presbyterianism than a 'top-down' theory as in Anglican episcopalianism. Did authority (whether in church or state did not matter) flow upwards or downwards, upwards from God's people, the laity, or downwards from God's anointed, the princes and prelates who ruled in his name? This was a conflict of ideas that was to bring on civil war and two revolutions in the next century (Oliver Cromwell's, and the 1688 'Glorious Revolution' against James II); and it is the argument of *The Cousins' Wars* by Kevin Phillips[16] that therein also lay the seeds both of the American Revolutionary War and the American Civil War. Nor is the argument over yet.

Medieval European Christendom had relied upon the top-down model, but had nevertheless evolved a dual system of power, the monarchical and the papal, whereby each acted as a check and balance on the other. The dual system prevented either side from having absolute (i.e. unchecked) power. If a king went too far in exercising his powers, the church, which was outside his control, could seek to rein him in. The opposite was also theoretically possible, though it was usually the king who had effective power on the ground and therefore the greater temptation to abuse it. Needless to say, in practice the operation of these checks and balances often required a good deal of crude pushing and shoving, and occasionally even war. Not long before Henry's own crisis with papal authority, the Holy Roman Emperor, Charles V, had gone so far as to march against Rome, which his troops sacked, capturing Pope Adrian VI (whom Henry VIII had previously strongly supported). The twelfth-century story of Thomas à Becket, and the thirteenth-century role of Archbishop Stephen Langton in helping to bring King John to the point where he agreed to sign Magna Charta, are two instances where a monarchical thrust leading towards tyranny was turned aside by the opposition of the church. Charles V also provides an example of the other – of secular power acting to rein in the church. His pressure was primarily responsible for the convening of the Council of Trent in 1545, which set about a root and branch reform of the Catholic Church, its worship, practice and doctrine, partly in the light of Protestant criticism (which it did not, nevertheless, succeed in satisfying).

The constitutional issue raised by Henry VIII's break with Rome was that if the church was not independent, it could no longer function as a check on a king's power, which would rapidly become absolute and, indeed, tyrannical. This, according to the Anglican historian and Canon of St Paul's Cathedral, Canon John Halliburton, was precisely what Thomas More foresaw when he resigned the Chancellorship of England rather than co-operate with Henry's seizure of power over the church. In a sermon at Chelsea Old Church in 1992, Canon Halliburton said:

> The spectre before More's eyes as he discharged himself from the greatest office in the land was undoubtedly that of tyranny. Much earlier in his life, he had placed great hopes in the young Henry. Henry's rather grim father had been a threat to More; More had seen him as a tyrant, and had welcomed his death, welcomed the new reign, welcomed the literate and intelligent prince with the beautiful wife, welcomed his interest in music and dancing, welcomed his sociability and reverence for the church which both married him and crowned him. More, one suspects, hadn't bargained for Wolsey, hadn't reckoned on that prelate's hold over the young king, sweeping him into wars he could not afford, financial relationships he could not sustain, and into doubts even about his home life and his marriage.
>
> Wolsey was undoubtedly unscrupulous, piling up livings and preferments to afford him an income commensurate with his political programme. But the cardinal, it would seem, had led the king to the brink of the apotheosis of power; and when Europe and the papacy said a very firm 'No' to Henry's projects and ambitions, Henry, like the child he was, claimed kingdom and church for his own. His power was absolute; nobody could say him nay. And More saw in this the beginning of the ruin of the reign. Five marriages later, with the economy in tatters, the monasteries ruined, the church plate melted down, the intelligentsia clamouring for reform and the country people sparking revolts, Henry was to die of syphilis. His madness had achieved nothing. Suspicion and vanity had led him to put to death those who could have been his closest allies.
>
> So it is with all tyrants; and if there is any lesson we can learn today from the wisdom of Thomas More, then it is that tyranny brooks no

criticism, and that the ingrained selfishness of the tyrant is only overcome by the self-sacrificing integrity of the martyr.

Henry's death and the succession of Edward VI unleashed a far more radical overhaul of English Christianity. Nor were the reformers gratified by Thomas Cromwell's historical claim to continuity between the post-Reformation church and the medieval church. They preferred what became the received view (referred to above), namely that the medieval church was rotten to the core. But Cromwell's preambles and their re-written English history were still a useful foundation.

John Foxe, the prince of Protestant propagandists, found other work just as useful for his complete reconstruction of English national identity, especially that of his friend John Bale. Cromwell's version of history had too many holes in it. In outline, Bale's history of English Christianity went back to Joseph of Arimathea, who on the instructions of St Philip the apostle was said to have brought the gospel straight to England at the time of Christ, certainly not via Rome. In medieval legend Joseph was guardian of the Holy Grail (in which Christ's blood had been shed at the Crucifixion) and was buried in Glastonbury. There are strong links here with the Arthurian legend. Joseph was recorded in the Gospels as a well-placed but secret supporter of Jesus who provided his own tomb for Jesus's burial. Bale's recruitment of Joseph for his own version of English history would have set up powerful resonances in the national subconscious. It all, so to speak, 'began to make sense'.

Thus the English church was established by one King Lucius, a near contemporary of Constantine; after that, the story of England is of perpetual heroic struggle between native kings and their people on the one hand (Arthur among them), and alien invaders of various kinds representing the forces of Anti-Christ. The pagan Saxon invasion, St Augustine's 'corrupting' mission at the end of the sixth century, even the Norman Conquest with its insidious train of bishops, monks and friars, were all chapters in this epic tale. Thus was it demonstrated that English Christianity was of the purest kind, coming direct from Christ and the apostles and preserved down the centuries (though sometimes driven underground), for the sixteenth-century English Protestants to emerge into the light and proclaim it as the authentic faith that Christ intended. It was an apocalyptic vision, and it gave to English kings a triumphant role as brave defenders of the sacred national heritage against the constant harassment of foreign rulers, the papal Anti-Christ in particular. John Foxe followed Bale faithfully, writes Jones:

His massive work [*The Book of Martyrs*] was written within the same national-erastian framework of thought. There is the familiar description of the papacy as a tyrannical power, representing the force of Anti-Christ and threatening the independence, freedom and true religion of the English people. There is also the erastian statement of the supremacy of the king as God's vice-regent over church and state. These were the old pillars of Cromwell's structure. Now, however, under Bale and Foxe a new and essential element had been added to the myth.[17]

Foxe adopted Bale's apocalyptic version of English history: that

> the whole of English history had led providentially to the reigns of Henry VIII and Elizabeth I, who had been appointed by God to lead the English people out of the land of bondage (foreign papal control) into freedom and national success . . . This incorporation of the Protestant interpretation of history into English history, to serve the needs of his apocalyptic vision, turned Foxe's book into a philosophy of history. This gave a crusading appeal to the folk myth of the English past. English Protestants could now become part of the apocalyptic vision in the present and the future . . . This apocalyptic tradition was destined to become ever more important to English nationalism.

The reference to Moses in the typology of Henry 'leading the people of England out of the land of bondage' is obvious. Those whom the new Moses led were successors of the ancient Israelites.

At the outset this new apocalyptic national ideology placed England alongside other Protestant nations, as a leader, supporter, refuge, ally, and foe of Catholic Spain and France. The chosen – the 'elect' in Calvin's language – were at first transnational. But the ideology of Henricianism (if one may thus label the ideas behind the Reformation statutes of the 1530s) pulled it towards a particular focus on England's role to the exclusion of others, as did the historical narrative devised by Bale. Members of other nations may be among the elect, but there was only one Chosen Nation, one place where the true gospel had been providentially preserved since the time of Christ: England.

Thus Thomas Brightman in a pamphlet published in 1615 – five years before the Pilgrims landed at Plymouth Rock, Massachusetts, and planted these ideas on American soil – referred to the special place given to the reformed English Church in God's apocalyptic plan, saying 'there was no parallele to match her, as being a peerless Paragon'. It was a religion still beset by enemies (directly or indirectly in league with Rome) that would take a civil war to defend itself against them. Thus did these two streams – the erastian, Henrician need for a constitutional settlement, and the Puritan, apocalyptic vision of a nation with a destiny – converge (and also collide) in the late sixteenth and early seventeenth centuries. The ambiguities and contradictions that resulted from these various incompatible ideas were actually for a time a source of strength – refute one side of the contradiction, and the other side shone forth all the more brightly. And their first great flourishing, showing just how virile these ideas were to prove in world history, arrived in the reign of Good Queen Bess, Protestant England personified. As Jones writes:

> Nothing did more to inspire the Elizabethan concern with nationhood than the idea that the cause of true religion was identified with the rise of the English sovereign state under its queen, appointed by God to protect the Protestant nation against the evils of Catholic powers such as France and Spain who were in the grip of Anti-Christ – the papacy. One Elizabethan bishop, John Aylmer, felt confident enough to announce that 'God is English'.[18]

Jones is himself a Catholic, but his demolition of the false 'Protestant' history of English Christianity perpetrated for political reasons is largely endorsed by the theologian and historian Ian Bradley, a Scottish Presbyterian (and a minister in the Church of Scotland). Bradley notes that the supposedly ancient form of 'pure' Christianity which the first Protestant reformers claimed to inherit was largely what is now called Celtic Christianity. He suggests, having come across no use of the term prior to John Foxe's friend John Bale, that the very term 'Celtic' was a Protestant invention. Whether there was ever such a thing as a 'Celtic Church', as popularly understood today, is, he states, a matter of some uncertainty. Nevertheless it proved a useful idea, not least because it was a blank screen on to which people could project whatever they wanted. The early English Reformers, says Bradley,

> found the Celtic Church to be a Protestant institution in all but name, characterised by evangelical purity and wholly independent of Rome. Far from bringing in new-fangled Continental principles, as its opponents claimed, they argued that the Reformation represented a return to the values of an indigenous British Christianity in its golden age.
>
> The process of rewriting history to give it a new Protestant spin was begun by William Tyndale. In his *The Obedience of a Christian Man* and *Practice of Prelates*, written in exile in Holland, he presented a picture of an independent British Church which had steadily succumbed to the shackles of Roman domination during the Middle Ages. Tyndale's particular hero from the Celtic golden age was Gildas, the sixth-century British monk, whom he portrayed as a prophetic figure sent by God to rebuke his countrymen for having deserted the Scriptures. His strongly pro-Roman sympathies overlooked, Gildas became for many of the

apologists of the Reformation a proto-Protestant prophet calling his countrymen to repentance and preaching the true Gospel.

Tyndale's pioneering efforts to find a precedent for Protestantism in early British Church history were taken up and developed by John Bale ... His most important work ... presented an idyllic picture of a pure and primitive British Church uncontaminated by Rome. Picking up the Glastonbury legends he located the conversion of Britain in apostolic times and specifically the mission of Joseph of Arimathea in AD 63 ... The notion that this was the route by which Christianity had first come to the British Isles was to remain a major plank in Protestant history and propaganda for the next 150 years or so.[19]

The legend of Lucius is attributed to the medieval myth-maker Geoffrey of Monmouth (twelfth-century chronicler of the King Arthur legend), who reports that Christianity was brought to England in the second century at the invitation of that king, who wrote to Pope Eleutherius asking for missionaries. The papal ingredient in the story was dropped, but, says Bradley,

several leading figures in the post-Reformation Church of England, notably Matthew Parker and John Jewel, enthusiastically took up the notion of Lucius as the first Christian king of Britain and argued that it showed the British Church to have been from the first a national institution in which the initiatives and leadership came from the monarch rather than the Pope ... whatever their differences about how and when the faith had arrived here, there was agreement among Protestant historians that the British Church had originally been independent and free of Roman influence. [Parker was Elizabeth I's first Archbishop of Canterbury, and Jewel was her Bishop of Salisbury.]

The 'fatal contamination' with popery had happened with the arrival of Augustine in 597, Bradley goes on, who was authorised by Pope Gregory the Great to set up a new episcopal hierarchy based at Canterbury, to which existing British bishops would be subject. Vilification of Augustine became a marked feature of Protestant Church history throughout the sixteenth and seventeenth centuries. It was as a result of his mission, said the Protestant historians, that British Christianity had for the first time to submit to the jurisdiction of Rome, and compromise the pure character of its worship and beliefs by accepting Roman idolatrous practices such as candlesticks, vestments and relics, which were hitherto unknown.

But as Bradley makes clear, the Protestantism of ancient Celtic Christianity (if such a thing ever really existed) would not have been apparent to the ancient Celts. First, their religion was strongly monastic, and monasticism is not a Protestant trait. They would have been as nonplussed by *sola Scriptura* as they would by 'salvation by faith alone': for them, getting to heaven was a lifetime's work. Celtic Christianity was based largely on cults of local saints, usually holy monks or bishops or both, which were built up after their death, with prayers said to them, their shrines and relics venerated, holy wells dedicated in their names, and many miracles (some of them quite bizarre) attributed to their interventions in heaven. The cult of a Celtic saint like St Brigit appeared to have been strongly influenced by the example of the Virgin Mary. They had a Catholic doctrine of the Real Presence and of purgatory. All this would have been anathema to a true Protestant. Nor did Celtic Christian leaders really ignore Rome. At the Synod of Whitby in 664 they accepted that the pope had authority to fix the date of Easter, and various other matters. Indeed, though Bradley does not make the connection, Celtic Christianity begins to sound suspiciously like medieval Catholicism as portrayed by Eamon Duffy in his *The Stripping of the Altars*.[20]

Nevertheless whole shelfloads of books were written from the sixteenth century onwards extending or revising the theories of Bale, Parker and Jewel, to show, for instance, that if Joseph of Arimathea did not bring Christianity to Britain then it must have been St Paul, that Irish Christianity had originally been Protestant (indeed, Anglican), or that the ancient Celtic saints were in reality good Scots Presbyterians. Any evidence to the contrary of whatever theory the Celts were being called upon to prove was simply ignored, or explained away. One such explanation proposed that the Celtic use of the very unprotestant word 'mass' for the Communion service was in fact not derived from the Latin formula *Ite missa est* with which the Catholic mass concluded, but was a modification of 'mistletoe' which had been used in pagan rituals and taken into Celtic Christianity when paganism was supplanted.

From the English point of view, the most important conclusion to draw from this rewriting of history was that God had providentially preserved the true Protestant faith in England since the time of Christ, which now, under the leadership of Protestant kings and queens (starting with Henry), was being restored to its rightful place. In the light of that amazing fact, how else could England be described but as a chosen people, a royal priesthood and a holy nation? And of course, the only one.

5

Myths and More Myths

To understand the New Israel mindset it is necessary to look more closely at the content of early Jewish history, to see exactly what it was that the English and Americans regarded as their own story – to see, that is, how they thought God had dealt with their predecessors and therefore how he would deal with them. It is no less important because the Old Testament contains a comprehensive set of moral teachings that were adopted by the Protestant pioneers of Anglo-Saxon democracy as applicable to themselves.

It might be advisable first, however, to take a pinch of salt from the archaeologists' table, especially the Egyptologists. The significance of Old Testament history for Protestantism's self-understanding is not that it was true but that it was thought to be true. It is because of this principle that this chapter relies largely on the Authorised Version (AV) of the Bible, known in America as the King James Version (KJV). Far more accurate translations exist, though not necessarily with the same quality of English prose. But until the end of the nineteenth century the only version the great majority of the population of Britain and America would have been familiar was the 1611 one, 'appointed to be read in churches' by King James I. Because we are concerned here primarily with what they thought the Bible said, rather than what it actually said, this is the version we shall quote from. The price is some loss of clarity in some places: but if it is not quite clear to us what the text meant, then it would not have been clear to readers in previous centuries.

The archaeological evidence is that many narratives in the Old Testament correspond hardly at all to historical fact, or are at best vast amplifications or conflations of small incidents. Oral history no doubt grew better in the telling. As has happened many times since, the foundation narrative of the new nation assumed greater significance than may be historically justified. As Ernest Renan remarked in 1863 in his celebrated *Life of Jesus*: 'Nothing great has been established which does not rest on a legend.' Nations need myths, and look to historical events for the raw material to create them. The creative process is in the hands of poets and storytellers, whose skill lies in capturing the imagination, not in their command of dry facts. Myths work best, however, if those accepting them believe them to be factually true. The problem is that while such myths exalt the nation they belong to, they often do so by denigrating other nations. Thus myths easily turn into long-standing grievances towards their neighbours, long-standing reasons for prejudice or hatred which may have little or no basis in fact. This is not a plea for a myth-free history. There is no such thing. But it is an argument for the endless re-excavation of every national story to move it gradually nearer to the truth, and for a general awareness that 'self-evident truths', no less than 'things every schoolboy knows', should never be trusted absolutely.

There are similar historical problems here. Did the Hebrews ever acquire a title deed made in heaven for the land called Canaan? Did the ancient Egyptians ever really oppress the Hebrews? Despite the some-times strenuous efforts of partisan archaeologists in the nineteenth century to vindicate the biblical story – even Sigmund Freud had a go, in his monograph *Moses and Monotheism* – there is no trace in ancient Egyptian writing of the presence of large numbers of Hebrews before the events described in the Book of Exodus, nor any mention of the Exodus event itself. As for Canaan, the archaeological evidence suggests that the process of settlement and acquisition was very gradual. That is not the pattern of sudden conquest of one tribe by another described in the Old Testament. And a truth by no means conveyed by the biblical accounts but revealed by archaeological evidence is that the Canaanites were a rather more advanced and cultured society than the Hebrews. It is probable that the Canaanites were the first to use a systematic alphabet in their written language.

In nineteenth-century England the Egyptian Exploration Society, the most famous of all the international sponsors of Egyptian archaeology, came into existence to find traces of the 'treasure cities' Pithom and Rameses, said in the Bible (Exodus 1:11) to have been built by Hebrew slaves. The sites of those cities are known – the biblical Rameses is fairly obviously Pi-Rameses, built as a new capital city for the great Pharaoh Rameses II. But no evidence that Jews helped in their construction has emerged. However, that does not alter the intriguing possibility that the Pharaoh of the Exodus was indeed the greatest Pharaoh of them all. Needless to say, there is no evidence for Hollywood's version of the myth that Hebrew slaves built the pyramids. They date from more than a thousand years earlier.

Neither Joseph, who became Vizier to the Pharaoh after correctly interpreting his dreams, nor Moses, who also rose to high rank after being adopted by the Pharaoh's daughter, figure in Egyptian recorded history (at least not until Cecil B. DeMille's film *The Ten Commandments*). The Israelites' dramatic departure from Egypt and the crossing of the Red Sea are ignored, though some of the plagues which preceded the Exodus do correspond to fairly common naturally occurring events, such as catastrophic Nile floods, of which archaeologists have evidence. It is little more than speculation that there could be some connection between the presence of the (monotheist) Hebrews and the brief monotheist cult of the Pharaoh Akhenaten (*c.* fourteenth century BC). The best hard evidence, and 'hard' is rather overstating it, is the curious parallel between the *Hymn to the Aten* (attributed to Akhenaten himself; Aten, the sun, is also the One God who created the Universe) and the Old Testament's Psalm 104. For instance:

Thou makest darkness, and it is night: wherein all the beasts of the forest do creep forth. The young lions roar after their prey, and seek their meat from God. (Psalm 104:20–1)

When thou dost set in the western horizon, the Earth in darkness, like to death . . . Every lion has come forth from his lair. (*Hymn to the Aten*)

The parallels, which Egyptologist John Romer describes as 'clear and subtle',[1] are not only in such textual similarities but also in the sequence of ideas. The inference is that the author of the Psalm knew the *Hymn to the Aten*, or some version of it, and took it as a model. This suggests that the Israelites were well aware of the short but spectacular monotheist period in Egypt's history. Furthermore this was likely to have been contemporary knowledge as subsequent Pharaohs regarded Akhenaten as a heretic and took great care to expunge his memory. It also suggests the Hebrews could read hieroglyphic inscriptions: the *Hymn to the Aten* is engraved on the walls of the tomb of the Pharaoh Ay at El-Amarna in Middle Egypt.

Nevertheless it is inconclusive evidence. The only indisputable reference to Israel in any ancient Egyptian text is the so-called 'Israel stele' now in the Cairo Museum, which seems to describe the Israelites as having been laid waste – 'his seed is not', says the hieroglyph, with succinct finality – by the Pharaoh Merenptah, Rameses II's successor, possibly in Canaan. But there is no such episode recorded in the Old Testament.

Even allowing for the principle that each warrior would exaggerate his own successes and not record his failures (or make them into victories too), it is striking how little trace major upheavals described in the Bible have left on the ground. Did they actually happen at all? The sequence to the escape from Egypt related in Exodus was the Israelites' forty-years stay in the wilderness of Sinai, which was unlikely to leave much archaeological evidence behind. But what happened next should have done. As Romer argues:

> Contrary to the biblical story that a savage Israelite army destroyed Canaan's wicked old cities and established a new faith and a new nation in their place, archaeology shows that the reality of change between Bronze Age and Iron Age Palestine was a gradual transformation in which the traditional forms of worship were maintained, as powerful expressions of men's relationship to the sacred, whether to biblical Jehovah or to the ancient Gods of Canaan . . . So, although the Bible stresses the novelty, the uniqueness of Jehovah, archaeology shows that the differences between the biblical ritual of his faith and the old cult of Canaan was slight – and this indeed was doubtless why the prophets attacked the ancient Gods for century after century, so that the new faith was not absorbed into the ancient ways.[2]

Which is a point not dissimilar to that already quoted from Rabbi Louis Jacobs. It may be noted, however, that Rabbi Jacobs had long been in trouble with the Orthodox Jewish authorities for questioning whether Moses was the real author of the first five books of the Bible (or Pentateuch).

This throws into sharp relief the question – if the Bible is history, what sort of history is it? The conventional answer among both Jewish and Christian theologians outside the fundamentalists' camps in both faiths is that it is 'salvation history', a special category of history most people (including most followers of both faiths) are unlikely to have heard identified as such. This is a narrative whose main focus is the interactive relationship between humanity and God. Almost the entire Old Testament is concerned not with God's relations with the whole of humanity but with one small section of it, a group of Middle Eastern tribes which claimed a common ancestry from one patriarchal figure, Abraham. Other tribes and nations appear and disappear as they impinge on the main story. God came into it because most of the successes and failures of these tribes are attributed to his intervention, directly or indirectly. Sometimes things go right for them; sometimes he lets them go wrong. Along the way they learn more about him, and their religious ideas become more and more sophisticated and subtle, more complex and more interesting. It is also true that along the way they pick up influences from other tribes, other religions, and some of this sophistication may come from these external sources. But they rarely if ever acknowledge that fact, as if to do so might compromise the uniqueness of their relationship to God.

What further complicates the notion of the Old Testament as salvation history is that much of it is told as if it was real history, as we understand the term. It is still a characteristic of fundamentalists, especially in the United States, to treat it as literally true as if it claimed to be a scientific record. It is full of reports of the type 'X did Y to Z, and the result was ABC'. The right way to approach salvation history masquerading as real history is with a pinch of salt as far as the facts are concerned, but with an open mind as to what the author was really trying to say. At a distance of 3000 years, the exact detail of what X did to Z matters not at all. What might still be interesting is why X did it, why did Z react as he did, and what was God's purpose in it all? Was ABC the result he wanted, and if so why? And for us – assuming we are in a frame of mind to ask such questions – what does that tell us about God?

There is further meaning to be extracted if we are interested in God's dealings with this particular group of Semitic tribes precisely because they were, or thought they were, specially chosen. Because if we are a part of a group that also feels itself to be specially chosen, even more so if that group regards itself as the successor of the original group, then we could learn from the experience of that earlier group how God expects our group to behave. And we could even predict the future, for while 'real' history may not repeat itself, salvation history has a habit of doing so. And to complicate the matter further, this exercise will involve the continual blurring of the line between real history and salvation history.

Did Moses write the Pentateuch? Yes, if the question is asked within the rules of salvation history – in other words salvation history invites us to read the first five books of the Bible as if they were written by Moses. But No, if it is to be regarded as real history, because the answer Yes does not fit the facts as real history has uncovered them. (Nor does it explain how a book written by Moses could describe Moses's own death.)

All this alters the way the Bible is read and interpreted. For those who want the Bible to be true or false, without lingering over these grades of meaning, that is very unsatisfactory. This is a pressing problem for modern Protestantism, as we shall later discuss. Are modern Christians, for instance, bound to believe that God gave the Promised Land (formerly Canaan) to the Hebrews? Given the eventual outcome – in the twentieth century the return of the Jewish people to their ancestral homeland has been the cause of prolonged bloody conflict in the Middle East – this is by no means an academic question. But modern Christianity is not well equipped to answer it.

A systematic comparison between the history of ancient Israel and the two main contenders for the title 'New Israel', England and America, is complicated by several factors. In the first place, the chronological order of events is different. If we follow the sequence of situations and events as told in the Old Testament, searching for situations and events in English and American history which were understood at the time they happened to be comparable to them, the sequence is bound to be different. In the Bible, for instance, Moses came before Gideon. In Anglo-American history, Oliver Cromwell is identified with Gideon in the seventeenth century, George Washington with Moses in the eighteenth, which in historical terms is the wrong order. But because our interest is primarily in salvation history rather than 'history as it actually happened', it makes more sense to follow the Old Testament sequence, accepting as a consequence that that means telling Anglo-American history in what may seem to be a rather confusing fashion, out of its chronological order. So because Moses came before Gideon we shall deal with Washington (typologically, that is) before we deal with Cromwell.

This non-linear approach is further justified by the fact that salvation history has a cyclical pattern to it. There may be a progression from one cycle to the next – salvation history never quite repeats itself – but similar patterns keep coming around. Thus the American Civil War is prophetically foretold by Harriet Beecher Stowe as divine chastisement for American wickedness in allowing slavery; British setbacks on the western front in the First World War are seen by the Bishop of London as divine chastisement for British laxity in religious and moral matters. These two occurrences, separated by more than sixty years and having no causal connection whatever, are two examples of the same idea – that God punishes his chosen people when it misbehaves. The fact that pre-Civil War America and First World War Britain cannot both be the Chosen People, though this consideration may drive us to the conclusion that in fact neither of them were, need not deflect us. We are dealing with what people believed about themselves and how that influenced their actions at the time, not what we believe about them now.

The Bible starts with a brief account of the creation of the world. Following various Babylonian 'creation narratives' which it resembles, the first book describes how everything was created in six intervals, or 'days', the last of which saw the arrival of Man (and soon after, Woman). They lived a life of marital bliss and primal innocence until, tempted by the devil, they broke the rules and were expelled from the Garden of Eden, their original perfect home. The symbolic act of disobedience was the eating of an apple from the tree of the knowledge of good and evil, from which the phrase 'forbidden fruit' entered the English language. This disobedience and its consequences were known as the Fall. All humanity is descended from this original pair, the Bible asserts, which is one piece of biblical information that modern genetic research appears to have supported. In modern times the common ancestry of the whole of humanity is taken to be a theological argument against racism, but that does not seem to have occurred to Christian interpreters of the Bible much before the twentieth century. Genetic research lends no scientific weight to the theory of the Fall itself, however.

The consequence of Adam's and Eve's disastrous transgression was that they and all their successors were marked by sin (Original Sin). Because in the original story it was Eve who tempted Adam (she in turn having been enticed to do so by Satan), the Judaeo-Christian treatment of femininity was always marked by distrust. In cases of sexual mis-behaviour the prejudice set in that the woman was usually the seducer, man the seduced: the woman bore the greater share of the blame, therefore. One of the cruel and unusual punishments that God chose to inflict on women as a result of the Fall was the monthly pain of menstruation, still commonly called the 'curse' for that reason. It is characteristic of both the Lutheran and Calvinist versions of Pro-testantism to take Original Sin to mean that humanity was utterly depraved and incapable of performing any act of merit, sinful in character as well as sinning in individual acts. Unredeemed, therefore, mankind was condemned to hell, and could do nothing about it. Only God could reverse the sentence. Catholicism and liberal Protestantism have taken a more benign view of humanity. Needless to say, biblical texts can be quoted to justify either view. (But that should not lead us logically to conclude that therefore both are untrue. Human nature is more complicated than that, and so is Christian theology.)

The biblical description of the creation famously collided with the theories of Charles Darwin in the mid-nineteenth century, inflicting lasting damage on public perceptions of the reliability of the Bible as history. It is now only possible to maintain the literal truth of the Bible by denying evolution completely, and the theory of Creationism still has surprisingly many American adherents (though few elsewhere, including Britain). Once the Bible is read as allegory, whose meaning is true at some other level than science or history, the difficulties subside, though not completely. The doctrines of the Fall and of Original Sin still pose serious problems that 'modern' (i.e. post-Darwinian) Christianity has yet to unravel fully. But there are unsolved problems about the origins of humanity no less serious for Darwinism. It is too soon for either side to claim complete victory, much more likely that wisdom will eventually settle on something that reconciles them both. Outside the funda-mentalist camps, and even to some extent within them, the broad truth of Darwin's theory is now generally accepted. It would be fair to say that having undermined the biblical account of creation through Darwinism, science then handed it back some credibility with its twentieth-century theory of the Big Bang, and later still with the so-called Anthropic principle (which states that the universe seemed to have been pre-programmed for the eventual evolution of life, as the odds against it happening by chance are demonstrably astronomical).

After the Fall, Adam and Eve started their numerous family with two sons, Cain and Abel, who had a quarrel in which Abel was murdered. Cain was banished, and made to wear a permanent mark (which was also carried by his descendants). The story of Cain the first murderer was very popular with Protestant preachers, though there was divergence among them about its typological interpretation. Some saw Cain as the archetype of Roman Catholicism, in other words the source of all iniquity in the Protestant world-view; others claimed to know that the famous 'mark' was in fact black skin, so that Cain was the forebear of black Africans. The treatment of Cain was also used to justify the marking or branding of outcasts. Aside from the original act of disobedience by Adam and Eve, Cain's killing of his brother is the first sin recorded in biblical history, the archetype of all other sins committed since. The fact that God did not require the death of Cain and ordered that he should not be molested might seem a powerful argument against capital punishment, but the original Puritans, who liked a good hanging from time to time, were not looking for such inspiration. The fact that it was Abel's brother who killed him supplied powerful biblical ammunition against the 'enemy within', and fuelled the paranoia about plots and conspiracies which was characteristic of biblical Protestantism in its hey-day – especially when families were divided by civil war.

If Cain had descendants, the Bible does not explain how they survived the primeval cataclysm, the Great Flood, which is the next major event in biblical pre-history. God so despaired of the mess Adam's and Eve's progeny were making of the world, he decided to start again. The flood was designed to kill every living thing except those saved in a boat built by Noah, who was judged to be the one decent human being of an otherwise bad lot. Preachers found rich material in this legend. Modern scholars now regard it as a synthesis of various Babylonian myths, except for the new factor that Noah was spared because he was a good man who 'walked with God'. The myths may or may not relate to some actual happening in the region where the myth originated, now thought to be bounded by the Tigris and the Euphrates in what is now modern Iraq.

The conclusion to be drawn from the Noah story was that God punishes the wicked with destruction but spares the righteous remnant – a regular theme of later biblical texts. The idea of a remnant was powerful – it was a remnant of the Jews that survived the Babylonian Exile. The first Christians saw themselves as a remnant of Israel which was to become a New Israel. New England settlers clearly saw themselves as another righteous remnant, spared from the sinful state that was England under

James I and Charles I. In modern times Protestant loyalists in Northern Ireland still understand their position as that of a faithful remnant in this Old Testament sense, loyal to an imagined ideal of Protestant Britain that holds their imagination in the way the dream of Jerusalem lingered in the minds of Jewish exiles during the Babylonian captivity. 'People of God' typology is still a feature of Northern Ireland Protestant preaching.

Christian theology has traditionally seen the waters of the flood as an allegory for the waters of baptism; and the destruction of everyone, with the exception of the righteous few (Noah and his relations), as a metaphor for the Last Judgment. From a Puritan perspective, the story has the advantage that it emphasises that the 'elect', those chosen to be saved, are far outnumbered by the condemned. From a more modern, 'green', point of view, the story emphasises how the misdeeds of humanity can threaten the whole living world – the Flood was the first recorded environmental catastrophe.

After the survival of Noah and his family, the Bible describes how God then entered into a covenant with him and through him with the whole human race. In return for not destroying the world a second time, God demanded an end to the shedding of human blood and abstention from eating food that contained animal blood. It is an amusing detail that the New Jerusalem Bible heads this chapter of Genesis with the title 'The new world order'. Indeed in the Jewish tradition the covenant with Noah is enlarged into a covenant binding the whole human race, which has become a common Jewish response to the complaint that in entering a covenant only with the Jews, God was showing favouritism to a small group and ignoring the rest.

Subsequently the Bible tells how Noah's son Ham came across him naked when he was in a drunken sleep, and told his two brothers (who did not look at his nakedness, but covered their father with a cloth). On the basis of this trivial incident Noah put a curse not on Ham but on his son Canaan: 'Cursed be Canaan; a servant of servants shall he be unto his brethren' (Genesis 9:25). Canaan later gave his name to a land to the south; his subjugated status may explain why his tribe's title to the land is never regarded as valid, so the Canaanites could therefore be pushed aside whenever they were in the way. The country called Canaan later became the Promised Land, which God gave to the Hebrews.

The Noahide Laws, as the Rabbinic tradition called the human side of the bargain, are not expressly stated in the Bible but were worked out from other biblical evidence. Thus assembled, they constitute 'the Torah of the Gentiles' (the Torah of the Jews being the Ten Commandments). By these seven commandments Gentiles are prohibited from idolatry, blasphemy, murder, adultery, incest, robbery, and the eating of meat with blood in it. They are also commanded to set up a system of justice.

Because they are not expressly stated in the Bible and rely on the authority of Jewish teachers, the Noahide Laws have not received the attention they deserve in the Christian world. That may be because Christians do not feel the force of the problem that the Noahide covenant exists to resolve – why God chose only the Jews. It may be that as a result of the debate about supersessionism, referred to in the previous chapter, the Noahide covenant is due for a come-back among Christian scholars. The story of Noah is also part of the Muslim faith.

The final story, before Genesis turns its attention to Abraham, is about the Tower of Babel, thought by modern scholars to have been somewhere in Mesopotamia. God saw a great tower being built, and decided the human race was getting above itself once more. In order to obstruct future collaboration of this sort he broke up the unity of language that the race had enjoyed until then. Preachers would frequently employ the Tower story as a metaphor for the evils of city life. Again, the lesson is that God will intervene to punish human beings who misbehave (but not, since his pledge to Noah, by wiping them out completely). Both the story of Ham and the story of the Tower of Babel would suggest, to anyone taking them literally, that the God of the Old Testament was easily upset and unpredictable, the sort of irritable father-figure a child would be very careful not to cross. That was, indeed, just the impression Puritan preachers wanted to give.

Abraham, often spoken of as the spiritual ancestor of Jews, Christians and Muslims (i.e. the three 'Abrahamic faiths'), began life as Abram, a tribal elder who lived in the city of Ur, southern Mesopotamia. Archaeologists have been able to reconstruct elements of the cult and culture of the natives of the region at about the time of Abraham, and these show a surprising degree of conformity with the biblical account. This has altered the previous view held by scholars that Abraham and his contemporaries were really just mythical archetypes, invented in order to personalise and bring to life some dimly remembered story of Hebrew origins.

Genesis presents Abraham as the founder of what was in effect a new religious movement. It had its own God, with whom Abraham made a covenant. Faithfulness to the covenant was to be sealed in the ritual of circumcision, and in return God promised Abraham that he would found a nation. At God's command he led his tribe (largely an extended family plus concubines and servants) out of Ur; and after some delay, they settled in Canaan. God made a gift of Canaan to Abraham and his descendants in perpetuity, a gift that was to be renewed under Moses. After Noah, this was the second divine covenant between God and Man, the first to be made exclusively with one people.

Round the figure of Abraham revolve several important biblical stories, which became favourite allegories in later Jewish writing and, in the course of time, in both Catholic and Protestant typology. The most famous concerns the occasion when Abraham was ordered by God to prepare to sacrifice his beloved son Isaac, a scene which seemed to appeal particularly to the imagination of pious Victorian Protestants. Abraham would have gone through with it except that God intervened, and told him it was only a test of his obedience and faith. It is a regular Old Testament theme that the 'first fruits' belong to God, and in a sense Isaac is a first-fruit, or firstborn. So Abraham gives him to God, who gives him back again. There are also overtones here of the rejection of ritual child sacrifice, which may have been part of the religious practices of the Canaanites. God was dramatically teaching Abraham that that is not what he wants from him. In the early church the sacrifice offered by Abraham was likened to Christ's sacrifice ('God gave his only begotten son...'). Taken at face value, a man who sets about killing his son because the voice of God tells him to would quickly be recognised today as suffering from severe paranoid schizophrenia. What is to his credit is not that he obeyed the voice of God but that he broke out of the paranoid delusional state and returned to reality just in time.

Another story, the destruction of Sodom, became the basis for the traditional Christian condemnation of homosexuality. Abraham's nephew Lot settled in the city of that name. When two men – described as angels – came visiting, Lot welcomed them to his home. But the men of the town gathered outside, and called for the visitors to be brought out 'that we may know them'. ('Know' is the common biblical euphemism for sexual intercourse.) Instead Lot offers them his daughters, all virgins, to do with whatever they wished. It seems clear that, either way, the crowd had gang rape in mind. Evidently, offering one's daughters as substitutes in order to save two male strangers from such a fate was in the morality of its time deemed highly laudable, for when God proceeds to destroy the city to punish it for its sins – it turns out that the angels were divine *agents provocateurs* – he first arranges for Lot to escape. This is to honour a deal he has done with Abraham. As they get away they are ordered not to look back; Lot's wife does so, and is turned into a pillar of salt.

Again, God's sense of justice seems a little haywire, but there are plenty of other moral lessons for preachers to draw from this extra-ordinary tale (not least, about what happens to disobedient wives, and that sexual intercourse with men, willing or not, is vastly more wicked than raping women). The association of Sodom with homosexuality was strongest in Protestantism, present to a lesser extent in Catholicism, and lesser still in Jewish scholarship where the Sodomites' real offence against morality is regarded as the refusal to respect a stranger, hence a sin against the duty of hospitality. 'Sodomy' is not found in Jewish writing as a synonym for homosexual intercourse, as it is in Christianity. Elsewhere in the Old Testament Sodom is used as an example of more generalised iniquity (though still without protest at the atrocious way Lot proposed to use his daughters). Lot is another reminder of the 'righteous remnant' motif in Jewish typology. In the New Testament (Luke 17:29) the destruction of Sodom is mentioned as a foretaste of the Last Judgment; and as an example of unparalleled wickedness (which was a ready temptation to Protestant preachers to equate it with Rome).

Abraham had a son, Ishmael, by his wife's maid Hagar. Isaac was Abraham's son by his chief wife, Sarah. When Hagar feared that the birth of a legitimate heir threatened her own son she prayed to God for help, and he replied: 'Arise, lift up the lad, and hold him in thine hand; for I will make him a great nation' (Genesis 21:18). The Old Testament does not pursue this much further, but more than 2000 years later the Prophet Muhammad incorporated the story of Ishmael into his account of the origins of Islam. This was none other than the pristine religion of Abraham, who was the father of Ishmael and progenitor of the Arabs, as well as of Isaac from whom the Jews descended. He declared that the true Abrahamic religion had been distorted both by Judaism and Christianity; and he, Muhammad, the 'seal' of the prophets, had been called by God to restore it to its purity. In Islam, the Abrahamic covenant presents yet another version of the Chosen People theory, the new claimant to that title being the so-called Muslim nation (or *ummah*). Like the others, this claim excluded and repudiated all other claims. There could be only one Chosen People, and any other group claiming that title was usually perceived as a deadly threat. Just as the Jews derived their rite of circumcision of the foreskin from Abraham, as a sign of the covenant, so did Muslims. The Bible specifically records the circumcision of Ishmael (Genesis 17:23).

Jacob was the youngest of Isaac's sons; and Jacob acquired the additional name of Israel. In due course the wives, children, and children's children came, in Jacob-Israel's lifetime, to constitute a family of seventy souls. This was the nucleus of the Israelite people. Jacob's son Joseph (great-grandson of Abraham) was sold into slavery by his brothers, but rose (with the help of Providence, obviously) to a high post in the Egyptian court. Ultimately he helped his family to settle in Egypt to escape famine. The story of how he recognised his destitute brothers and forgave them is a powerful piece of literature. The sons of Jacob-Israel were the twelve ancestors of Israelite tribes (after whom the tribes were named). Because the notion of a tribal God was normal, it took time for ideas of the local divinity to broaden into the conception of one universal God, not only the God of Israel but also the Creator of the

Universe. By the time of the Egyptian captivity – Joseph's family was at first made welcome, but a later Pharaoh decided to enslave them – salvation history was ready for the third element in the unfolding story to be put in place. The God of Israel and Creator of the Universe was about to be revealed also as the Author of the Moral Law: the authority behind the Ten Commandments.

First the Hebrews had to be rescued from the Egyptians. The story of the Exodus was among the most important in Old Testament Judaism, regularly referred to in later texts. The most significant Jewish festival of the year was Passover, by which the deliverance of the Hebrews out of Egypt was remembered and symbolically re-enacted, with transcendental meaning attached to almost every twist and turn. The text was a rich source of typological material both in Judaism and in Christianity. Before the Reformation, the Exodus was used typologically to refer to baptism (the waters of the Red Sea which parted), Easter (which happened at the time of the Passover, and with some borrowing from Jewish liturgy), and the Eucharist. And the servitude being escaped from was bondage to sin (actual as well as original). Thus the heroes of the Old Testament – Abraham himself, Moses, Gideon, Saul, David and so on – were all types (in this theological sense) who foreshadowed Christ. They struggled against Israel's physical enemies, while he struggled against Israel/New Israel's spiritual enemies, who were deemed far more dangerous. Before the Reformation, no Christian leader would be comfortable calling himself 'another Moses': if he did, the church would quickly remind him that only Christ was entitled to that name.

In Protestant typology, Egypt (and therefore Pharaoh) stood for every tyrant since, and the Israelites were every group that had resisted and escaped from tyranny. Egypt could be Rome, therefore, to sixteenth-century Protestants, or England to eighteenth-century Americans (and so George Washington could be Moses). The Catholic 'escape from sin' motif was dropped, because in Protestantism of both the Lutheran and Calvinist varieties, sin was escaped from 'by faith alone' in the act of surrendering to God's grace. To escape by one's own efforts – at least up to the point where God parts the waters – suggested the much disapproved of Catholic doctrine of 'good works'.

So the designation of 'Moses' as an archetypal liberator is available in Protestantism to be attached to any worthy claimant. Both Oliver Cromwell and Charles II had been likened to Moses, but Washington's claims were strongest (or so his contemporaries thought). One of many to make the connection was the great Yale scholar Timothy Dwight, who included Deuteronomy 34:10–12 in his 'Discourse' on Washington's death in 1800 – 'And there arose not a prophet since in Israel like unto Moses, whom the Lord knew face to face' – adding: 'Washington, like

Moses, was born of simple, but worthy parents; like Moses, he was trained in the wilderness; like Moses, he reluctantly answered God's call to serve the people', and so on. Dwight had already dedicated his *The Conquest of Canaan* to Washington: it was an attempt to relate biblical prophecy to the progress of the American people and their escape from British tyranny under the leadership of the new Moses.

How much historical truth is there in the Old Testament story of the Israelites' escape from servitude under the Pharaoh? The Bible omits any mention of a major political upheaval in the life of Egypt to which this could refer. The matching of dates between ancient Egyptian history and history as told in the Bible has always been highly speculative – with occasional bouts of wild theorising – because of the lack of evidence. But the authorities have by no means decided that the Hebrew exile in Egypt did not happen. There is still too much to explain away. Joseph Mélèze Modrzejewski, professor of ancient history at the Sorbonne, states in *The Jews of Egypt*, 'In contrast to the absence of references to political events, the Bible faithfully depicts many features of Egyptian social life under the New Empire, in language that can pass the acid test of historical and archaeological verification with a reasonable degree of probability.'[3] He finds a possible prototype of the biblical Joseph in the person of Aper-El, an Asiatic foreigner who rose to be vizier under Amenophis III of the eighteenth Dynasty. In the nineteenth Dynasty under King Mineptah, an Asian (i.e. non-Egyptian) called Ben-Azen rose to the high rank of royal cup-bearer. It cannot be supposed that these are Joseph and Moses, but they show that the promotion of Joseph and Moses to high office was not impossible. Similarly, the story of the infant Moses, son of a slave, being rescued from a floating basket in which he had been hidden to escape the routine killing of male children (an early population control measure) is quite compatible with other Egyptian narratives. High personages did sometimes adopt stray slave children.

There were several subordinate groups of non-Egyptians in the country, of which the Hebrews were not necessarily the most numerous. Known at various times as the *Shosu*, they worked as labourers or as soldiers. The word 'slave' over-simplifies their status. According to Modrzejewski they

> were not an ethnic group or a nation as such, but rather a social category with a common lifestyle. The ancestors of the Israelites were part of a larger marginal group, ambiguous but integral, suspect but occasionally useful . . . The day was to come when a few handfuls of these immigrants, no longer willing to lead lives of drudgery in an inhospitable country, would take leave of Egypt under the aegis of a certain Moses. For the Pharaonic government it was a minor incident:

the departure of one among several groups of *Shosu*. For the sons of Israel it was, on the contrary, a historic moment of capital importance.[4]

Moses may not have written the entire Pentateuch but he must have been the source for such stories as this. His struggle with the Pharaoh to allow the Hebrews to leave turned on his ability to threaten various trials ('plagues') on the Pharaoh's family and subjects. The significance of this is not what precisely they were, though the boils, frogs, vermin and locusts lovingly described in Exodus are a rich store of metaphors for later preachers, but the fact that Moses could not have conducted his campaign of progressively worse threats and terrors without God's direct help and collusion. Archaeologists have little difficulty in finding natural explanations, so none of these plagues need have been directly miraculous. But their timing indicates that God's Providence was working overtime on behalf of the Israelites. This is in keeping with the central role that the escape from Egypt plays in salvation history: it is virtually the hinge of the entire plot. Nowhere does God intervene more directly to save his people from imminent destruction than when they stop at the Red Sea, the Egyptian cavalry hot in pursuit, and the waters suddenly part to let them through, closing again on the pursuers as they try to cross. However, as Modrzejewski says:

> the fact is that, for the armies of the Pharaoh, this episode was a simple skirmish with a band of forced labourers who had managed to flee, an incident of negligible importance. For the Hebrews, on the contrary, it was a major event in which the Divine Hand had manifested itself, permitting them to escape from servitude and become a nation. This was the veritable birth of Israel. Its remembrance is engraved forever in its profession of faith.[5]

Typologically, Moses was more attractive to myth-makers in America than in England, and his name was invoked in comparisons with individuals as diverse as John Winthrop, George Washington (already referred to) and Martin Luther King. The latter has been raised to the altars by the Episcopal Church of the United States as a prophet – he has his own feast day in the Church's official calendar, 5 April, the Collect for which states:

> Almighty God, by the hand of Moses your servant you led your people out of slavery, and made them free at last; Grant that your Church, following the example of your prophet Martin Luther King, may resist oppression in the name of your love, and may secure for all your children the blessed liberty of the Gospel of Jesus Christ . . .

The attribution of the role of Moses to John Winthrop was his own idea. In his famous sermon *A Modell of Christian Charity,* written on board the *Arabella* as he approached the American coast in 1630 (which contained the immortal line 'For wee must consider that wee shall be as a citty upon a hill'), he concluded:

> I shall shutt upp this discourse with that exhortation of Moses, that faithfull servant of the Lord, in his last farewell to Israell, Deuteronomy 30. Beloued there is now sett before us life and good, Death and evill, in that wee are commanded this day to loue the Lord our God, and to loue one another, to walke in his wayes and to keepe his Commandements and his Ordinance and his lawes, and the articles of our Covenant with him, that wee may liue and be multiplied, and that the Lord our God may blesse us in the land whither wee goe to possesse it.

An event of even greater significance took place during the long march of the children of Israel through the desert towards their Promised Land, the land of Canaan they had left hundreds of years before when famine drove them south. In an encounter of great mystery and transcendence, Moses saw God face to face at Mount Sinai and received from his hands the Tablets of the Law on which were inscribed the Ten Commandments. These were the moral and religious principles by which the People of God were henceforth to be bound. God was thereby renewing his covenant with them, and fleshing out the duties that went with it. From then on, the duty of the People of God to God and the duty of the People of God to each other were part of a unified system of belief and practice. 'Ethical monotheism' – the unique contribution of Judaism to human civilisation – dates from that moment. It would have been by no means obvious to those coming before, that the right way of worshipping God had anything to do with moral behaviour.

It might be objected that the covenant between humanity and God transacted by Noah after the Flood, with its seven commandments resembling some of the Ten, indicates an earlier birth to ethical monotheism. But if by the most conservative reckoning the story of Noah was written by Moses, he must have done so after the revelation of the Tablets on Mount Sinai. Up to that point, ethical monotheism was a secret Moses had kept to himself. The same point applies to the story in Genesis in which Abraham was 'chosen' as the father of a new people and promised the land of Canaan for them, foreshadowing the same promise to Moses. It may be assumed that the author or editor of Genesis (if not Moses himself) was not working separately from the author of Exodus and therefore the two stories cannot be regarded as independently corroborating one another. Rather, the author of Genesis may be regarded as providing earlier historical material to reinforce the gift of the Promised Land recorded in Exodus, of which he was, by the time of writing, well aware.

The Ten Commandments, especially those which prohibit perjury, murder, theft and adultery, lie at the very core of Western civilisation. The command not to take the name of the Lord in vain has for generations defined the concept of bad language; the commandment to rest on the seventh day has given Western civilisation its basic pattern of a seven-day week, with the seventh day covered by different rules – some tighter, some more relaxed – from the others. Though not so easily understood by the secular mind, the commandment not to make idols of false gods has a powerful resonance in contemporary ethical debate. Even the commandment to honour father and mother, like the command-ment to avoid adultery, is still regarded as a valid principle even if now honoured more often in the breach.

But a curious feature arising from the origins of these commandments is not so obvious. When they were first delivered, they were considered to apply only to the People of God who were the Israelites, just as the one God was the God of the Israelites. This becomes clearer if the Ten Commandments are seen in the biblical context, as part, albeit the central part, of a much more complex set of ritual laws and customs for the correct worship of the true God. Some of the laws would strike a modern reader as bizarre. Leviticus 20:24–7, for instance, reads:

> But I have said unto you, Ye shall inherit their land, and I will give it unto you to possess it, a land that floweth with milk and honey: I am the Lord your God, which have separated you from other people. Ye shall therefore put difference between clean beasts and unclean, and between unclean fowls and clean: and ye shall not make your souls abominable by beast, or by fowl, or by any manner of living thing that creepeth on the ground, which I have separated from you as unclean. And ye shall be holy unto me: for I the Lord am holy, and have severed you from other people, that ye should be mine. A man also or woman that hath a familiar spirit, or that is a wizard, shall surely be put to death: they shall stone them with stones: their blood shall be upon them.

Hence 'Thou shalt not kill', for example, originally meant 'Thou shalt not kill fellow Israelites.' That it did not apply outside the limits of the Chosen People is illustrated by various texts, such as Leviticus 26:3–8 –

> If ye walk in my statutes, and keep my commandments, and do them; then . . . I will give peace in the land, and ye shall lie down, and none shall make you afraid: and I will rid evil beasts out of the land, neither shall the sword go through your land. And ye shall chase your enemies,

and they shall fall before you by the sword. And five of you shall chase an hundred, and an hundred of you shall put ten thousand to flight: and your enemies shall fall before you by the sword.

This is a much more difficult ethical world to understand than might have at first seemed the case. One interpretation of the Mosaic Law in its entirety would be to see it as designed to bring about the harmony of the Israelites internally, and victory over their enemies whatever the cost. Indeed, subsequent events seem to exclude any more generous reading. Otherwise not only is God showing reckless disregard for his own ethical teachings, but he is leading the Israelites to do likewise. The principle seems to be that the People of God must treat each other properly and fairly. But they can treat the rest of humanity however it suits them.

Leviticus is not just about ritual. It is in Leviticus that the so-called law of love, 'Thou shalt love thy neighbour as thyself' (Leviticus 19:18), first appears – though the immediately preceding passage, 'Thou shalt not avenge, nor bear any grudge against the children of thy people', seems to limit the concept of 'neighbour' to fellow Israelites. It was on this text that Jesus preached his sermon on the Good Samaritan, challenging the accepted view about who was the neighbour and who was not by extending the category to include the Samaritans, a semi-Jewish sect that orthodox Jews looked down on as unclean. Though he was pushing back the boundaries, even he did not make it clear that the neighbour referred to in Leviticus 19 was any human being on the entire planet.

That is actually a modern interpretation. Even by the Christian Middle Ages, the label 'neighbour' had not been extended to apply to Jews and Saracens, whom Christians felt free to murder by the thousand at the time of the Crusades. Nor were heretics neighbours, as the Albigensians discovered. As at the time of Moses, a neighbour had to be within the household of faith, another member of the People of God. After the Reformation, and especially in the colonies where the Puritans settled, the concept of neighbour (whom one should love as oneself) did not generally apply to native 'savages'. Nor, a little later and further south, did it apply to slaves. One of the charges against the rule of George III contained in the Declaration of Independence not only refers to the Indians in such beyond-the-pale terms, but obliquely mentions the allegation that the British had tried to stir up slaves to rebel against their masters – 'He has excited domestic insurrections amongst us, and has endeavoured to bring on the inhabitants of our frontiers, the merciless Indian Savages, whose known rule of warfare, is an undistinguished destruction of all ages, sexes and conditions.' Native Americans, so-called Indians, were soon to discover, like the Canaanites, the force of the text: 'Five of you shall chase an hundred, and an hundred of you

146

shall put ten thousand to flight: and your enemies shall fall before you by the sword.' Even the French Canadians, invaded by an American revolutionary army, had a brief taste of being a Canaanite in 1776.

Indeed, the general principle still applies. Those nations which either now or in the past have formed their identities under the rubric 'Chosen People' are still in the business of defining 'neighbour' to mean 'people like us', members of the national household. The universal, global duty of solidarity – the concept of a set of human rights that apply equally to everyone regardless of which national or ethnic group they belong to – is a very recent idea. All that the Old Testament gives authority for, at least in the plain meaning of its text, is a set of rights for those already within the *laager*.

Yet the clear message of the best Jewish leaders has been consistent down the ages: the point of being the 'Chosen People' is not to lord it over others but to be 'a light unto the Gentiles' (Isaiah 49:6 et al.). God did not and does not choose one people out of all others because, like some vain aristocrat, it pleases him to have favourites. The Chosen People have a duty to use their status and position for the benefit of the whole of humanity. They have to communicate by example the lesson of morality, and the lesson of the worship of the one true God – the two lessons Moses brought down from Mount Sinai. But if the advantage to humanity disappears, and all that those who look at the Chosen People can see is corruption, injustice, abuse of power and wealth and a general abandoning of higher things in favour of short term material or carnal pleasures, then God will withdraw his protection and the Chosen People will be plunged into a time of woe. Before he despairs of them, God will try to bring them back to a true sense of their vocation. He will send prophets to warn them, calamities to punish them, rewards to comfort them. If they are faithful he will send them victories over their enemies, internal and external peace and harmony, and a time of prosperity.

His crucial judgments will be about how the Chosen People have treated the weak and defenceless – in Old Testament society, the defenceless ones, cripples, widows and orphans. (Exodus 22:22 declares: 'Ye shall not afflict any widow, or fatherless child.') Justice in the sight of men is closely related to justification in the sight of God. That is the true meaning of the covenant, in the eyes of those Jewish leaders who are most steeped in the wisdom of their faith. They know better than most, because they know their Bible better than most, that mere wallowing in the privileges of Chosenness is likely to invite God's wrath. The Israelites tried it many times, and always the result was catastrophic.

The Chief Rabbi of Great Britain, Dr Jonathan Sacks, said in an article in *The Guardian* written in the light of the terrorist attacks on the World Trade Center, New York:

Religion has become a major force in shaping world events – and if it does not become part of the solution, it will certainly be part of the problem.

The creative and destructive powers of the great faiths often go together. Religions bind people together as communities; that is their strength in an age when other structures of meaning and relationship are in disarray. But the very walls we build around ourselves for mutual protection, divide us from those who stand outside; every 'us' creates a 'them'. That is why religions, though they promote peace within their borders, can inspire war across them.

Humanity has been here before. The pages of history are stained with the blood shed in crusades, jihads, inquisitions, pogroms, and the wars of religion that scarred the face of Europe in the sixteenth and seventeenth centuries. In the past, most people were surrounded by others with whom they shared a history, traditions and a creed. Today, our lives are enmeshed with conflicts far away and cultures utterly unlike our own. Never before have religions been confronted more fatefully with the challenge of making space for difference – the other, the infidel, the unredeemed.

Can we see God's image in one who is not in our image? Can we hear His voice in accents unlike our own? Can we learn to love the stranger? God has given us many faiths, but only one world in which to live together, and it is getting smaller all the time.[6]

6

War Crimes and Slavery

If salvation history is the story of the Chosen People moving slowly, erratically but inexorably towards some higher goal, the actual history that accompanies it – history as we normally understand the term – can look pretty bloody. Chapter 31 of Numbers, for example, records how the Israelites, under Moses's command, defeat and then destroy one of the pagan tribes, the Midianites, that had corrupted some of the Israelites into pagan practices – evidence suggests the Canaanite religion was focused on fertility gods and ritual sex. They killed all the men and seized all their property, part of which had to be made a thank-offering to God. Then Moses ordered every male child and all the married women to be killed as well. Among the booty to be distributed to the victors were 32,000 virgins. But they could not be enjoyed until the requirement for ritual cleansing after killing had been carried out: how to do this was carefully explained.

Modern scholars have suggested that this is the point of a story with no factual basis – it is a teaching aid, illustrating ritual practices and designed to teach the Israelites repugnance for the fertility cults of the native tribes. Nevertheless the degree of callous brutality and blood-thirstiness displayed – and reported without disapproval – is shocking. Nor is this an isolated text. Thus:

> When the Lord thy God shall bring thee into the land whither thou goest to possess it, and hath cast out many nations before thee, the Hittites, and the Girgashites, and the Amorites, and the Canaanites, and the Perizzites, and the Hivites, and the Jebusites, seven nations greater and mightier than thou; And when the Lord thy God shall deliver them before thee; thou shalt smite them, and utterly destroy them; thou shalt make no covenant with them, nor shew mercy unto them. (Deuteronomy 7:1–2)

> But of the cities of these people, which the Lord thy God doth give thee for an inheritance, thou shalt save alive nothing that breatheth: But thou shalt utterly destroy them; namely, the Hittites, and the Amorites,

the Canaanites, and the Perizzites, the Hivites, and the Jebusites; as the Lord thy God hath commanded thee: That they teach you not to do after all their abominations, which they have done unto their gods; so should ye sin against the Lord your God. (Deuteronomy 20:16–18)

The last instruction makes clear that total destruction of these neighbouring tribes is ordered because otherwise their religion will be a standing temptation to infidelity, as indeed turns out to be the case. Pagan deities exerted a permanent fascination for the Israelites, who were regularly seduced away from the worship of the one true God. The word 'abominations' suggests the cultic sexual practices that these religions may have involved.

There was ample biblical sanction here for massacre, genocide, enslavement, and what is nowadays called ethnic cleansing, all committed 'in the name of the Lord' and often at his direct command.

Deuteronomy 32:49–50 and 34:1–5 record the defining moment at which Moses, just before he died, gazed across from the top of Mount Abarim at the land God promised to the Israelites:

Get thee up into this mountain Abarim, unto mount Nebo, which is in the land of Moab, that is over against Jericho; and behold the land of Canaan, which I give unto the children of Israel for a possession: And die in the mount whither thou goest up, and be gathered unto thy people . . . (32:49–50)

And Moses went up from the plains of Moab unto the mountain of Nebo, to the top of Pisgah, that is over against Jericho. And the Lord shewed him all the land of Gilead, unto Dan, And all Naphtali, and the land of Ephraim, and Manasseh, and all the land of Judah, unto the utmost sea, And the south, and the plain of the valley of Jericho, the city of palm trees, unto Zoar. And the Lord said unto him, This is the land which I sware unto Abraham, unto Isaac, and unto Jacob, saying, I will give it unto thy seed: I have caused thee to see it with thine eyes, but thou shalt not go over thither. So Moses the servant of the Lord died there in the land of Moab, according to the word of the Lord. (34:1–5)

Moses passed command of the ferocious Israelite army to Joshua, whose first task was to circumcise all those males who had not been circumcised previously – the practice had obviously been neglected during their stay in Egypt. His second was to conquer Canaan by force. Joshua 6:21 records the fate of the city of Jericho, after it had been captured by the curious strategy of marching round its walls in procession, blowing trumpets and accompanied by the ark of the covenant. 'And they utterly destroyed all that was in the city, both man and woman,

young and old, and ox, and sheep, and ass, with the edge of the sword.'
The city was then burnt.

No doubt these were the customary privileges of victory in the ancient
world. Egyptians, Greeks and Romans behaved no differently. But it
would have been by no means clear, to those who suffered from such
God-sanctioned savagery, exactly what message the People of God had
been divinely chosen to deliver – except a primitive (and hardly
monotheistic) 'our God is better than your God'.

If interpretation of the Bible is to be guided by the Christian or Judaic
religious authorities rather than left to each individual, as was the case
until the Reformation, then the savagery which is often described in the
Old Testament can to some extent be explained away. Thus the narrative
that unfolds the military and political fortunes of the tribes of Israel also
unfolds their spiritual journey towards a better understanding of what
God wants of them. At first God is shown to be at best indifferent to the
sufferings of Israel's enemies (even their women and children), at worst
causing them, relishing them and expecting to be thanked for doing so.
Gradually a softer tone enters the story. The sword of righteous anger is
blunted, so to speak, and the Hebrews learn that their God is a God of
compassion and mercy who prefers peace to war: 'And they shall beat
their swords into plowshares, and their spears into pruninghooks: nation
shall not lift up sword against nation, neither shall they learn war any
more' (Isaiah 2:4).

As their understanding of God deepened, their understanding of
humanity deepened too. The texts start to concern themselves with
emotional states – happiness, grief, depression, joy, longing, even
romantic love – as well as political and military matters. The God of war
was gradually emerging into the light as a God of justice and love.

But until the nineteenth century at least – and not even then in some
cases – Protestant Christianity tended to treat the Bible as a body of
religious teaching of uniform value, every part of equal weight to every
other, without a concept of development. Even if a theory of development
was regarded favourably by biblical scholars, the principle that every
Protestant was entitled to interpret the Bible in his own way was
paramount. This was especially true when salvation history was treated
as identical to 'real' history as an accurate description of what actually
happened. A biblical account of an intervention by God was just that, not
a record of what people at the time believed but had possibly misunderstood. As a result the barbaric behaviour which mainly occurs at the
beginning of the post-Exodus period could be given just as much weight
as an example to be followed as the Hebrews' later more peaceful and
civilised behaviour. The sacking and massacre at Jericho, for instance,
could be cited as divine sanction for Cromwell's sacking and massacres

at Drogheda and Wexford in 1649 during his Irish campaign. Nor was the biblical example regarded as unhelpful as white settlers confronted the indigenous peoples of America whom they called Indians. They were just like the Canaanites, standing in the way of the Chosen People taking possession of their Promised Land.

In fact Cromwell identified not so much with Joshua as with Gideon, who enters the story after the settlement of Canaan is becoming well established. After Joshua came a period of rule by so-called 'judges', who combined, as Moses had done, political and spiritual leadership in one. The Midianites, the old enemy routed by Moses, were still active in Canaan, and grew so strong that, aided by the Amalekites, they subjugated the Israelites and kept them in fear for seven years. Gideon was a farmer who was hiding his wheat after thrashing it so the Midianites would not take it, when an angel came to him and commanded him to overthrow the oppressors. The Midianites still worshipped their deity Baal, and had seduced many Israelites, including Gideon's father Joash, into their pagan ways.

Joash had built a large altar (or 'tower', see Marvell's poem below) as an idol for the worship of Baal, and Gideon was instructed to demolish it. When the crowd clamoured for him to be put to death as a punishment, he was protected by his father who pleaded for him and spoke against Baal. After further traffic with angels, who performed miracles to prove they were genuine, Gideon assembled a force to fight the Midianites. But the 32,000 men at his disposal were deemed by God to be far too many, and all but 300 were dismissed so that God could prove his power. With divine help – the men were ordered to storm into the enemy camp with lighted torches, blowing trumpets and shouting 'The sword of the Lord and of Gideon' and creating great confusion – the Midianites were vanquished, their two kings were captured and slain, and eventually there were the usual massacres.

Because the people of the town of Succoth had refused to offer his army food and drink, Gideon went back and chastised their leaders with thorns and briars, and having lectured them on the errors of their ways, slew them by his own hand. Thus it was shown that it was God's will that righteous armies should live off the land (taking provisions from the territories they passed through). With all this success, Gideon was asked to become king of the Hebrews. He declined, saying 'The Lord shall rule over you' (Judges 8:23), but served as their leader, in the role of 'judge', for forty more years. Thus he was a type of ideal Christian ruler and commander in battle.

Not surprisingly, Gideon was a favourite biblical character with the English Puritans as he had been with John Knox and the Scottish Reformers, who used his example to justify their resistance to the

Catholic Mary Queen of Scots. Typologically, the Midianites equalled the Catholics because of their supposed idolatry (Calvinists were bitterly opposed to all forms of religious imagery) and worship of false gods. Gideon had smashed the pagan altar, the crowd had been won round to his side by preaching, and he had defeated the enemy with a tiny band of dedicated men fighting in the name of the Lord. This appealed very much to Oliver Cromwell. At the crucial battle of Marston Moor in 1644, honours had been about even until Cromwell, at the head of his fanatical Ironside troops, attacked the Royalist lines with the cry 'The sword of the Lord and of Gideon!'; and they broke. This was a decisive moment in the king's fortunes – his first major defeat – and in Cromwell's ascendancy to his eventual domination of the Roundhead forces. To the sixteenth- or seventeenth-century Protestant mind, Gideon's story fitted their situation neatly. Gideon's declining of the role of king also inspired Cromwell's personal decision not to be made king, but to rule England 'in the name of the Lord'.

Andrew Marvell devoted his long poem 'The First Anniversary of the Government under His Highness The Lord Protector' to saluting Cromwell in precisely these typological terms – for instance:

> When Gideon so did from the War retreat,
> Yet by Conquest of two Kings grown great,
> He on the Peace extends a Warlike power,
> And Is'rel silent saw him rase the Tow'r;
> And how he Succoths Elders durst suppress,
> With Thorns and Briars of the Wilderness.
> No King might ever such a Force have done;
> Yet would not he be Lord, nor yet his Son.
> Thou with the same strength, and an Heart as plain,
> Didst (like thine Olive) still refuse to Reign . . .

Just as Gideon's victory over the Midianites was really God's, so Cromwell's victories over the king's forces were also God's. After the Battle of Naseby in 1645 he wrote to Speaker William Lenthall: 'This [victory] is none other but the hand of God; and to him alone belongs the glory, wherein none are to share with him.'

Gideon's story was the foremost biblical precedent for the view that it was God's will that oppressive or idolatrous rulers of the People of God – such as the Midianites or the sixteenth-century English Royalists (and their supposed papist allies) – could be overthrown by force. Like Gideon, Cromwell felt personally called to be a warrior in God's service – Milton named him 'God's Englishman'. And before the call, both had been farmers.

The blood-thirstiness of Civil War Puritans when they were convinced they were doing God's work is exemplified in Milton's poem 'On the Proposals of Certain Ministers at the Committee for Propagation of the Gospel'. It dwells on the glory of Cromwell's victories including his bloody defeat of Royalist, including Scots, forces at Dunbar in Scotland, in 1650 and earlier at Preston, Lancashire, on the River Darwen:

> Cromwell, our chief of men, who through a cloud
> Not of war only, but detractions rude,
> Guided by faith and matchless fortitude,
> To peace and truth thy glorious way hast plough'd,
> And on the neck of crowned Fortune proud
> Hast rear'd God's trophies, and his work pursu'd,
> While Darwen stream with blood of Scots imbru'd,
> And Dunbar field, resounds thy praises loud . . .

The relationship between the English Civil War of the seventeenth century and the American War of Independence in the eighteenth has already been mentioned. In Cromwell's case the Midianites were the Royalists, tainted by idolatry. In the following century in North America the Midianites were the British, the typological similarity this time being not idolatry but tyranny, though at the outset a Catholic – hence idolatrous, hence Midianite – threat to American Protestantism was felt in the background.

But there was less personal identification with Gideon in the latter case: instead, one of the most common biblical allusions was the link between George Washington and Moses, previously noted. One instance of a reference to Gideon's example dates from before the battle of King's Mountain in the Blue Ridge Mountains in South Carolina in 1780, when the local patriots, a mainly Presbyterian force ranged against the British, were rallied before battle with a sermon from the local minister which climaxed with the old Cromwellian battle cry, 'The sword of the lord and of Gideon!', which the congregation shouted back in a frenzy. Needless to say, they won. And like Marston Moor, it marked the beginning of the end for the Royalists (in this case, known as the Loyalists). As was usual with Protestant typology, once a biblical archetype had been identified, God could be assumed to want events to be acted out the same way and could be called upon to help. And no doubt those who knew God was on their side wielded their swords and bayonets with that much greater fury.

The end of the Battle of King's Mountain was one of the most savage episodes of a savage war. One Loyalist survivor, quoted by Robert Harvey in *A Few Bloody Noses*, had told a colleague how 'as the mountaineers passed over him he would play possum; but he could plainly observe their faces and eyes; and to him those bold, brave riflemen appeared like so many devils from the infernal regions, so full of excitement were they as they darted like enraged lions up the mountain'.[1] The British (that is to say, mainly Americans loyal to the Crown) eventually surrendered, but many were killed despite that, as revenge for a British massacre earlier in the campaign. The battlefield lay littered with the British dead and wounded, many of whom died of neglect or ill treatment, and nine Loyalists were hung. Many of the 700 prisoners died as they were later marched north. General Cornwallis, the overall British commander, realised that the number of Americans loyal to the Crown joining his forces was dwindling, and the savagery inflicted on Loyalist prisoners after King's Mountain was thought to be one of the main reasons. But the behaviour of the Loyalists towards the patriots, had they won, would not necessarily have been any better: such is the nature of civil war. Ferguson, the Loyalist commander, had already issued a proclamation threatening to hang the patriot leaders and 'lay the country waste with fire and sword'. It is indicative of Harvey's whole approach, as of very many other historians of the period, that he does not mention the religious dimension in this bitter fight, and so leaves the perpetrators of the ensuing atrocity apparently motiveless save for sheer bloodlust. In fact they were fired up by the religious conviction that their cause was just and that God willed them to win (and hence would tip the odds in their favour).

A theology of salvation history shows up clearly in Judges. It indicates a pattern in the relationship between God and the Chosen People which occurs again and again both in the Old Testament and in the story of the 'new' Chosen Peoples of England and America. It is so much a cyclical pattern of spiritual health lost and regained that one could label it the Chosen People Syndrome or Chosen People Paradigm.

Either the People of the Covenant remain faithful and obedient to God, or else they must suffer the consequences of disobedience, which could be by a deliberate act or by mere carelessness in keeping to the Covenant promises. Obedience brings peace and prosperity; in turn that leads gradually to slackness, and eventual unfaithfulness; the community is weakened in its unity and its moral fibre, and hence in its ability to resist aggression. Conquered and oppressed by 'pagan' – i.e. 'non-Chosen' – enemies, the community reassesses its position and realises the cause of its troubles (thanks often to the intervention of a wise man or prophet). So the community repents, returns to the practices of the true religion and regains the strength to resist and free itself. Parallel with this human cycle is God's cycle. Seeing his people becoming first slack and then unfaithful, he gradually withdraws his protection, allowing bad things to happen. Directly, or through an intermediary like one of the prophets, he sends them clues as to what has gone wrong until they understand the message. As they return to faithfulness, he forgives them and helps them to overthrow their enemies once more, thereby returning the situation to the start of the cycle (which sooner or later begins again).

Sacvan Bercovitch, in *The Puritan Origins of the American Self*, speaking of England in the seventeenth century, describes it thus:

> Were not the English, like the biblical Hebrews, summoned by God to a terrestrial goal, under conditions of legal outward behaviour? And did not that correspondence convey England's special role, without trespassing on the rights of the elect? The spiritual Israel would inherit the kingdom; the English Israel could clear away obstacles to Christ's return. It was true that the Israelites had failed in their contract; with Nehemiah's death, piety had given way to hypocrisy, and in time God had justly revenged himself for their broken promises. But that was no reason to suppose that the perishable ship of England would follow the Hebrews' course to shipwreck. On the contrary, the precedent girded them doubly for success: as a reminder of the benefits of obedience and as a warning against falling short of their commitment. If Englishmen lived up to their part of the bargain – reforming the church and state in accordance with Scripture and Calvin – God would grant them the worldly protection, power and privilege he had once granted the Hebrews. More than that, he would make them his two-edged sword against the dragon of Rome, his instrument of political and ecclesiastical progress towards the millennium.[2]

This pattern was adopted as a typological warning describing the way Protestant societies – acting out their role as the new People of God – would fare if they too became slack and unfaithful. It is not so conspicuous in Catholic typology – perhaps it ought to be – where there was a long-standing assumption that the Church, as such, could not sin (though individual church leaders and members obviously could).

The fear of losing God's favour – known as 'declension' – was real among the early New England Puritan settlers, whose chances of survival were always precarious. As Deborah Madsen writes in *American Exceptionalism*:

> The signs of declension and so of God's wrath would be war, famine, disease, just as the signs of God's grace would be prosperity and plenty. The federal covenant was always at risk from the disobedience of the community; if the community were to become depraved then it could call down upon itself its own destruction at God's hand and, of course, the cancelling of the covenant. Puritans looked to biblical precedents

such as the destruction of Sodom and to more contemporary examples of colonial settlements that failed to survive. The risk of catastrophic failure was quite real and ever present.[3] [The most famous settlement failure was at Roanoke island off Virginia in 1588.]

The development of colonial life inevitably brought about the widening of the cultural gap between England and America, which increasingly lacked a sense of a common identity and common destiny. Nevertheless it was still possible to believe in one Anglo-American chosen nation, open to the risk of 'declension' and the wrath of God. It was to that joint entity that Protestant typology could still be applied. American Episcopalians, using the *Book of Common Prayer*, would still have prayed at Evensong, for instance: 'O Lord, show thy mercy upon us. And grant us thy salvation. O Lord, save the king. And mercifully hear us when we call upon thee. Endue thy ministers with righteousness. And make thy chosen people joyful. O Lord save thy people. And bless thine inheritance . . .'

The Revolutionary War necessarily brought this common Anglo-American sense of chosenness to an abrupt end. The American assumption was that chosenness had passed from Britain because of its breach of the divine covenant by falling into tyranny. Henceforth that unique status would belong to America alone. But the British saw it in reverse. The loss of the American colonies had been a chastisement of God on his (still) Chosen People, punishing them for their misconduct. They were called upon by a prophet – as it happened, an outstanding MP called William Wilberforce – to make amends, in order to regain God's favour. This was to be done by abolishing slavery. If America continued to practise slavery while Britain banned it, who would then be the tyrant among nations?

Thomas Jefferson had tried to include the promotion of the slave trade as one of the charges laid against George III in the *Declaration of Independence*. He included a passage which had accused the king of waging 'a cruel war against human nature itself, violating its most sacred rights of life and liberty in the persons of a distant people who never offended him, captivating and carrying them into slavery in another hemisphere'. It was deleted from the final document as a result of pressure from a combination of southern slave-owners and northern merchants. But it made no judgment about the actual ownership of slaves. Jefferson was a slave-owner himself.

The first petition for the abolition of the slave trade was collected by British Quakers and delivered to Parliament in 1783, the year the Treaty of Paris brought Anglo-American hostilities to a formal end. Considerable support for these petitions came from the people called Methodists, largely through the influence of John Wesley who had set out his detestation of slavery in a tract called *Thoughts Upon Slavery* in 1774. He had asked:

> Where is the justice of inflicting the severest evils on those that have done us no wrong? of depriving those that never injured us in word or deed, of every comfort of life? of tearing them from their native country, and depriving them of liberty itself, to which an Angolan has the same natural right as an Englishman, and on which he sets as high a value? Yea, where is the justice of taking away the lives of innocent, inoffensive men; murdering thousands of them in their own land, by the hands of their own countrymen; many thousands, year after year, on shipboard, and then casting them like dung into the sea; and tens of thousands in that cruel slavery to which they are so unjustly reduced? . . .
>
> Is there a God? You know there is. Is he a just God? Then there must be a state of retribution; a state wherein the just God will reward every man according to his works. Then what reward will he render to you? O think betimes! before you drop into eternity! Think now, 'He shall have judgment without mercy that showed no mercy.'

He had made no attempt to address the issue in biblical terms, appealing to an innate English sense of justice. Nor did he make anything of the fact that by the time he was writing, numerous slaves had been converted to Christianity (though the high tide of such conversions was yet to come).

By 1788 – six years after the peace treaty which formally ended the American war – further anti-slavery petitions were being drawn up all over the country. That was the year the first legislation to regulate (in other words to humanise) the British slave trade was brought in. Linda Colley, in *Britons, Forging the Nations, 1707–1837*, states:

> The loss of the American colonies also precipitated a rise in enthusiasm for parliamentary reform, imperial reform, for religious liberalisation, for the reform of gaols and lunatic asylums: for virtually any change, in fact, that might prevent a similar national humiliation in the future. Yet the new enthusiasm for anti-slavery was bound up with the experience of defeat in a special way. As we have seen, Britons retained a strong belief in Providence. Just as they had attributed their success in earlier wars to Divine favour for the leading Protestant nation, many of them now sought to explain what appeared to be almost inexplicable defeat at the hands of colonists by reference to their own failings in the sight of God. They had been corrupt and presumptuous, and they had warred against fellow Protestants. And they had been duly punished. In this mood, the slave trade, so obviously questionable in moral terms, and so productive of worldly profit and luxury, seemed far more of a liability.[4]

The Bishop of Durham, supporting the successful bill for the abolition of the slave trade in the House of Lords in 1807, declared: 'We were a people more favoured by heaven than any other nation had been from the commencement of time, but we should beware how we forfeited the protection of Providence by continual injustice.' Britain risked losing the assistance of God, which had secured it victories over the French fleet at the Nile and Trafalgar. This was serious stuff if you believed it, obviously, as national survival depended on it. If Britain fell below the standard of behaviour expected of it as the Chosen People, God would allow misfortune in war to fall upon it. And Wilberforce, who became one of the most influential churchmen of his generation, argued that the abolition of slavery would be a necessary act of atonement if Britain was to be redeemed and recover God's favour. As Colley remarks: 'For this overwhelmingly Protestant culture, anti-slavery became a particularly rigorous contract with the Almighty. If Great Britain prospered, then clearly it must persevere with the good work.' So anti-slavery became a way of demonstrating that the mantle of 'chosen nation' was still with Britain, not America, and a reason for treating it as morally inferior.

It is a moot point whether Wilberforce was recruited to the anti-slavery cause by a former sea captain, John Newton, or the other way round. Newton had had the characteristic Evangelical conversion experience – known as the Great Change – while in charge of a slave ship, though unusually for a Protestant he had also been influenced by the celebrated fourteenth-century Catholic devotional book, *The Imitation of Christ*, attributed to one Thomas à Kempis. Newton was the author of the famous hymn 'Amazing Grace' – which appropriately enough played a not insignificant role in the American civil rights movement in the 1960s – and wrote a book denouncing slavery, *Thoughts Upon the African Slave Trade*. Newton confessed his shame for 'the misery and mischief' to which he had been an accessory. His close friend William Cowper wrote a poem, 'The Negro's Complaint', which demanded to know by what God-given right the English had enslaved Africans. The central section reads:

> Is there, as ye sometimes tell us,
> Is there one who reigns on high?
> Has he bid you buy and sell us,
> Speaking from his throne, the sky?
> Ask him, if your knotted scourges,
> Fetters, blood-extorting screws,
> Are the means that duty urges
> Agents of his will to use?
> Strewing yonder sea with wrecks,

Wasting towns, plantations, meadows,
Are the voice with which he speaks.
He, foreseeing what vexations
Afric's sons should undergo,
Fix'd their tyrants' habitations
Where his whirlwinds answer — No!

Wilberforce, at the time of his own Great Change, decided God had put before him two chief objectives, 'the abolition of the slave trade and the reformation of manners'. In aid of the latter he took up a list of other good causes ranging from prison reform to child labour, and including, perhaps oddly considering his convinced Protestantism, relief for Catholics from the penal laws. He in turn recruited his well-connected friends in the so-called Clapham Sect – Evangelicals were usually middle or upper class – and together they launched their campaign in Parliament. At the outset they met considerable derision. The Society of Friends (Quakers) in Britain had been campaigning against the slave trade for many years. Of the twelve original members of the Society for the Abolition of the Slave Trade formed in 1787, nine were Quakers. Most of Wilberforce's Tory colleagues in the House of Commons were against restrictions on the slave trade and he had to rely on Whigs such as Charles Fox, William Grenville and Richard Sheridan. His first bill for the abolition, presented in 1791, was defeated by 163 votes to eighty-eight. He presented similar bills again and again, accompanied by an ever-growing public clamour – meetings, petitions, leaflets – in support. He eventually gained a House of Commons majority, in 1805, only for the measure to be defeated in the House of Lords. In 1807, however, it passed that final hurdle.

By that time a large share of the slave trade was in British hands – the wealth of ports like Bristol was built on it – and it fell to the Royal Navy to stamp it out. The penalty for carrying slaves was £100 per slave. When faced with the risk of being boarded and in order to reduce the fines, some slave captains forced slaves to jump overboard, where they drowned. The naval patrols to enforce British policy – which had to be maintained in equatorial latitudes in intense summer heat, with considerable risk from disease – took a heavy toll of British seamen over the years. This increased interest in the more radical measure of abolishing not just the traffic in slaves but slavery itself. Wilberforce at first disagreed, saying, 'To grant freedom to them immediately, would be to ensure not only their masters' ruin, but their own. They must be trained and educated for freedom.' But he eventually joined the new Society for the Mitigation and Gradual Abolition of Slavery. One month after he died, in July 1833, the Slavery Abolition Act was passed, freeing all slaves in the British

Empire – which meant, in his context, mainly the British West Indies in the Caribbean. Slavery continued for another generation in the southern states of the United States, though the supply of new slaves was effectively cut off by the British blockade of the African coast.

Wilberforce's motivation had an outward and an inward aspect. In his snappily named *A Practical View of the Prevailing Religious System of Professed Christians in the Higher and Middle Classes in This Country Contrasted with Real Christianity*, published in 1797, he took from the Old Testament the principle that the fortunes of the nation were dependent upon God's favour, which in turn depended on it behaving in an appropriately Evangelical moral and religious manner. He wrote:

> My firm persuasion is that to the decline of Religion and Morality our national difficulties must both directly and indirectly be chiefly ascribed; and that my only solid hopes for the wellbeing of my country depend, not so much on her fleets and armies, not so much on the wisdom of her rulers, or the spirit of her people, as on the persuasion, that she still contains many who love and obey the gospel of Christ – that their intercessions may yet prevail – that for the sake of these, Heaven may still look upon us with an eye of favour.

Thus the success of the nation was the primary reason for reforming its manners. But the success was in the hand of God, not of man. So it was with individuals too. His inward motivation was that taught him by the Evangelical movement, which – unlike Methodism – stayed within the Church of England and tried to reform it from inside. In a variation of the Calvinist doctrine, Evangelicals felt that nobody could 'earn' salvation but they could respond – by 'Greatly Changing' – to the divine impulse (called grace). Unlike the Puritans, Evangelicals were less fixated on the Old Testament and cultivated a sense of a personal relationship with Christ. Once saved, they then manifested their saved-ness by their good works, which were therefore a response to salvation, not a way to achieve it. Evangelicals, like most Protestants until at least the middle of the twentieth century, were firmly convinced that the Catholic Church taught a strict doctrine of salvation by works; and as good Protestants they were duty bound, therefore, to shy away at all costs from any religious idea that hinted at it.

Like the Calvinists, Evangelicals were both certain of their own salvation – which became known as the 'doctrine of assurance' – and desperately worried about it. Many of them kept notebooks in which they recorded every slight sin, fearful that it might be a sign that they were backsliding. The chosen remedy was ever greater dedication to public service. The result was they were wholly committed to a 'religion of works' while wholly denying it. Wilberforce himself founded or led countless philanthropic societies as well as the anti-slavery campaign, and was a driven workaholic on behalf of all these causes. He also believed – long before John Wesley, the founder of Methodism, wrote to him to tell him so – that he was God's chosen. Wesley's letter was virtually the last thing he wrote, and expressed his own dedication to the anti-slavery cause. The reason Wesley and Wilberforce ended up in different churches was that Wesley pitched his appeal to the common man, Wilberforce to the gentry. According to Wilberforce, Christianity taught the rich to be liberal and beneficent, the poor to be humble, diligent and patient. He believed that all human distinctions would disappear in the next world, not in this.

Not surprisingly, Wesley had the greater following in America. In a powerful tribute to his faith in God's providence, he told Wilberforce that he would not succeed unless God chose to aid him:

> Unless the divine power has raised you up to be as 'Athanasius against the world,' I see not how you can go through your glorious enterprise in opposing that execrable villainy, which is the scandal of religion, of England, and of human nature. Unless God has raised you up for this very thing, you will be worn out by the opposition of God and devils. But if God be for you, who can be against you? Are all of them stronger than God? O be not weary of well doing! Go on, in the name of God in the power of His might, till even American slavery (the vilest that ever saw the sun) shall vanish away before it.
>
> Reading this morning a tract wrote by a poor African, I was particularly struck by the circumstance, that a man who has black skin, being wronged or outraged by a white man, can have no redress; it being a law in our Colonies that the oath of a black man against a white goes for nothing. What villainy is this!
>
> That He who has guided you from youth up may continue to strengthen you in this and all things is the prayer of, dear sir, Your affectionate servant, John Wesley.

The tract referred to was by an ex-slave, Gustavus Vassa, who was captured in Africa, taken to Barbados, brought to England, and converted to Evangelical Christianity. He was convinced that Christianity and slavery were incompatible. At about that time an influential pamphlet by James Ramsay on the *Treatment and Conversion of Slaves in the British Sugar Colonies* argued that slavery was preventing conversions to Christianity. In an argument reminiscent of that used by Harriet Beecher Stowe some seventy years later, Ramsay argues 'that men will not respond to lessons of eternal redemption from those who enslave them on earth, or about heaven when kept in hell'.

Yet the original justification of slavery had been biblical, and for centuries Christians had relied on it. This somewhat balances the claim that Christianity in general and Evangelical Christianity in particular can take great moral credit for being in the lead of the movement to abolish slavery, both in Britain and America. If it was an evil Christians abolished, it was equally an evil Christians had created and defended. The fact that not many of them were Evangelicals, while strictly true, is more than adequately explained by the fact that Evangelicalism was a relatively late phenomenon in the history of Protestantism. It is also true, however, that Evangelicalism, with its particular interest in adult conversion experiences, had a theology which did not limit Protestant Christianity to any one race or faith. Strict Calvinistic predestination – that God had decided in advance who was to be saved and who not – and the Anglican emphasis on membership of the church by virtue of being born English, were both unfavourable to the idea, though they did not rule it out, that anyone might be saved whatever their race, colour or nation. Evangelicals were especially interested in converting people. It is also true that their faith was more centred on the New Testament than the Old. The church of the New Testament is described as a church open to all comers, whereas conversion to Judaism, though not impossible, was not easy. And the Evangelicals would have been less swayed by arguments based on Old Testament support for slavery. They would be more inclined to see the discontinuity, even contradictions, between the Old and New Testaments than the continuity and agreement between them – they were, in a word, more supersessionist. Nevertheless there is no obvious conflict between what the Old Testament said about slavery and what the New Testament said. The Old allowed it: the New did not disallow it.

The Old Testament justification of slavery was not what would nowadays be called racist, that one race was superior to another. But Calvinism in particular made an appeal to the Old Testament on not dissimilar grounds, citing the story of Noah's curse on Ham's son Canaan, after Ham had disgraced his father by drawing attention to his nakedness. The black races were presumed to have been descended from Ham, though there never was the slightest evidence for such a theory. The particular text they relied on was Genesis 9:25-7 – 'And he said, Cursed be Canaan; a servant of servants shall he be unto his brethren. And he said, Blessed be the Lord God of Shem; and Canaan shall be his servant. God shall enlarge Japheth, and he shall dwell in the tents of Shem; and Canaan shall be his servant.' This text was relied upon by Protestants in the Deep South of the United States (and also by the Calvinist Afrikaners in South Africa) not only to justify slavery when it existed, but also the perpetual subservience, and hence racial segregation, of black people once slavery had ended.

There are repeated Old Testament instances of the victorious Israelites taking captives into slavery, a standard custom in the ancient world. Leviticus laid down strict rules for the taking of slaves. An Israelite could only take a fellow Israelite into bondage with his permission (for instance to settle a debt), and then only until the next jubilee year, which came round every seven years. Such a one might not be sold to another, and must not be treated harshly. But slaves might be taken from pagan tribes without limit and their children and children's children kept as slaves. They could be bought and sold, and the rule about avoiding harsh treatment did not apply. In certain medieval Catholic states, some interpreted the rule in Leviticus about freeing an Israelite at the next jubilee as meaning that a slave who became a Christian (i.e. joined the Chosen People) must eventually be set free. Needless to say this did not apply in Protestant America or the Protestant British West Indies, and was one of the reasons why Christian slaves could not see their masters as Christians like themselves.

> And if thy brother that dwelleth by thee be waxen poor, and be sold unto thee; thou shalt not compel him to serve as a bondservant: But as an hired servant, and as a sojourner, he shall be with thee, and shall serve thee unto the year of jubilee. And then shall he depart from thee, both he and his children with him, and shall return unto his own family, and unto the possession of his fathers shall he return. For they are my servants, which I brought forth out of the land of Egypt: they shall not be sold as bondmen. Thou shalt not rule over him with rigour; but shalt fear thy God. Both thy bondmen, and thy bondmaids, which thou shalt have, shall be of the heathen that are round about you; of them shall ye buy bondmen and bondmaids. Moreover of the children of the strangers that do sojourn among you, of them shall ye buy, and of their families that are with you, which they begat in your land: and they shall be your possession. And ye shall take them as an inheritance for your children after you, to inherit them for a possession; they shall be your bondmen for ever: but over your brethren the children of Israel, ye shall not rule one over another with rigour. (Leviticus 25:39–46)

Exodus also refers to the rule about Hebrew slaves being freed every seven years. It indicates how far an owner may go in the severity of his treatment of his (non-Hebrew) slaves, and declares the principle that a slave is an owner's private property:

> And if a man smite his servant, or his maid, with a rod, and he die under his hand; he shall be surely punished. Notwithstanding, if he

continue a day or two, he shall not be punished: for he is his money [property]. If men strive, and hurt a woman with child, so that her fruit depart from her, and yet no mischief follow: he shall be surely punished, according as the woman's husband will lay upon him; and he shall pay as the judges determine. And if any mischief follow, then thou shalt give life for life, eye for eye, tooth for tooth, hand for hand, foot for foot, burning for burning, wound for wound, stripe for stripe. And if a man smite the eye of his servant, or the eye of his maid, that it perish; he shall let him go free for his eye's sake. And if he smite out his manservant's tooth, or his maidservant's tooth; he shall let him go free for his tooth's sake. (Exodus 21:20–7)

The New Testament was milder. In Galatians 3:28, St Paul seems to suggest it does not matter whether someone was a slave, when he declares: 'There is neither Jew nor Greek, there is neither bond nor free, there is neither male nor female: for ye are all one in Christ Jesus.' In Colossians 3:22 he stresses the duty of obedience: 'Servants, obey in all things your masters according to the flesh; not with eyeservice, as menpleasers; but in singleness of heart, fearing God: And whatsoever ye do, do it heartily, as to the Lord, and not unto men.' But his teaching reproaches slave owners who lord it over their slaves, indeed who rejoice in their possessions whatever they are. Acquisitiveness, pride and arrogance are unworthy of a Christian.

Let as many servants as are under the yoke count their own masters worthy of all honour, that the name of God and his doctrine be not blasphemed. And they that have believing masters, let them not despise them, because they are brethren; but rather do them service, because they are faithful and beloved, partakers of the benefit. These things teach and exhort. If any man teach otherwise, and consent not to wholesome words, even the words of our Lord Jesus Christ, and to the doctrine which is according to godliness; he is proud, knowing nothing, but doting about questions and strifes of words, whereof cometh envy, strife, railings, evil surmisings, perverse disputings of men of corrupt minds, and destitute of the truth, supposing that gain is godliness: from such withdraw thyself. But godliness with contentment is great gain. For we brought nothing into this world, and it is certain we can carry nothing out. (1 Timothy 6:1–7)

And in 1 Peter 2:18–20, St Peter takes the same line:

Servants, be subject to your masters with all fear; not only to the good and gentle, but also to the froward. For this is thankworthy, if a man for conscience toward God endure grief, suffering wrongfully. For what glory is it, if, when ye be buffeted for your faults, ye shall take it patiently? But if, when ye do well, and suffer for it, ye take it patiently, this is acceptable with God.

Historians of slavery have frequently asserted its economic advantages to the slaving nations, especially the way it made labour-intensive crops such as sugar, tobacco and cotton highly profitable, and hence slave trading highly profitable too. This emphasis on the economics of slavery has obscured the religious aspect, which may have been even more significant. The first slave-owners on the American continent were the Spanish and Portuguese, who felt entitled to own slaves not merely on biblical grounds but because it was compatible with the teaching of the Catholic Church. St Augustine and St Thomas Aquinas condoned it; some popes, Gregory the Great included, had been slave owners themselves. There can be little doubt that had the Catholic Church condemned the practice at the outset, slavery would have gained no foothold in the Catholic part of the New World and it may very well not have spread to the Protestant colonies in the north, who initially disapproved of Spanish and Portuguese slave practices as further examples of Catholic tyranny.

The enslavement of natives especially by the Spanish quickly became a Protestant horror story. According to Edmund S. Morgan in *American Slavery American Freedom*:

> The natives were reduced to a species of slavery or serfdom and declined in numbers catastrophically. In their place the Spanish brought in slaves of other regions, especially Africa. As the story spread through Europe in the wondering pages of the Spanish chronicler Peter Martyr and in the withering pages of the Dominican friar Bartolomé de Las Casas, it added new dimensions to the traditional European image of Spanish cruelty.[5]

During the reign of Mary Tudor (Bloody Mary) who was married to the King of Spain, the persecution and burning of heretics in England was associated in the public mind with the cruelty of the Spanish towards their enslaved Indians. John Ponet, former Bishop of Winchester, borrowed from Peter Martyr (an early Italian Protestant) the story of slaves being made to work at sifting for gold under a hot sun without rest, with the result that many of them died. The English would not be so compliant: Mary Tudor should remember she ruled 'a body of free men and not of bondmen', warned Ponet.[6] He used biblical examples to show how Scripture authorised the overthrow of a tyrannical ruler.

When piracy against Spanish shipping and general troublemaking in the Spanish possessions became state policy under Elizabeth, her admirals, Francis Drake chief among them, fomented rebellion among escaped African slaves and freed Indians. But this was not quite in aid of the pure cause of freedom and anti-slavery: Drake too had dealt in slaves.

Efforts by the Catholic Church in Spain to specify the limits of the rights of an owner over a slave were only partially effective; but at least they set up a theoretical standard with which priests in central and South America could nag the consciences of their slave-owning parishioners. Thanks to the lobbying of the Spanish Dominican priest Las Casas, to whom belongs the prize of being the first European to appreciate the true enormity of African and Indian slavery, Spanish laws were changed so that the status of slave was no longer inherited. On becoming bishop of Chiapas in Guatemala in 1545 he brought in regulations under which the Sacraments were to be refused to slave owners who failed to comply. His denunciation of slavery and Spanish colonialism generally, which gained some sympathy from the Spanish authorities including the king, was nevertheless thwarted by the machinations of Spanish settlers. He wrote an extensive account of the evils of colonialism that he had seen, with a warning that God would punish Spain if she did not mend her ways. His name became an inspiration to the anti-slavery movement once more in the nineteenth century.

According to *The History of the Negro Church* by Carter G. Woodson, Maryland, being originally a mainly Catholic state, was the only American colony that took seriously its duty to preach the gospel to black slaves, accepting that the consequence would be the eventual manumission of Christian converts.

> After some opposition the people of that colony early met the test of preaching the Gospel to all regardless of color. The first priests and missionaries operating in Maryland regarded it their duty to enlighten the slaves; and, as the instruction of the communicants of the church became more systematic, to make their preparation adequate to the proper understanding of the church doctrine, some sort of instruction of the Negroes attached to these establishments was provided in keeping with the sentiment expressed in the first ordinances of the Spanish and French sovereigns and later in the Black Code governing the bondmen in the colonies controlled by the Latins.
>
> Although the attitude of the Catholic pioneers was not altogether encouraging to the movement for the evangelisation of the Negroes, still less assistance came from the Protestants settling the English colonies.
>
> Few, if any, of the pioneers from Great Britain had the missionary spirit of some of the Latins. As the English were primarily interested in founding new homes in America, they thought of the Negroes not as objects of Christian philanthropy but rather as tools with which they

might reach that end. It is not surprising then that with the introduction of slavery as an economic factor in the development of the English colonies little care was taken of their spiritual needs, and especially so when they were confronted with the unwritten law that a Christian could not be held a slave.[7] [By 'Latin' he appears to mean Roman Catholic.]

In the Protestant northern settlements, there were to be no religious constraints over an owner's excesses, except, to a degree, over his use of slaves for sexual purposes (which had nothing to do with recognising the rights of slaves but with the maintenance of white racial purity). Nevertheless many individual slave owners who were good Protestant Christians did try to treat their slaves in a generally humanitarian way, and in particular the use of slaves as house servants and children's nurses sometimes produced bonds of real affection between owner and owned.

In fact the philosophical basis of slavery, treated as a pure idea, is not so obviously wrong. The Ottoman Empire is one example of a society where slaves could rise to high office, own property, marry and have families. Some slavery practised in Africa was similar. Even in modern Western societies, prisoners can be made to work. Conscription into a national army in wartime is a kind of bondage: British troops ordered to dig ditches on the Western Front in 1916 were no freer to refuse than Pharaoh's slaves would have been, and just as liable to be executed for disobedience. A paid labourer sells his labour by the hour; it is not immediately obvious why he should not sell a whole lifetime of it, if he wants to. But this theoretical gloss on slavery disguises the reality of what was actually done to millions of captured African slaves in the European colonies in the New World, and later in independent America. They were not treated as humans but as animals, beasts of burden. It was not their labour that was legally owned but their whole being, their life, body and soul. Even the Romans had not subjected their slaves to such degradation.

Given how often in the history of the Anglo-American myth of the Chosen People the Protestant love of freedom is opposed to Catholicism as a bogey-man which represents tyranny and slavery, it is worth examining more fully the Catholic Church's actual record on slavery. The debate in Spain in the sixteenth and seventeenth centuries happened elsewhere in Catholic Europe, with much intellectual discussion of what was, and what was not, permitted in the way of slavery. The background was the fact that since Imperial Roman times slavery was by no means uncommon in the Mediterranean area, and was widely practised by Muslim states including the Turks. But few if any such slaves would have become so by straightforward capture, which was the method employed in West Africa to acquire slaves to be sold in the New World. In the Middle Ages fine distinctions were drawn between the various routes into slavery – one of the most common was capture in battle (slavery was the common fate of prisoners of war), and another was conviction as a criminal, which could be a life-time sentence or for a period. Prisoner-of-war slaves could be ransomed (released on payment), at the request either of their home country or of their families. Either way, slaves could be bought and sold. But an early distinction was brought in between chattel-slavery (where ownership of a slave was just like ownership of a beast of burden), or 'Christian' or ameliorated slavery, where owners were allowed to own and dispose of the slave's labour, but could not kill or maim a slave, or injure his or her morals (which prohibited sexual slavery).

Owners purchasing a slave were commanded to investigate whether the slave was enslaved justly, by the above criteria, or unjustly. As an unjustly enslaved slave had to be released, this discouraged owners from buying them. Owners were allowed to buy unjustly enslaved slaves, however, on condition that they released them after they had done enough work to pay back their purchase price. There was much discussion whether native Indian slaves in central and southern America were just or unjust, which depended on whether they had been captured in a proper war (and hence were in one of the permitted categories, prisoner-of-war slaves), or just snatched by a raiding party. In practice these fine theories were often disregarded, but they are a good deal more civilised compared with later Anglo-American slavery practices. Sometimes the Vatican intervened forcefully on behalf of slaves. In 1591, for instance, a papal bull was addressed to the Bishop of Manila, in the Philippines, on the subject. According to John Francis Maxwell in *Slavery and the Catholic Church*, this showed

> that many of the Spaniards of the Philippine Islands appreciated that they had a duty of making restitution to the Indians for the injuries and damage to property which the latter had suffered at their hands. Following the terms of a Royal Decree the Pope ordered on pain of excommunication the emancipation of all Indian slaves held by the Spaniards in the Philippines.[8]

Less than a hundred years later, in 1686, the Vatican became concerned about the African slave trade (then in its early stages), and the Holy Office of the Inquisition issued instructions to Catholics who might find themselves engaged in it. Maxwell states:

In general, Catholic traders must discriminate between Negroes who have been justly enslaved and those who have been unjustly enslaved. The capture by force or fraud and subsequent trade in harmless and innocent Negroes and others who live in forest regions is morally unlawful. Traders who hold such unjustly enslaved persons are bound to emancipate them and make compensation to them for the injuries they have sustained. If purchasers suspect that some of those offered for sale are unjustly enslaved, they are bound to inquire about the justice of the title by which they are held.

Furthermore the Church insisted on the rights of an unjustly enslaved slave to refuse to be bought by a Christian if that was against his conscience. Where this highly moral approach to slave ownership faltered, however, was when it came to consider the rights of slave children. Within the Catholic Church it was generally held until the nineteenth century that the child of a justly-enslaved slave could also be justly owned, even for the remainder of its life.

All this is somewhat irrelevant to the trans-Atlantic slave trade, of course, as no one was seriously pretending that the slaves transported from Africa to be sold in America were justly enslaved as prisoners of war, criminals, or children of the same. And they were full chattel-slaves, with no rights over their person, life or limb, and no protection for their morals or regard for their souls whatever. After the abolition of the slave trade by the British, Pope Pius VII agreed at the request of the British government to support efforts at the Congress of Vienna in 1815 to have the trade outlawed internationally.

It is no coincidence that slavery had a long history as an issue for moral debate. Many of the first Christians were from the lower orders in the Roman Empire – Christianity itself became known as 'the religion of slaves' – and did not regard it as part of the teaching of the new faith that they should rebel against their masters. Indeed, this example was often put forward when defenders of slavery in the southern states of America replied to the growing religious campaign for abolition from the north, in the first sixty years of the nineteenth century.

Yet they lost the debate, and part of the reason was the adoption by the abolitionists of religious arguments remarkably similar to those that had prevailed in Britain half a century before – that if the Chosen People acted unjustly they risked losing God's favour, and the nation would then be threatened by calamities. It was not slavery *per se* which was clearly contrary to God's will, but the actual poverty and cruelty that, in practice, always seemed to accompany it.

In America's case, in particular, the issue of slavery became mixed up with the question of the rights of property. Any attempt to raise the quality of life of slaves by forcing their owners to behave better was met by the complaint that this interfered with the free exercise of property rights, something of a sacred cow among property-owning Americans. As a result of this reluctance to regulate slavery, the disparity of power between slave and owner was so vast that the grossest injustice was inevitable.

No work was more influential on the abolitionists' side than *Uncle Tom's Cabin* by Harriet Beecher Stowe – greeted by Abraham Lincoln during the American Civil War as 'the little lady who made this big war'. In her introduction to the Penguin edition, Ann Douglas writes: 'Almost no-one in ante-bellum America wrote about slavery in secular terms. Its defenders explained slavery as economically necessary and divinely ordained; they pointed proudly to all the Africans converted from heathenism to Christianity by bondage to Christian masters. Many of its opponents felt it was a curse on master and slave alike.'[9]

Harriet Beecher Stowe's novel, the first of any distinction by an American female author, was a sensation when it was published serially, and ultimately became the American best-seller of the nineteenth century. Lincoln's description of her as 'the little lady' tells more about his attitude to female success than about her physical size or literary stature. Except for the predictable scenarios of romantic love and female self-sacrifice, women writers in America were not expected to tackle serious subjects, though for more than a generation women had stood at the top of the literary landscape in England (albeit, in the case of the greatest of them all, Mary Ann Evans, under her masculine pseudonym, George Eliot). Nevertheless Stowe's passionate tale of slavery and freedom was so influential that it mobilised Northern feeling eventually to overturn the Compromise of 1850, not least because of its provision that slaves who fled to the north should be returned to their masters. Stowe (like some of the northern Protestants she quotes in her book) did not object to slavery in coinage recognisable in the moral currency of today. She did not speak of human rights. In dealing with a central character of the novel, the slave George Harris, Douglas explains:

> What concerned Stowe most about George Harris was not whether or not he had the right to run away (she clearly believed he did) or even whether or not he should go back to Africa (on this, according to friends, she wavered). What interested her most was whether or not the injustice so violently done him would make it impossible for him to believe in any version of the God that his owners theoretically believed in, and what, if he rejected Christianity, he would have to live for and how. For the gravest charge Stowe levelled against slavery was that it would kill the soul in slaves . . .

Her interest is that of a missionary and evangeliser, not a campaigner for civil rights. But also, in a religious sense, it is as an American patriot. In the closing page of her novel she lays aside the conventions of mid-nineteenth-century fiction and mounts her pulpit. She believed, writes Douglas,

> that God would accomplish the act of retribution [punishment for the sin of slavery] that mid-nineteenth century blacks would have been both incapable of achieving and which from every viewpoint it would have been profoundly unwise for them to attempt. At this point in her development Stowe was still adhering as much to the Calvinism in which she was partly reared as to the kindlier Anglican creed she would later adopt; she believed in a Last Judgement. For her as for Lincoln, the crucial biblical text on the subject of slavery and sin was Matthew 18:7 – 'For it must needs be that offences come, but woe to that man by whom the offences come.'

For all its political significance, it should surprise no one that it has become fashionable, following modern black criticism, to dismiss *Uncle Tom's Cabin* as a demeaning portrayal of black people. For W. E. B. Du Bois, celebrated black writer and a founder of the National Association for the Advancement of Colored People (NAACP), the damage done by submissive black spirituality was fundamental.

> This deep religious fatalism, painted so beautifully in *Uncle Tom*, came soon to breed, as all fatalistic faiths will, the sensualist side by side with the martyr. Under the lax moral life of the plantation, where marriage was a farce, laziness a virtue, and property a theft, a religion of resignation and submission degenerated easily, in less strenuous minds, into a philosophy of indulgence and crime. Many of the worst characteristics of the Negro masses today had their seed in this period of the slave's ethical growth. Here it was that Home was ruined under the very shadow of the Church . . .[10]

This objection focuses attention on the character of Tom himself, who is depicted as polite, child-like, obedient and passive, even placid, in the face of extremes of cruelty and injustice. At the end of the book, dying in pain after a vicious flogging, Tom forgives his white owner and tormentor, Legree, and experiences a vision of Christ. Stowe is presumed by modern black critics to be urging this spirit of forgiveness on blacks then and now – forgiveness even before white people have accepted that they have done anything to forgive.

Douglas suggests this was not her intention, though perhaps does not give full weight to the theological significance of Stowe's approach. She is working within a Calvinist ethos to depict the slave Tom as one of the predestined elect, a saint (in Calvinist terms), who is assured of his place in heaven. The presence of Christ at his deathbed could mean nothing else. That black people could be among the elect was itself a strongly anti-racist point to make, and challenged the common assumption among northern Calvinists that the covenant God had entered into was with the white race alone. This was a live issue: in 1857 in the famous Dred Scott case the Supreme Court was to rule that neither slaves nor free blacks could be American citizens. She was aware – and said so in her book – that racism in the North was as much part of the problem of justice for black people in America as slavery in the South. Stowe comes close to saying that Tom was Christ-like, even an *alter Christi*, but that was probably too close to a Catholic understanding of sainthood – a typology a Protestant such as her would not have been familiar with.

Jesus's manner of death on the cross at Calvary was submissive, obedient to his fate, forgiving those who sentenced and executed him. Many a Christian martyr since has faced death in an 'imitation of Christ', trying to recreate in him or her self the state of mind and soul – acceptance of a fate that cannot be altered – that Jesus displayed. But this has never been assumed to mean that there was only one manner of death fitting to a Christian. Those who have criticised Stowe, on the grounds that her portrayal of the death of Tom was in effect an exhortation to all black slaves to live and die passively and forgivingly like that, have misunderstood her theology. Tom 'died that others might live' because he refused to betray his friends. Stowe would be entitled to argue that it is permissible for Christians in other circumstances not just to die for such a reason, but to kill for such a reason. Righteous anger is not unchristian. In other words this is not an advocacy of pacifism or submissiveness in the face of evil *per se*.

Nevertheless the ambiguity in the narrative that has given her critics a purchase was her doing, and she did not say enough to remove it. Probably, she did not know enough to remove it. And generations of black people were indeed exhorted even by their own leaders and pastors not to rebel against harsh treatment, when at least measured resistance to it might have served them better in the long term. So the permanent legacy of Stowe's great work has not been the universal recognition of her unique contribution to the ending of slavery – qualified though that would have to be by seeing her as a creature of her time – but the derogatory use of 'Uncle Tom' as a type of submissive, polite, forgiving but essentially gutless black victim of slavery, the sort of example the black community in America has quite rightly been taught to despise. This will need more exploring when we consider the real black experience of the struggle against slavery and racism, rather than white imaginings of it, in particular the powerful and moving typology of the American black community as yet another version of God's Chosen People. The preferred image was not to be Uncle Tom as the 'suffering servant', but black slaves as a tribe sold into bondage, needing to be led by one of their own out of Egypt and towards the Promised Land.

Stowe was blind to all this. She wound up her story with a solemn warning to white America – still God's Chosen People in her eyes – of its likely fate, in terms that astonishingly anticipate, indeed prophesy, the horrendous civil war that was less than a decade away:

> This is an age of the world when nations are trembling and convulsed. A mighty influence is abroad, surging and heaving the world, as with an earthquake. And is America safe? Every nation that carries in its bosom great and unredressed injustice has in it the elements of this last convulsion.
>
> For what is this mighty influence thus rousing in all nations and languages those groanings that cannot be uttered, for man's freedom and equality?
>
> O Church of Christ, read the signs of the times! Is not this power the spirit of Him whose kingdom is yet to come, and whose will to be done on earth as it is in heaven?
>
> But who may abide the day of his appearing? 'For that day shall burn as an oven; and he shall appear as a swift witness against those that oppress the hirelings in his wages, the widows and the fatherless, and that turn aside the stranger in his right; and he shall break in pieces the oppressor.'
>
> Are these not dread words for a nation bearing in her bosom so almighty an injustice? Christians! Every time that you pray that the kingdom of Christ may come, can you forget that prophecy associates, in dread fellowship, the day of vengeance with the year of his redeemed?
>
> A day of grace is yet to be held out to us. Both North and South have been guilty before God; and the Christian church has a heavy account to answer. Not by combining together, to protect injustice and cruelty, and making a common capital of sin, is this Nation to be saved – but by repentance, justice and mercy; for not surer is the eternal law by which the millstone sinks in the ocean than that stronger law, by which injustice and cruelty shall bring on nations the wrath of Almighty God!

Her scriptural quotations were from the book of the prophet Malachi, completed with a phrase from Psalm 73. To supply the context that her devout Protestant readers would be instantly aware of, it deserves to be given more fully here. This is after all, if President Lincoln was right, the key text in the book that caused the war that abolished slavery. In this expanded version, the quotation from Malachi becomes clear as a threat by God to destroy a nation that betrays its covenantal calling. In a country which regarded the special protection of God as the key to its past and future, this is as dire a warning as it is possible to deliver. Stowe's prophecy of imminent divine punishment would also reinforce the North's reluctance to accede to the southern demand for independence, when their differences over slavery became insuperable. 'Letting the South go' might have relieved the political impasse, but would not have postponed God's judgment. Similarly, in this light the fight to 'save the Union' can be interpreted not just as an attempt to prevent the splitting of the United States into two. It was also a fight to save the Union from the wrath of God – salvation in the strict religious sense:

> Give the king thy judgments, O God, and thy righteousness unto the king's son. He shall judge thy people with righteousness, and thy poor with judgment. The mountains shall bring peace to the people, and the little hills, by righteousness. He shall judge the poor of the people, he shall save the children of the needy, and shall break in pieces the oppressor. (Psalm 72:1–4)

> Behold, I will send my messenger, and he shall prepare the way before me: and the Lord, whom ye seek, shall suddenly come to his temple, even the messenger of the covenant, whom ye delight in: behold, he shall come, saith the Lord of hosts. But who may abide the day of his coming? and who shall stand when he appeareth? for he is like a refiner's fire, and like fullers' soap: And he shall sit as a refiner and purifier of silver: and he shall purify the sons of Levi, and purge them as gold and silver, that they may offer unto the Lord an offering in righteousness. Then shall the offering of Judah and Jerusalem be pleasant unto the Lord, as in the days of old, and as in former years. And I will come near to you to judgment; and I will be a swift witness against the sorcerers, and against the adulterers, and against false swearers, and against those that oppress the hireling in his wages, the widow, and the fatherless, and that turn aside the stranger from his right, and fear not me, saith the Lord of hosts. For I am the Lord, I change not; therefore ye sons of Jacob are not consumed. Even from the days of your fathers ye are gone away from mine ordinances, and have not kept them. Return unto me, and I will return unto you, saith the Lord of hosts. (Malachi 3:1–7)

> For, behold, the day cometh, that shall burn as an oven; and all the proud, yea, and all that do wickedly, shall be stubble: and the day that cometh shall burn them up, saith the Lord of hosts, that it shall leave them neither root nor branch. But unto you that fear my name shall the Sun of righteousness arise with healing in his wings; and ye shall go forth, and grow up as calves of the stall. And ye shall tread down the wicked; for they shall be ashes under the soles of your feet in the day that I shall do this, saith the Lord of hosts. Remember ye the law of

Moses my servant, which I commanded unto him in Horeb for all Israel, with the statutes and judgments. Behold, I will send you Elijah the prophet before the coming of the great and dreadful day of the Lord: And he shall turn the heart of the fathers to the children, and the heart of the children to their fathers, lest I come and smite the earth with a curse. (Malachi 4:1–6)

Discounting the books known as the Apocrypha, these are, dramatically enough, the very last words of the Old Testament. Stowe was, of course, speaking from within a tradition which was steeped in the Bible. She, and even more significantly those who read her book, were living through a period of heightened religious expectation connected with the Second Great Awakening, a revivalist movement which had swept across America from New England in the first half of the nineteenth century. Its mainstream form developed into the phenomenon of the camp meeting, the gathering of local people that collected round an itinerant preacher with much hell-fire sermonising and ecstatic hymn-singing. Camp meetings and the revivalist fervour they produced brought many slaves into Christianity for the first time, and the moral improvement that seemed to follow was much appreciated by local slave owners. Uncle Tom himself, wrote Stowe, had been converted at a camp meeting. The Second Awakening spread New England-style Evangelicalism into the south and mid-west, areas that were later to be defined as the Bible Belt. One by-product of the over-heated religious climate produced by the Second Awakening was the appearance of various strict sects preaching millenarianism, pentecostalism and ever more literal readings of the Bible. The most distinctive were the Mormons, who added their own revelation (the Book of Mormon) to the Old and New Testaments and revived the ancient Israelite practice of polygamy. In their insistence that the salvation of the world was coming through the 'chosen' Anglo-Saxon race, they were by no means alone. That particular detail of their beliefs was widely shared.

The Second Awakening also gave a new impetus to abolitionism, though some historians believe its effect was waning by the time of the 1850 Compromise. Stowe herself felt it needed relaunching, which was why she wrote her book. But a more subtle, if longer lasting, influence came by a less direct route. Just as the First Great Awakening was said to have encouraged republican ideals in the years before the War of Independence, so the Second was widely seen as having laid some of the ideological ground that led to the Civil War. As has already been noted, there is a tension within Christianity, Protestant as well as Catholic, between salvation regarded as an aspiration and achievement of the whole Christian community – so that individuals were saved by their being in membership of that community – and salvation as an individual matter, outside of, and even despite, the community. The spiritual danger of the first form is that individuals are tempted to become lax, leaving salvation to be the work of the group. The Second Great Awakening was addressed to the alleged collective spiritual torpor into which the people had sunk, and called upon them to rise up individually, not to wait for the group around them. This stress on individualism became, as a result of the Second Awakening and the victory of the Yankee Protestant North, a permanent mark of the American character. But it did not, as might have been expected, develop in opposition to the idea that the American people, as a Christian community, was special in the sight of God. The lifting up of the individual carried the whole community with it.

But this again is precisely the insight of the Old Testament. The promise given through Abraham was a collective promise, the deliverance secured through Moses was a collective deliverance. In the voice of the Psalmist, 'my' God is equally the 'God of Israel', 'our' God. The movement back and forth between the 'I' and the 'we', the individual and the collective, is a characteristic feature of the Psalms. Psalm 5 is representative. It opens, as many of them do, in the singular, with the individual calling upon the Almighty for help. 'Hearken unto the voice of my cry, my King, and my God: for unto thee will I pray. My voice shalt thou hear in the morning, O Lord; in the morning will I direct my prayer unto thee, and will look up.' But it ends in the plural: 'But let all those that put their trust in thee rejoice: let them ever shout for joy, because thou defendest them: let them also that love thy name be joyful in thee.'

But ultimately, these two strands are never completely reconcilable. They can only co-exist in tension, either destructive tension or creative tension. In the case of Wilberforce and Stowe, the righteousness of the individual eventually led to the righteousness of the whole community. There are also instances of the opposite: where the righteous community was let down – and pulled down – by the unrighteous behaviour of individuals. One example would be the failure of Oliver Cromwell's experiment in 'government by saints', during the mid-seventeenth-century period of the English Commonwealth (sometimes called the Protectorate). Cromwell wanted to crown his Puritan revolution by handing sovereign power to a state council, which later called itself a Parliament, a title expanded by its critics into the 'Barebones Parliament'. As the state was Christian, so would the council be. Nearly 200 worthies, supposedly of impeccable Puritan credentials, were called together and addressed by Cromwell. He told them that their taking power was the culmination of his mission.

'Truly you are called by God to rule with him and for him,' he declared. 'I confess I never looked to see such a day as this – it may be nor you neither – when Jesus Christ should be so owned as he is this day and in this work . . . This may be the door to usher in the things that God has promised, which have been prophesied of, which he has set the heart of the people to wait for and expect . . . You are at the edge of the prophecies and promises.' Plainly, Cromwell felt the time had come to announce the arrival of the Millennium – the return of Christ (or Second Coming) and the start of his thousand years of rule. The righteousness of the English nation, the Chosen People, was about to be guaranteed for ever. And the theory was, equally plainly, that the righteousness of the nation would make the people righteous, as individuals. (Righteous in this context means vindicated, saved, but it also means morally pure.) But it did not work, the millennium did not arrive, and instead of the community pulling individuals up, individuals pulled the community down. It was the old Adam at work. Factions emerged, conservatives on the one side and radicals on the other; proposals to abolish church tithes and to stop paying the army met strong resistance from vested interests. The gentry felt the rights of property were at risk. After five months the Barebones Parliament – England's only experiment at a total theocracy – fell apart and was dissolved. The Thousand Year Reign of Christ was not merely indefinitely postponed. Cromwell, deeply disillusioned, abandoned the whole idea of it.

Some historians of Puritanism, Bercovitch and Christopher Hill included, treat Cromwell's abandonment of the belief that the English nation, as such, was capable of becoming the kingdom of Christ as meaning that all ideas of England being 'chosen' were henceforth off the agenda. Bercovitch[11] does acknowledge that the restoration of Charles II after the death of Cromwell was likened, in a typological way, to Moses' delivery of the Chosen People from the bondage of Pharaoh in Egypt. This to say the least was pushing it, even though the release from the grip of Puritanism must have felt like a liberation at the time. But that was state-Anglican rather than Puritan-Protestant typology, and did not carry the millennial or apocalyptic implications the idea had had previously. Charles II had led the Chosen People from the bondage of righteousness into the freedom of licentiousness: an ironic sort of Exodus indeed.

7

Empire, Mission and War

The phenomenon we identified as the Chosen People Syndrome (or paradigm) was as much a factor in English history as in American. Alongside trade and military expansion, it provided an impetus to the establishment of what was later to be called the Second British Empire, the first being the North American one (of which only Canada and Nova Scotia remained). The impetus for the founding of the First Empire was largely religious – the desire of the Puritans to have a land where they could practise their beliefs unmolested – and so was the Second, though with quite different reasons. As with the first one, higher motives were mixed with lower, idealism with the pursuit of profit, which were conveniently reconcilable under the principle that 'God helps those who help themselves', or in more Calvinistic terms, that God showers his blessings on those who do his will. But the Puritans had a Calvinistic belief in predestination – the idea that God had ordained in advance those who were to be chosen, the 'elect', to go to heaven. Though the eighteenth-century Evangelicals had strong roots in Calvinism, they generally differed on this point.

The archetypal Evangelical preacher was George Whitefield, an Anglican clergyman whose sermons stirred up the First Great Awakening in both England and North America in the middle of the eighteenth century. He was closely allied to John and Charles Wesley, and like them his primary interest was not in church rules but in preaching the Gospel with enthusiasm. They broke the rules where necessary – John Wesley's decision to ordain ministers for the American church led to a definitive break with the Anglican authorities and the emergence of a separate denomination called Methodism. It seems that none of the early Evangelicals took a strict Calvinist line over predestination, though Whitefield would call himself a Calvinist and the Wesleys did not. They leant towards the modified Calvinism of Jacobus Arminius, a near contemporary of Calvin who wished to emphasise the role of free will in the salvation process.

Arminianism was becoming the standard deviation from strict Calvinism in Anglicanism at that time, as a solution to the dilemma that pure predestination seemed to condemn to hell a great many people who had no choice in the matter, which seemed a poor advertisement for God's love. Whitefield, Wesley and the Evangelicals believed that God loved every human soul and wished for the salvation of everyone, not just an elect few. This salvation was gained through faith, most of all displayed at a particular moment in time, the moment of conversion, when the soul responded radically to the preaching of the Word of God. At that moment it was (as if) reborn, or 'new born' as they themselves described it. Thus the importance they all placed on emotionally charged public prayer meetings, when a noted preacher would strive there and then to 'win souls for Christ' by the power of his oratory. Jonathan Edwards was the leading American example of the type, though he never abandoned predestination entirely but developed it into a more optimistic concept. Edwards, as well as being a stirring preacher, was also a great philosopher and theologian, and was made President of Princeton shortly before he died.

At the time of the First Awakening the difference between Wesley's modified Arminianism and Whitefield's and Edwards's modified Calvinism may have been more theoretical than practical. In each case the theory was that what mattered was the individual's response to the preaching of the Word of God. Whether he was predestined to make that response, or he made it of his own free choice, made little difference to the practical outcome. He was transformed, converted. The significance of this idea was enormous, because it meant the opportunity for salvation was – or had to be assumed to be – available to everyone. Protestant Christianity had become a universal road to salvation, no longer restricted to a pre-ordained 'elect'. It could be preached to 'Indian savages'. It could be preached to African slaves. It was no longer in theory the preserve of the white man. And in the process, the concept of the Chosen People underwent a revolution. But it was far slower than it might have been, as old habits died as hard in this area as in any other. The theoretical expansion of the concept of the Chosen People by conversion did not alter the custom of regarding it as primarily, if not exclusively, the preserve of the white race.

Indeed, as has often happened before in Christian history, two conflicting ideas, in this case Predestinationism and Arminianism, existed side by side, sometimes even overlapping within the same person. It is easier to deal with people who are logical, but more often they harbour mutually incompatible ideas with equanimity (but are never in a hurry to thank the person who points this out). The idea that the 'chosen' constituted the entire body of believers throughout the world coexisted with the (technically incompatible) idea that the 'chosen' were the English nation or the white race (in practical terms, more or less the same thing), and especially that part of the white race which belonged to the upper middle or upper classes. Inevitably this tended towards a first-class and second-class status amongst the saved – the first-class were chosen individuals within the chosen nation. The closer one was to England, culturally, spiritually or geographically, therefore, the closer one was to God. This was at a time when fine gradations of social rank were commonly accepted as part of the natural order. Not only were there First, Second and Third class railway carriages, but most people knew instinctively into which class they fitted and would have been uncomfortable travelling in the wrong class, whether too high or too low. So it was with the allocation of seating in churches. So it was on the road to heaven. So it was, indeed, in the distinctions between denominations, with 'chapel' – meaning Nonconformist, especially Methodist – occupying a lower social status than 'church', which meant Anglican. In religion as in much else, social status was implicitly measured in England by 'distance from the Crown', the wearer of which was, by definition, at the pinnacle of the pyramid of class.

The people of the Old Testament had to be born into it in order to be Chosen. It was possible to become a Jew by conversion, but not easy and very rare. Under the complete fusion of church and state in England post Henry VIII, every English citizen was assumed by the law of the land to be an Anglican Christian. The status of the non-English in this respect was very uncertain. In Ireland for instance, membership of the Church of England – now renamed the Church of Ireland – was almost completely confined to those of English descent. No way did it ever occur to Cromwell to convert the Catholics of Drogheda or Wexford instead of murdering them: they were Canaanites. In both Wales and Ireland the local branch of the Church of England was established by law, which meant all citizens had a duty to pay church taxes to it – tithes – whatever their religious belief. Neither in Ireland nor Wales did the Church of England achieve a mass following. The Church of Ireland was disestablished in 1871 as part of a process of trying to relieve Catholic grievances; the Anglican Church in Wales in 1920 as part of a similar process of trying to relieve Nonconformist (mainly Methodist) grievances. The Scottish Episcopal Church is Anglican but not established, and has no connection with the Church of Scotland which is Presbyterian (but is established).

Until the Evangelicals came along with their universally accessible Protestantism, neither the Anglicans nor the Puritans (nor, indeed, the Puritan Anglicans) had shown much interest in missionary work. Indeed, the work of Christianising the North American Indian population had until then been largely confined to French or Spanish-based Catholic missionaries. There was no Protestant equivalent to the chain of Catholic mission stations stretching up the coast of California which were established by Spanish Franciscan missionaries in the eighteenth century (and still commemorated in the names San Francisco, Los Angeles, Sacramento, San Diego, Santa Barbara, Santa Clara, Santa Maria and so on).

The difference was not just a matter of style or personality. Protestantism itself was going through a profound revolution, whose origins were various and to some extent mysterious. The shift in emphasis from predestination to free will was only part of it. Even more significant was a shift in emphasis from the Old Testament to the New. With this went far greater interest in, and stress on, the salvific significance of Jesus Christ himself. It may not be purely coincidence that what first inspired John Newton in the direction of Evangelical Christianity was his reading of the *Imitation of Christ*. It was a call to holiness of life – a call which became characteristic of Evangelicalism especially in its Methodist form, but which also greatly fascinated Wilberforce. With a renewed interest in Jesus went a decline in interest in the Old Testament, and a subtle shift back towards the old medieval, Catholic, way of reading it as a prophecy of the coming of Christ himself, rather than as the foretelling of political events in the lives of nations.

Barbara Tuchman, in *Bible and Sword,* credits the English Puritans with having laid the foundations for two key principles of modern Western society, Parliamentary government and the right to freedom of worship. The case is more tenuous than she makes out – it was the Puritans who hanged Quakers and flogged Baptists; and it was Cromwell, Puritan in chief, who ordered his armed men into the chamber of Parliament to break it up by force. The Puritans discarded mercy and forgiveness in favour of the more bellicose qualities of the Old Testament: but like the Israelites, says Tuchman, they too were fighting against odds to establish a new way of life. She quotes the nineteenth-century economic historian William Cunningham who said in his *Growth of English Industry and Commerce* in 1896, that 'the general tendency of Puritanism was to discard Christian morality and to substitute Jewish habits in its stead'. The Puritans, he continued, followed 'the letter of an ancient code instead of trusting to the utterances of a divinely instructed Christian consciousness . . . and there was in consequence a retrogression to a lower type of social morality which showed itself at home and abroad'. (It is arguable that the common English misrepresentation of Judaism as a religion interested more in strict ritual compliance than in true morality was acquired not from direct knowledge of Jews at all, but from their imitators, the Puritans.) Tuchman goes on:

Although the Puritans did not by any means reject the New Testament, some of the extremists among them did reject the divinity of Jesus. Even the moderate Puritans included as one of their demands in the millennium petition to James I that they be no longer required in church to bow at the name of Jesus. In their effort to purify religion of vestments, sacraments, genuflections and so on, the extremists returned to a belief in God whose divinity could not be shared, the same belief expressed in the synagogue: 'Hear, O Israel, the same Lord thy God, the Lord is One'.[1]

Similarly Matthew Arnold, in his *Culture and Anarchy*, wrote of Puritanism that it was a revival of the Hebraic spirit in reaction to the Hellenic [Greek] spirit that had animated the Renaissance. Its lasting effect on the English nation was to give it 'a strong share of the assuredness, the tenacity, the intensity of the Hebrews. This turn manifested itself in Puritanism and has had a great share in shaping our history for the last two hundred years.'

There is no doubt that the Old Testament is more open to predestination than the New. It is true that Old Testament theology never restricted salvation to the Israelites, though it never displays much curiosity about how the salvation of pagans might be brought about. But to be an Israelite was certainly to be favoured, compared with a pagan. And one became an Israelite by being born one. One did not choose to be so born: it was, so to speak, a choice already made for one. It was here that Jewish belief was closest to Calvinist predestination. And the lack of curiosity about the salvation of pagans is also in evidence. The stress is on backsliders, renegades – people who reject the salvation God has chosen them for. Again, the Old Testament is on parallel lines. There were no Jewish missionaries, and very few Jewish converts. But there are always Jewish backsliders.

But the new post-Puritan Protestantism of Whitefield, Newton, Wesley and Wilberforce represented a rediscovery of the New Testament. And with it, the idea of 'evangelism' – spreading the word by preaching it, seeking out converts wherever they may be had. The hitherto closed boundary of the Chosen People became, like Abraham's tent in the desert, open on every side for the welcoming of strangers. Preaching until then had been approached much more in terms of warnings – the so-called jeremiad – about what dreadful things God would do if people did not shape up. There was not much love in it, nor what modern Evangelicals would later call 'outreach'.

Hence the significance of Whitefield's and Wesley's Evangelicalism for the future of the British Empire was enormous. Without their preparation, Wilberforce and his Clapham sect would have had nothing like the same effect. It was the Anglican Evangelicals' victory over slavery at the beginning of the nineteenth century that really unlocked the missionary doors. The banning of the slave trade became the jumping off point for the next expansion of empire. The British saw themselves as a people so noble that they had banned the trade in slaves, so honourable that they would maintain a naval blockade for that purpose for another forty years, so sacrificial that they did both these things at considerable cost to themselves, and concluded they were surely fit to rule the world and teach it their religion. Indeed, such words – noble, honourable, sacrificial – were precisely the conscious motives of those who expanded, settled and ruled this empire. Above all stood the concept of duty. It was as if the English felt a conviction that they were so fortunate to be of that race and nation that they owed it a debt; and it was a debt so large that it was unrepayable no matter what they did, though they had to make their best effort. So dying for the cause was nothing exceptional: indeed many of them spoke about it as if it were a privilege.

The fact that some of them also got very rich in the process, and that without exception they all acquired a profound conviction of the effortless superiority of the English over every lesser breed, was merely the result. David Edwards, in his *Christian England*, says:

> In the end, the prestige acquired by these great moral victories helped Wilberforce and his Evangelical companions to open up Africa and India to Christian missionary work, understood as another kind of liberation. They had to concentrate first on Sierra Leone, which they founded in 1778 as a colony on the coast, to enable ex-slaves facing destitution or crime in England to settle in Africa as farmers and traders. The small colony around Freetown suffered many calamities and was virtually destroyed by a French squadron in 1794, to be rebuilt by Zachary Macaulay who was willing to spend five years there as governor. The Evangelicals remained inflexible in their support until at last in 1808 missionary work that proved permanent was established, using a mighty river, the Rio Pongas – and in the same year the colony was taken over by the Crown. Gradually the conviction spread that whites owed something to the 'dark continent' after all the horrors of the slave trade; and that the Christian Gospel was among the white man's blessings which he ought to share with Africans despite the violence often encountered, despite the degradation which the trade in human flesh had left behind, and despite the killer diseases including malaria. And this mission was planted on African soil during the great war against Napoleon.[2]

The persistence of high ideals behind the British colonial effort in Africa was illustrated by Dr David Livingstone, the greatest explorer and missionary of his day, who shared entirely the Evangelical disgust at slavery. He was one of the most famous men of his generation, explorer of the Nile, discoverer and namer of the Victoria Falls, a man who loved Africa and the Africans and was loved in return. He wanted to civilise Africa, but not to conquer it. He would not have wanted it to be exploited and despoiled, yet he was chiefly responsible for the fact that that was to be its fate. In an address at Cambridge University in 1857 he had declared: 'I beg to direct your attention to Africa. I know that in a few years I shall be cut off in that country, which is now open. Do not let it be shut again! I go back to Africa to try to make an open path for commerce and Christianity, do you carry out the work which I have begun . . .'[3]

Livingstone's journeys of exploration were motivated by – considering his strict Scottish Calvinist upbringing, 'driven by' is probably nearer the mark – a passion for spreading the gospel and for closing down the slave trade. He quickly discovered, notwithstanding the British abolition of slavery, that the practice was widespread, indeed endemic. He called it 'the open sore of the world'. Slavers were usually the Arabs and the Swahili, and they harvested their crop of slaves by the simple expedient of catching them. A slaving expedition would drive a swathe through the African countryside, capturing the fit and killing the unfit; the captured slaves would then be marched northwards or to a convenient port on the coast. At times Livingstone noticed that the countryside he was travelling through with his bearers was surprisingly empty and apparently recently vacated – because local people had left to hide in the jungle, assuming he was just another slaver. Or one tribe would raid the territory of another, capturing slaves ready to sell to the slavers when they next came through. Livingstone perceived that slavery was not just a curse upon the continent; it was also economically important as a source of wealth and revenue. Hence extinction of the slave trade would require an alternative economy. He conceived his famous 'three Cs' – Commerce, Christianity and Civilisation – as that alternative. But he was not quite far-sighted enough to see that commerce meant exploration and trade, which sooner or later meant control. Control in turn meant conquest. In the end, the only way to ensure the extinction of the slave trade was to make it illegal and enforce the law. And that meant colonisation.

It was indeed high-minded, though the middle and low-minded soon saw their chance to go in on the back of it too – diamonds, gold, land, glory, and eventually, settlement and farming. And markets for European goods. But almost until the death of Livingstone in 1873, Africa had remained a closed continent, the Dark Continent, a place of nameless horrors and fabulous beasts. But then there began suddenly and mysteriously the so-called Scramble for Africa (a phrase apparently coined in 1884), when all the leading nations of Europe decided, more or less simultaneously, that they had to have their share. But none more than the British were so convinced of their divine mission. As Thomas Pakenham puts it:

> In Britain, the Scramble was taken calmly – at first. Then there was growing resentment towards the intruders. Britain had pioneered the exploration and evangelisation of Central Africa, and she felt a proprietary right to most of the continent. Besides, there was a vital interest at stake for Britain. As the only great maritime Empire, she needed to prevent her rivals obstructing the steamer routes to the East, via Suez and the Cape. That meant digging in at both ends of Africa.
>
> And it was in Protestant Britain, where God and Mammon seemed made for each other, that Livingstone's words struck the deepest chord. The three Cs would redeem Africa.[4]

But Africa was not enough. The Evangelicals had long had their sights on India. Until late in the eighteenth century, says David Edwards, it was assumed that the English were in India simply to make money. The English word 'loot' comes from India. In terms of trade and political and military influence, the British presence in India had already had many moments of glory. But this changed, not least when making money in the sub-continent grew harder. The English East India Company, which had been Britain's surrogate ruler, made losses, proved incompetent, and was widely suspected of corruption (which high-minded Englishmen had thought until then was an activity exclusively reserved for foreigners). Towards the end of the eighteenth century – the trial took over a decade – the Governor General of Bengal, Warren Hastings, was impeached before Parliament for corruption, his chief adversary being Edmund Burke, the most famous parliamentarian of his day. The prosecution failed, but in the course of it concern was whipped up in England about the standards of the British administration in India (conducted via the East India Company), which looked decidedly shoddy. Hence by the turn of the century the British were in a mood to raise the moral tone of their presence and influence. Hastings's policy had been not to interfere in local customs and cultures, though he had provided access to English standards of justice for those who wanted it. This deliberate refusal to be high-minded in India was soon to be challenged by the Evangelicals, led once more by Wilberforce, for whom high-mindedness was next to godliness. Edwards writes:

> The belief that the English were in India to exercise a trusteeship mysteriously placed in their hands by Providence now began to prevail. It was much encouraged by the Evangelicals who penetrated India's new government. The most influential of these was Charles Grant, who

had gone out to India in 1767 and had undergone an Evangelical conversion in the course of his grief over the deaths of two young daughters . . . His well trained son Robert became Governor of Bombay, and the spirit in which Sir Robert Grant governed Indians is shown by his authorship of the hymn 'O worship the King all glorious above'. [The first two verses of which are as follows]

> O worship the King
> all glorious above!
> O gratefully sing
> his power and his love!
> Our shield and defender,
> the Ancient of Days,
> pavilioned in splendour,
> and girded with praise.
>
> O tell of his might!
> O sing of his grace!
> Whose robe is the light,
> whose canopy space.
> His chariots of wrath
> the deep thunderclouds form,
> and dark is his path
> on the wings of the storm.[5]

The effect on the natives is not recorded. Other senior administrators followed in the same vein: Governor General Lord Teignmouth 'made no secret of his religious convictions', according to Edwards. His successor Lord Wellesley explicitly declared that England had a 'sacred trusteeship', which justified him annexing or 'protecting' a large part of the subcontinent. Meanwhile British determination to reform Indian society and morals was further spurred on by stories of temple prostitution, the enormous vehicle called a Juggernaut under which devotees of Krishna threw themselves to be crushed, the activities of *thuggees* who strangled travellers as a sacrificial offering to Kali, and above all the horrific custom of *sati*, the ritual burning alive of a widow on her husband's funeral pyre.

There was an outcry when the East India Company, still formally in control, refused to intervene to outlaw such customs, on the grounds that to do so might affect its profits. Needless to say the humanitarian instincts of the Evangelicals dovetailed nicely with their desire to make converts and their sense of superiority over lesser mortals. And all this, at a time when England was slipping away from the hedonism of the

Regency period into the much more puritan (with a small 'p') Victorian era, with Evangelicals sitting smugly on top of the pile.

Until then, Protestant missionary activity in India had been left mainly to German Lutherans, sponsored by the (Anglican) Society for Promoting Christian Knowledge and salaried chaplains paid by the East India Company. Apart from that, the company did not see itself as a Christian bridgehead in Hindu India; nor did its employees want to be preached to about their morals. Irregular sexual relations with local girls had become customary, leading, over the generations, to an increasing population of people of mixed race descent who were regarded as neither really Indian nor really English.

But there then approached the year 1813, when the East India Company's charter was due for revision; and the Evangelicals, led by Wilberforce, saw their chance. Edwards goes on:

> Anticipating this, one of the company's own chaplains, Claudius Buchanan, devoted himself to propaganda in favour both of missionary work and of a much enlarged 'Indian Ecclesiastical Establishment' to convert the godless English; and when 1813 came, the Evangelicals seized the opportunity to secure the admission to India not only of merchants who were not members of the company but also persons wishing to enter it 'for the purpose of enlightening and reforming Indians' . . . To lead the chaplains still to be appointed by the East India Company, and to exercise an undefined influence over any other missionaries, there was to be a Bishop of Calcutta on a noble stipend, £5,000 a year, assisted by three archdeacons.

And the charter itself was amended to give the British presence in India the high moral purpose the Company had declined to acknowledge, by declaring: 'It is the duty of this country to promote the interests and happiness of the native inhabitants of the British Dominion of India; and such means ought to be adopted as may intend to the introduction among them of useful knowledge and of religious and moral improvements.'

Addressing the Commons during the debate on the new charter, Wilberforce had declared that 'Christianity assumes her true character . . . when she takes under protection those poor degraded beings on whom philosophy looks down with disdain.' He promised that future missionary activity in India would not try to spread the gospel by force. 'Compulsion and Christianity? Why the very terms are at variance with each other – the ideas are incompatible. In the language of Inspiration itself, Christianity has been called the "law of liberty".'

Thus was the character of the new British Empire established at the beginning of the century in which it rose and flourished to its peak, as India became the Jewel in the Imperial Crown. The Raj, as the British administration in the Victorian era became known, held a peculiar fascination for the English, which was, perhaps surprisingly to modern political tastes, not entirely unreciprocated by the Indians. There was resentment: there was indeed violent mutiny in the army in 1857–58, when Western reforms (some of them Christian-inspired) seemed to have become a comprehensive threat to Indian culture. But the relationship had many positive sides to it from the Indian point of view. Indian intellectuals were particularly attracted to the study of English law. The fact that the English were at least nominally Christian did not lead to the widespread adoption of that faith, but it did mean the Protestant English were well equipped to hold the ring in the many and various disputes between Indian tribes and religions – Hindus, Buddhists, Muslims, Sikhs, Jews, Jainists, Syrian Christians and others – which often had the potential to turn violent.

On the whole Muslims preferred a British government of India to a Hindu one, and vice versa. Nevertheless life in India seemed only to encourage in the English themselves a sense of their own superiority, which from time to time manifested itself in disgusting and degrading displays of racism. This was closely allied to an extreme class consciousness that fitted neatly with the Hindu caste system, which already (for reasons unconnected with European white racism) placed lighter skins at the top of the religious and social hierarchy, darker at the bottom.

Prejudices that are now called racism would have seemed to those who held them to be merely a proper part of class-consciousness. The English of that time would have regarded race as a sub-set of class, and both would have been dominated by assumptions about breeding and blood. These gave an objectivity and permanence to class gradations – they were a transmogrified form of predestination. To be 'well born' was to be blessed for life with a moral character that others who were equally well born could recognise. The poor were not just poor because God had decreed that was to be their status: they were born to be poor, born not to be gentlemen. It was in their blood. (There is of course no scientific basis for this claim: high-class blood is much the same as low-class blood.) Victorian literature abounds with examples where good breeding surmounts social disadvantage, of which *Oliver Twist* is probably the most celebrated. Even in the twenty-first century the English working class dislike of those who 'get above their station' is not completely extinguished. The English still distinguish amongst themselves on the basis of accent, for instance, which is the most telling of all the codemarks of class, in many ways much stronger than race. The notion of 'blood' and with it the notion of 'breeding' has proved surprisingly tenacious, despite the fact that any suggestion of a factual basis for it has long ago been abandoned.

Expatriate communities are inevitably conservative. The English under the Raj were dangerously reactionary, and their manner towards the local population – the derision reserved for Indians who 'tried to be English' was unbelievable – caused such resentment that it eventually blew the Raj away completely. One of the last but not the least of the wanton acts of arrogance inflicted on an increasingly restive Indian population was that which followed the Amritsar massacre in 1919. It may serve as a summary of British attitudes throughout the Raj era, which by then had been set in stone.

Serious nationalist unrest in Amritsar, a city in the Punjab, had gone on for several days when Major General Dyer, the local British commander, ordered his troops to open fire on a large crowd of demonstrators, killing between 500 and a thousand of them. His tactics were intended to show British firmness towards Indian agitators; in fact they showed British contempt for Indians in general, as a curious sequel was to underline. In the previous mayhem a woman Christian missionary, Marcia Sherwood, had been set upon by a mob shouting 'kill her, she is English' and knocked off her bicycle. Despite one cry from the crowd of 'No, she is one of God's chosen people who is educating our children and doing God's work', the assaults on her grew increasingly frenzied and life-threatening. Eventually she was rescued by friendly Indians, hidden from the mob, and after dark, conveyed to safety.

General Dyer, hearing of this affront to innocent English womanhood, declared the lane in which the assault had happened to be hallowed ground. In order to impress on the Indian population the importance of respect for white women, he ordered British sentries with fixed bayonets to patrol the lane in which the assault had happened, and then announced that any Indian wanting to pass down the lane, some 150 yards long, would have to crawl on his belly in the dirt (and it was very dirty, with considerable amounts of human sewage). This indignity was inflicted on hundreds of innocent Indians, including several who had helped save Miss Sherwood's life. A wooden trestle was erected in the middle, and six youths, who might or might not have been part of the original mob, were tied to it and publicly flogged. The 'Crawling Lane' incident became notorious throughout India and the world, and it was as much for that as for the reckless firing on the demonstrators that Dyer was soon to be relieved of his command by the London government. The English population in India was solid in its support for him and outraged at his dismissal.[6] It thought the Crawling Lane idea was particularly sound.

Thus did the Raj come eventually to mock Wilberforce's Evangelical dream of a converted and humanised India. The undoing of it was due perhaps to the one detail of Wilberforce's own life of which he was not sufficiently self-critical – his belief in privilege, wealth and breeding, as divinely ordained aspects of the English social and class structure. As much as anything, these paramount English vices eventually spelled the downfall of the Raj, as indeed they did when they turned local native populations against white settlers and their colonial governors all over Africa and elsewhere. A proud people might consent to be ruled, but not at the price of insult and humiliation.

Nevertheless India gained much from the British presence, and acquired a taste for the English language, parliamentary democracy, cricket and the rule of law which has endured and flourished, sometimes despite enormous difficulties. It would be impossible to define an 'Indian identity' that did not take full account of this British – indeed mainly English – legacy, including the formative experience of having thrown off that colonial yoke in what was essentially a moral battle, won by the side with better weapons. It was completed largely without bloodshed (though much blood was spilled in bitter conflict between Muslims and Hindus at the time of independence). These were their gains: and largely because of the British they gave up (or were forced to give up) the more barbaric features of Hindu society that had so alarmed the early Victorians, such as widow-burning (*sati*). Though Christianity as a formal religion made few inroads, many of the values that the colonists drew from Christianity and applied to India were successfully assimilated. Christian schools were particularly popular among high-caste Hindus. Perhaps Wilberforce was more successful than at first appeared. He had reformed Indian manners. Hinduism, meanwhile, had proved once again its genius for learning from contact with other cultures and systems, preserving its essence while adjusting its practices.

The conviction that English civilisation was superior to any other had an obvious and close relationship with the idea that the English were God's Chosen. In international affairs, this had two aspects to it: it was a case either of 'he who challenged God challenged England' or of 'he who challenged England challenged God'. The Napoleonic Wars were very much an example of the latter. England found itself the leading nation upholding a monarchical and aristocratic model of society, which the French dismissed as the *ancien régime*. Napoleon's objective was to spread French revolutionary ideas throughout the nations of Europe through political influence, through military intimidation and above all by conquest. Because divine Providence was believed to be decisive in such matters, to defeat him England had to have God on its side. England felt it had a duty to use its military power in defence of a form of government which the English regarded as ordained by God. This is the argument referred to above used by the Bishop of Durham for abolishing the slave trade, and was regularly used in other connections.

The reverse principle – that 'he who challenged God challenged England' – was one of the factors behind the Crimean War (1853–56), which pitted Britain, France and the Turkish (Ottoman) Empire against Russia for control of ports in the Black Sea. The real issue was a Russian desire to become protector of the religious rights of Christian, mainly Orthodox, subjects of the Ottoman (i.e. Muslim) Empire. This meant, to the alarm of British Protestants, that Russia would become a dominant power in the Holy Land and able to control the Holy Places, the sites and shrines mentioned in the Bible, not least those in Jerusalem.

Russia, both because it was opposed to British interests worldwide but also because it was thought to be undeveloped and tyrannical, was a favourite *bête noire* of the British press. The Russian threat to control Palestine, or at least those parts and places in Palestine special to Christians, was regarded as a direct threat to British interests – which were, self-evidently to a mid-nineteenth-century Englishman, the interests of God. Curiously, they did not so much mind a Muslim country ruling Palestine; and France, though Catholic, was more acceptable as a guardian of the Holy Places than Russia. (Not that the English had gone soft on Catholicism: far from it.) But the British had been gently wooing the Ottoman rulers, with a view to a gradual British take-over in Palestine (as they had gradually taken over Egypt). Russia was no part of such a plan.

Then, as more recently, conflict frequently erupted between the two traditions which regarded themselves as guardians of the Holy Places – Greek Orthodox, and Latin Catholic. Spectacular quarrels broke out, while arguments over access and precedence sometimes turned violent. Some of the sacred places in the Holy Land such as the Holy Sepulchre, where Jesus was said to be buried between the Crucifixion and the Resurrection, were under shared management; some, like the Church of the Nativity, were mainly Orthodox; some, like the Garden of Gethsemane, were under Catholic control – the Franciscan order held the papal appointment. (By the end of the nineteenth century, thanks to the visionary cartography of General Gordon, Protestants had at least one of their own Holy Places, the so-called Garden Tomb which Gordon claimed to have discovered by noticing that one of the contour lines on the map of Jerusalem seemed to follow the shape of a skull. By a curious quirk, the British army were official map-makers in Palestine under the Ottoman rulers. Being much more like a picture-book tomb than the garish Sepulchre, it is particularly popular with American tourists. Gordon was a devout Protestant, and his success in finding the 'real tomb' was, to Victorian Evangelicals, all the evidence they needed of God's approval, both of him and of the British nation.)

So allowing the Russians to take charge in Palestine would seriously threaten the Franciscans, who on this occasion the British preferred. As Barbara Tuchman says in *Bible and Sword*: 'The quarrel over the Holy Places that brought on the Crimean War was one of the most ridiculous causes of a major war in all history.'[7] But as she also points out, it falls into the larger context of long-term British designs on Palestine in order to enable the return of the Jews, a desire that culminated in the Balfour Declaration in 1917 and the British Mandate not long after.

The heir to the Evangelical legacy of William Wilberforce was Lord Shaftesbury, known for the first part of his life as Lord Ashley. He was one of the most influential politicians of the age – bishops were often said to have been appointed merely on his personal recommendation to the Prime Minister. He campaigned tirelessly to oppose the rise of the Anglo-Catholic movement in the Church of England, even having Parliament make illegal certain ritualistic practices such as making the sign of the cross, associated until then with the Roman Catholic Church. His conviction that the English were the Chosen People was strongly held, and he was also affected by the rise in millenarial expectations – that the Second Coming of Christ was imminent – among English Evangelicals in the latter half of the Victorian era. A careful combination of selected prophecies from the books of Daniel, Revelation and elsewhere was widely held to define certain conditions which would be necessary before the Millennial event – Christ's return – could occur.

Protestant interest in converting the Jews dated from the seventeenth century, when English Puritan exiles encountered Jews in Amsterdam and were impressed by the faithfulness of their lifestyle to Old Testament teachings. Under Oliver Cromwell the medieval edict banning Jews from England was lifted, and the first few Jews were seen in London. Even then, one of the reasons for encouraging Jews to England was to convert them, in order to meet one of the necessary conditions for the Second Coming. It was felt they would be strongly attracted by the Puritans' own faithfulness to the biblical way of living.

Shaftesbury shared this desire, and even wore a gold ring inscribed with the words 'Oh pray for the peace of Jerusalem!' But he saw the two things – Jewish return to Palestine, and Jewish conversion to Christianity – happening together. Hence his ardent desire for British foreign policy to foster the return of the Jews, and his equally ardent support for the idea of a bishopric in Jerusalem, whereby the Church of England could bring about the conversion of the Jews *in situ*, as it were. This was the logical extension of the Evangelicals' London Society for Promoting Christianity Among the Jews, which dated from Wilberforce's time.

Barbara Tuchman says of him:

Like all men in the grip of an intense belief, Lord Shaftesbury felt the touch of the Almighty on his shoulder, a commandment to work personally for the 'great event'. In company with other great Victorians he never doubted that human instrumentality could bring about divine purposes . . .

Eighteenth century scepticism had given way to Victorian piety; eighteenth century rationalism was again surrendering to Revelation. And as an inevitable accompaniment of the return to Hebraism we find Lord Shaftesbury espousing the restoration of Israel . . . Whenever Christians returned to the authority of the Old Testament they found it prophesying the return of its people to Jerusalem, and found themselves duty-bound to assist the prophecy.[8]

Old Testament and New, indeed. Thus the point of the English being the Chosen People was not just that they had a superior civilisation and religion which they felt a duty to share with the less fortunate: it was also, among the Evangelicals who were influential in English politics, nothing less than to bring about the end of time and inaugurate the reign of God. Israel may have carried the messianic baton of salvation in the early days before Christ, but now it was firmly lodged in London.

What were these prophecies that so powerfully influenced events? Given that they were instrumental in the actual restoration of the Jews to a land now again called Israel, they are worthy of closer study – even though modern Christian scholarship, outside the narrow self-absorbed circles of American Fundamentalism – has almost completely ignored them. It is hard to avoid the impression, in this as in so many other areas, that modern Christianity – Anglo-Saxon Protestantism in particular – has airbrushed out of its own memory many ideas and events which shaped world history in fundamental ways, because they are no longer thought to be (and, it has to be admitted, no longer are) intellectually respectable.

Both Old and New Testaments are rich in apocalyptic material (that is to say, material foretelling the end of time), and hence there is an almost inexhaustible combination of prophetic texts that can be brought together, apparently to predict something in the future. Nineteenth-century Protestant readers of the Bible would have been able to identify at least these, even if they did not wholly understand them:

And in the days of these kings shall the God of heaven set up a kingdom, which shall never be destroyed: and the kingdom shall not be left to other people, but it shall break in pieces and consume all these kingdoms, and it shall stand for ever. (Daniel 2:44)

And the kingdom and dominion, and the greatness of the kingdom under the whole heaven, shall be given to the people of the saints of the most High, whose kingdom is an everlasting kingdom, and all dominions shall serve and obey him. (Daniel 7:27)

And at that time shall Michael stand up, the great prince which standeth for the children of thy people: and there shall be a time of trouble, such as never was since there was a nation even to that same time: and at that time thy people shall be delivered, every one that shall be found written in the book. And many of them that sleep in the dust of the earth shall awake, some to everlasting life, and some to shame and everlasting contempt. And they that be wise shall shine as the brightness of the firmament; and they that turn many to righteousness as the stars for ever and ever. But thou, O Daniel, shut up the words, and seal the book, even to the time of the end: many shall run to and fro, and knowledge shall be increased. (Daniel 12:1–4) [The 'Michael' here is the Archangel Michael.]

And this gospel of the kingdom shall be preached in all the world for a witness unto all nations; and then shall the end come. When ye therefore shall see the abomination of desolation, spoken of by Daniel the prophet, stand in the holy place (whoso readeth, let him understand:) . . . (Matthew 24:14–5)

For I would not, brethren, that ye should be ignorant of this mystery, lest ye should be wise in your own conceits; that blindness in part is happened to Israel, until the fulness of the Gentiles be come in. And so all Israel shall be saved: as it is written, There shall come out of Sion the Deliverer, and shall turn away ungodliness from Jacob: For this is my covenant unto them, when I shall take away their sins. (Romans 11:25–7)

And there shall be signs in the sun, and in the moon, and in the stars; and upon the earth distress of nations, with perplexity; the sea and the waves roaring; men's hearts failing them for fear, and for looking after those things which are coming on the earth: for the powers of heaven shall be shaken. And then shall they see the Son of man coming in a cloud with power and great glory. And when these things begin to come to pass, then look up, and lift up your heads; for your redemption draweth nigh. (Luke 21:25–8)

And I saw an angel come down from heaven, having the key of the bottomless pit and a great chain in his hand. And he laid hold on the dragon, that old serpent, which is the Devil, and Satan, and bound him a thousand years, And cast him into the bottomless pit, and shut him up, and set a seal upon him, that he should deceive the nations no more, till the thousand years should be fulfilled: and after that he must be loosed a little season. And I saw thrones, and they sat upon them, and judgment was given unto them: and I saw the souls of them that were beheaded for the witness of Jesus, and for the word of God, and which had not worshipped the beast, neither his image, neither had received his mark upon their foreheads, or in their hands; and they lived and reigned with Christ a thousand years. (Revelation 20:1–4) [This is the source of the word 'millennium', which did not originally refer to dates with three noughts but to the thousand-year reign of Christ after the Second Coming.]

So Shaftesbury lobbied for a return of the Jews to Israel. Tuchman sums up his ambitions as being for 'an Anglican Israel restored by Protestant England, at one stroke confounding popery, fulfilling prophecy, redeeming mankind'.

This is not to suggest that the entire population of England was captivated by the idea. Indeed, Shaftesbury and his Evangelicals were usually looked down upon, certainly in London intellectual circles, as anti-modern reactionaries with a streak of fantasy. Among Shaftesbury's many philanthropic interests was the reform of the laws on mental illness, then called lunacy. As in many other areas of reform which held his passionate interest, he was successful in humanising cruel and foolish legislation which treated the mentally deranged as objects of scorn or hilarity. As the pioneer in this field, he was chairman of the official Lunacy Commission, whose job it was to decide who was mad and who was sane. One day the case of a woman was brought before him, about whom it was said, to prove her insanity, that she 'supported the Society for Converting the Jews'. Shaftesbury retorted: 'Are you aware that I am the President of that society?' He must have known that the Evangelicals whose leader he was were generally regarded as a faintly ridiculous bunch of zealots. It was they, above all, who gave the Victorian era its reputation for prudery and puritanism, and who whipped up the fury of anti-religious campaigners like Thomas Huxley.

Shaftesbury's ideas about the return of the Jews lingered after his death. Barbara Tuchman describes in *Bible and Sword* how they had stood in the background of British foreign policy in the Middle East for a generation, as Britain twisted and turned in its traditional manner to extract something for itself from the regional conflicts, primarily between Russian and the Ottoman Empire but with Germany and France also as important players. The end of the Ottoman control of areas outside Turkey itself seemed not far off: it was already seen as 'the sick man of Europe'. This instability seemed an opportunity, but for what? A Jewish return to the ancient homeland after nearly two thousand years of exile certainly did not seem the most likely outcome at the time. Jews themselves seemed hardly interested: British Jews in particular disliked the Balfour Declaration of 1917 and tried to have it stopped.

But a number of factors were in place to make it conceivable, of which Shaftesbury's support for the idea, and his time at the helm of British foreign policy as Foreign Secretary under Disraeli, was of great importance. For meanwhile, anti-Semitism was manifestly on the increase, not just with pogroms in Russia and unrest in Poland, where conservative Jewish communities lived traditional, almost tribal, lives; but also in France and Germany, where more liberal Jewish ideas of assimilation as a solution to anti-Semitism were being put to the test – and failing. Thus wide swathes of opinion in Europe – anti-Semites in church and state, liberal and traditional Jews, pro-Jewish Evangelical Christians, British diplomats looking to keep Germany and Russia at bay – were becoming aware of a 'Jewish Problem' in a way they had not been before.

Meanwhile Jewish religious opinion, which had hitherto taken the view that a return to the Promised Land was in the hands of God alone, began to be open to the possibility of a more do-it-yourself approach to messianic prophecy. Perhaps Jewish destiny could be helped by a bit of organisation. So the Ottoman government – known as the Porte, after the palace it occupied in Istanbul – was persuaded that Jewish immigration to Palestine might be good for the local economy. Out of all these factors, plus some political dreaming of their own, the founders of Zionism constructed a political movement which aimed, on the one hand, to foster Jewish settlement in Palestine (largely by the purchase of land), and on the other, to look towards the building of a Jewish nation. Zionism was at that point a secular movement, largely because Jewish religious opinion still tended towards 'waiting on Providence'. So there was no explicit ideological aim of reuniting the Jewish Chosen People with the Jewish Promised Land. Except, that is, on the part of a post-Shaftesbury generation of Evangelicals in high places in the British establishment. They had their own, very unjewish, agenda – to trigger the Second Coming of Christ by returning the Jews to Israel and then converting them to Christianity. And that was the agenda of an English Protestant 'Chosen People', not a Jewish-Judaic one.

But not only English. Thus General Jan Smuts, despite having fought for the Boers against the British in South Africa, was invited to help integrate Empire and Commonwealth contributions into the British war effort in the First World War, and even became a member of the small inner War Cabinet which, under Lloyd George, was conducting the campaign. He had great influence, therefore, over decisions affecting British policy in the Middle East, and at one point was invited to command British forces in the region.

Boer national ideology, based on strict Calvinist principles, had its own version of the Chosen People mythology. In the 1830s they had set out on their Great Trek across hundreds of miles of uncharted country to escape the British, and then and afterwards they saw themselves as the ancient Israelites led by Moses out of the clutches of Pharaoh (the British), who were beset by Canaanites (black natives) on all sides as they reached their Promised Land (the Transvaal). David Fromkin, in *A Peace to End All Peace*, states:

> As a Boer, steeped in the Bible, Smuts strongly supported the Zionist idea when it was raised in the Cabinet. As he later pointed out, the 'people of South Africa and especially the older Dutch population has been brought up almost entirely on Jewish tradition. The Old Testament . . . has been the very marrow of Dutch culture here in South Africa.' Like Lloyd George, he had grown up believing that 'the day will come when the words of the Prophets will become true, and Israel will return to its own land,' and he fully agreed with Lloyd George that the Jewish homeland should be established in Palestine under British auspices.[9]

Two key landmarks lay ahead: first, the Balfour Declaration at the end of 1917, which promised British support in principle for the creation of a Jewish Homeland; secondly the British military victory over the Turkish army under General Allenby in 1918, which brought Palestine under British military control and therefore gave the British the unexpected chance to put the Balfour Declaration into effect. The Declaration had many parents – even American President Woodrow Wilson was consulted by Smuts in its drafting – but the man who bore its singular name was the British Foreign Secretary (and former Prime Minister) in the wartime coalition government led by David Lloyd George. Tuchman says of his role:

> In Balfour the motive was Biblical rather than imperial. If the Biblical culture of England can be said to have any meaning in England's redemption of Palestine from the rule of Islam, it may be epitomised in Balfour. Though he was the reverse of Shaftesbury, not ardent but a sceptic, not a religious enthusiast but a philosophical pessimist, he was nevertheless strongly infused, like the Evangelicals and the Puritans, with the Hebraism of the Bible. Long before he ever heard of Zionism, Balfour, steeped in the Bible from childhood, had felt a particular interest in the 'People of the Book'. According to his niece, companion and biographer, Mrs Dugdale, it was a life long interest that 'originated in the Old Testament training of his mother and his Scottish upbringing. As he grew up his intellectual admiration and sympathy for certain

aspects of Jewish philosophy and culture grew also and the problem of
the Jew in the modern world seemed to him of immense importance.
He always talked eagerly on this and I remember in childhood imbibing
from him the idea that Christian religion and civilisation owes to
Judaism an immeasurable debt, shamefully ill repaid.'[10]

His motives were not millennial, therefore: he was not contemplating a
Second Coming, merely paying a debt. Nor was his Declaration an effort
to relieve the acetone shortage by doing a favour for Chaim Weizmann,
the Zionist leader who was also a distinguished research chemist (as
Lloyd George was to suggest in his memoirs). Nor indeed was it a sop to
American Jewish opinion, which was, at that time, hostile to the whole
Zionist project. For Tuchman the most likely motivation on the British
side was a combination of Balfour's moral debt argument and the fact
that a British army was approaching Jerusalem. Britain needed a
convincing story as to what it would do with the Holy Land it was about
to conquer (or liberate).

> To proclaim that Britain would enter Palestine as trustee for its Old
> Testament proprietors would fulfil this purpose admirably and above
> all quiet the British conscience in advance. The gesture, far from being
> insincere or cynical, was essential to the British conscience. No advance
> in Britain's imperial career was ever without a moral case, even if the
> pretext were only the murder of a missionary or a native's insult to a
> representative of the Crown. How much more necessary was a good
> moral case when it came to the Holy Land, which of all places on earth
> had the most precious associations in men's minds. The conquest of
> Palestine would be the most delicate and unusual of imperial acquisi-
> tions, as Allenby signified when he dismounted at the Damascus Gate
> in order to enter the Holy City on foot.

By then the Declaration had been issued. It was to become the explicit
basis of the League of Nations Mandate agreed in 1922, under which
Britain administered the territory until it handed the mandate back to
the League's successor, the United Nations, on Israel's birth as an
independent nation in 1948. The difficulty was that the British had
already indicated something different to the Arabs, and could not keep
faith with both parties (though the Declaration had nodded in that
direction). It read:

> His Majesty's Government view with favour the establishment in
> Palestine of a national home for the Jewish People and will use their
> best endeavours to facilitate the achievements of this object, it being
> clearly understood that nothing shall be done which may prejudice the

civil and religious rights of existing non-Jewish communities in Palestine, or the rights and political status enjoyed by Jews in any other country.

It may well be the case that the final steps towards the Declaration and the adoption of the Palestinian mandate were taken for moral rather than millennial reasons – Balfour's, not Shaftesbury's. But without the latter's manipulations to move British foreign policy to where it was by the turn of the century, the circumstances would have been so different that such a Declaration would have been inconceivable (or absurd). Balfour's position not only followed Shaftesbury's in time, but the one became the prior condition of the other. In the imagination of the English, God still had a providential purpose for the nation as a prime civilising force and policeman in the world, the righter of wrongs, the bearer of what Rudyard Kipling had half-ironically called the 'White Man's Burden'. Whether it would eventually trigger the Second Coming or not, putting the Jews back into Israel was fitting work for the English to do.

In his *The Church of England and the First World War*, Alan Wilkinson records that:

> The Crimean war was the last English War to have begun with the proclamation of a General Fast; during the war military disasters prompted the holding of another general fast. Two main views of the spiritual significance of the war were proclaimed by the clergy: the war was a solemn duty laid upon the nation by God; it was a divine punishment for a variety of national sins. Though sermons mostly proclaimed the war was just, they also emphasised the evils and sufferings of war. In Evangelical circles it was widely believed that England had replaced the Jews as God's Chosen People and instrument. The failures or successes of the war were frequently explained in terms of divine punishments or rewards. As the war proceeded, and it became more difficult to present it as a crusade, clergy turned to expound it as human folly which God could use for his purposes, for example in order to rouse England from selfishness and complacency – sentiments which found eloquent expression in Part III of Tennyson's *Maud*, which were often echoed during the Great War.[11]

By the middle of the nineteenth century the Evangelicals had a strong presence in national life, both in the country and in Parliament. But though he shared some of this national sentiment, Alfred Tennyson, by this time universally recognised as England's finest poet, was no Evangelical. His leanings were towards a broad and liberal style of Anglican churchmanship, more Kingsley than Shaftesbury. The exact identification of England with the Chosen People may have been confined to those who still regarded the Bible as a useful guide to contemporary politics. But a more vague and general sense that England was special with a special role, and that this specialness had in some sense implicit divine endorsement, was much more widely spread and Tennyson evidently shared it. Indeed, it became the principal characteristic of the Victorian era. This is how the poet, in Part III of his famous poem *Maud*, described how he came to recognise his and his country's duty to go to war for what was right (though none of its business):

> For the peace that I deemed no peace is over and done,
> And now by the side of the Black or Baltic deep,
> And deathful-grinning mouths of the fortress flames
> The blood-red blossom of war with a heart of fire.
> Let it flame or fade, and the war roll down like a wind,
> We have proved we have hearts in a cause, we are noble still,
> And myself have awaked, as it seems, to the better mind.
> It is better to fight for the good than rail at the ill;
> I have felt my native land, I am one with my kind,
> I embrace the purpose of God, and the doom assigned.

[The 'Black and Baltic' were the seas affected by the Crimean war.]

Later, the Boer War, fought against Dutch settlers for control of South Africa (1899–1902), caused a bitter division in British public opinion, though both sides couched their argument in religious terms. Some of the Christian Socialists who disowned the war greeted news of British reverses on the battlefield as a divine chastisement for British imperial arrogance. There is more than a hint of Chosen People ideology behind such views. Others supported it, on the grounds that imperialism exemplified the virtues of brotherhood and service; while Professor H. E. J. Bevan in a famous sermon exalted war as a means whereby Britain could once more be ennobled – again, a glimpse of the Chosen People idea:

History lent but scant support to the theory that a great nation is necessarily demoralised by war such as this. Rather does it arouse a slumbering patriotism, and call citizens from the luxurious enjoyment of peace, and from the petty and selfish interests, to sacrifices and self-denial for a common cause. It awakens in many a lively consciousness of the perishableness and insecurity of human affairs, destroys the artificial barriers between class and class, and teaches multitudes to pray.[12]

This was still very much the mood when Britain went to war in 1914. But the churches, the Church of England in particular, also had in mind the significant lesson of Old Testament salvation history – that misfortune falls on a nation that has lost God's favour. It was therefore not just in pursuit of their calling as men of God but also as English patriots desiring victory in battle that the Church of England's leaders started to worry about the moral tone of the nation as the Great War developed. Nor was this simply a matter of producing a better class of soldier who would fight more diligently. God controlled those things which were outside men's control, on which victory in battle often turned – the weather, happy coincidences, lucky guesses, troops happening to be in the right place at the right time, and so on. All these were at the disposal of Divine Providence – provided Divine Providence was well disposed. When the war was not 'over by Christmas', as had been widely predicted when the British Expeditionary Force first set out for France that summer, what the church could do to help was to call the nation to prayer and repentance, to ensure that God, so to speak, would fight on Britain's side.

At the outbreak of war, writes Wilkinson, a national religious revival was widely expected; and indeed, at first, church attendance seemed to increase. But by 1915 no revival had arrived, and the Archbishop of Canterbury, Dr Randall Davidson, set up a committee to advise him on 'the spiritual call to the Nation and to the Church, on what was being done by the war and what could be done'. It recommended a National Mission, designed to trigger the religious revival that was by then thought to be overdue. Opening with a passage from Deuteronomy 30 – 'See, I have set before thee this day life and good, and death and evil . . . therefore choose life' – it declared that God had a purpose for the nation but the nation had ignored God:

> Our great social cleavage and industrial strifes show that something is fundamentally wrong in our national life. We have a righteous cause in the Great War; but the civil war which seemed to be imminent in Ireland in the summer of 1914 and the great industrial war, for which preparation was then being made, were evidence of something wrong among ourselves.[13]

It hardly needs saying that such a committee did not look for the cure of this unrest through the satisfaction of the just grievances of the Irish or by supporting the trade unions in their long struggle to give British workers a living wage. The nation, the missioners said, must repent its sins and return to God. By sin, as literally countless sermons preached from every Anglican pulpit in the land made clear, the clergy meant drunkenness, sexual promiscuity, gambling, the neglect of church attendance, failure to pray, and refusal to submit the interests of self to the good of the whole. The last point had obvious implications at a time when enormous efforts were being made to rebuild the strength of the army by voluntary recruitment. One way a young man could repent of his sin was by joining up – going to war, said one leading cleric, was itself the beginning of a surrender to God's will.

The National Mission of Repentance and Hope was an enormous success inasmuch as it managed to mobilise almost every muscle and sinew the Church of England possessed, every last ounce of its energy. It was, so to speak, the spiritual version of total war. For an institution noted for its sluggishness, such an effort was extraordinary. But it was a failure in almost every other respect – except, as a by-product, Parliament restricted the hours that public houses could sell intoxicating drink. Churchmen began to notice that those stirred by the Mission were those already within the church's embrace. It did not make contact with the man in the street. Even the message, repentance and hope, became as much a liability as an asset. Why, newspaper editors and writers began to ask, did Britain have to repent, given that the war was started not by Britain but by Germany's brutal and unjust aggression against 'poor little Belgium'? What had Britain to say sorry for? And as the casualty figures grew with the military campaigns of 1916, and news arrived of the disaster on the Somme in particular, British public opinion became less tolerant of the notion that its citizens in uniform at the front were sinners, and their dreadful fate was somehow brought upon them as God's punishment. An embarrassed silence stifled the strict application of Protestant ideas of salvation – that soldiers who died without accepting Christ as their Saviour were doomed to everlasting punishment. Instead, death in battle for king and country was thought somehow to equate with that Christian act of faith, the cause of Christ and the cause of the chosen nation being so closely related.

Hurried official explanations were offered for the tactless choice of 'repentance' in the Mission's title – one suggestion was that people should repent of the 'sins of European civilisation' which had led to war – but the imagination of the country was not captured. Why should God punish the British for the sins of the Germans? The tone of an address by Archbishop Cosmo Lang of York was typical of many such failures:

We have called it a National Mission of Repentance and Hope: repentance because we are called to bid men and women everywhere to repent of the sins that have stained our civilisation and brought upon it the manifest judgment of God; and Hope because, during the closing period of this terrific ordeal in the midst of increasing strain and sacrifice and sorrow, our people will need the strength of Hope, and in those difficult days that are coming, when the old order will have gone and the duty will be laid upon the nation of seeking a new order in a new world, we must present before the minds of the nation the one hope, Christ, His Mind, his Spirit, for the rebuilding of a new world.[14]

By the end of 1916, Wilkinson states, certain uncomfortable truths had become clear. 'Throughout the country few really outside the churches had attended the special services, though more outsiders had attended the public (and often open air) meetings.' On the other hand the church's internal life had received a stimulus, and as a result of the Mission church leaders gained a much more realistic impression of the gap that had opened up between themselves and the common man. So the repentance the Mission had urged upon the nation really only occurred inside the church itself, with a great deal of breast-beating which included no less than five commissions of inquiry. But the Church of England displayed then, as it has displayed since, a maudlin and indeed almost masochistic interest in dwelling on its own faults, as if a perverse comfort was thereby to be gained at this sign that the doctrine of the total depravity of man – the clergy were exclusively male – had once again been vindicated.

The special challenge to the Church of England in this war was that, as the established national church whose supreme governor was the king, it could only throw its weight behind the war effort. Every other option – pacifism, neutrality, detachment, prophetic criticism, opposition, even seriously qualified support – was therefore closed. If the public judged at the end that the war had been worth it, then the Church of England could bask in the glow of having been proved right. But if national sentiment was unsure of the merits of the conflict, above all of the way it had been waged, then the church's conspicuous display of solidarity with the state was likely to prove a millstone. The church's general posture towards the war had been crystallised in the National Mission, which had raised the stakes considerably. Perhaps the gamble was justified, though those who took it, so significantly misjudging their chances of success, cannot be credited with much moral courage for it. As it happened, the gamble failed. Two quotations, one from 1915 and one from 1916, show church leaders adopting a tone that looks astonishingly misjudged, now we know how people felt about the war once it had ended.

The first, from 1915, is from the Bishop of London, Dr Winnington-Ingram, whom Wilkinson describes as 'the voice which rose above that of all other churchmen'. Writing in a church paper called the *Guardian*, he declared:

I think the Church can best help the nation first of all by making it realise that it is engaged in a Holy War, and not be afraid of saying so. Christ died on Good Friday for Freedom, Honour and Chivalry, and our boys are dying for the same things. Having once realised that everything worth having in the world is at stake, the nation will not hesitate to allow itself to be mobilised. You ask for my advice in a sentence as to what the Church is to do. I answer MOBILISE THE NATION FOR A HOLY WAR.[15] [His capitals.]

The second is from Hensley Henson, later to be Bishop of Durham and widely supposed to be the voice of modernism and moderation. In an essay in 1916 in which he prophesied (correctly) that 'organised Christianity does not come well out of the world crisis', Henson went on to outline the hopes he held out for the church's future role in the nation:

The name of England will emerge from the world conflict with fresh titles to human veneration, dearer than ever to the thought of Englishmen, more richly freighted than before with associations of public service, and glorious memories of personal heroism. The Church of England will catch a certain lustre from its historic character as a national institution. Men will be disposed to give it a fair trial, willing to admit its right to express the Christian religion to and for Englishmen . . . A new link between the church and the nation will have been forged in the furnace of affliction.[16]

Those who led the church in the First World War were in all sorts of ways similar to – and often personally known to – those who led the British army. They had the same stubborn determination to reinforce failure, the same unwillingness to consider a change of tactics, the same lack of imagination, and above all, the same lack of self-reflective irony. That was indeed the spirit of the age, or at least of the upper and upper-middle classes who supplied English dioceses and English regiments with leadership. But it changed in wartime, and it changed largely from the bottom up, so the last to hear of and adjust to this radical change of mood and style were those at the top.

It is a commonplace that the Great War smashed into the self-confidence of a British Empire near its peak as devastatingly as the iceberg had smashed into the side of the *Titanic*, the 'greatest ship ever built', two years earlier. It is less obvious that the collision suddenly made obsolete a set of assumptions which constituted almost an entire culture, summed up an entire race. Many of those assumptions were pious ones. Among them was the belief that God had England in his special protection, because God had given England a special purpose. It was in obedience to that purpose that England had gone to war. Thus England was fulfilling generously and enthusiastically its side of the covenant bargain that defined it as the Chosen People. God's role was to keep his side of the deal, to see that England came through. If some correction was due in the process, it was meant to be light chastisement, sufficient to cure laxity and sin. It was not meant to be Hell on Earth. But that is what it became.

Dramatic irony happens in the mutual interaction of what is in the mind and what is actually happening – the heroine thinks she is recovering, we know she is dying. The combination produces a kind of tragic satire, a commentary on the foolishness of optimism. Aside from the military historians, undeniably the best book on the First World War is *The Great War in Modern Memory* by an American professor of English literature, Paul Fussell. All war, he states, is ironic, because all war is worse than expected:

> Every war constitutes an irony of situation because its means are so melodramatically disproportionate to its presumed ends. In the Great War, eight million people were destroyed because two persons, the Archduke Francis Ferdinand and his Consort, had been shot . . . The Great War was more ironic than any before or since. It was a hideous embarrassment to the prevailing Meliorist myth which had dominated the public consciousness for a century. It reverses the idea of progress . . .[17]

Meliorism, the belief that humanity can be improved and is improving, is closely allied to what is called the Whig view of history. Popularised by Lord Macaulay in the mid-nineteenth century, the Whig interpretation of history sees English civilisation as the pinnacle of political progress. With a sturdy Evangelical piety and commitment to continuous political reform, Macaulay and the many subsequent generations of English people that he influenced were quite sure God was on England's side – so much so that they prescribed English political institutions and English religion, language, manners and culture as the highest goal of civilisation all over the world. It was of course God who had shaped all those things providentially, not least by bringing the English the benefits of the 'Glorious Revolution' of 1688 (which kicked out the Catholic king James II) from which all subsequent good fortune flowed (partly through the logic of events, partly as a divine reward).

But the irony arrived, with the shelling, the bullets, the tanks, the barbed wire and the mud of the eternal battlefield. 'We seen 'em, we seen 'em, hangin' on the old barbed wire' sang British troops merrily on the march, describing the gruesome fate of an entire lost battalion. The

British quickly acquired a talent for black humour, to the puzzlement of their more earnest allies. 'The more revolting it was,' wrote the writer Philip Gibbs, 'the more people shouted with laughter.' This was 'the laughter of mortals at the trick which had been played on them by an iron fate'; he went on:

> They had been taught to believe that the whole object of life was to reach out to beauty and love, and that mankind, in its progress to perfection, had killed the beast instinct, cruelty, blood-lust, the primitive, savage law of survival by tooth and claw and club and axe. All poetry, all art, all religion had preached this gospel and this promise. Now the ideal was broken like a china vase dashed to the ground. The contrast between That and This was devastating . . . The war-time humour of the soul roared with mirth at the sight of all that dignity and elegance despoiled.[18]

That was ominous news for nationalistic religion. Militarily the war begun well enough. The British, preferring to regard the Royal Navy as the principal weapon of self-defence, maintained only a small professional army in peacetime, and very good it was. Nearly 100,000 soldiers went to France and Belgium in the first stage of the war, and soon found themselves engaged in the supreme test of battlefield discipline, an organised fighting retreat (the so-called Retreat from Mons). What in most military textbooks would later be regarded as an ignominious withdrawal in the face of superior force became quickly elevated to the status of another glorious episode in British history. And under what was popularly assumed in Britain to be divine protection – an angel in the clouds ('the Angel of Mons') was reported to have appeared to some of the marching troops – the army held together and was intact and coherent enough eventually to stand and fight, and give a good account of itself. In an early outbreak of British wartime irony, the surviving regular soldiers took the Kaiser's reported description of the British Expeditionary Force as a 'contemptible little army' and immortalised it by calling themselves, for evermore, the Old Contemptibles. By the end of four and a half years of war not many Old Contemptibles were left, but the survivors maintained an annual peacetime parade in honour of their fallen comrades for the next half century or more; and remained very proud of what the Kaiser had called them.

The following year saw the first major British reverse of the war: the bold but poorly planned expedition to capture the Gallipoli peninsula that guarded the Dardanelles sea channel between the Mediterranean and the Black Sea. The soldiers who went to France in 1914 were almost all regulars; those who fought in Turkey were partly regulars but also territorials (part-time militia, many of whom had served as regulars in peacetime) and regulars and volunteers from the Dominions, primarily Australia. Both the 1914 and 1915 British armies had been so weakened by ceaseless conflict and mounting casualties that it was decided to start again and form a new one, partly from volunteers and eventually also by conscription. This was the so-called Kitchener's Army, named after the colonial war hero who was also by then Minister for War, Lord Kitchener. Its purpose was to prepare and train for, and then execute, the one Big Push on the Western Front that British commanders were convinced was all it would take to turn the tide of war in their favour. In any event the French were taking a dreadful hammering at Verdun, and a major British effort elsewhere in the line was essential to draw off some of the German forces facing them.

Thus it was that Britain and its army squared up to the enemy for a battle that was meant to turn the war, but which, in failing to do so, nevertheless turned British history. The Battle of the Somme was rehearsed in every detail. Aware that very many units had not been in action before, and that they were relying for their officers on men who were not quite of the same social class as the regular officers of 1914 and 1915, the British high command issued precise instructions as to what was to happen in battle as each stage developed. Fussell notes what several military historians have remarked upon: the lack of confidence, even lack of respect, that senior British officers showed for the men they commanded as they went into battle. Another cause, he writes, was traceable to the class system and the assumptions it sanctioned. The regulars of the British staff entertained an implicit contempt for the rapidly trained new men of 'Kitchener's Army', largely recruited from workingmen from the Midlands and the north.

> The planners assumed that these troops – burdened for the assault with 66 pounds of equipment – were too simple and animal to cross the space between opposing trenches in any way except in full daylight and aligned in rows or waves. It was felt that the troops would become confused by more subtle tactics like rushing from cover to cover, or assault firing, or following close upon a continuous creeping barrage.[19]

Fussell does not say so, but it is possible to detect in the stubborn over-confidence of the generals more than a hint of Chosen People thinking – that with so much at stake, things could not go too badly wrong. God's divine protection would be available to the British troops once more, as always before. Douglas Haig, the British Commander-in-Chief, was supremely confident. His preparations left no room for mistakes, no detail of military planning was neglected. 'I feel that every step in my plan has been taken with Divine help,' he wrote to his wife shortly before the battle. The proposition that 'God helps those who help themselves' should have earned him a very large slice of divine assistance from the God of Battles. Such sentiments were universally shared. An entire nation was about to stake the lifeblood of its manhood on the proposition that it was indeed the Chosen People.

And everything went wrong. German artillery, and above all German machine guns and barbed wire, repelled wave after wave of advancing British infantry, who, almost incredibly, kept going through a battlefield soon littered with corpses and the dying. The first day of July 1916 became the worst day in the history of the British Army, before or since. Of the 110,000 men in the initial attack, there were more than 60,000 casualties. A large number of those not killed outright were left lying on the battlefield for days, their massed cries of pain and thirst generating an eerie screech by night that could be heard way behind the lines – it was too dangerous to try to rescue more than a handful. By day their cries were drowned in the noise of resumed battle, as the generals concluded that their perfect plans for Day One were still good for Day Two or Three. And the battle went on until November, with attack after attack brought to a standstill, or a few yards' progress all there was to show for endless effort and massive losses. It is difficult to avoid the impression that Divine Providence was still being relied upon to win the day, and that Haig, a dour Scots Calvinist, felt that God had to be given sufficient time to join the battle and deliver the victory. God, it seemed, had temporarily left his post. That he would eventually return to it, Haig never doubted. Indeed, the best way of ensuring his assistance was to remain faithful to the plan, to keep Britain's side of the bargain. Keeping going was literally a trial of faith. Failure in it could have meant losing the war.

The end of the agony of 1916 was but a prelude to the renewed horrors of 1917, the most frightful battle the British have ever fought, Passchendaele (officially the Third Battle of Ypres). Haig had not lost his conviction of eventual British victory, but came to regard the enormous losses sustained as the necessary blood sacrifice. The popular myth that he was ignorant of conditions at the front is not sustainable. He was well briefed at all stages, and in his private correspondence he often expresses distress at conditions at the front, and at the scale of the losses. (The final British and Commonwealth total of fatalities was little short of a million.) But it seems likely that only a man who was certain he had God on his side could have gone on ordering thousands of soldiers to their deaths, day after day. The reaction against Haig after the war owes something to the way Lloyd George chose to blame him for the conduct of a war for which he was himself ultimately responsible – he could have sacked Haig at any time – and also to the general British abandonment of the notion that their participation in the conflict had anything to do with the designs of God. Haig was seen to be following to its logical conclusion a theological view of Britain's place in the world that the rest of the population had turned its back on, sometime between 1916 and the end of the war.

Kitchener's recruiting campaign had emphasised that friends could join up and fight together, the so-called 'Pals' Battalions'. Whole streets in the industrial towns of central and northern England received the dread news together that hardly any of their menfolk had survived. It was a national disaster. Fussell recognises the turning point. 'The innocent army fully attained the knowledge of good and evil at the Somme on 1 July 1916. That moment, one of the most interesting in the whole long history of human disillusion, can stand as the type of all the ironic actions of the war.'[20]

In fact Haig fought stubbornly on; the British steadily grew in sophistication and skill, they discovered air warfare, the creeping barrage, the power of the machine gun, the use of cover, the uselessness of cavalry; and they invented the tank. By the autumn of 1918 the British Army (which included substantial forces from Australia, New Zealand and Canada) was the primary war-winning force on the European battlefield, and in a series of smashing victories almost completely ignored both at the time and subsequently, it brought the exhausted German army to the point of rout, capitulation and unconditional surrender.

But never again would it trust God to win its battles for it. Henceforth the belief in the general population that the English were a Chosen People was sustainable, if at all, only ironically. It was equally likely to produce furious anger. The damning final verdict on pre-war British God-and-glory patriotism was delivered by Wilfred Owen, in one of the most famous – and most bitter – poems of the First World War, 'Dulce et Decorum est':

> Bent double, like old beggars under sacks,
> Knock-kneed, coughing like hags, we cursed through sludge,
> Till on the haunting flares we turned our backs,
> And towards our distant rest began to trudge.
> Men marched asleep. Many had lost their boots,
> But limped on, blood-shod. All went lame, all blind;
> Drunk with fatigue; deaf even to the hoots
> Of gas-shells dropping softly behind.

Gas! GAS! Quick, boys! – An ecstasy of fumbling
Fitting the clumsy helmets just in time,
But someone still was yelling out and stumbling
And flound'ring like a man in fire or lime. –
Dim through the misty panes and thick green light,
As under a green sea. I saw him drowning.

In all my dreams before my helpless sight
He plunges at me, guttering, choking, drowning.

If in some smothering dreams, you too could pace
Behind the wagon that we flung him in,
And watch the white eyes writhing in his face,
His hanging face, like a devil's sick of sin,
If you could hear, at every jolt, the blood
Come gargling from the froth-corrupted lungs
Bitten as the cud of vile, incurable sores on innocent tongues, –
My friend, you would not tell with such high zest
To children ardent for some desperate glory,
The old Lie: *Dulce et decorum est
Pro patria mori.*[21]

Alan Wilkinson[22] sees the period of the Great War not only as the point from which the statistical decline of the Church of England can be measured: it was the point beyond which 'whatever the church did, it could never re-establish its old type of authority in the nation'. He charts the decline in Easter Day adult (over fifteen) communicants in the Church of England as 98 per 1,000 in 1911; 90 per 1,000 in 1925; 73 per 1,000 in 1939; 63 per 1,000 in 1958; 42 per 1,000 in 1973. The equivalent 1997 figure was approximately 29 per 1,000, or 2.9 per cent of the population.

And as Wilkinson also acknowledges, after seventy, eighty, nearly ninety years, the English sense of themselves is still haunted by that war and its imagery; and by the unresolved question, 'What went wrong?' In the aftermath of the Holocaust, Jews were later to ask themselves: 'Where was our God at Auschwitz?' Years before, the British had coined the same question – 'Where was our God at the Somme?'

8

Sex and Savages

The period when Israel was ruled by its judges was a time of constant inter-tribal warfare, carefully recorded in Scripture though apparently not always in the correct sequence. This supplied much ammunition for militant Protestant sermons, as England's enemies could be variously described as the Moabites, the Canaanites, the Philistines, the Amalekites, the Ammonites and assorted Assyrians. As Linda Colley says:

> Adam Ferguson sent the King's Highland regiments off to do battle with what was left of the Jacobite army in December 1745 with a Gaelic sermon based on Joab's speech to the army of Israel in advance of its battle with the Ammonites ... Alexander Webster, the staunchly pro-government minister of Tolbooth church in Edinburgh, dedicated his sermons on Culloden to those filled with 'concern for the welfare of our Jerusalem and zeal for British Israel'. While another clergyman, an Englishman this time, trumpeted the cosmic significance of the Seven Years War in the title of his sermon in celebration of the Peace of Paris in 1763 – '*The Triumph of Israelites over Moabites, or Protestants over Papists*'.[1]

The assumption that anyone who resisted the power of the English Protestant nation-state could be regarded as a Canaanite – and therefore dealt with equally ruthlessly – was readily transferred to the United States of America, especially when it confronted the original occupiers of the territory, the native Americans or Indians.

Against powerful enemies, rule by religious judges was felt to be a source of weakness, as was the disunity of Israel because each Hebrew tribe had its own leader. This led the last of the judges, Samuel, to agree reluctantly that Israel should become a united kingdom, and he consented to Saul as the first king. Nevertheless he warned of the dangers of centralism and tyranny; it was not long before he and Saul were at

213

loggerheads. One of the main duties of the king was to organise and lead an army, which Saul did for a while with great success. But a falling out with Samuel became inevitable.

The actual circumstances were peculiar. Samuel asked Saul to avenge the attacks by the Amalekites on the Israelites during their journey in the wilderness after the Exodus 200 years earlier. Saul defeated the Amalekites but did not destroy everyone and everything as custom (and Samuel) demanded. Agag, the captured Amalekite king, was brought before Samuel, who accused Saul of disobedience in letting him live. He proceeded to hack him to pieces himself, to show what it was that God had commanded. The way the story is told, there is no doubt readers are expected to side with Samuel, and with his cruel and vengeful act. Saul and Samuel went their separate ways, and Samuel eventually sought to undermine Saul by appointing his successor, David (he who had slain the giant Goliath, thereby providing further ammunition for generations of Protestant sermons thousands of years later).

David established his capital at Jerusalem and moved the Ark of the Covenant there to make the city the focus of religious national identity. His victories over neighbouring tribes gave him virtually a mini-empire to rule. But the peak of power and glory in the kingdom was not reached until the reign of Solomon, David's son. Israelite civilisation began to make great progress. And of course, eventually, the cycle of salvation history – the Chosen People Syndrome – began once more to assert itself. The people grew less faithful as they grew more prosperous. Solomon tolerated pagan practices, and allowed non-Hebrew settlements in the kingdom. His rule was increasingly resented, not least his reliance on forced labour. Solomon's reputation as a scourge of the lazy was based on the text, attributed to him, of Proverbs 6:6–8, which became so much quoted by Protestant clergymen that it almost became the basic text of the so-called Protestant work ethic: 'Go to the ant, thou sluggard; consider her ways, and be wise: which having no guide, overseer, or ruler, provideth her meat in the summer, and gathereth her food in the harvest.'

Eventually some parts of King Solomon's mini-empire revolted. On his death, the kingdom was split in two: the north (which kept the name Israel) and the south (the kingdom of Judah). So disobedience by the Chosen People was once more punished by misfortune.

The separation into the two kingdoms of Israel and Judah gave them separate histories, both of which, however, were dominated by the power and influence of stronger pagan neighbours, first the Assyrians and later the Babylonians. (The Egyptians also intervened.) There followed a long period of wars, coalitions and failed alliances, aimed at an accommodation with the Assyrians. Prophet after prophet arose to warn the Chosen

People that their increasing flirtations with the more exciting pagan deities of their neighbours – whose worship usually included a strong sexual element – would bring on their doom.

The most colourful and memorable of these struggles between good and evil (as the biblical narrator would have seen it) was the bitter conflict between the prophet Elijah and Queen Jezebel, wife of King Ahab of the northern kingdom, the archetypal *femme fatale*, described as a whore and a witch. She was opposed to the God of Israel and killed several hundred of his followers (called prophets in the text); Elijah out-magicked the followers of Baal in a bizarre competition on Mount Carmel, and then killed several hundred of them (also called prophets) in turn. Jezebel threatened his life, and he cursed her back, saying the dogs would eat her flesh. And so eventually it came to pass. There was not even enough left of her to bury. Jezebel personifies not just a religious distaste for open displays of female sexuality. She is also the personification of the temptation of pagan religion, with its magic sexual cults and false gods waiting to seduce the Israelites away from the worship of the True God.

Jezebel reappears in the Book of Revelation as a woman of sin and fornication, a type therefore that Protestant preachers easily applied to the Roman Church and its supposedly wicked ways. She is also a clue to a more subtle kind of association: that between sexual sin and religious infidelity. The Old Testament is not very interested in sexual sin *per se*, at least not the heterosexual sort. In a patriarchal polygamous society, a man who wants to have intercourse with an unmarried woman, whether he is himself married or not, has to marry her, which would be done by arrangement with her father. A man who had intercourse with an unmarried woman before or outside marriage could be forced to marry her, if she was a person of standing; otherwise he could make her his concubine. Or he had to pay her father a penalty. Exodus 22:16–17 lays down: 'And if a man entice a maid that is not betrothed, and lie with her, he shall surely endow her to be his wife. If her father utterly refuse to give her unto him, he shall pay money according to the dowry of virgins.' A man who had intercourse with a woman married to someone else would be guilty of adultery, and both were liable to be stoned to death. But the adultery was on her account not his: unless the woman he had intercourse with was already married to someone else, a married man could not be guilty of adultery. Nobody was very interested in the woman's consent. But if she believed her body was the property of others, she was presumably not very interested in it herself. It is significant that rape, as such, is not mentioned as a crime in the Old Testament anywhere.

These extreme double-standards only make sense if a woman is regarded as male property. If she (or her sexuality) 'belongs' to someone else, then to have intercourse with her is akin to an act of theft. If she does not belong to someone else, she can be acquired by a financial arrangement with her father, who, so to speak, 'sells' her virginity to her new husband. Hence the loss of virginity ruins her value.

The strict application of these rules in New England Puritan society had unexpectedly lenient results. John Winthrop, Governor of Massachusetts, records in his *Journal* for 21 June 1641: 'There arose a question in court about the punishment of single fornication, because, by the law of God, the man was only to marry the maid, or pay a sum of money to her father; but the case falling out between two servants, they were whipped for the wrong offered to the master in abusing his house . . .'

The most famous adulteress from the Puritan period is the fictional Hester Prynne, made to wear the infamous Scarlet Letter in the novel of that name by Nathaniel Hawthorne. She was married (albeit to a man who had disappeared) and had had a child by another man whose identity was not disclosed. Under Old Testament law, which the Puritans of Massachusetts accepted but did not strictly apply, she could have been put to death by stoning. The sentence laid down in Massachusetts law was that she be 'whipt at a cart's tayle through the town streets, and weare a badge with the capital letters AD cut in cloth upon her left sleeve'. In this case Hawthorne has Hester Prynne sentenced by the magistrates to a period of public shaming – standing on the town scaffold – and the requirement to wear a letter A on her dress at all times. Prynne defies her punishment by making a letter A that is richly embroidered and wearing it not with shame but with a certain defiant pride.

In Old Testament societies and those that were later modelled on them, the man who married acquired sexual rights over his wife, but she had no sexual rights over him. The treatment of women as male property in such a society was in turn part of a system of ownership and inheritance within families. It safeguarded the family fortune. A man would not want to be succeeded by another man's children as a result of his wife's adultery. And virginity at marriage guarantees that she is not already pregnant by another man.

Understood in the later Christian sense to mean intercourse outside marriage, fornication is not an Old Testament concept. Where the word occurs, it usually means sexual intercourse with temple prostitutes, or during other ceremonies in honour of pagan fertility gods. It is not so much a sexual crime or sin, therefore, as a religious one. The kings and prophets who fought against the attraction to their people of the highly sexualised pagan religion that was all around them were not primarily interested in sexual morality, in the modern sense. They wanted Israel to stay faithful to its God. Intercourse with a temple prostitute was akin to intercourse with the god she represented.

Nobody personalises that pagan-sexual allure better than the beautiful Jezebel. It is quite clear Elijah did not oppose her because she was so blatantly sensual, though obviously she was that (just before she was killed, she is described as having painted her face) (2 Kings 9:30). He opposed her because she drew the Hebrews towards false idols. But in Protestant preaching, reflecting a highly Manichean distaste for all things sexual that was characteristic of the Puritans and to some extent of all other varieties of Christianity too, 'Jezebel' came to stand for the archetypal female temptress. Any woman who took pains to make herself look sexually attractive was liable to be compared with her, and reminded of her dreadful fate. It became the fashion for women to dress plainly. Cosmetics were of the devil.

The equation of fornication with unfaithfulness to God is a coin with two sides. There is a parallel tradition in the Old Testament of gradually coming to understand God's relationship with the Israelites as like the love of husband and wife – not just romantic love, but marriage with all its ups and downs. This becomes apparent from the prophet Hosea onwards. His thoughts began with reflections on his own wife's infidelity, which he forgave her for. Despite his pain he stayed faithful, and this crisis in his marriage led him to think about God's love for the Israelites. There is a touching pen portrait of him in *Who's Who in the Bible* by Peter Calvocoressi:

> Hosea struck a comparatively compassionate note even though inveighing strongly against idolatry, luxury, debauchery, and the irresponsibility of rulers who betrayed their trust. He urged Israel to concentrate on religious and moral reform and stop dabbling in international politics . . . He believed that God's function was to punish but also to show mercy; that God was pulled two ways by Israel's sins and by its sufferings. Hosea himself was not a happy man and, uncharacteristically for a Hebrew prophet, his private life was entangled with his prophecy. He was ordered to marry a harlot, Gomer, by whom he had three children, and later to redeem a fallen woman who may have been Gomer lapsing again or another adulteress. Whether or not he knew of Gomer's past before marrying her, he became bitterly hostile to sexual irregularity and developed a parallel between earthly marriage and the relationship – compounded of passion and disappointment – between God and his Chosen People.[2]

While illuminating the relationship between the people of God and God himself, showing it to be one of forgiveness, intimacy and tenderness as well as power, this key idea also elevated the status of marriage.

The gradual decline in polygamy and predominance of monogamy (well established by the time of the New Testament, though polygamy was not finally abolished in Judaism until the eleventh century AD) has been attributed directly to this enhanced status of marriage following Hosea and also indirectly to the enhanced status of women that went with it.

When Christianity considered itself to have superseded Judaism, this God-Israel relationship was transformed typologically into the relationship between God and the church (specifically, Christ and the church). It did not, however, preserve the idea that the church might from time to time be unfaithful, or that Christ might need to forgive it. Rather, the church is seen as a spotless bride, incapable of sin (the 'holy' part of the creed's list of adjectives for the church, 'One Holy Catholic and Apostolic'). Instead of resembling the reality of married life, the relationship between Christ and the church becomes, like romantic love of popular fiction, a perpetual honeymoon.

This has undoubtedly weakened the value of the metaphor, as well as reinforcing a theoretical view of the church that contradicts the actual, proud, sinful and often unfaithful institution with which we are familiar from church history. Much misunderstanding, some of it deliberately created, flowed from this dichotomy, and still does. The theory rests upon a metaphysical and sacramental understanding that the church is both an outward sign, which may be partial or flawed, and an inward reality, which must be perfect. The early Protestants rejected this sacramental metaphysics, most of all because of their rejection of the Catholic theology of the Eucharist – which distinguished between the outward sign of the Blessed Sacrament, bread and wine, and the inward reality, the body and blood of Christ. Even today, when the Catholic Church speaks of itself it tends to mean the church's hidden (perfect) essence rather than the visible (often all too human) surface appearance. It was for such reasons that in its Millennium statement of apology for Catholic anti-Semitism, the Vatican blamed 'members of the church' rather than 'the church' itself, a distinction which manifestly left many Jews feeling that the apology was less than wholehearted.

Protestantism, while not identifying 'the church' as the institution of that name centred on Rome (rather the opposite), applied to its own concept of church the Lutheran principle of *ecclesia reformata – semper reformanda*, meaning that the church needs to be in a process of continuous reform. This is closer to the Old Testament model of the People of God, and compatible with the cycle of decay and renewal which we have labelled the Chosen People Syndrome. It is a mark of the Catholic Church beginning to move closer to this way of understanding the church that the Second Vatican Council (1962–65), while also using the People of God terminology for itself much more than previously, also went some way towards the Lutheran notion of *semper reformanda* by adopting the similar formula of *semper purificanda* (continuous purification). What it has not done so far is to appropriate for itself the Old Testament model of prophecy – that an inspired individual could stand in the place of the prophets and be God's mouthpiece for the work of *semper purificanda*. But that may be a development to look forward to. The Catholic Church needs another Hosea, to tell it not of a divine bridegroom constantly dazzled by the church's beauty but of a broken-hearted husband repeatedly forgiving an unfaithful wife.

Until modern biblical scholarship altered the accepted interpretation, it had been assumed that this typological marriage relationship (God-Israel equals husband-wife) explained the presence in the Old Testament of some fairly explicit love poetry, the so-called 'Song of Songs' or 'Song of Solomon'. The romantic (indeed erotic) feelings being described were assumed to be an allegorical or typological reference to the passionate marriage of God and Israel (or Christ and the church). In fact this interpretation is missing from the Old Testament, and it seems may not have occurred to Jewish scholars until they heard Christian scholars applying it to the church in about the second century AD. In both cases the motive may well have been to explain away a text that seems to exalt eroticism, an idea with which neither the Jewish nor the Christian religious authorities were comfortable.

The explanation that the author, King Solomon himself perhaps, was trying to compete with Canaanite fertility rites was fashionable for a while but is not now accepted. There are parallels in ancient Egyptian love poetry, but no direct borrowings. In so far as it has a teaching role in religious terms, the 'Song' simply demonstrated that there was nothing sinful about sexual desire *per se*, nor was God offended when men and women enjoyed each other this way. There is also a reciprocity and equivalence about the sexual feelings of the man for the woman and vice versa. It is not a relationship of dominance or possession, but of passion, desire and humble devotion. Scholars now think it most likely that the 'Song' was collected from verses originally performed as entertainment at wedding celebrations. This is a fair sample of the style:

Behold, thou art fair, my love; behold, thou art fair; thou hast doves' eyes within thy locks: thy hair is as a flock of goats, that appear from mount Gilead. Thy teeth are like a flock of sheep that are even shorn, which came up from the washing; whereof every one bear twins, and none is barren among them. Thy lips are like a thread of scarlet, and thy speech is comely: thy temples are like a piece of a pomegranate within thy locks. Thy neck is like the tower of David builded for an armoury, whereon there hang a thousand bucklers, all shields of mighty men. Thy two breasts are like two young roes that are twins, which feed among the lilies. Until the day break, and the shadows flee away, I will get me to the mountain of myrrh, and to the hill of frankincense. Thou art all fair, my love; there is no spot in thee. Come with me from Lebanon, my spouse, with me from Lebanon: look from the top of Amana, from the top of Shenir and Hermon, from the lions' dens, from the mountains of the leopards. Thou hast ravished my heart, my sister, my spouse; thou hast ravished my heart with one of thine eyes, with one chain of thy neck. How fair is thy love, my sister, my spouse! how much better is thy love than wine! and the smell of thine ointments than all spices! Thy lips, O my spouse, drop as the honeycomb: honey and milk are under thy tongue; and the smell of thy garments is like the smell of Lebanon. (Song of Solomon 4:1–11)

The uninhibited ecstasy of the verse meant it was not a Puritan's preacher's favourite text. Nor does it lend much weight to the traditional Catholic view that the only justification for sexual pleasure was procreation, and that too much passion, even in the marriage bed, was sinful. The reduction of the 'Song' to theological allegory, showing how much God loved Israel or Christ loved the church, was a convenient way of burying the poet's obvious delight in sensuality.

As time passed this softening in attitudes towards women, marriage and sex in the Old Testament was mirrored by a softening of attitudes towards war; indeed, by a general increase in wisdom and reduction in savagery across the board. Political and military developments were the spur, but the product was a body of religious literature by the major and minor prophets of Israel of a profundity and imaginative ingenuity unsurpassed in the literature of any other civilisation of the time. It was as if the woes of the people, caused by a series of minor kings who were either fools or knaves, generated an equivalent outburst of creative energy in favour of goodness on the part of the learned and wise men of the era (some of whom, for all their wisdom, appeared quite deranged to their contemporaries). Much of it was devoted to correcting the stupidities of kings and warning the people of the consequences of their folly, but its scope transcends its immediate context and like great art everywhere, it speaks to the human condition in every circumstance. Nothing has influenced and shaped the mental landscape of Western culture as much as the psalms, proverbs and prophecies that were generated by the events known as the Babylonian Exile, a period of acute political and military crisis in the life of the Israelite nation in which it almost came to be extinguished for ever. It was during that period that most of the Old Testament came to be written down and edited into the form in which we know it.

Having noted the barbarism of the ancient Israelites, the murders and massacres routinely carried out apparently with the consent of or at the command of God, it is important also to recognise their growing moral depth and sophistication, the sense of justice, the awareness of the pathos of human life, the importance of mutual dependence. If the barbarism was a dangerous example for later nations which thought of themselves as chosen by God, the growing moral and spiritual insight which also began to characterise the ancient Israelites was a powerful factor in the evolution of civilisation under Christianity.

Those prophets were unsparing as they castigated the rulers of their day. It is entirely likely that it was from their example that Protestants in Britain and later in America considered they had a divine right to speak their minds about the shortcomings of their own rulers.

At times the office of 'prophet' was almost considered an authorised one, part of the Temple establishment in Jerusalem. Given that the main job of the prophet was to castigate the king and the people for their bad behaviour, it was a kind of 'official opposition'. To talk of freedom of speech is an exaggeration, however, for prophets denounced kings at their peril and could pay with their lives for it. Nevertheless their denunciations are reported at length in the Old Testament, usually as utterances in the mouths of humans but coming directly from God. Invariably, the author of Scripture is on the side of the prophet. As a record of prophecy, the Old Testament is a powerful catalogue of political dissent against the abuse of government. Because it was regarded in Protestant societies as the Word of God, this gave dissent (at least when expressed in the name of true religion) something akin to divine sanction. The king and his ministers may not have liked it but with such biblical examples to hand, they could not so easily argue that to criticise the king was, as such, wicked or contrary to the will of God.

Given how steeped the populace was in the example of the Bible, the notion of a permanent tension between king and prophet, government and opposition, was an important formative influence in the emergence of parliamentary democracy in England. Although criticism of state policy became secular as the subject matter politics itself became secular, it first emerged when almost the whole business of politics was with religion. The lack of a similar scriptural metaphor for political debate in the Catholic understanding of biblical prophecy may explain why parliamentary democracy was for a long time regarded in Catholic countries as an alien system. The prophetic tradition is as hostile to ideas of monarchical absolutism – that the king can do no wrong – as it is to ecclesiastical absolutism – that the church can do no wrong. Anyone who knows his Old Testament and applies it to his own situation knows differently: kings and churches do wrong all the time. This may explain why Catholic societies were both more reactionary and more revolutionary than Protestant societies, and why Protestant societies were thought to be more faithful to the Bible. A parliamentary system provides a method by which government institutions may bend under pressure. Without it, they have little alternative but to resist to the death, or break.

This may also explain why biblical Protestantism became closely identified with the idea of freedom and liberty. The case is not entirely proved. In the name of Protestantism ghastly crimes against humanity were committed, and if one includes Protestantism as the driving ideology behind colonialism in Africa, say, or the elimination of native resistance to American expansion westwards, or Anglo-American involvement in slavery, then such crimes may exceed the crimes committed in the name of Catholicism (heinous though they were too). Catholicism was the flag under which Bloody Mary persecuted the Protestant martyrs in the mid-sixteenth century, a story vividly chronicled by John Foxe; and even that death toll, some two to three hundred, was a pale shadow of the monstrosities committed in the wars of religion in Central Europe, the persecution of Huguenots in France or the fate of Jews and heretics in Spain under the Inquisition. But in subsequent (Protestant) reigns, more Catholics were put to death in England and Wales than the total of Mary's victims. Whether death by hanging, drawing and quartering (the fate of most of the Catholics) was any less cruel than death by fire (the chosen method for disposing of Protestants) is moot. The point is not who killed most people, or which form of execution was more painful, but that Catholics under Elizabeth I or James I were no more free to express their opinions than Protestants under Mary. There was much talk of 'tolerance' as the seventeenth century drew on, but it was never – apart from the brief reign of James II – tolerance of Catholics. It was, in other words, tolerance of those who were easiest to tolerate, tolerance on the cheap.

Catholics, of course, really existed. One cannot say the same for the other hate crime that stands against Protestantism's good name in England and America in the seventeenth century – the persecution of witches. Such liberty or freedom as was claimed in Protestantism was liberty for the People of God, just as in the Old Testament, most of the prohibitions contained in the Law of Moses, including freedom from slavery, applied only to the Hebrews. Someone beyond the pale, whether an outsider or a traitor, had no such protection. Catholics (being members of a rival Chosen People) were by definition not included, nor were Jews (for similar reasons). Witches were almost worse than either, being secret enemies within rather than obvious enemies without. Witchcraft, like heresy, is a thought-crime: the act itself is invisible, though it may be inferred from other evidence.

For the first thousand years of Christianity witchcraft was regarded either as simply a survival of pagan belief in magic, or as absurd. This is despite the clear injunction in Exodus 22:18 – 'Thou shalt not suffer a witch to live,' which implied that witches were real. Neither the Roman nor the Spanish Inquisition took witchcraft seriously, and areas of Europe under their sway were spared the witch-manias that broke out elsewhere, especially in Germany (largely under Catholic auspices) and Scotland (under Protestant auspices). The high point of witch-burning in England occurred during the period of Puritan rule under Cromwell. The famous Salem trial of 150 suspects in Massachusetts, also dominated by Puritan biblical literalism, occurred somewhat later, in 1692, and resulted in nineteen hangings – and not long after, in as many pardons.

The fierce opposition of the Puritans to witchcraft has been variously interpreted, and it offers a rich field of pickings for psychoanalysts and anthropologists (an example of this approach is quoted at the start of this book). One religious explanation could be that it was a product of belief in predestination. Those who are of the 'elect' – predestined for salvation – were naturally curious about those who were not, who could not all be Roman Catholics. The saved and the damned jostled together through life, scarcely able to tell each other apart. Yet if the saved were already chosen by God, then the damned were, by inference, already chosen by the devil. The devil being cunning, he would not have revealed his selection too obviously, for instance by making them all extremely wicked. So some of them would have lived outwardly modest and pious lives, while maintaining their links with him in secret. Part of the devil's work was to snatch the souls of the elect from the road to heaven – predestination was only an indication of a state of grace that could be lost, not a solid guarantee of salvation come what may. Thus those engaged in witchcraft were either 'Christians gone wrong' – who could be preached at, brought to confess, reconverted, punished and eventually redeemed – or those predestined to be condemned, who would not repent, or after pretending to do so, would relapse. The idea that witchcraft was a survival of some previous pagan religion seems fanciful – there is no way the famous 'witches of Salem', for instance, could have been in contact with pre-Christian English religion.

The paranoia about witches that had gripped Europe and touched New England for about 200 years eventually faded, after having claimed something like 50,000 victims. Belief in witches required an active faith in the devil, an evil spirit able to take human or animal form who wandered the world spreading evil, and with whom witches had sexual intercourse. The devil, of course, was closely related to the Anti-Christ. In Protestant England and America, the peak of the witch-hunting mania coincided with the peak of paranoia about Catholicism, especially the fear that a lot of people pretending not to be Catholics really were. They were known as 'church papists', meaning those who conformed to the Church of England without really abandoning the Old Religion, which they continued to practise in private. Given the severe penalties for failing to attend the services of the established church, including the risk of disinheritance, such outward conformity was widespread.

Nor was Protestant suspicion of Charles II and his regime entirely fanciful. He had accepted financial help from his French cousin Louis XIV, which came with the condition that he should convert to Catholicism, which, on his deathbed, he duly did. But as a result of this climate of suspicion everything that went wrong that could not be attributed to witchcraft could be put down to Catholics and their secret activities. Or to Catholicism and witchcraft in satanic alliance. Catholics were at first officially blamed for the fire which destroyed most of London in 1666. Purcell's opera *Dido and Aeneas*, probably written before the death of Charles II in 1685 when feverish Protestant agitation against the incoming Catholic king James II was at its height, has a role for a 'Sorceress and her witches' that has always been interpreted as a reference to the dark and sinister menace of popery in popular imagination.

The idea that Protestantism stood unambiguously for freedom is therefore doubtful, unless it means, somewhat tautologically, freedom to be a good Protestant. Even at the height of the Spanish Inquisition, a Catholic could claim an equivalent definition – freedom to be a good Catholic. In both cases, the limited freedom that existed was only given to those within the 'People of God', howsoever defined. Those outside its boundaries had no such freedom. Catholics did not tolerate Protestants, nor Protestants Catholics, and on the whole neither of them tolerated Jews.

Whether Catholic or Protestant, however, freedom did have a particularly *English* provenance. Freedom here means not specifically freedom of speech – the English had long had laws against seditious speech or writing – but a structure of laws which erected barriers against the powers of the king in defence of the subject. The Magna Charta of 1215 was not the beginning of this tradition. Many of its requirements are couched in terms of obliging the king to respect existing rights and conventions, showing that they had existed since anyone could remember, some since pre-conquest times. The most significant of the rights granted under Magna Charta did indeed go some way to guaranteeing the rights of subjects. Three crucial clauses declare that:

(38) No bailiff shall in future put anyone to trial upon his own bare word, without reliable witnesses produced for this purpose.
(39) No free man shall be arrested or imprisoned or disseised

[dispossessed] or outlawed or exiled or in any way victimised, neither will we attack him or send anyone to attack him, except by the lawful judgment of his peers or by the law of the land.
(40) To no one will we sell, to no one will we refuse or delay right or justice.

Not only did the Archbishop of Canterbury, Stephen Langton, organise the protests of the barons which led to Magna Charta, but he acted as one of the witnesses and guarantors of it (though it was also subject to papal confirmation). So it did sometimes fall to leaders of the medieval church to offer a prophetic voice against the tyranny of the king, and the church fought strenuously to maintain sufficient freedom to do so. This was the central issue in the quarrel between Henry II and Langton's famous predecessor of the century before, Thomas à Becket. Thus the final clause of Magna Charta begins by repeating the guarantee previously given, that the English church shall not be under the power of the English state.

Wherefore we wish and firmly enjoin that the English church shall be free, and that the men in our kingdom shall have and hold all the aforesaid liberties, rights and concessions well and peacefully, freely and quietly, fully and completely, for themselves and their heirs from us and our heirs, in all matters and in all places for ever, as is aforesaid . . .

And Magna Charta also set up a council of twenty-five barons, who were to watch over the king's observance of its terms and who were given the right to wage war on the king if he defaulted on his promises. These were the various ways in which the English constitution began to build in checks and balances in order to withhold absolute power from the king, and punish him if he tried to exercise it. There are unmistakable signs here that the barons, and Stephen Langton in particular, were conscious of the example of the Old Testament, where the prophets had licence to monitor, and where necessary protest at, the way the king exercised his powers. Although Magna Charta gives no sanction to republicanism, the drafters of the American constitution, and the constitutions of many individual American states, regarded it as central to their own philosophy. It did give legal sanction for taking up arms against a king who trampled on the liberties it guaranteed, which may be why it has always been better preserved in historical memory in America than in England.

On the other hand the English constitutional system with a permanent 'official' opposition – it is actually called 'Her Majesty's Loyal Opposition' – is even closer to the Old Testament model of the tension between king and prophet than the American system, where the party out of power in Congress or the White House does not see itself with a mission to oppose the government at all costs. That role belongs more to the American press.

The first of the prophets was Moses, and it did not fall to him to criticise the ruler as that was himself; but the greatest was Isaiah, to whom it did so fall. In fact there was more than one of him, for among the sayings attributed to someone of that name are some describing incidents hundreds of years apart. Isaiah was a favourite prophet of later Christian commentators because many of his prophecies are capable of being taken as predictions of the coming of Jesus Christ, such as Isaiah 7:14: 'Behold, a virgin shall conceive, and bear a son, and shall call his name Immanuel.' The most famous use of Isaiah in this way was attributed to Jesus himself:

> And there was delivered unto him the book of the prophet Isaiah. And when he had opened the book, he found the place where it was written, The Spirit of the Lord is upon me, because he hath anointed me to preach the gospel to the poor; he hath sent me to heal the broken-hearted, to preach deliverance to the captives, and recovering of sight to the blind, to set at liberty them that are bruised, To preach the acceptable year of the Lord. And he closed the book, and he gave it again to the minister, and sat down. And the eyes of all them that were in the synagogue were fastened on him. (Luke 4:17–20)

Isaiah and the later prophets contributed profoundly to the development of Judaism, especially in the gradually emerging emphasis on ethical behaviour and social justice as the mark of true righteousness (instead of mere ritualism and the avoidance of pagan influences). Under some of the later prophets the thought began to emerge that God's ethical rules applied not just to Jews but to everyone, and that Jews had to behave ethically towards non-Jews as well as towards their own kind. The Old Testament model of social justice was to have a deep influence on such later (nineteenth- and twentieth-century) developments as Christian Socialism in England and the Social Gospel movement in America.

It is hardly necessary to say, however, that the Old Testament model for the treatment of women did not form part of that example. Nor, as in Roman Catholicism with its high status for the Virgin Mary (sometimes verging on regarding her as 'co-redeemer' of the human race with Christ), are there any compensating features in Protestantism to redress this strongly male bias.

In the two creation narratives in Genesis, one describes the first male and the first female being created at the same time, but the second describes Adam created first and Eve being made from a rib taken from his body when he slept. The text describes Adam as 'ruler' (sometimes translated as 'master') of Eve, and the story of the Fall depicts her as the author of Adam's downfall when she seduced him into eating the forbidden apple.

As well as the rules favouring men in sexual relations and marriage customs as already described, Mosaic law includes numerous other discriminatory regulations. After childbirth, a woman who had given birth to a male child was unclean for forty days; after a female child, for eighty days (Leviticus). In a census, males over a month old were counted, girls were not (Numbers). A male child under five was worth five shekels, a girl three shekels (Leviticus). Sons were to inherit from their fathers, and daughters inherited only if there were no sons. If there were no direct descendants, then brothers inherited, sisters did not (Numbers). Vows taken by women could be cancelled by their fathers or husbands, vows taken by men were binding (Numbers). A woman losing her virginity before marriage could be stoned to death, but not a man (Deuteronomy). Divorce could only be initiated by a man, not a woman (Deuteronomy). After the end of the Babylonian Exile the second temple was rebuilt with a separate, inferior, area reserved only for women; and women were not allowed to testify in court (Chronicles). It became forbidden for women to talk to strangers or appear in public unveiled; and so on.

At the start of the Christian era, when the detailed regulations of the Old Testament were generally regarded as no longer binding on Christians, it was open to the emerging Christian church to dismiss all these discriminatory rules concerning women, and start again. Instead most of them were confirmed. St Paul in particular was careful to repeat the rule that women were subject to their husbands. In addition, the Christian church's adaptation to itself of the prophet Hosea's metaphor – that God's relationship to Israel was like a husband's relationship to a wife – underlined even further that wives owed obedience to their husbands as the church owed obedience to Christ.

There are other discriminatory elements in the New Testament, such as that women should not be 'the head of' men, women should keep silent in the assembly, women should have their hair covered at all times, and so on. Protestants inclined to take the New Testament as literally as the Old were unable to allow much leeway in the interpretation of such rules. Protestantism became an exceedingly masculine religion as a result. Catholicism, with its freedom to reinterpret Scripture, its numerous female saints, its large women-only religious orders with their powerful abbesses, and above all its devotion to Mary as the supreme human being (albeit one who was immaculately conceived), was never so unambiguously male-orientated. On the other hand since at least the thirteenth century compulsory male celibacy in the priesthood left the government of the Catholic Church not only exclusively in the hands of men – that was just as true of Protestant churches – but of men who were cut off from close contact with women as wives and daughters. That inevitably led to a tendency not just to look down on women excessively but to look up to them excessively too. In Catholic cultures women were either madonnas or whores, or a bit of both. In Protestant cultures they were housewives.

In neither case, however, were women denied membership of the People of God or excluded from the Chosen People just because they were women. For that, they had also to be black, or North American Indian, or Catholic (especially Irish). For these were three of the main categories who felt the full force of the English or American belief that they were the Chosen People, and permitted by God to act towards the non-Chosen just as Moses, Joshua, Gideon and other rulers of ancient Israel had done.

The likening of the North American continent to a Promised Land is a strong element in the emerging sense of American nationhood, before and after the Revolutionary War. It was a regular theme of sermons. Timothy Dwight had dedicated *The Conquest Of Canaan* to George Washington, but was not felt to have said anything new. The analogy between the land of Canaan, already populated by numerous tribes but claimed as a result of divine donation by God's first Chosen People, and this vast and wealthy 'land flowing with milk and honey' claimed by God's new Chosen People, was all too obvious.

It might have been different. In Virginia, the marriage between John Rolfe and Pocahontas, daughter of the local chief, suggested the beginning of a relationship of peace and partnership. It did not last, but the breakdown was not unilaterally the fault of the English. The real deterioration started, naturally, with the Chosen People *par excellence*, the first Puritan settlers in Massachusetts. The Indians at first took pity on them – a fact commemorated every year at Thanksgiving – but their repayment was fast and harsh. Dee Brown, in *Bury My heart at Wounded Knee*, describes the rapid progression towards conflict and confrontation in this most tragic of all colonial relationships:

For several years these Englishmen and their Indian neighbours lived in peace, but many more shiploads of white people continued coming ashore. The ring of axes and the crash of falling trees echoed up and down the coasts of the land which the white men now called New England. Settlements began crowding upon each other. In 1625 some of the colonists asked Samoset to give them 12,000 additional acres of Pemaquid land. Samoset knew that land came from the Great Spirit, was as endless as the sky, and belonged to no man. To humour these strangers in their strange ways, however, he went through a ceremony of transferring the land and made his mark on a paper for them. It was the first deed of Indian land to English colonists. Most of the other settlers, coming in by thousands now, did not bother to go through such a ceremony. By the time Massasoit, great chief of the Wampanoags, died in 1662, his people were being pushed back into the Wilderness. His son Metacom foresaw doom for all Indians unless they united to resist the invaders.[3]

Metacom created an alliance of Indian tribes and then went to war, attacking fifty settlements and destroying twelve. After months of fighting, the superior firepower of the white men overwhelmed the Indian tribes. Their menfolk were killed – Metacom's head was exhibited upon a stake at Plymouth for twenty years – and women and children sold into slavery, just as the Bible said they could be. 'For two more centuries these events were repeated again and again as the European colonists moved inland through the passes of the Alleghenies and down the westward-flowing rivers to the Great Waters (Mississippi) and then up the Great Muddy (Missouri),' says Brown.

From the Indian point of view, one calamity towers over all the others in the history of their dealings with the white man. As Reginald Horsman starkly declares in *Expansion and American Indian Policy*: 'The American victory in the Revolution was a disaster to the Indians.'[4] At the outset of the war, the Indians calculated that they had less to fear from British traders and officials than from American land speculators and farmers. Hence they joined forces with the British, sometimes even as regular units under commissioned Indian officers but more often as war-parties fighting by their own rules. But when the British lost, they lost too. They were not consulted about the peace settlement – Indian matters are not mentioned in the 1782 Treaty of Paris between Britain and the United States – but the American government proceeded to treat them as a defeated enemy whose land could be occupied.

In response to unauthorised incursions, the British colonial administration had drawn a so-called Proclamation Line on the map in 1763 as part of the take-over of French Canada, which prohibited the confiscation of Indian land and appropriated the entire area west of the Appalachians to native Americans. Robert Harvey describes 'burning resentment' over the Proclamation Line as 'one of the main, if unstated, motives of the rebellious colonists in the war'. He goes on:

Once war broke out between the British and the Americans, from north to south along the Western border a no-holds-barred systematic holocaust was carried out against the Indian tribes across the Proclamation Line – largely by militia raised from among the land-hungry white border settlers with the full support of Washington and the American high command. This was devastatingly successful, and opened the way to the full-scale occupation of Indian lands during the following century. Thousands of Indians were massacred in the process, hundreds of their villages burnt and levelled, vast acreages of land laid waste, thousands of tons of crops destroyed, and probably tens of thousands of Indians deliberately starved to death as a result.[5]

An even worse killer was smallpox. The Puritans in Massachusetts had noticed how vulnerable the Indians were to this devastating disease, one of them describing the rapid depopulation it caused as 'the wonderful preparation of the Lord Jesus Christ, by his providence for his people's abode in the Western world' ('His people' being the Puritans). The British had tried to spread smallpox among the Indians allied with the French who were besieging Pittsburg in 1763, by giving them smallpox-infected blankets. It is by no means certain they succeeded, and smallpox was widespread already. Smallpox was often referred to as a providential aid to the settlement of Indian lands by white people, and evidence suggests the giving of infected blankets to Indians has become part of the folklore of America, both white and native peoples, whether true or not. And a certain tardiness on the part of the American government in fighting the disease among Indians in the nineteenth century, after vaccination became possible, suggests a reluctance to stand in the way of 'God's purposes' in this respect. Could the Indians have been saved, had the American authorities seen it as being in their interests to do so? It is quite probable. Using the primitive medical procedure known as inoculation, Washington took steps to stamp out smallpox in his army fighting the British, which undoubtedly helped him to victory.

The Indians whose land was stolen were no mere nomads. Much of the land was under cultivation, and the standard of living of the people was advanced. It was all the more valuable, therefore; and in the critical financial situation of the early days of the United States, the selling of Indian land to settlers was a good way to raise revenue (payments went by and large not to the Indians but to the new government). Though the British were not famous for their love of Indians, they had granted them a legal status and recognised their 'right of soil' – ownership through occupation. The new American government was reluctant to do so, and used the argument that the Indians were now a defeated enemy whose rights had been extinguished.

Horsman describes the situation thus:

> Yet, though the eastern half of the Mississippi Valley was for the most part unsettled by the Americans, it was no deserted wilderness. Its

history is sometimes written as though settlers were to pour into a vast empty valley but actually much of the eastern half of the Mississippi Valley was occupied by Indian tribes. Many of these tribes had fought successfully on the British side in the Revolution; others, on the banks of the Mississippi, hardly knew a revolution had taken place. Few of them could comprehend how the signing of a treaty in Paris between the English and the Americans could result in the transfer of their villages and hunting grounds to the new United States.[6]

It is striking how Euro-centric was the attitude of both British and Americans with regard to Indian rights. The British did not own the land that was ceded to the Americans at the Treaty of Paris in 1782, but the real owners, the Indians, were invisible to a European mind. The key to this mindset is the assumption that the British (and hence their successors, the Americans) had a God-given right to the land, compared with which Indians were mere squatters ('right of soil' notwithstanding). They could be driven off or killed. Usually the process started, as in Massachusetts a century earlier, with efforts to drive them off which were resisted; having taken up arms against the white men, they had declared themselves to be an enemy; they could therefore be brought to battle and defeated.

Washington himself favoured land grants to those who had fought on the side of the Revolution. Being fighting men, they would be able to protect other white settlers in the frontier territories 'and more than probably prevent the murder of many innocent families, which frequently, in their usual mode of extending our settlements and encroachments on the hunting grounds of the Natives, fall the hapless victims to savage barbarity'. No thought here about the right of the Indians to protect their hunting grounds by force, despite the settlers using methods which Washington himself was admitting were provocative.

What is surprising about American policy towards the Indians, both at the outset of the new republic and later, is the repeated and never really abandoned pretence that the acquisition of Indian territory was somehow being conducted according to civilised rules. There was endless talk of treaties and agreements, boundaries and guarantees, and after each agreement the Americans tended to sound as if they really meant to stick to it this time. Always some reason cropped up, usually sooner rather than later, as to why what had been conceded by the Indians was not enough, and further concessions had to be made. As Horsman remarks:

Agreements with Indian tribes were made to be broken, because in the eyes of the 'civilised world' the United States already had sovereignty over the lands westward to the Mississippi river. The only questions were how, when, and under what terms actual Indian dispossession would be arranged. For white negotiators, treaty language was merely a means of obtaining land with the least conflict and expense, and a means for deflecting Indian resistance until the next, inevitable cessions were necessary. For Indian negotiators, treaty language often represented solemn promises that they believed would be carried out.[7]

In fact the progress of American settlement into Indian territory would have proceeded little differently had the declared policy been one of naked and ruthless plunder, without regard for any legal niceties. In other words all these treaties and agreements brought little benefit to the Indians. Instead they merely persuaded those doing the encroaching that they were behaving honourably; which in turn encouraged them to further encroach, ever more eagerly.

This was part of the conviction that in some sense the Indians were being done a favour, because they were being exposed to the advantages of American civilisation. Thomas Jefferson in particular wanted an Indian policy which would not 'violate his own concept of the mission of the United States to show Europe that a nation could live without war and could bring happiness to its people'; in Horsman's words:

> That he viewed American expansion in terms of the spreading of civilisation, the bringing of a new and better way of life, is not surprising . . . The sense of 'Manifest Destiny', of moralistic expansion, is plainly evident in Jefferson's Indian policy. To Jefferson expansion was desirable not only for the Americans, but also for those whom it would engulf. This confidence often blinded Jefferson to the realities of everyday relations with the Indians.[8]

Horsman's summing up of America's Indian policy is that it started with high principles which proved harder and harder to apply, and that acceptance of the idea that Indians had rights was incompatible with the land hunger which it was government policy to stimulate. And land hunger won. But the high principles were somehow treated as if they still applied, and as if the Indians had been treated fairly. America not only had to be seen abroad to have kept faith with the Enlightenment; it had to be able itself to believe it had done so. That demanded some rearrangement of the facts.

So the history of the north American continent had to be adjusted, to avoid reminding people of the century or more of cruelty and bad faith that had in fact been required in the building of the new country, and instead substituted an empty wilderness, waiting to be populated and tamed by the bringers of Christian civilisation. American frontier culture treated an Indian as a particular awkward kind of natural hazard in the way of progress, somewhere between a bear and a rattlesnake, a drought and a thunderstorm, not as a human being whose right to life, liberty and the pursuit of happiness was self-evident. Yet these were precisely the touchstones of the civilisation the Americans were trying to spread. The best explanation of this contradiction is not hypocrisy, though that must have been present, nor racism in the modern sense, though confidence in the inherent superiority of the white race was more or less universal, nor even sheer wickedness. For this was a time that took righteousness very seriously, a time of intense Evangelical earnestness and Bible-based piety. People wished to act well.

The best explanation is simply that the standards of civilisation that America wished to identify with applied only to those within the American family, those who were already members of the Chosen People. Those outside were not covered by them. And there is an exact parallel here with the behaviour of that earlier Chosen People, the ancient Israelites, whose Ten Commandments were indeed a moral leap further forward than other cultures to date had achieved, but who saw them as applicable only to themselves. Canaanites and Indians were outside the covenant, not among the beneficiaries. Their lands could be taken, and if they resisted, they could be killed. Not being among the Chosen People, when viewed through the moral lenses of ancient Israelites or pious American Evangelicals, they became more or less invisible.

Simon Schama deals with the American veneration of empty wilderness in his *Landscape and Memory*.[9] It was epitomised in the 1852 discovery, and the extraordinary national reaction to it, of a remarkable area of forest in what became known as the Yosemite Valley in the foothills of the Sierra Nevada in Central California. (The name Yosemite appears to come from an Indian expression for the white race meaning 'some of these people are murderers'.) In the national imagination, it had to be empty, unspoilt by human hand. It contained groves of vast trees, some of the largest living things ever discovered anywhere on the planet, which were eventually to be catalogued as *sequoia gigantea*. Because of their great age – some were thousands of years old – they filled a gap in the American imagination and balanced the national fascination with novelty. Some poets claimed they were, indeed, the original 'indigenous Americans', thus conveniently displacing the Indians from that embarrassing title. They were, as one tree-struck observer remarked, the 'Hebrew Tree', as old as the Old Testament. The fancy grew that God had planted them long ago in anticipation of the arrival of white men who would appreciate them.

In fact the valley was not at all empty of human habitation, having been the home of the Ahwahneechee people since time immemorial.

The meadow floor of the valley, which dazzled white visitors with its lush vegetation, actually looked the way it did because this was managed forestry, land cleared by burning in order to allow cultivation. But visitors wanted it to be 'natural', not the product of the skill of the despised Indian. The Indians were quickly chased out of Yosemite valley, which was declared a state (later a national) park.

> Only the sense that Yosemite and the Big Trees constituted an over-powering revelation of the uniqueness of the American republic can explain Abraham Lincoln, in the midst of the Civil War, signing an unprecedented bill that on July 1, 1864, granted them to the State of California 'for the benefit of the people, for their resort and recreation, to hold them inalienable for all time.'
> ... it was the aura of heroic sanctity, the sense that the grove of Big Trees was some sort of American monument, a botanical pantheon, that moved Lincoln and the Congress to act as they did ... The sequoias seemed to vindicate the American national intuition that colossal grandeur spoke to the soul. It was precisely because the red columns of this sublimely American temple had not been constructed by the hand of man that they seemed providentially sighted, growing inexorably ever more awesome until God's new Chosen people could discover them in the heart of the Promised Land.[10]

What Americans were looking for, in other words, was some way of signifying that the land they inhabited was not just beautiful but actually *holy*. Katharine Lee Bates, who wrote the patriotic hymn 'America the Beautiful', described its creation thus: 'One day some of the other teachers and I decided to go on a trip to 14,000-foot Pikes Peak. We hired a prairie wagon. Near the top we had to leave the wagon and go the rest of the way on mules. I was very tired. But when I saw the view, I felt great joy. All the wonder of America seemed displayed there, with the sea-like expanse.'

> O beautiful for spacious skies,
> For amber waves of grain,
> For purple mountain majesties
> Above the fruited plain!
> America! America!
> God shed his grace on thee
> And crown thy good with brotherhood
> From sea to shining sea!

It was in the wild forest, above all, that Americans felt they could be in touch with their souls and relate to their God. The first generation of indigenous American artists often painted rural scenery, woodlands in particular, as natural temples or cathedrals – silent and still, numinous, transcendental, mystical. Poems inspired by such sentiments speak of a profound humility, almost unworthiness, when the poets contemplate how much God has done for them as Americans, not least by giving them such a wonderful wild country to inhabit. Walt Whitman expressed this American dream when he wrote in 'Song of Myself':

> Alone far in the wilds and mountains I hunt,
> Wandering amazed at my own lightness and glee,
> In the late afternoon choosing a safe spot to pass the night,
> Kindling a fire and broiling the fresh-kill'd game,
> Falling asleep on the gather'd leaves with my dog and my gun by my
>   side.

That God gave it to them, and that they did not have to steal it from someone else, is of course of the essence of such feelings. Manifest Destiny could not afford a conscience.

9

The Chosen Meet the Modern

In the spirit with which America went to war in 1941, it is possible to recognise some of the innocent and righteous zeal with which the British army was sent forth in 1914. In each case the ensuing conflict was beyond the shores of the nation and did not seem to threaten national survival, at least not foreseeably. Unlike Britain, the United States had not had its fateful 1916 summer on the Somme, and its shocked disillusionment with dreams of military glory and national destiny. The Britain of 1914 was still a great power, possibly still the greatest – industrious, wealthy, cultured, self-satisfied (at least, apart from what were generally called the 'lower orders'). The national response to the plight of Britain's ally, 'poor little Belgium' invaded by Germany at the start of the war, was that of a magnanimous powerful friend towards a weaker neighbour in trouble.

America in December 1941 had been brutally attacked; there was anger, not magnanimity, behind its declaration of war – though also a sense of relief that the time had come to help a friend in need, Great Britain. But American national self-confidence was undiminished, whereas, by that time, England's had been for ever overshadowed by the apparently senseless carnage on the Western front a generation earlier. England in 1940 had about it the sense of a biblical Faithful Remnant, precariously clinging to the True Faith when the rest of Europe, twenty-one miles from the coast of Kent, was under the Nazi jackboot. Such a sense of vulnerability has not been felt in America before or since, not even as a result of domestic or international terrorism.

Just as Field Marshal Douglas Haig could command his armies to attack and attack again, sure that God was on his side and eventual victory would be his whatever the cost; so American generals and admirals went after the Japanese with the same faith. One thing the story of the Chosen People tells us is that military historians have not paid enough attention to the prayers of the military commanders they write about, and their troops. Those prayers, and the ideological and theological framework in which they are said, would reveal a great deal about military motivation and morale.

Kevin Phillips's thesis in his book *The Cousins' Wars*[1] is that three conflicts which changed the direction of Western civilisation, the English Civil War (or wars, as some historians say), the American War of Independence (or Revolutionary War), and the American Civil War, were closely linked. Each represented a collision of two religious ideals or principles which existed among the Anglo-Saxon peoples of England and America. In each case it is possible to identify the winning side as the more religiously zealous side, the one most convinced God was with it, the more radically Protestant (indeed, more Calvinist) of the two. Cromwell's armies were well known for riding to battle singing psalms; so did the troops of Massachusetts fighting the British. No image of George Washington is more famous or more revealing than that of him at prayer during his army's winter ordeal at Valley Forge. *Gone with the Wind* perceptively begins with an analysis of the war between northern and southern states of America as a reopening of the feud between Roundhead and Cavalier, a rerun of Cromwell versus Charles I, Puritan versus Episcopalian, the common man versus the gentry, Yankee versus Reb.

In America that spirit still lives. The 'Battle Hymn of the Republic', written by the Northern abolitionist Julia Ward Howe in 1862 and sung to the tune she heard troops singing, 'John Brown's Body', became the anthem of the victorious Union armies in that war. But it was still sung with feeling by American GIs in the Second World War. There is no record of it capturing the American army's imagination in the Vietnam war, which may throw light on the disastrous outcome, but it has come back strongly into favour since the events of September 2001. It is a clear statement that God is uniquely on America's side because America is uniquely on the side of right. In the light of our advice to military historians, it deserves to be considered in full.

> Mine eyes have seen the glory of the coming of the Lord,
> He is trampling out the vintage where the grapes of wrath are
>   stored,
> He has loosed the fateful lightning of His terrible swift sword.
> His truth is marching on.
> Glory! Glory! Hallelujah!
> Glory! Glory! Hallelujah!
> Glory! Glory! Hallelujah!
> His truth is marching on.
>
> I have seen Him in the watch-fires of a hundred circling camps,
> They have builded Him an altar in the evening dews and damps,

I can read His righteous sentence by the dim and flaring lamps,
His day is marching on.
Glory! etc.

I have read a fiery gospel writ in burnish'd rows of steel,
'As ye deal with my contemners, So with you my grace shall deal;'
Let the Hero, born of woman, crush the serpent with his heel
Since God is marching on.
Glory! etc.

He has sounded forth the trumpet that shall never call retreat,
He is sifting out the hearts of men before His judgment-seat,
Oh, be swift, my soul, to answer Him! Be jubilant, my feet!
Our God is marching on.
Glory! etc.

In the beauty of the lilies Christ was born across the sea,
With a glory in His bosom that transfigures you and me:
As He died to make men holy, let us die to make men free,
While God is marching on.
Glory! etc.

This is a plainly a battle hymn for an elect nation, a Chosen People. It is at the opposite pole of national sentiment from the ironic, indeed cynical, post-1916 British army marching song of the First World War: 'I seen 'em, Hanging on the old barbed wire ...'[2] or its contemporary, the innocent but equally ironic 'We're 'ere, because we're 'ere, because we're 'ere, because we're 'ere' (sung to the tune of 'Auld Lang Syne'). The contrast between the two moods is an identifying mark of national personality that still applies in the modern age, and explains the quite different reactions of two apparently similar nations – both still, at their core, Anglo-Saxon and Protestant.

The difference is not simply that the British have a sense of irony and the Americans do not. The difference is not simply that the Americans still believe in their 'chosenness' and the English do not. It is possible, rather, that the English have started to believe in the chosenness of the Americans, though they would not admit to it in as many words. Certainly, the phrase 'the white man's burden', used in England ironically (of course), is now regarded as applicable to the United States; the phrase *Pax Americana* – meaning the American willingness to act as the world's policeman – has become a common cliché of the British newspaper columnist, with an implied nod in the direction of the old (superseded) phrase *Pax Britannica* (which in turn originated in the *Pax Romana* – peace enforced by the Roman legions – of classical times).

The 'Battle Hymn of the Republic', which to the English sounds like sheer Jingoism, in fact belongs within the same religious tradition as Harriet Beecher Stowe's stirring epilogue to *Uncle Tom's Cabin* which we have already discussed. She had declared America to be under judgment unless it righted the wrong of slavery; Howe shows the wrong actually being righted. It also offers a link or cross-over to another Chosen People tradition, also one that links the nineteenth century with the twenty-first, namely the American black consciousness of itself in biblical terms as a 'people in bondage' awaiting deliverance. The typology of Howe's hymn is not Moses as liberator, but the classical Christian typology of Christ as liberator (though in classical typology, Moses was a type prefiguring Christ). This is unusual; the typology is more Catholic than Protestant. And in the line 'In the beauty of the lilies Christ was born across the sea' there is a hint of Renaissance symbolism: the lily, the flower of purity and chastity, was a traditional mark of the Virgin Mary.

The thrust of the 'Battle Hymn' is about 'dying to make men free', which is a clear Christ-reference. It is not about those denied their freedom, taking it for themselves. Certainly there were black uprisings in the Civil War, and by its end a vast straggling tail of black refugees had attached itself to the rear of the triumphant Union army in the south. But the liberation of the black slaves was essentially an act of the white race, functioning as the 'redeemer nation' – in the place of Christ, therefore. But that other more Protestant typology, of the blacks as the Hebrews in bondage awaiting their Moses, was not far below the surface.

W. E. B. Du Bois, born within five years of the end of slavery, describes how as a young man he came across a Negro church service in the Deep South – not his native territory (he was originally from Massachusetts):

> The black and massive form of the preacher swayed and quivered as the words crowded to his lips and flew at us in singular eloquence. The people moaned and fluttered, and then the gaunt-cheeked brown woman beside me suddenly leaped straight into the air and shrieked like a lost soul, while round about came wail and groan and outcry, and a scene of human passion such as I had never conceived before. Those who have not thus witnessed the frenzy of a Negro revival in the untouched woods of the South can but dimly realise the religious feeling of the slave; as described, such scenes appear grotesque and funny, but as seen they are awful.[3]

Black slave Christianity grew out of pagan African religion with its chants, sacrifices, voodoo priests and witch women. The vibrant sense of the presence of unseen but powerful spirits was transferred to a primitive Christian context by the Great Awakenings stirred up by Evangelical preachers in the eighteenth and early nineteenth centuries (with the unseen powers now identified as the Holy Spirit driving the worshipper into a mad frenzy of supernatural joy). The Negro revival produced the Negro preacher, 'the most unique personality developed by the Negro on American soil', wrote Du Bois. He was 'a leader, a politician, an orator, a "boss", an intriguer, an idealist'. Secular black leaders, of which Du Bois was himself a type, were not always comfortable with this tradition of minister as leader – as was still the case in the 1950s, at the start of the civil rights movement, when there was some vying for supremacy between black ministers like Martin Luther King and secular politicians connected with Du Bois's own NAACP.

Du Bois records how slaves used to sing:

> Children, we shall be free
> When the Lord shall appear!

But he was mistaken to dismiss this as mere millennialism – deliverance postponed to the end of time, in human terms more or less for ever. What he did not recognise was the power of Protestant typology to turn Bible stories into present reality, to make Christianity a force for real liberation, not pious submission. The biography of the escaped slave Harriet Tubman, *Harriet, The Moses of Her People*, by her contemporary and friend Sarah Bradford, describes how she began to relate her slave condition to the message she had heard preached in church:

> Already in her mind her people were the Israelites in the land of Egypt, while far away, somewhere in the north, was the land of Canaan; but had she as yet any prevision that she was to be the Moses who was to be their leader, through clouds of darkness and fear, and fires and tribulations to that Promised Land? This she never said.[4]

She decided to flee, with her brothers; but as conversation among slaves was regarded by the overseers with suspicion, she communicated by song, slightly adapting well-known words to say what she intended. To the unsuspecting ear these were still innocent millennial dreams, ultimate freedom 'when the Lord shall appear'. So Harriet Tubman, in the dialect attributed to her by Bradford, could sing out loudly, without fear of detection, her coded message – 'The time has come.'

> When dat ar ole chariot comes,
> I'm gwine to lebe you,
> I'm boun' for de Promised Land,
> Frien's, I'm gwine to lebe you.

> I'm sorry frien's to lebe you,
> Farewell! oh, farewell!
> But I'll meet you in de mornin',
> Farewell! oh, farewell!
>
> I'll meet you in de mornin',
> When you reach de Promised Land;
> On de oder side of Jordan,
> For I'm boun for de Promised Land.

They remembered it long after she had gone. She got clear that night, and eventually reached sanctuary where she could not be recaptured and returned. At first this meant New York – and the Jordan of her song would have been the Ohio River which divided Kentucky (slave state) from Ohio or Illinois (free). In time she became organiser of one of the Underground Railroads (as they called them) which spirited slaves to safety along that route. Her biographer credits her with numerous successful missions and hundreds of individual slaves led to freedom, always in conditions of greatest danger. Had she been captured she would have been killed, presumably by hanging or flogging. After the 1850 Fugitive Slave Act allowed escaped slaves to be returned even from free states, there was no security to be had short of Canada – and the mythical 'Jordan' to be crossed to freedom became the Niagara River which separated the United States from British soil. Bradford gives a moving description of Tubman's vision of Queen Victoria, whom she imagined standing like a regal mother on the Canadian side of the river to welcome the escaping slaves. To the slaves in the South, Canada was a symbol or a concept as much as a place, a Promised Land. Jordan was the frontier of biblical Canaan, the land promised by God to the Israelites after their escape from Egypt under Moses and their forty years wandering in the wilderness of Sinai: 'Until I shall pass over Jordan into the land which the Lord our God giveth us' (Deuteronomy 2:29).

On their way north they sang the spiritual 'Oh Go down, Moses', which had been banned in the south:

> Oh go down Moses,
> Way down into Egypt's land,
> Tell old Pharaoh
> Let my people go.
>
> Oh Pharaoh said he would go cross,
> Let my people go,
> And don't get lost in de wilderness
> Let my people go.

You may hinder me here, but you can't up dere,
Let my people go
He sits in de hebben and answers prayer
Let my people go!

The lifetime of Du Bois, 1868–1963, overlapped both Harriet Tubman (1820–1913) and Martin Luther King Jnr (1929–68). King was the son of a minister, and would have been immersed from childhood in this kind of Exodus typology. Keith D. Miller in *The Voice of Deliverance* writes:

> King learned about slave religion from his father, a folk preacher, and adopted its vision of deliverance as the foundation of his thoughts and oratory... Over long decades slaves exercised their religion under extremely difficult circumstances. Laws usually prohibited them from learning to read and write, leaving most unable to read the Bible. Sermons thus served not only as an important means of religious instruction but, for many blacks, the only means of instruction apart from music. Like their fellow slaves, most preachers had no recourse but to imbibe religion from other preachers – not from the Bible or other texts.[5]

This had one remarkable result: every preacher would have a repertoire of sermons in his memory from which he could draw or adapt as need arose; and these sermons were often compounded of sermons he had himself heard preached by others. So his stock of sermons was a kind of accumulation of the wisdom of the people. This would add to his authority, even among those who recognised the sources he had borrowed from. It was not customary to give references, as if a sermon was an academic tract with footnotes, but nor was this practice of unattributed borrowing regarded as unfair plagiarism. It meant a particularly effective metaphor or image – or biblical quotation – could be recycled as necessary. One might liken this to the way in which a papal encyclical will be peppered with quotations from other encyclicals from previous popes. The purpose is to show the continuity of the papal teaching tradition – just as a black preacher, by using and adapting the words of preachers before him, was showing the continuity of a preaching tradition of which he was the guardian and spokesman.

The *double entendre* of Harriet Tubman's 'coded' farewell to her fellow slaves in the song quoted previously actually contains a profound theological message. Slave religion was both this-worldly and other-worldly: it was both about liberation from sin and liberation from physical captivity (indeed, just as Old Testament religion had been). Words or phrases which could apply to either meaning were common, and the play of ideas was appreciated and enjoyed. A Christian slave-owner would find it difficult to object to Christian slaves singing about Moses delivering the Hebrews out of Egypt, even if he knew they were also singing about walking out on him.

Individuals would rejoice in, and rapturously recount to the enthusiasm of the congregation, their personal experience of conversion. 'Slave preachers sometimes exulted in the rewards of the afterlife,' says Miller.

> They also offered hope for this life. One clear manifestation of slaves' this-worldly religion was an intense and widespread identification with Old Testament figures. Slaves sympathised profoundly with the struggles of Mary, Daniel, Noah, Ezekiel, Joshua, Jonah and Moses – most of whom participated in social upheavals and each of whom figures prominently in spirituals. Along with Jesus, the Old Testament heroes favoured by slaves faced terrible hardship and difficult odds before achieving resplendent victories. Slaves saw these hardships as parallel to their own oppression and viewed Biblical success stories as a harbinger of their own eventual Biblical-style liberation . . .
>
> Expressing a particular fascination with Moses, African Americans pervasively identified with the Chosen People held captive in Egypt – an identification evident in many spirituals about Moses, the Pharaoh, the Red Sea, the wilderness and/or Promised Land . . . In 1808 the eminent African American preacher Absalom Jones interpreted a national law banning the slave trade as an act of providence equivalent to the Exodus. Just as God 'came down to deliver' the Israelites from the Egyptians, Jones declared, he 'came down into the British Parliament' when it outlawed slave ships and 'came down into the Congress of the United States' when it approved a comparable ban.[6]

Even before the end of slavery, according to Miller's evidence, mainly illiterate black preachers had perfected a full-blown Protestant typology that would have done credit to a Puritan preacher in Cromwell's New Model Army, two hundred years earlier. How this transmission of ideas actually took place we shall probably never know, as the process would have been oral and largely unrecorded. The Second Great Awakening made deep inroads into the black slave population in the Deep South from the 1790s onwards. Slaves could neither read nor write but their culture was already a culture of song and chant, and the expression of religious feeling in song came naturally to it.

The tradition was largely carried forward by Negro Spirituals. One of the earliest known references to Protestant typology being applied to black slavery is in a collection of such spirituals published by Methodist Richard Allen, himself a black preacher and later a bishop, in 1801. Excluded from his local (white) Methodist church, he founded what became the African Methodist Episcopalian Church. But this typological 'Exodus paradigm' for black slavery was apparently unknown to the founder of Methodism, John Wesley, though he was an early English opponent of slavery. So Protestant typology may have been introduced into black Christianity from the Baptist tradition with its roots in Calvinism, rather than from the Methodist side.

The accuracy of this transplant of typology from white Protestantism to black even extended to the concept of 'sacred time' – which would be known theologically as salvation history – by which past events are made contemporary. Miller describes how black preachers adopted these principles:

> Typology can also apply to the present, for Christians may treat biblical figures and events as types recurring throughout human existence, up to the present moment. Thus, typology patterns history according to knowable and repeatable forms of experience. It does not merely present a system of symbols, for believers view typological events as literally true. Nor does typology entail analogy, for, unlike analogy, typology introduces and sustains an entire and coherent world-view, fitting human experience into a system of interpretation both sturdy and flexible.[7]

Typology, he says, enables speakers to create extremely powerful arguments because it serves not only as a system of persuasion but as a system of knowledge provided by God. 'Typology turns the universe into a clean, well-lighted place where people can recognise and understand themselves.' Miller does not quite make the connection that might have been expected between personal liberation from sin and communal liberation from oppression, probably because he has only one model of typology – that of the black Protestant preacher – before him. While he notes the blurring of the line between the two forms of liberation, spiritual and political, he does not perceive that the classic Protestant typology of a Chosen People implies a bargain or covenant, one side of which is that the people have to be worthy of their God, and the other, that God will, in recognition of this obedience, safeguard, assist and liberate them. Being converted, in the individual spiritual sense, was therefore a necessary condition before God would engage himself to fulfil his side of the bargain. In reverse, if the Chosen People slid back into sin and idolatry, God would chastise them to recall them to the true path. Chastisement could include renewed captivity, just as the Israelites were taken into exile in Babylon some hundreds of years after their liberation from Egypt. But they returned to the worship of the true God, earned their freedom (through the providential intervention of Cyrus the Great) and returned to Zion. As a scheme of social justice, this is at odds with the modern secular view that possession of a human right does not depend on good behaviour (though for instance in the case of a prison sentence, the modern view does envisage the loss of a human right as a result of bad behaviour).

The role of Divine Providence in this black typological system is clear. What is less clear is who exactly fulfils the other roles in the typological drama of black salvation/liberation – who are the Canaanites, for instance, and where is the Promised Land? What is the relationship between this black Chosen People and its predecessor claimants to the title, especially the white Chosen People who originated from the early Puritan settlements in New England? Have they been superseded, with all the supersessionist implications discussed in chapter three? And are the new Chosen People to be defined racially (like the Chosen People of the Old Testament) or can anybody join?

The black preacher's answer may have to be that the drama has only unfolded so far, and the Chosen People are still on their post-captivity journey through the wilderness, not yet having espied where they are headed. The questions above may have answers, but they have not yet been arrived at. It is more likely that the typology has started to break down and become a mere metaphor, losing the revelatory quality that Miller refers to; and that the Promised Land has been spiritualised into an emotional, political or economic condition – enfranchisement, equality, the end of racial prejudice, equal opportunity, and all the other goals of the secular civil rights movement. For instance fifty years after the Emancipation Proclamation, the black preacher L. J. Coppin declared that they had reached the borders of the Promised Land 'and the Canaan of our citizenship is just before us'. Hence those who opposed giving blacks equal citizenship were the Canaanites who resisted the entry of the Chosen People.

That is fine imagery, but the significance of the Canaanites in the Old Testament is primarily that they were idolatrous, worshipping false gods and seducing the Israelites to do likewise. They wanted the Israelites to become like them. In Coppin's model, the Canaanites (white supremacists, and not just extremists but majority white opinion at the time he was speaking) are specifically refusing to let the black people become like them – that is to say, refusing to let them believe in the creeds, and worship the gods, of American white society (democracy, equality, capitalism, materialism, whatever else they may be) rather than insisting that they do so. This is a curious reversal.

White theologians having abandoned Protestant typology as a subject worthy of serious theological reflection some time in the nineteenth century, black theologians are handicapped if they wish to subject their own tradition to a degree of rigorous interrogation. But they are not entirely without allies: the last thirty years has seen the development of several modern schools of 'Exodus theology', most notably the so-called Theology of Liberation among Roman Catholics in Latin America. It is much less literal, however, in that it does not argue directly from specific biblical events and characters to modern day events and characters. There are reasons to think, from his education and the intellectual circles he moved in, that Martin Luther King was aware of this, even if he was assassinated just as liberation theology was beginning to attract intellectual interest – and ferocious attack – in the wider world.

King assumed a religious shape to the civil rights movement that was more apparent inside the black community than from the outside. Even now, the white treatment of civil rights in popular culture – Hollywood films such as the 1988 blockbuster *Mississippi Burning*, for instance – tends to sentimentalise black religion as a naïve source of comfort, not as the cutting edge of black protest. Nor does popular culture – here Alan Parker's film is again guilty – give credit to King's creed of non-violence and the redemptive power of undeserved suffering. His chosen method of political activism was carefully modelled on Mahatma Gandhi, but directly inspired by New Testament teaching such as Jesus's Sermon on the Mount. Even now, the true implication of this has not yet been properly appreciated. As a society that respects violence and those who use it, non-violence does not seem to appeal to the American temperament. Hence non-violence, however successfully used, becomes invisible and almost forgotten.

King worked within the already well-established doctrine that blacks were a 'people' and not just a collection of individuals with similar origins and skin colour. And 'people' was used typologically to mean 'We are the modern Israelites, the People of God, His Chosen ones.' (This raises the question whether the word 'black' should be capitalised, and indeed whether, in the name of consistency, the word 'white' should be, too. In a text such as this chapter there are no entirely satisfactory answers to such questions.) 'People' is not necessarily equivalent to a race in a narrow genetic sense, not least because many of those accepted as members of it may in fact be only half or a quarter 'pure' black in parentage or grandparentage. It comes closer to the idea of 'nation' as used by Benedict Anderson in his theory of 'imagined communities'[8] – as a 'deep, horizontal comradeship' which defines 'people like us' and separates them from 'people not like us'.

In the case of the black people – 'black community' or 'African-American community' would be the contemporary expression – the definition of who the 'we' are has historically had quite a lot to do with who 'they' say 'we' are. Blacks have accepted as black those whom the white community has said were black, which in American race relations, at least in the past, has meant those (of mixed racial ancestry, perhaps) who were rejected because they were not white enough. The Anglo-Saxon white 'imagined community' imagined itself as white-skinned, or at least did so since Emancipation. Before that, under the slavery codes the status of slave or free in the case of inter-racial parentage was determined by the status of the mother. (It is no coincidence that this matches the definition of a Jew contained in the Oral Torah of the Halakhah, or ancient Jewish law.) At least in the eighteenth century, the tradition in England itself – where slavery was illegal – was different: one could well be accepted as a black (or mixed-race) English gentleman if one had the right social credentials.

Under slavery, if a white woman had a mixed-race child by a black man, the child would not be a slave; vice versa, and it would be. As far as appearance went, however, it would not be possible to tell the two cases apart, so even a free mixed-race person, with a white mother, would have some difficulty avoiding being taken for a slave. It is perhaps not surprising that such a person's membership of the white community was regarded as somewhat tentative. Any black or mixed-race person was treated as a slave unless he or she could prove to the contrary. After the slave codes were abolished, when segregation was formalised under the Jim Crow system, black parentage on either side of a mixed-race combination determined the individual's status as legally black. There is no logic to it, as someone half and half could theoretically be regarded as a member of either group or both. But the rule underlines a perception of blackness as something that has tainted, contaminated or polluted whiteness: the Nazis had a similar approach to people of mixed Jewish and Aryan parentage. One Jewish grandparent was enough to deprive someone of the status of 'pure' Aryan.

So membership of the black community was extended to all those excluded from the white community. Again, taking into account Anderson's definition of an 'imagined community', the 'deep horizontal comradeship' he speaks of here refers to a shared experience of racial exclusion and prejudice. This is recognisably Christian in a profound way, and suggests a sophisticated grasp of solidarity as a moral principle (and some careful meditation on, for instance, the parable of the Good Samaritan). It does not mean that the white community has been allowed to define the black community by its policy of exclusion; it means the black community has decided for itself to adopt 'shared racial suffering' as the identifying mark of those with whom it chooses to feel 'deep horizontal comradeship'.

What reinforced this sense of a separate black Chosen People was the failure of white Protestants, even liberal Social Gospellers (the American equivalent of English Christian Socialists), to identify and protest at increasing evidence of racial segregation and bigotry in the post-Civil War South. There was insufficient pan-Protestant solidarity to break down the walls of religious separation which had already divided the major denominations (except Episcopalian and Roman Catholic) into distinct black and white branches of the same churches. In any event, black Protestantism was not particularly liberal, neither theologically nor ethically; black Protestantism would have seemed distastefully Fundamentalist to a mainstream white theologian in an Ivy League college. Hence the crossing of racial boundaries to reach out to white liberal sentiment was not easy. 'Race never emerged as a dominant religious issue for whites prior to the [1955] Montgomery bus boycott,' writes Miller. It was that event which brought Martin Luther King to international fame.

King regarded the Social Gospel as putting back the essential missing ingredient in white Protestant individualism, condemning as spiritually moribund any 'religion that deals with the souls of men and is not concerned with the slums that damn them . . .' But his brand of black Protestantism did not need a Social Gospel to remind it of that, and his public endorsement of the Social Gospel was designed to make common cause with liberal white Protestantism rather than a significant addition to his own faith. To put it another way, black Protestantism had its own Social Gospel, long before white American theologians like Walter Rauschenbusch (author of *Christianising the Social Order* in 1912) coined the term. The preaching of social justice would have marked every black sermon King ever heard, for that had been the normal black interpretation of the Old Testament since slavery days. It was the direct consequence of regarding blacks typologically as a biblical people – as the ancient Israelites escaping from Egyptian bondage.

King's problem was not that of having to convince black Christians that racial segregation was contrary to the Word of God. His problem was with white Christianity, especially the majority opinion in United States Protestantism (though more among grass roots than among its leaders) that wished not just for a 'wall of separation' between church and state (to recycle Jefferson's phrase) but a wall of separation, built even higher, between religion and politics. There was no sanction for such a wall in the Bible – 'render therefore unto Caesar the things that are Caesar's and unto God the things that are God's' of Matthew 22:21 comes nowhere near meeting the case. But the Calvinism of the New England pioneers, by now spread widely if thinly over the Deep South, did pass on the message that if prosperity was a mark of God's approval, then failure, destitution, ignorance and social inferiority, were marks of God's disapproval. A useful pseudo-scientific piece of reinforcement was supplied by the spurious theories of the Social Darwinists, who believed that the pecking order in American society – having abolished aristocracy and inherited class privilege – was a reflection of the principle of the survival of the fittest. Those who survived least well were thus the unfittest, and the low economic status of blacks revealed them to be in that category.

All this seemed to be reinforced by the curse on Ham's descendants – descended from his aptly named son Canaan – pronounced in Genesis 9:25, which condemned them all to perpetual servitude. But above all, Calvinism had not entirely shed the predestinationism that defined the 'elect' as those already known to God, the closed group, the white English tribe, the visible Chosen People who were the first Anglo-Saxon Protestants. John Bale's and John Foxe's historical theories about the original pure Christians being the English,[9] whose faith was planted within living memory of Christ himself by Joseph of Arimathea, had left at least a rumour that those who could claim good Anglo-Saxon blood were especially favoured by God. And that rumour had been expanded in the Deep South into the core ideology of the Ku Klux Klan.

The extreme version of such mythological speculation was the so-called 'British Israelite' movement, which first attracted attention in the nineteenth century with its claim that the British were the actual (genetic) descendants of the mythical 'ten lost tribes' of Israel, who disappeared from biblical history after the Northern Kingdom was captured by the Assyrians. Thus the Stone of Scone, used in British coronations, was said to have originated with King David and carried to Scotland for safe keeping. And at some point Jesus himself visited the lost tribes. This invention – the term 'myth' does it too much credit – appears to lie behind William Blake's famous question in the hymn 'Jerusalem':

> And did those feet in ancient time
> Walk upon England's mountains green?
> And was the Holy Lamb of God
> On England's pleasant pastures seen?

The British Israelite claim was popular for a time as part of the patriotic basis for the British Empire. Among those who disapproved of it were those who felt it diminished the force of the more common, and semi-official, view that the British were the spiritual (but not literal) descendants of the Hebrew people. There are American far-right groups which profess a home-grown version of the original British-Israelite belief, mixing it with Nazi Aryan mythology; they are, needless to say, fascist. A very different version appears in the belief system of the Church of Jesus Christ of Latter-day Saints (Mormons).

The neo-Calvinist 'Chosen People' idea of a white American covenant with God had certain consequences. It defined the Promised Land – the North American subcontinent – and it also defined who white Protestant America's enemies were. They were either the classic supersessionist categories, British, Jews and Catholics – whom God had repudiated – or the classic Canaanite categories, native Americans and blacks – whom God had cursed and labelled inferior. In each case Protestant typology made clear how they could be treated. Catholics, Jews and blacks deserved no better handling than the ancient Chosen People's enemies had received under Moses, Joshua, Gideon and the rest. An enemy of the white Protestant tribe was an enemy of God: in defence of the white tribe, it was ultimately permissible to kill. This typology – which could claim to be rigidly biblical – had taken off in the South after the civil war, having supplanted the old ideology of class, breeding, hierarchy and *noblesse oblige* that had 'gone with the wind' once Sherman had marched through Georgia destroying all he met.

By the 1950s, therefore, there were two mature but rival and utterly incompatible assumptions of 'Chosen People' status in the South, each claiming the Bible as its source and each with its own biblical typology. And they were opposed, with daggers drawn, as the civil rights movement started to demand the completion of the post-Civil War agenda spelled out by Lincoln in his Gettysburg Address. This religious depiction of the race relations crisis in America in the 1950s and 1960s is not the secular or indeed Marxist one usually favoured by commentators, but it undoubtedly has greater power to explain or illuminate it. It also has important implications for British race relations.

If the most important sermon preached in America in the eighteenth century was 'Sinners in the Hands of an Angry God' by Jonathan Edwards (discussed in chapter four), the most important American sermon preached in the twentieth was surely 'I Have a Dream' by Martin Luther King, delivered before a rally of 200,000 people in Washington in August 1963. It is a beautifully composed piece of oratory, at least the match in craftsmanship of any speech by Winston Churchill (widely recognised as the greatest English language orator of the twentieth century), and it is constructed by someone with a fine ear for the balance of every phrase and the sound of every syllable. That is what a lifetime of black preaching had taught him, plus a rare talent of his own.

'I Have a Dream' begins by reminding his audience – but primarily the unseen audience that was white America – of its promises to black America. He refers to and quotes tellingly from the Declaration of Independence, the Gettysburg Address and the Emancipation Proclamation. At first it sounds largely secular, though with a strong moral focus. The speech only begins to become a sermon half way through, though

King has already adopted a preacher's way of presenting his case, such as the use of repeated rolling phrases:

> There are those who are asking the devotees of civil rights, 'When will you be satisfied?' We can never be satisfied as long as the Negro is the victim of the unspeakable horrors of police brutality. We can never be satisfied as long as our bodies, heavy with the fatigue of travel, cannot gain lodging in the motels of the highways and the hotels of the cities. We cannot be satisfied as long as the Negro's basic mobility is from a smaller ghetto to a larger one. We can never be satisfied as long as our children are stripped of their selfhood and robbed of their dignity by signs stating 'for whites only'. We cannot be satisfied as long as a Negro in Mississippi cannot vote and a Negro in New York believes he has nothing for which to vote. No, no, we are not satisfied and we will not be satisfied until 'justice rolls down like waters and righteousness like a mighty stream'.

. . . which is when the address becomes a sermon, for those are the words of the prophet Amos. 'But let judgment run down as waters, and righteousness as a mighty stream' (Amos 5:24). (The Authorised Version regularly uses 'judgment' where more modern translators use 'justice'.) When he reaches the most famous passage of all, the repetitive phrase is that of his title, 'I Have a Dream'. But he has a preacher's surprise at the end. Who exactly is the dreamer?

> I say to you today, my friends, so even though we face the difficulties of today and tomorrow, I still have a dream. It is a dream deeply rooted in the American dream.
>
> I have a dream that one day this nation will rise up and live out the true meaning of its creed: 'We hold these truths to be self-evident, that all men are created equal.'
>
> I have a dream that one day on the red hills of Georgia, the sons of former slaves and the sons of former slave owners will be able to sit down together at the table of brotherhood.
>
> I have a dream that one day even the state of Mississippi, a state sweltering with the heat of injustice, sweltering with the heat of oppression, will be transformed into an oasis of freedom and justice.
>
> I have a dream that my four little children will one day live in a nation where they will not be judged by the colour of their skin but by the content of their character. I have a dream today.
>
> I have a dream that one day down in Alabama, with its vicious racists, with its governor having his lips dripping with the words of 'interposition' and 'nullification', one day right there in Alabama little black boys and black girls will be able to join hands with little white boys and white girls as sisters and brothers. I have a dream today.

I have a dream that one day 'every valley shall be exalted, and every hill and mountain shall be made low; the rough places will be made plain, and the crooked places will be made straight; and the glory of the Lord shall be revealed, and all flesh shall see it together'.

And that is the vision not of M. L. King Jnr but of the prophet Isaiah. His audience would have recognised it at once. It is a valuable contribution to understanding how his words would have been heard to provide the wider scriptural context. This also answers the question – who is doing the dreaming? It is King; but he is dreaming Isaiah's dream; and Isaiah is repeating the Word of the Lord. It is, in short, God's dream. Isaiah 40:1–5 reads in full:

> Comfort ye, comfort ye my people, saith your God. Speak ye comfortably to Jerusalem, and cry unto her, that her warfare is accomplished, that her iniquity is pardoned: for she hath received of the Lord's hand double for all her sins. The voice of him that crieth in the wilderness, Prepare ye the way of the Lord, make straight in the desert a highway for our God. Every valley shall be exalted, and every mountain and hill shall be made low: and the crooked shall be made straight, and the rough places plain: And the glory of the Lord shall be revealed, and all flesh shall see it together: for the mouth of the Lord hath spoken it.

It is not just the announcement of imminent justice. This passage, like others in Isaiah, looks forward to a new messianic age. These words (as his hearers would know) are quoted again in the Bible, by John the Baptist, who is predicting the imminent coming of the Christ and demanding that the people prepare for it by repentance:

> ... the word of God came unto John the son of Zacharias in the wilderness. And he came into all the country about Jordan, preaching the baptism of repentance for the remission of sins; As it is written in the book of the words of Isaiah the prophet, saying, The voice of one crying in the wilderness, Prepare ye the way of the Lord, make his paths straight. Every valley shall be filled, and every mountain and hill shall be brought low; and the crooked shall be made straight, and the rough ways shall be made smooth; And all flesh shall see the salvation of God. (Luke 3:2–6)

Then a third biblical prophet made his appearance: Daniel. Keith Miller's exposition of the text needs no further comment:

> Following the 'I have a dream' litany, King again evoked biblical eschatology by reworking imagery from the prophet Daniel. 'With this faith we will be able to hew out of the mountain of despair a stone of

hope.' Interpreting a famous dream of king Nebuchadnezzar, Daniel describes a stone that smashes a figure made of precious metals, iron and clay. Hewn from a mountain by God, the stone symbolises God's ideal kingdom that destroys all petty earthly kingdoms and itself endures forever. In King's speech, however, human beings extract the stone from the mountain without waiting passively for God to create a new kingdom entirely by himself. Represented by the stone from the mountain, the arrival of Daniel's ideal kingdom coincides with the arrival of Isaiah's realm of valleys uplifted and mountains levelled. King expertly manipulated the mountain symbols from Daniel and Isaiah as he created the image of a perfected community.[10] [The story is told in Daniel 2.]

This is, in other words, the old dream of Protestant Millenarianism: the vision of a perfect world in which Christ reigns for a thousand years. And, as Protestant typology makes clear time and again, it is the role of the Chosen People to bring it in. They are the midwives of the Second Coming, by their work for justice.

And it is America, still, that is the Promised Land where this will all take place: King's salvation faith is in the end the same American faith as all his predecessors, black or white. Any doubts are removed by his peroration, when the Isaiah theme of mountains transfigured becomes the American dream itself, a fusion of Old Testament prophecy and the American national anthem:

This will be the day when all of God's children will be able to sing with new meaning:

> My country tis of thee
> Sweet land of liberty
> Of thee I sing.
> Land where my fathers died,
> Land of the Pilgrims' pride,
> From every mountainside
> Let freedom ring.

So let freedom ring from the prodigious hilltops of New Hampshire,
Let freedom ring from the mighty mountains of New York,
Let freedom ring from the heightening Alleghenies of Pennsylvania,
Let freedom ring from the snowcapped Rockies of Colorado,
Let freedom ring from the curvaceous slopes of California,
But not only that: let freedom ring from Stone Mountain of Georgia,
Let freedom ring from Lookout Mountain of Tennessee,
Let freedom ring from every hill and molehill in Mississippi,
From every mountainside, let freedom ring.

And then he finally returns to his roots as a black preacher, to 'proclaim the acceptable year of the Lord' and summon the millennium:

> And when this happens, when we allow freedom to ring, when we let it ring from every village and every hamlet, from every state and every city, we will be able to speed up that day when all of God's children, black men and white men, Jews and Gentiles, Protestants and Catholics, will be able to join hands and sing in the words of the old Negro spiritual: Free at last! Free at last! Thank God Almighty, we are free at last!

For that, as every black Christian who heard it would have known, is the song of the End of Time. Thus has Martin Luther King produced in his sermon not only a stirring and noble call to action to right racial wrongs; he has provided a renewed and completed 'theology of America' that is directly in line with a long tradition of apocalyptic Protestant preaching, as much white as black. Black America is to be the redeemer nation, a 'light unto the Gentiles': white America the nation redeemed. Its redemption heralds the end-time, the onset of the kingdom of Christ on earth. It would have been a remarkable synthesis even had it been the only thing he ever did.

In the theory of biblical typology, it was as a people – akin to the Israelite people in the Old Testament – that black people were persecuted, and as a people therefore that they would be liberated (from 'bondage in Egypt' etc.), with God's help but by their own efforts. The American civil rights movement provided a model which was taken up by other campaigners, who saw similarities between themselves and their grievances and the grievances of black people.

The solidarity and sense of empowerment that the notion of 'peopleness' gave to the black civil rights struggle was regarded as valid for homosexuals, the disabled, the elderly, women and so on, and gave rise to such concepts as 'the gay community' and 'the disabled community'. Hostility to this community was regarded as akin to the racial hostility that the black community was subjected to. Political correctness began as the language of anti-racism, and was applied by analogy to these disparate peoples who also saw themselves as resisting group oppression. In the theory, the source of the oppression was the same in the case of homosexuals, the disabled, women etc. as it was for blacks. It was the body of conservative White Anglo-Saxon Protestants (WASPs) whose most virulent manifestation had been in white male working class culture in the Deep South, and whose most extreme symbol had been the Ku Klux Klan. For they too were a 'people' in the biblical sense, albeit a majority one.

Most of these new 'oppressed communities' – the inverted commas are to signify that they are imagined communities in the Benedict Anderson sense, not that the injustice was not real – developed their philosophies apart from the religious tradition which had been the basis of the original oppressed community, black Protestantism. But they kept some similarities. They had to seize their freedom, not be given it (as the Hebrews had seized their freedom from the ancient Egyptians); they had a sense of journeying, at least metaphorically, towards a promised land; they had to be 'better than their enemies' otherwise they would not deserve their freedom; they had to operate in hostile territory (among Canaanites). They developed a group consciousness and a group way of thinking, even a group language. Though they were mainly secular, some of their more religious-minded campaigners even developed theological systems which went back to biblical typology in order to adapt the Exodus mythology for their own purposes. It is no coincidence that observers of politically correct thought-systems have occasionally likened these systems to religious movements, with their own codes of orthodoxy and the occasional witch-hunt or heresy hunt for deviant doers or thinkers.

In America political correctness became a powerful force in academic and literary circles. In Britain it became for a while the official ideology of professional social workers, under the sponsorship of the Central Council for Training and Education in Social Work. Its technical name was Anti-Oppressive Practice. It received its inevitable come-uppance in 1999 when Terry Philpot, editor of *Community Care,* the magazine read by the social work profession in Britain, edited a collection of articles[11] by experts pointing out how much harm was being done by trying to fit the world and all its diverse problems into one theoretical strait-jacket. More than one of his contributors likened the 'politically correct' mindset to Puritanism. This inadvertently draws attention to the fact that the Puritans who fled to New England also felt themselves to be an oppressed people fleeing from persecution, and worked out their consciousness of this experience in biblical terms. They were the archetypal Oppressed Community. If America's ideological origins as a haven from persecution go back to the Puritans, then political correctness is bred into its very soul.

The theoretical conviction of British social workers that non-white people automatically constitute a single social and political community, defined by its racial oppression, could not survive contact with the reality – that Asians in Britain do not regard themselves as black or as one community, and usually prefer either to be defined by their national origins or religion, or simply as 'British Asian'; that black people of Caribbean origin in Britain do not naturally have a shared group identity, and do not easily integrate with black people from Africa (an increasingly significant proportion of the whole); and finally that, at least in major metropolitan centres, racial intermarriage and interbreeding between blacks and whites is approaching the point where it is impossible to define who belongs to what community. As Darcus Howe, who emigrated to Britain from the West Indies in the 1950s, wrote in *The Observer*: 'This ease of presence which characterises the new black and Asian population means we are less and less given to the solidarity of skin.'[12]

Several times Martin Luther King linked the campaign for American civil rights with the international anti-colonial movement. There were indeed points of similarity. Black people in Africa did not have equal rights with whites. Nowhere was this more true than at the southern end of the continent. By the 1960s the (white) Afrikaner majority in South Africa – blacks had no vote – had installed the world's only fully racist state, where discrimination was more deeply enshrined even than under the Jim Crow laws in the southern United States. The Afrikaners based themselves on their Calvinist reading of the Bible, specifically the concept of a white 'Chosen People' occupying, under a divine covenant, a Promised Land, with native Africans cast as the Canaanites. In their Great Trek of the 1830s, they had, like the ancient Israelites, escaped from the 'Pharaoh' (who appears in this drama in the unlikely guise of Harriet Tubman's hero Queen Victoria). Such beliefs were close to the political theology of grass-roots white Protestantism that Martin Luther King was combating in his own land. Although the Boers did not practise slavery in American terms, they also believed 'Canaanites' were put there by God to be ruled, and to be turned into workers and servants.

It was the Afrikaner 'Chosen People' ideology, derived from the Calvinism of the Dutch Reformed Church, that lay at the foundations of the apartheid system. But it was, ironically, from within the Calvinist Chosen People *laager* (originally, a ring of wagons encircled protectively for the night) that apartheid began to fall apart. And the reason was theological. It was not possible, in the light of such texts as Acts 10:34–5, to exclude blacks from conversion to Christianity if they sincerely sought it 'with a pure heart': 'Then Peter opened his mouth, and said, Of a truth I perceive that God is no respecter of persons: But in every nation he that feareth him, and worketh righteousness, is accepted with him.'

So for a long time the Dutch Reformed Church in South Africa had sought to accept Africans, 'Cape coloureds' (mixed race), and other non-Afrikaner groups as Christians by founding single-race daughter churches into which they could be admitted. But this very concession had built into Afrikaner Calvinism a profound anomaly. How could there be two or more 'Chosen People' in the same place? Afrikaner biblical scholars went back to the original texts on which they had based the apartheid theory, and saw that other interpretations – including that which had led to the long-standing repudiation of apartheid by their Dutch Reformed mother church in Holland – were possible. While the popular perception, especially in the English-speaking world, was that apartheid had been undermined by international sanctions, the militancy of the ANC, the heroism of Nelson Mandela and the solidarity of international black civil rights and anti-colonial movements, the truth is that the leaders of the Afrikaner people were already losing confidence in it as the will of God. When Mandela offered the Afrikaner leadership a way out, they took it.

The employment of blacks under inferior conditions to whites, and the denial of most of their political rights, had been a feature of European colonialism throughout Africa and Asia, and the situation in South Africa, though extreme, was by no means unique. But unlike the colonies, that country was independent, and therefore isolated. It had not been through what the rest of the world had been through. The rest of the world had had a severe fright, which had shaken up its thinking especially over relations between peoples and races. The defeat of the Nazi 'master-race' in the Second World War had for ever discredited the idea that one branch of the human race was innately superior to any other. Hitler's troops had been out-fought by the British and the Americans; but their worst defeat was at the hands of the Red Army, consisting almost wholly of Slavs, who, in Nazi racial theory, ranked well below the Aryans and should have been easily beaten. In Fascist ideology, fighting spirit was one of the chief indicators of racial prowess. Meanwhile the West saw the hellish logic of racial superiority as it recoiled in horror from what had been discovered inside the concentration camps as the war ended. It is impossible to understate the shock of realising what the Germans, once one of the most civilised nations in the world, had been led to do. Indeed, the shock had not worn off fifty years later. And though not Christian, the Nazis had presented yet another version of the Chosen People scenario. They believed they had been chosen – by history, 'the light of perverted science', fate, destiny, the ancient gods of the Rhine, it is not clear which – to rule the world.

The revulsion against Nazi racial theory had a profound and lasting effect in the West. From then onwards, any theory or proposition had only to be shown to be akin to Fascism for it to be regarded as evil beyond debate. Indeed, in Europe, the lessons to be learned from that era were incorporated into the European Convention on Human Rights, which quite deliberately outlawed, clause by clause, practices associated with the Nazi regime. If all historical evidence of Nazism was somehow lost or forgotten, it would be easy to reconstruct simply by reversing the principles of the European Convention. As a result, the old certainties of white supremacy that had hardly been called into question in the formative years of the British Empire now looked a lot more tentative.

There had been little expansion of the Empire after the First World War. But there was little understanding that the Empire's foundations rested on wrongs committed against other peoples and societies. Winston Churchill, as leader of the Opposition, had opposed the independence of India in 1947. This did him no damage: he won a general election in 1951 (by which time, admittedly, it was too late to reverse). Nor had Attlee's Labour government of 1945–51, despite its Socialism, been anti-colonial in principle. Correlli Barnett, in *The Verdict of Peace*, writes:

> The [Labour] Government was not alone in believing, in the euphoric aftermath of victory, that as a power Britain could have a future like her past. So also believed the Conservative Party in opposition; so also believed the British people. The mental chains of imperial history shackled them all. Although the Labour Government did at least dump India in 1947, it tenaciously but indiscriminately preserved all the rest of Britain's traditional military and naval commitments in the Mediterranean, Middle East and Far East – on the score that these were the essential buttresses of (in Bevin's words in 1948 about the Middle East) Britain's 'position as a great power'.[13] [Ernest Bevin was Labour's Foreign Secretary at the time.]

A soft and benign version of the Chosen People theory – that England's destiny was to shine 'a light unto the gentiles' and that that shining was best done on the spot rather than at long range – still generally prevailed. It was still a Whig theory. It presumed that, whatever had recently happened in Germany, the natural direction of English civilisation was towards progress. Gradually, inch by inch, British-type institutions had been established and built up in the African and Asian colonies still ruled from London – institutions like schools and colleges, courts and legal systems, local assemblies (some with delegated legislative powers, some merely consultative), and local branches of the main British Christian denominations. The English language was taught in preference to local languages. At some distant point far ahead, most British officials would have conceded, local people would begin to move into senior positions, but not overnight. For instance by 1958, every part of the British Empire had bishops of the Church of England, usually appointed from London. None were black, though that was the colour of the overwhelming mass of the church's African membership. Nor was this remarkable. At the start of the Second Vatican Council in 1962, the Roman Catholic Church had only one black cardinal.

In fact the Chosen People theory of British colonialism, right back to the time of Wilberforce at the end of the eighteenth century, contained within itself the seeds of its own destruction. Sooner or later the 'light unto the gentiles' would be seen and responded to. The redeemer nation would do the business of redeeming. And as the benefits of English civilisation were spread and absorbed among the colonies, there would be a corresponding demand for political rights to match. The lessons of 1776 were obvious enough, even if the Americans had failed to point them out (which they did not).

The most salutary lesson of this kind came during the so-called Suez Crisis (which was in fact a war). Britain, with French and Israeli military assistance, had decided to reconquer the Suez Canal which the firebrand Egyptian nationalist leader, Gamal Abdel Nasser, had nationalised (i.e. taken from foreign ownership) in 1956. There was abroad in the nation, in the words of Winston Churchill earlier in the decade, 'a growing sense of the need to put Britain back in her proper place, which burns in the hearts of men far beyond the ranks of any political organisation'. The England which had felt national self-confidence returning to the national mood at the time of the coronation in 1953 was not about to be bested by a petty foreign dictator, as Anthony Eden, Churchill's successor as Prime Minister, labelled Nasser.

Militarily it was a messy sort of success, but America strongly disapproved. The essence of American feeling was probably similar to the liberal feeling in Britain that opposed the project: that this was an out-of-date way for any nation to behave. The British establishment still had a colonial mentality. But because of its history, America, despite its own experiments in empire-building, had a deep-seated hostility to colonialism in its standard European form and an instinctive sympathy for any people trying to throw it off.

Some of the British government's instincts were indeed pretty imperialist. In response to Nasser's nationalisation, the British and French governments did their best to stop all traffic through the Canal by withdrawing the British and French pilots, which every vessel had to carry. Correlli Barnett comments: 'It was their arrogant belief that this would demonstrate to the world that the backward Egyptians could not run the enterprise they had nationalised. To Franco-British chagrin the Egyptians simply hired pilots from other nations to supplement their own, and the merchant ships and tankers steamed through as usual.'[14]

So the decision was taken to seize back the Canal by force, in a complex charade of intervention to defend international assets from the Israelis (whom the British and French were secretly encouraging to attack Egypt, to supply a pretext for the military action to follow). By such manoeuvring Britain assumed it could act independently of America. It could not. One effect of the world war had been to convert a major part of Britain's currency reserves into debts owed to the United States, and even ten years after, the British economy still needed propping up. A run on the pound in international currency markets could not be corrected by Britain alone, as it did not have the reserves to do so. It relied on American help, which on this occasion was not forthcoming. As President Dwight D. Eisenhower crisply put it: 'no ceasefire, no loan'. (He was referring to a British request to draw on its International Monetary Fund credit facility in order to shore up the currency markets, which America vetoed.) He set out his reasons in a broadcast which made clear his conviction that what was behind this dispute was old-fashioned colonialism – primarily British. He complained that the United States had not been consulted about the intention to make an armed attack on Egypt, which was not as shocking as it might have seemed, given that the United States had gone to war over Korea in 1950 without consulting the British. He went on:

> As it is the manifest right of any of these nations to take such decisions and actions, it is likewise our right – if our judgment so dictates – to dissent. We believe these actions to have been taken in error. For we do not accept the use of force as a wise or proper instrument for the settlement of international disputes . . . The action taken can scarcely be reconciled with the principles and purposes of the United Nations to which we have all subscribed. And, beyond this, we are forced to doubt that resort to force and war will for long serve the permanent interest of the attacking nations.

President Eisenhower was a pragmatic man, but the Suez Crisis revealed him to be profoundly convinced of the unique moral role of America in world affairs. Its old ally in the Second World War, which it had fought alongside on the basis of parity and whose soldiers he had personally commanded in the invasion of Normandy, was no longer an equal but now a junior partner. He had the means to impose his will – and he now had God on his side. That summer he had proclaimed 'In God We Trust' to be the national motto of the United States.

In Britain in 1956 colonialism was not a dirty word. But the American desertion of its closest ally (as it seemed in London) was a severe blow to national prestige. The truth appears to be that Eisenhower and the State Department in Washington had become increasingly irritated by British pretensions to equality with America, which were simply getting in the way of America's freedom to act 'for the protection of the entire free world' (as the State Department put it).

It was during this period that British thinking about America shifted from 'equality' with America as another world power, to the 'special relationship' between a lesser and a greater power. After the crisis in the relationship of 1956 and the subsequent resignation of Prime Minister Eden, it fell to his successor, Harold Macmillan, to try to repair things. His strategy was simple: to agree with America that the days of colonialism were over.

Two former British colonies had already reached independence – Ghana and Malaya (in the Far East) – and Nigeria was on the way. But there were serious problems elsewhere, not least when the interests of white settlers were colliding with the increasingly militant demands of African nationalist politicians in central and southern Africa. In 1959 General de Gaulle offered self-determination to the Algerians, bringing a considerable risk of civil war both in mainland France and its North African possessions.

So the writing was on the wall for the British Empire. Macmillan went on a tour of Africa at the start of 1960, which was to end with his famous 'Wind of Change' address to the South African Parliament. His tour was an excellent opportunity to observe how far the self-appointed British mission to civilise Africa had gone, since its conception in the days of William Wilberforce and later of David Livingstone. Livingstone's call for white volunteers to go to Africa to renew its economy on modern lines – in his mind, the only real answer to slavery – had resulted in a large expatriate population in most central and southern African colonies. Some countries had made progress in building up a political class, including a new generation of black civil servants and black lawyers; some countries were further behind. Few whites got poor in the process: there was wealth and luxury to be had in the colonies.

Everywhere the Union Flag flew, the British churches had planted their own missions, which in time had become the base for schools, colleges and hospitals. The Church of England was usually not present as such, but through one or other of the two major Anglican missionary bodies, the Church Missionary Society (CMS) which was Low Church (Evangelical) and the United Society for the Propagation of the Gospel (USPG) which was High Church (Anglo-Catholic). Both were based in England. By and large they did not compete. Instead of having various brands of churchmanship (as the preference for High, Low or Broad style of Anglican Christianity is called) side by side as in the mother country, the Anglican church in each part of the continent developed under just one of these banners. The Anglican church in Kenya, for instance, became almost uniformly Evangelical (Protestant), having been missionised by the CMS, while South Africa had been USPG territory and so Anglicanism there was High Church (Anglo-Catholic). This partly explains why the black struggle for freedom in South Africa, though strongly supported by the English-speaking churches, was not accompanied by biblical typology about 'Moses leading the Chosen People out of Pharaoh's bondage' (Moses could have been Nelson Mandela, probably), as it undoubtedly would have been if the prevailing Christian presence had been more Protestant.

In most colonies there were also smaller Church of Scotland, Methodist and Baptist missions; and in virtually all of them, Anglicans and other varieties of Protestants found themselves outnumbered by Roman Catholics, whose main efforts were concentrated on education. So to a considerable degree the early vision of the pioneer missionaries was being fulfilled as Africa was gradually Westernised and Christianised. In most cases the protection of the European colonial power had been a significant factor. At the same time, as seemed to be the universal pattern with European colonialism, the idealism of white engineers, lawyers, doctors and churchmen had to be offset against the selfishness and arrogance of some white settlers and farmers and of the exploitation of local resources by Western mining interests. Attitudes of racial superiority were very widespread, intermingled with English snobbery (strengthened, no doubt, when the children of wealthy white families were sent back to English public schools to complete their education).

During his visit to Nigeria, at the start of his tour, Macmillan had a conversation with Sir James Robertson, the British Governor-General, which he often referred to later. It is very telling, both about the state of Africa at the time and for what it reveals about the paternalistic and patrician attitudes of the English ruling class. In his own words:

> after attending some meeting of the so-called cabinet or council, I said, 'Are these people fit for self-government?' and he said, 'No, of course not.' I said, 'When will they be ready?' and he said 'Twenty years, twenty-five years.' Then I said, 'What do you recommend me to do?' He said, 'I recommend you to give it to them at once.'[15]

Expressions like 'so-called cabinet', 'these people', 'fit for' and the emphatic 'No, of course not', are all indicative of the effortless English superiority and disdain for native Africans that was a hallmark of Macmillan's style, and probably the Governor-General's too. It is also evidence of the continuing tradition of colonial paternalism: whites were the adults, Africans the children. Nevertheless it reveals that the sense of moral purpose behind British colonialism was still very much alive. The British 'had responsibilities'. Robertson explained his unexpected reply by saying that if self-government was delayed, African leaders would spend the next decade or two fighting for independence, not in learning the finer arts of government, and 'I shall have to put them all in prison,' which would, he imagined, do them no good at all. But doing the Africans good was the main reason for the British being there. The implicit British mission to civilise the world which was there at the start of the second British Empire was still being taken for granted at its end. And it was, few of Macmillan's generation would have questioned, a mission from God.

In South Africa he met a very different mission from God, which was spelt out to him by Prime Minister Verwoerd. To him, Macmillan noted afterwards, apartheid 'was more than a political philosophy, it was a religion; a religion based on the Old Testament rather than the New . . . he had all the force of argument of some of the great Calvinist leaders of our Scottish Kirk.'[16]

The heart of his speech was his conclusion, which he said was based on the experience of his tour but which must have existed in his mind when he set out, that 'a wind of change is blowing through this continent, and whether we like it or not, this growth of national consciousness is a political fact. We must all accept it as a fact, and our national policies must take account of it.' His message for South Africa was that while English civilisation was, like theirs, based on Christianity, 'that must in our view include the opportunity to have an increasing share in political power and responsibility, a society in which individual merit and individual merit alone is the criterion for a man's advancement, whether political or economic . . .'

So Britain proceeded with a systematic policy of divesting itself peacefully of its colonial territories in Africa, but of only relinquishing those elsewhere which served no strategic purpose. The only difference in practice was that it had to be prised out of useful staging posts, such as Cyprus and Aden, by force. But Macmillan's 1960 Wind of Change speech was the decisive moment when the British gave up on the idea of Empire, and instead turned to developing the idea of a voluntary association of independent states in a Commonwealth (at first the 'British' Commonwealth, but the adjective was soon dropped).

His journey towards this position had been accelerated by such events as the so-called Hola Massacre in 1959, named afer a detention camp in Kenya for Mau-Mau terrorists. After a riot, eleven of them had been beaten to death. The white colonial administration reacted much as the British in India had reacted after the Amritsar Massacre in 1919, with a defiant pretence that nothing much had happened. It nevertheless split the British Cabinet in an election year, which could have been a dangerous turn of events for Macmillan. But while liberal opinion in Britain was angry, the public at large was not so upset. Opinion in Britain was still overtly racist, and a 'colour bar' was widely practised in housing and employment. 'No blacks or Irish' signs were common at the entrances to public houses and elsewhere.

Not wanting to disturb a general British sense of self-satisfaction,

Macmillan famously remarked 'They've never had it so good.' And the British voted to keep it that way. This year also saw the highest level of attendance at weekly worship in the Church of England since the end of the war: what was good for the national body was evidently also good for the national soul.

In the period between the coronation in 1953 and Macmillan's 'They've never had it so good' election in 1959 the national religious mood was complacent to say the least. Little was allowed to challenge the comfortable assumptions of Anglican England that the coronation itself had set forth, as a curious episode in 1955 illustrated. Margaret Knight, a psychologist from Aberdeen University, was signed up to deliver two radio talks under the general heading 'Morals Without Religion'. She wished to express her disagreement with a current Ministry of Education circular that the 'natural setting' for the moral education of children was in the course of religious instruction, and to offer advice to non-believing parents on how to inculcate moral standards in children outside such a framework. She later described the problems such parents faced, surrounded by 'organised indoctrination' in schools and the mass media:

> This high-powered propaganda has not made us a nation of believers, but it has created strong deterrents to the expression of unbelief. In some cases the threat is financial; a teacher, for example, who is openly agnostic finds his chances of promotion threatened. But more subtle than the financial deterrent is the effect of mass suggestion – the feeling, sedulously fostered, that 'inability to believe' is a regrettable and slightly embarrassing condition, to which it is best not to refer. Thus many honest sceptics feel ashamed and furtive about their doubts; and all over the country, perplexed and uneasy parents are creating similar conflicts for the next generation by teaching their children doctrines they do not themselves believe.[17]

It was in this spirit she gave her two talks, and there was national uproar. As so often happens when the condition termed 'moral panic' occurs in the media and public opinion, it started slowly. First there was a short and objective report in one newspaper, the *News Chronicle*. Then things started to warm up. The *Daily Express* headlined a story 'Woman Psychologist Makes Remarkable Radio Attack on Religion for Children'. The *Daily Telegraph* piled in with a report which described her talk as 'one large slab of atheistical propaganda' and called for the second broadcast to be banned. And then the *Sunday Graphic* published a front-page character assassination of extraordinary vehemence. Under a banner front-page headline which captioned her picture as 'The Unholy Mrs Knight', the paper declared:

Don't let this woman fool you. She looks – doesn't she – just like the typical housewife; cool, comfortable, harmless. But Mrs Margaret Knight is a menace. A dangerous woman. Make no mistake about that . . . The misguided BBC had allowed a fanatic to rampage along the air lanes, beating up Christianity with a razor and a bicycle chain . . . Let's have no more of her twaddle. She is due to dish up a second basinful on Wednesday. The BBC should pour it down the sink. [Bicycle chains and razors were, at least in the tabloid imagination, the weapons of choice of the lowest sort of street thug.]

It is undeniable that Mrs Knight used the pretext of a talk on moral education to mount an attack on basic Christian beliefs, which she did in uncompromising terms. If she was dealing with doubters, her goal seemed to be to turn them into confirmed atheists. But it was also a curiously dated, not to say daft, argument. To teach a child that morality depends on Christianity ran the danger that he might reject Christianity for Communism, she said in her talk. 'He may well decide that it was all just old wives' tales; and now he does not know where he is. At this stage he could be most vulnerable to communist propaganda . . . far from being a protection against communism, tying up morals with religion could help to drive people into its arms.'

At first church reaction followed the press, and was equally indignant, no one more so than the Archbishop of Canterbury, Dr Geoffrey Fisher. But as she herself later acknowledged, the old English virtue of tolerance began gradually to surface. One of the most favourable comments – possibly even prophetic, in the light of subsequent trends – came from the *Church of England Newspaper*, doughty champion of Anglican Evangelicalism:

If the Christian faith can only reply to such a person as Mrs Knight with personal abuse and can find no compelling answer, it deserves to fail and will in fact disappear. The suggestion that the BBC erred in allowing Mrs Knight to broadcast only plays into the hands of Christianity's critics by implying that the Church is a vested interest with the power of censorship. Big Brother is no less sinister for wearing a dog-collar . . . Those who share Mrs Knight's doubt about Christianity probably out-number those who do not in Britain at the present time, and include large numbers of our most highly respected and highly responsible citizens.

The overwhelming message of the large number of approving letters she received was that she had let fresh air into the national culture for the first time; many people said they felt liberated; some were ecstatic. Another clue to the future came in letters from teachers, particularly heads who had to organise religious assemblies and those who had to teach Religious Instruction (as schools were required to do by law) whether they believed in it or not. Religion in the 1950s, the postwar high point of 'official' Christianity in England, clearly also contained the seeds of its own destruction. Maybe an awareness of how fragile it was actually heightened the hysteria in part of the press. But like the monarchy, the Church of England had up until then been able to rely on a climate of uncritical deference. To probe it with frank criticism was to threaten to break a national taboo.

The Morals Without Religion furore of 1955 was the first sign of a thaw in this restrictive climate. It revealed the wide gap between what it was thought acceptable to say in public and what people actually thought in private. This was a time when the Church of England had its hands busy plugging leak after leak in the increasingly porous dam that was holding back the secular floodwaters.

Attention soon turned to the marriage plans of Princess Margaret, who had caused her sister the Queen, and even more the Archbishop of Canterbury, grave alarm by threatening to marry a divorced man, Group Captain Peter Townsend. Not only did the archbishop talk her out of it, but he also arranged for the Church Assembly, then the Church of England's regulatory body, to pass an Act of Convocation in 1957 banning the remarriage of divorcees in church. This reaffirmed earlier decisions – especially the church resolution passed after the Abdication of Edward VIII in 1936 – by declaring: 'In order to maintain the principle of lifelong obligation which is inherent in every legally contracted marriage and is expressed in the plainest terms in the Marriage Service, the Church should not allow the use of that service in the case of anyone who has a former partner still living.' There was no doubt that Archbishop Fisher wished to head off a growing social trend in favour of liberalised divorce laws. At the time, the state regarded marriage and divorce as the church's particular business, and would make no move without church consent. Fisher was making clear that no such consent would be forthcoming.

Much the same furore recurred in 1960, when, despite recent prosecutions which had resulted in a jail sentence for a bookseller, Penguin, the publishers, decided to publish an uncensored edition of *Lady Chatterley's Lover*. D. H. Lawrence's notorious novel's worst offence, beyond even its enthusiastic description of sexual intercourse, was the inclusion of obscene four-letter words (the words 'fuck' or 'fucking' no less than thirty times).

The establishment, including the Archbishop of Canterbury, strongly supported the prosecution, and the Tory ultra-establishment Attorney General, Sir Reginald Manningham-Buller, gave moral encouragement behind the scenes. In a passage much quoted against him afterwards, prosecuting Counsel Mervyn Griffith-Jones QC told the jury to 'ask yourselves the question: would you approve of your young sons, young daughters – because girls can read as well as boys – reading this book? Is it a book that you would have lying around the house? Is it a book you would wish your wife or servants to read?'

The defence was allowed to call literary and religious experts to show that the book had merits which outweighed its obvious, if superficial, obscenity, and the jury unanimously acquitted. Archbishop Fisher complained that the prosecution had not been tough enough, and should have matched 'don for don and bishop for bishop' in calling expert witnesses. Why keeping the f-word out of the vocabulary of English literature was such a high priority for the Church of England can only be explained if the established church felt itself to be responsible for the entire moral tone of the country, and not just for the religious beliefs of its members. Indeed, Fisher's easy and natural mindset ran precisely along those lines. Church and state were the spiritual and temporal aspects of the same English national entity (and 'spiritual' in this context largely meant 'moral').

The 'Lady C' trial was a landmark, not least because it came in the symbolic year 1960 – the start of the Sixties revolution in style and behaviour that removed many of the taboos which had given the post-war years such a stifling character. As Philip Larkin wrote in his poem 'Annus Mirabilis':

> Sexual intercourse began
> In nineteen sixty-three
> (Which was rather late for me) –
> Between the end of the Chatterley ban
> And the Beatles' first LP.[18]

It would seem that the character of Britain as a Christian nation was beginning to crumble. The next shock to the Anglican system was the publication in 1963 of the book *Honest to God* by the Bishop of Woolwich, Dr John Robinson. He had given evidence for the defence in the Chatterley trial and now he seemed to be spreading doubts about the truth of Christianity. An advance extract in *The Observer* set the scene with the headline, 'Bishop says the God up there or out there will have to go'.

Fisher had by now retired from Canterbury, but his successor, Michael Ramsey, was no less keen to enter the fray with denunciations. He said he was 'especially grieved at the method chosen by the Bishop for presenting his ideas to the public' which 'caused public sensation and did much damage. Many of us who read the article [in the *Observer*] and its slogans might not have had the opportunity or the necessary brains for reading the book referred to.' Robinson's book was a survey of some recent German-language liberal Protestant theology, by such scholars as Rudolf Bultmann, Paul Tillich and Dietrich Bonhoeffer (who had been executed by the Nazis).

They, and he, set out to update what they saw as primitive and childlike misconceptions of Christianity among the public. Ramsey clearly feared that instead of transmuting these ideas into something more sophisticated, and therefore better able to withstand the sceptical spirit of the age, people would simply conclude that Christianity was 'not true after all'. Such speculations were best confined to senior common rooms, where the best minds would know how to deal with them. It was an approach not very different from the prosecution line at the Lady C trial: 'Is it a book you would wish your wife or servants to read?' Archbishop Ramsey was right in one particular: some of the ideas put forward in Robinson's not specially well-written book were mind-bogglingly abstract and showed every sign of having been translated literally and clumsily from compound polysyllabic German words, such as 'ultimate ground of being'.

Philosophically, liberal Protestantism seemed to be groping its way back to some kind of metaphysics, having turned its back on that school of theology at the Reformation. Within the intellectual horizons of a tabloid sub-editor, however, Robinson appeared to be saying that God did not exist and Jesus was not his Son. If that was what he was being heard to say, leaders of the Church of England felt it was their business to stop him. Undoubtedly what gave the row its *frisson* was the fact that this seemed also to be an attack on the religion of the ruling establishment, from the Queen downwards, and hence was politically and socially subversive as well as religiously so. If there was still a strong residual belief in England as the Chosen People, then any suggestion that there was no God, or at least no God such as the Chosen People theory required, would be deeply threatening to national identity. And the establishment reacted accordingly, proving the point. Ironically, Robinson's actual intention was not to weaken religious belief but to strengthen it. He felt Christianity was not being presented in a way that intelligent people could respond to. He shared with his critics the view that a healthy society needed Christianity to make it function.

The *Honest to God* controversy established clearly how innocent of theology most church members were. These issues, not least the rejection of miracles and other supernatural elements in religion, had been in the public domain at least since George Eliot, if not from the time of the Deists[19] in the eighteenth century. Hence the public's confusion should have been a warning signal of the lack of depth to ordinary English religious belief that existed even among the core of the church's membership. Plainly the great majority of adults had ideas about Christianity that had not advanced since their primary school days. This put an enormous question mark against the church's investment in religious education. Without necessarily agreeing with them, they should have been able to take John Robinson's ideas in their stride, instead of being scandalised. The signal was sent, but not heeded. Religious ignorance among ordinary church-goers had created a vulnerability to cultural pressures and intellectual fashions that would, if not treated, have drastic results in the coming decades. It remained untreated.

These episodes had one thing in common. They demonstrated how much the powers-that-be wished to control how people behaved and what they thought, in the first instance concerning marriage and sexuality, and in the second with regard to religious faith. It was a trickle-down theory of religion and morality, which had strong echoes of the sixteenth-century assumption that when the king favoured divorce, everyone else had to favour divorce; when the religion of the monarch changed, everyone else had to change too.

The period since the 1950s had seen a gradual rise of the opposite sentiment: that ordinary people were increasingly resistant to having their beliefs and moral standards handed down from those above them in the social and political hierarchy. This was partly a rejection of social class and the old Victorian concept of 'breeding', an unwillingness to acknowledge any longer that those higher in the social spectrum were somehow morally better than those lower down, and indeed a refusal even to think in the language of 'lower' and 'upper' classes. But it was also partly a rejection of England's status as the Chosen People, and all that had been taken for granted as a consequence of that idea over more than three centuries. Explicitly, the idea had long disappeared below the surface. Implicitly, it continued to help shape the English people's perception of their rightful special place in the world even until the present day. But always less and less as the years passed. This decline in the ideology of chosenness presents enormous problems for the identity and destiny of the English nation. If it is not that, what is it? Being 'America's best friend' is hardly enough.

Perhaps it was Harold Macmillan's fault. After Suez, he clearly saw where the mantle of chosenness had moved to. Though the phrase existed before, his contribution to the long-term future of the British was to elevate the term 'special relationship' almost to the level of a substitute national definition. If Britain could not be the world's strongest power, it could at least be its closest ally. America still looked like the Chosen People, and believed in itself as such, even if the concept more usually lurked under such sentimental slogans as 'God's Own Country' or intellectual euphemisms like 'American Exceptionalism'. There was (and is) a breed of mainstream American politicians who have never seen reason to doubt their nation's God-given title deeds, or to question the view that the nation had a 'Manifest Destiny' to make the rest of the world as much like America as possible. Nor did they question that it was Providence that was moving them on.

The association of this faith in America with Christianity was much more explicit on the Republican side, though Democrats like President Jimmy Carter certainly shared it. Immigrant groups who had arrived since the Civil War, who were from other backgrounds than Anglo-Saxon and other religions than Protestant, found that identification with this ideology went with loyalty to the flag. They were eager to pass the test. Thus the large Jewish influx of the late nineteenth and early twentieth century quickly recognised the Chosen People theme as similar to their own, and felt all the more at home because of it.

And as we have seen in the course of this book, contemporary American politicians are still not shy about talking in these terms. We have quoted Presidents Reagan and George Bush Jnr in this vein, and also Mayor Giuliani of New York. We could equally have quoted Bush's Attorney General John Ashcroft, House Majority Whip Tom DeLay, or numerous others. On the left, belief in the unique moral destiny of America is no less confident, though less often expressed in religious terms. It shows up, for instance, in the unwillingness, which is as characteristic of the American left as it is of the right, to take heed of foreign criticism. For they believe the rest of the world represents the past while America represents the future – and therefore that the New World has nothing to learn from the Old.

10

Wider Still and Wider

Land of Hope and Glory, mother of the Free,
How shall we extol thee, who are born of thee?
Wider still and wider shall thy bounds be set;
God who made thee mighty, make thee mightier yet.[1]

The Chosen People paradigm was more than just a metaphor: it
described how people had behaved in the past, but it also prescribed
how they should behave in the future. 'Land of Hope and Glory'
illustrates it at work. It was written as a patriotic hymn for England. It
would look just as appropriate – maybe even more so, nowadays – as a
patriotic hymn for the United States of America. The history of England
over four centuries, and of America over at least three, is the story of two
societies living under the influence of this powerful guiding idea. Its
source was not just Protestantism but Protestant nationalism, the desire
to define a national community as coming into existence because God
willed it to do so, because he had a purpose for it. Protestants having
rejected the authority of the church in matters of religion, they turned
for their religious teaching in the only other direction available, to the
pages of Scripture. There they found the history of the ancient Israelites
becoming a holy nation under the guidance of God, and they appropriated that story for themselves. Thus did the first modern totally
self-contained nation-state appear in history, in the Kingdom of England
of Henry VIII in 1535.

For a long time this form of Protestant nationalism was taken to be
nothing less than Christianity itself. Yet by the end of the twentieth
century most spokesmen for mainstream Protestant Christianity in both
countries had come to regard Protestant nationalism as we have described
it as a deviation from the pure milk of Christian truth. In so far as there
is anything on the planet recognisable as a 'chosen generation, a royal
priesthood, an holy nation, a peculiar people' as in the first epistle of St
Peter, they would say it was the universal invisible shapeless mass of

believing Christians of every nationality and denomination added together. But that is a relatively modern view which largely dates from the period when Protestant Christianity developed global structures such as the World Council of Churches (founded 1948) and the Anglican Communion (the first Lambeth Conference was in 1867). Before they appeared, it would generally have been held that every Protestant denomination had to be rooted in the soil of its own land. This was one of the themes that distinguished Protestantism from Catholicism.

It is clear from history that religious ideas are generally stable and usually shift only slowly. They behave like the invisible deep ocean currents by which millions of tons of water are slowly transferred immense distances, sometimes halfway across the globe. They give little clue to their existence from the surface, yet they control the climate; and a permanent disturbance of the pattern of their flow could alter the destiny of entire continents and the living conditions of whole nations. What is visible on the surface are the waves and ripples which are largely the effect of wind and weather, but which may give a misleading impression of what is happening far below. This is a useful metaphor for religious ideas, and the Chosen People paradigm of Protestant nationalism can be regarded as one of the deep ocean currents. They may not be visible from the surface. Even violent storms may not disturb those currents; but sometimes, for mysterious reasons, they change by themselves. That is also true of religion. Who knows why the native Scots by and large embraced the Protestant Reformation, and the native Irish by and large did not?

Max Weber's principle that the explicit religious convictions of a particular generation usually become the implicit unexamined assumptions of the next one means that the Chosen People paradigm may continue to shape habits of thought and patterns of behaviour long after people have lost touch with the origins of these influences. They are, in the words of the British infantry on the Western Front, ''ere because we're 'ere because we're 'ere because we're 'ere'. Rarely is there a sharp break in religious belief or practice between one generation and the next. On the contrary, beliefs will often be retained even after they have lost their relevance. There are still parts of rural England where they call urgently for a priest or minister when someone is dying because 'that is what you do', even though the Church of England has no sacraments for a deathbed. But that is what they did before the Reformation, and the habit lives on. Friday is a busy day in the fish and chip shops of England, even though compulsory abstinence from meat on Fridays was abolished at the Reformation. Again, that is what they did before the Reformation, and again the habit lives on.

It might seem obvious that a necessary condition for believing that one's nation is the Chosen Nation, like the Jews in the Old Testament, is a belief in God. One cannot be chosen by God if there is no such thing. But this is not necessarily so; human beings are not as logical as that. Thomas Huxley, for instance, who was one of the leading scientists of the nineteenth century and lifelong advocate and propagandist of Charles Darwin's theories, believed he had a mission to replace Christianity with science, or even more specifically to deprive the Anglican establishment of its privileged status in English society and replace it with a Church Scientific, as he called it. His tone was Evangelistic, and even Protestant typology was enlisted to his cause. In a lecture in 1855 he castigated his audience (or congregation) as 'this idolatrous age', saying it 'listens to the voice of the living God thundering from the Sinai of science, and straightaway forgets all that it has heard, to grovel in its own superstition, to worship the golden calf of tradition, to pray and fast where it should work and obey, and, as of old, to sacrifice its children to its theological Baal'.[2] He went so far as to create the scientific equivalent of Sunday Schools, where children sang the scientific equivalent of hymns; and he founded the Natural History Museum in London as the scientific equivalent of a cathedral. He coined the term 'agnostic', meaning one who does not know whether there is a God or not; but judging from the religious opinions he actually expressed, he was really an atheist. An atheist with a destiny does seem like a contradiction, but it did not bother him. The thought that England had a destiny as the world's leading scientific nation, a thought derived from Sir Isaac Newton, would have seemed entirely natural to him. Both were to be Presidents of the Royal Society, which was pleased to regard itself as the world's leading scientific organisation.

Newton was one of the heroes of the Deists who believed the universe may have been constructed as if by a divine watchmaker – who wound it up and left it to tick. This scientific man *par excellence* was an expert on the design of the divine watch, yet that was only one way he spent his seventeenth-century afternoons. His other obsession was the contemplation of the mysteries of biblical prophecy, including trying to work out the end of time from obscure passages in the Book of Daniel. Any time over was spent plotting and intriguing either how to keep Catholics out of Cambridge (one of whom wished to be enrolled for a BA), or how to keep the Duke of York off the throne of England (for more or less the same reasons). Newton was convinced that his own destiny was to lead England into being the premier nation of scientific inquiry and hence the premier nation of world civilisation; and he foresaw that destiny in the pages of the Old and New Testament. He was a Chosen Person in the midst of a Chosen People. He was also convinced that this personal and national destiny would be destroyed if England tolerated Catholicism.

In line with respectable scientific opinion he saw the pope as the Anti-Christ. His personal take on world history, which set him a bit apart from his fellow Puritans, was that the Catholic rot set in, so to speak, with the papal condemnation of the Arian heresy (named after Arius, a third-century dissenter). He called himself an Arian and therefore did not accept the divinity of Christ: indeed, for this reason he had to obtain royal exemption from the oath that was required before taking up a professorial chair at Cambridge. This man of destiny was, for 300 years in England and America, the archetypal super-scientist. (Thomas Jefferson, the sceptical Deist, third President of America, was so impressed with Newton's work on the true application of the apocalyptic literature of Daniel and Revelation to the modern world that he had a new edition printed at his own expense.)

So belief in the Christian God is not necessary, though it helps. Hence there is no obvious reason why agnostic liberals in the United States cannot believe that Americans are the Chosen People, though as we have already noted they might prefer to describe this belief by the more academically respectable and neutral-sounding term American Exceptionalism. This applies also to the generation of English socialists before and after the Second World War who wanted to build what Correlli Barnett, in his *The Audit of War*, calls the 'New Jerusalem'.[3] Some of them were agnostics or atheists, but they shared the utopian, indeed, millennial vision of the Christian Socialists. They may be counted, therefore, as constituent parts of the Chosen People project even if they did not believe in a God who made such choices.

But if a Chosen People ideology is not strictly dependent on religious faith, it does much more depend on a certain type of nationalism. The full Chosen People syndrome set out in the Old Testament describes a nation or people that is rewarded when it remains faithful, but if it backslides it can expect to be pulled back to the mark by failure or defeat (perhaps the origin of 'learning one's lesson' after a good thrashing). Hence a nation that has little to show in the way of God's favours is being a trifle implausible if it claims God is on its side. On the other hand a nation enjoying success can easily convince itself it is basking in the benevolence of Providence.

That was certainly a believable claim by the English (or to be more complete, the British) until the First World War. That was when the first big doubt crept in. There are no statistical measures by which we may chart the decline in national confidence in a Chosen People definition of English identity. But it may be assumed that such statistics, if they existed, would have declined year on year since the end of the First World War. For, year on year, the evidence of the work of a benevolent Providence got thinner and thinner. It may also be assumed that such statistics would take on a very similar pattern to the statistics of Church of England membership quoted by Alan Wilkinson in his *The Church of England and the First World War*.[4] In other words a steady inexorable year-on-year decline. It is clear the two are closely related. Something happened in that war, Wilkinson implies, from which the Church of England never recovered.

Indeed, the authority that a national church needs in order to be able to preach the gospel compellingly rests not just on its own qualities but on the qualities of the nation to which it is attached (and of which it claims to represent the spiritual aspect). A mighty nation will have a mighty faith; and the combination will look formidable enough to be convincing. An all-too-human nation will have an all-too-human church, and not much sustenance will pass between them in either direction. According to a poll by the National Centre for Social Research published in 2000, only 48 per cent of people in the United Kingdom claim to belong to any religion, compared with 86 per cent of people in the United States. Attendance at Church of England services on Sundays fell below the one million mark for the first time in the late 1990s. It is no coincidence that the Church of England has sought, in the period under review, both to bolster its self-confidence by extolling its role as mother church of the Anglican Communion and also by playing 'best friend' to that spiritual superpower of the modern world, the Roman Catholic Church, just as British foreign policy has made much of the so-called 'special relationship' with that material superpower across the Atlantic. Those who noticed Prime Minister Tony Blair standing beside President Bill Clinton at the UN Millennium celebrations in New York in AD 2000 may also have noticed Archbishop George Carey standing beside Pope John Paul II at a similar event in Rome – in the words of the protocol for such events, in a position of honour, but in the words of reality, playing second fiddle – or, to be candid, basking in reflected glory. Is it any wonder that the two open forms of prejudice still commonly encountered among the English now they have learned to watch their language with respect to other racial, ethnic or religious groups, are anti-Americanism and anti-Catholicism? Is that the sour grapes of the superseded?

America, on the contrary, still makes a credible pitch for being the Chosen People, and almost the only factor restraining us from awarding it that title straight away is the nagging suspicion that in reality there are no Chosen People at all, and God (if we agree there is a God) does not work that way. Perhaps it does not matter too much whether outsiders agree that America is the Chosen People. What matters to the outcome is whether Americans believe it themselves. Chosenness is largely a self-appointed status and a self-fulfilling prophecy. Clearly they do, if not in the traditional biblical, Protestant typological way of previous generations, then closely derived from that (having stripped it, perhaps, of some of its more uncomfortable obligations).

The Chosen People paradigm is highly relevant to the problems of race relations and racial integration in both countries. Race is not a scientific fact of life but a human construct: there is only one race in the biological sense, and that is *homo sapiens*. 'Race' was used almost interchangeably with 'people' in the nineteenth century, and referred not just to inherited genetic characteristics but to shared cultures, beliefs and memories. Race took on its modern meaning only under the influence of Social Darwinism and early genetic theory, at the start of the twentieth century. So 'people', as a term describing the national community, is by far the older idea. And those who look to the Old Testament for their social model will find plenty of examples of the notion of a 'people' being used to divide 'us' from 'them', in most instances the Hebrews from the various tribes of Canaanites – even to the extent to saying that 'we' may make 'them' our slaves. And in contemporary language, because of matrilineal descent (one is a Jew if one's mother is a Jew), this definition of 'we' is also a racial definition.

The notion of a Chosen People therefore holds great dangers for race relations. This is surely the origin of the English uncertainty whether a black or Asian person can 'really' be English. Merely to admit them to Britishness is not enough, because that is too ill-defined and insufficiently significant (especially when the Scots, the Welsh and many in Northern Ireland are playing down the 'British' element in their identity and emphasising the Scottish, Welsh and Irish element). The English do genuinely wish to have good race relations; indeed they would rather like to be an example to other nations in this respect. Hence the more they hang on to any link with their past as a Chosen People, the more difficult this will be. This presents an acute challenge to two English institutions in particular, the monarchy and the Church of England, for their past identity is intimately bound up with the Chosen People paradigm of Englishness. If they are not careful, their very existence will become institutionally racist. And while this book has been careful to stay clear of the Middle East conflict, some of its conclusions about the consequences of Chosen People theory for race relations would apply to the Israeli attitude to the Arabs.

America, meanwhile, has attempted to transcend the singular and monolithic nature of American national identity as it was at the time, say, of the end of the Civil War. It has done so without abandoning the perception of itself as Chosen. The great achievement of Martin Luther King, as a theologian of chosenness, was to show how the grand design of America as a single chosen nation can contain within itself other tributaries, smaller groups who also wear the mantle of the elect but do so in a way that does not deny it to the whole. It is a model of convergence, or a 'people of peoples'. There is a biblical model for this too: the ancient Israelites were originally twelve tribes, but all were under the one covenant.

The 'American Problem', if one might define such a concept, is that while these twelve tribes were required to treat each other fairly and decently in accordance with Mosaic law, they were not required to deal that way with the non-Jewish tribes, the Canaanites, who shared the same living space. It is true the ethic of the Old Testament begins to be universalised – applied to Jew and non-Jew alike – in some of the later prophets. How unsuccessful they were may be judged from the fact that Jesus still saw the necessity for preaching the parable of the Good Samaritan, which is precisely addressed to the question 'Who is my neighbour?' To whom, apart from 'people like me', do I have moral responsibilities? The Jews of his time clearly did not think they had moral responsibilities towards Samaritans, and were somewhat shocked by a story that told them that the Samaritans felt they had moral responsibilities towards the Jews.

So while America may at last be trying to treat its own ethnic sub-groups fairly, it is a nation still very conscious of the boundaries of its own 'peopleness'. This can easily be simplified into the conviction that the rest of the world exists for America's benefit. This is different from the motivation behind the British Empire, which was based on the view – however inadequately acted out – that Britain existed for the rest of the world's benefit. It may be some consolation to know that the original Chosen People wrestled with precisely the same difficulty. They were Chosen, but for whose benefit? Early on, it was plainly for their own; as time passed, the truth dawned that it was for the benefit of all humanity. America too needs the Parable of the Good Samaritan preached to it, from someone it will listen to.

The Chosen People syndrome, as we have defined it, suggests that nations whose history is subject to that pattern will experience a cycle. Faithfulness will be followed by laxity, by idolatry and by infidelity (in the religious sense, at least); this will lead to suffering and misfortune as Providence intervenes to apply the corrective chastisement. (That is not to make God responsible for causing the misfortune; all he does is to lift his protection.) Prophets will arise to explain what has gone wrong and urge the Chosen People to return to their earlier obedience; as they do so, they are restored (redeemed) back to the earlier state of grace.

Whether or not this theory of history has any predictive value is a moot point. Did God really allow his Chosen People (the British) to lose their American colonies as a punishment for the slave trade? If that was

God's plan, how could he at the same time be freeing his Chosen People (the Americans) from British tyranny as a reward for American faithfulness? The two stories do not add up. If God wanted the slave trade ended, he would not have given the Americans victory in their War of Independence.

This leads to a wider difficulty about treating the Chosen People theory as true. Some of the key features of Protestant biblical typology, as applied in England as well as in America, are exaggerated to the point of fantasy. There was really no deep British plot to deprive Americans of their liberty in 1774, certainly no deep design to impose an absolute monarchy, even less to impose Roman Catholicism. America misread, and to a degree deliberately misrepresented, the signals. The proof was next door. The story of constitutional evolution in Canada and elsewhere was one of steady progress towards democracy and liberty under a monarchy: indeed, Canada was the American slave's Promised Land where they would be safe in the arms of Queen Victoria. Even native Americans recognised that they would have a better deal in Canada.

England's own biblical 'flight from tyranny' through most of the sixteenth, seventeenth and eighteenth centuries was motivated by the spectre of Roman Catholicism, seen as the tyrannical empire of the Anti-Christ. But the notion that Catholicism was diabolical in origin had been almost completely dropped by the start of the nineteenth century: one influence was the arrival in England of thousands of French Catholic refugees fleeing from the Terror. The English not only felt sorry for them, but found them civilised, cultured, learned, and manifestly Christian in a way even a dyed-in-the-wool Protestant could recognise. Perhaps they had an inferior political system, but agents of the devil they clearly were not. Yet the Catholicism of late eighteenth-century France was not very different from the Catholicism that emerged from the reforms of the Council of Trent even before the reign of Elizabeth I. That Council had set out to be a definitive event, a 'council to end councils': indeed, the next one was not held until 1870. If Catholicism at the start of the nineteenth century was not the embodiment of evil, then neither was it two centuries earlier.

Of course Foxe's famous *Book of Martyrs*, reprinted regularly throughout the period, had continued to spread its baleful message. Catholics were emancipated in 1829, but were still not trusted. When the Catholic hierarchy of dioceses and bishops was created in England in 1850, there was a storm of protest and mass meetings all over the country. But without the Catholics making a single concession, the wave of anti-Catholic paranoia soon passed and a workable but imperfect tolerance was restored. None of this proves that Catholicism is a perfect system, but it does make clear that the extreme fears which dominated English politics and religious feeling over three centuries – faithfully echoed on the other side of the Atlantic – were exaggerated to the point of paranoia. The Chosen People theory played a major part in the defence of England against 'popery' – the alleged conspiracy of the Catholic Church with England's European enemies – not least at the time of the deposition of James II and the 'Glorious Revolution' of 1688, and in the subsequent defiance of the continuous Jacobite threat. But would it really have been disastrous if James II had been allowed to complete his reign? Was his expulsion really the sublime turning point in English history that generations of Whig historians, following Macaulay, have said it was? Or was the excoriation of Catholicism simply a necessary condition for the Chosen People mythology to work its magic, with all that flowed from that? Was England's greatness really built upon such fanciful foundations?

So our final conclusion about the Chosen People theory has to be that while it is still influential, it is simply not true – and never was. The historical evidence alone refutes it, whatever we make of the theological issue. And while it injected a powerful dynamic into the life of the two nations that believed it about themselves, the theory let them also believe that they had the right to pursue their own interests even when that ran counter to the interests of others.

Such nations are a potential threat to others. Yet they will feel intensely righteous, convinced that the moral justification of their actions lies in their unique status. Nor will they allow others to call them to account. If 'an angel rides in the whirlwind and directs this storm', as John Page wrote to Thomas Jefferson, then George Bush's conclusion[5] is correct: 'We are not this story's author, who fills time and eternity with his purpose.' Is this not an oblique way of warning the world: to stand in America's way is to resist the will of God?

And while, if the Chosen People theory were true, God could be relied on to punish such a nation that abused its privileged status as he sometimes punished the ancient Hebrews, in the real world no such divine corrective operates. Proverbs 16:18 may warn that: 'Pride goeth before destruction, and an haughty spirit before a fall,' and Americans may believe it and be cautioned by it. That is some small comfort, but it is not a universal law. The effects of a powerful nation convinced it has God on its side are not self-limiting. It can often act, rightly or wrongly, with impunity. Indeed, in the extreme case, the Chosen People status can grow into a condition of zealous religious nationalism that is potentially Fascistic.

The best way of ensuring that that potential does not turn into actuality is to be aware of it, and to take steps to correct or resist it. That is as necessary for Americans themselves as it is for the rest of the world. But whether America and the world has the courage and wisdom equal to this daunting task is another matter.

Notes

Chapter 1: Destiny Versus Identity

1 Lipset, Seymour Martin, *American Exceptionalism, a Double-edged Sword* (W. W. Norton and Co., 1996).
2 Du Bois, W. E. B., *The Souls of Black Folk* (A. C. McClurg and Co., 1903).
3 Phoenix, Sybil, in Hooker, Roger and Sargant, John (eds), *Belonging to Britain, Christian Perspectives on a Plural Society* (CCBI Publications, 1991).
4 Maddox, Brenda, 'I'm glad to be here', *The Guardian*, 28 September 2001.
5 Anderson, Benedict, *Imagined Communities: Reflections on the Origin and Spread of Nationalism* (Verso, 1991).
6 Maier, Pauline, *American Scripture, How America Declared its Independence from Britain* (Pimlico, 1997).
7 Churchill, Winston, *The Speeches* (Penguin, 1989).
8 Paxman, Jeremy, *The English, a Portrait of a People* (Penguin, 1998).
9 Scruton, Roger, *England, an Elegy* (Chatto and Windus, 2000).
10 Paxman, op. cit.
11 Scruton, op. cit.
12 ibid.
13 Hodgson, Peter C., *Theology in the Fiction of George Eliot* (SCM Press, 2001).
14 Hattersley, Roy, 'Politics is no place for true faith', *The Guardian*, 30 July 2001.
15 White, Michael, 'The Holy Alliance', *The Guardian*, 7 November 2001.
16 *Daily Telegraph*, 11 January 2002.
17 Witchcraft is discussed more fully in chapter eight.
18 *The Book of Common Prayer* (Everyman's Library, 1999).
19 Clark, Jonathan C. D., *The Language of Liberty 1660–1832; Political Discourse and Social Dynamics in the Anglo-American World* (Cambridge University Press, 1994).

20 Koterski, Joseph, SJ, 'How Jefferson Honored Religion', *Crisis*, vol. 19 no. 3, March 2001.
21 *New York Times,* 27 December 2001.
22 de Tocqueville, Alexis, *Democracy in America* (Mentor, 1956).
23 Hastings, Adrian (ed.), *Oxford Companion to Christian Thought* (Oxford University Press, 2000).
24 Barr, James, *Fundamentalism* (SCM Press, 1977).
25 *New Bible Commentary Revised* (InterVarsity Press, 1970).
26 Text from Library of Congress website: www.lcweb.loc.gov
27 Lipset, op. cit.
28 Weber, Max, *On Methodology of Social Sciences* (The Free Press, 1949).
29 Weber, Max, *The Protestant Ethic and the Spirit of Capitalism* (1930).
30 Rahner, Karl (ed.), *Encyclopaedia of Theology* (Burns and Oates, 1975).

Chapter 2: New Jerusalem

1 Colley, Linda, *Britons, Forging the Nations, 1707–1837* (Yale University Press, 1992).
2 Wilkinson, Alan, *Christian Socialism, from Scott Holland to Tony Blair* (SCM Press, 1998).
3 Barnett, Correlli, *The Verdict of Peace* (Macmillan, 2001) [and elsewhere].
4 See chapter ten.
5 Kent, John, *William Temple* (Cambridge University Press, 1992).
6 Bagehot, Walter (1826–77), *The English Constitution.*
7 *Catholic Encyclopaedia* (Robert Appleton Company, 1908).
8 Kantorowicz, Ernst, *The King's Two Bodies: A Study in Mediaeval Political Theology* (Princeton, 1957).
9 Scruton, Roger, *England, an Elegy* (Chatto and Windus, 2000).
10 Colley, op. cit.
11 Eliot, T. S., *The Idea of a Christian Society and Other Writings* (Faber and Faber, 1982).
12 Doctrine Commission of the Church of England, *Believing in the Church* (SPCK, 1981).
13 Temple, William, *Citizen and Churchman* (Eyre and Spottiswood, 1941).
14 Raphael, Ray, *The American Revolution, a People's History* (Profile Books, 2000).
15 Phillips, Kevin, *The Cousins' Wars, Religion, Politics and the Triumph of Anglo-America* (Basic Books, 1999).
16 Clark, Jonathan C. D., *The Language of Liberty 1660–1832: Political Discourse and Social Dynamics in the Anglo-American World* (Cambridge University Press, 1994).
17 Bence-Jones, Mark, *The Catholic Families* (Constable, 1992).
18 Longley, Clifford, *The Worlock Archive* (Geoffrey Chapman, 1992).

Chapter 3: A Succession of Covenants

1 *The Complete Book of Bible Quotations*, edited by M. L. Levine and E. Rachlis (Robert Hale, 1986) runs to nearly 600 pages.
2 Hill, Christopher, *The English Bible and the Seventeenth Century Revolution* (Allen Lane, 1993).
3 Colley, Linda, *Britons, Forging the Nations, 1707–1837* (Yale University Press, 1992).
4 *The Revised English Bible* (Oxford University Press, 1989).
5 Lipset, Seymour Martin, *American Exceptionalism, A Double-edged Sword* (W. W. Norton and Co., 1996).
6 Madsen, Deborah L., *American Exceptionalism* (Edinburgh University Press, 1998).
7 Hill, Bridget, *The Republican Virago, The Life and Times of Catharine Macaulay, Historian* (Clarendon Press, 1992).
8 Baylin, Bernard, *The Ideological Origins of the American Revolution* (Harvard University Press, 1967).
9 Hill, Bridget, op. cit.
10 Hill, Christopher, op. cit.
11 *Oxford English Dictionary* (Oxford University Press, 1971).
12 Jacobs, Louis, *The Jewish Religion, a Companion* (Oxford University Press, 1995).
13 Shashar, Michael, *Lord Jakobovits in Conversation* (Vallentine Mitchell, 2000).
14 *The Missal in Latin and English* (Burns, Oates and Washbourne, 1958).
15 *The Book of Common Prayer* (Everyman's Library, 1999).
16 *The Jerusalem Bible* (Darton, Longman and Todd, 1966).
17 *Nostra Aetate*, Vatican official translation www.vatican.va
18 Jacobs, op. cit.
19 Foster, R. F., *The Irish Story, Telling Tales and Making It Up in Ireland* (Allen Lane, 2001).
20 Baylin, op. cit.
21 ibid.
22 ibid.
23 Phillips, Kevin, *The Cousins' Wars, Religion, Politics and the Triumph of Anglo-America* (Basic Books, 1999).
24 Baylin, op. cit.
25 ibid.

Chapter 4: Hope, History and Hatred

1 Edwards, Jonathan, *Sinners in the Hands of an Angry God* (US Library of Congress).
2 Cross, F. L. and Livingstone, E. A. (eds), *Oxford Dictionary of the Christian Church* (Oxford University Press, 1997).
3 Hastings, Adrian (ed.), *Oxford Companion to Christian Thought* (Oxford University Press, 2000).
4 *Luther's Works* (Fortress Press, 1971).
5 *Sharing One Hope? The Church of England and Christian Jewish Relations* (Church House Publishing, 2001).
6 Hastings, op. cit.
7 Walsh, Michael, *Dictionary of Christian Biography* (Continuum, 2001).
8 Hastings, Adrian, *The Construction of Nationhood, Ethnicity, Religion and Nationalism* (Cambridge University Press, 1997).
9 Madsen, Deborah L., *American Exceptionalism* (Edinburgh University Press, 1998).
10 Bercovitch, Sacvan, *The Puritan Origins of the American Self* (Yale University Press, 1975).
11 Colley, Linda, *Britons, Forging the Nations, 1707–1837* (Yale University Press, 1992).
12 Duffy, Eamon, *The Stripping of the Altars, Traditional Religion in England 1400–1580* (Yale University Press, 1992).
13 Jones, Edwin, *The English Nation, the Great Myth* (Sutton Publishing, 1998).
14 Davies, Norman, *The Isles* (Macmillan, 1999).
15 Jones, op. cit.
16 Phillips, Kevin, *The Cousins' Wars, Religion, Politics and the Triumph of Anglo-America* (Basic Books, 1999).
17 Jones, op. cit.
18 ibid.
19 Bradley, Ian, *Celtic Christianity, Making Myths and Chasing Dreams* (Edinburgh University Press, 1999).
20 Duffy, op. cit.

Chapter 5: Myths and More Myths

1 Romer, John, *Testament: The Bible and History* (Michael O'Mara Books, 1988).
2 ibid.
3 Modrzejewski, Joseph Mélèze, *The Jews of Egypt* (Princeton University Press, 1995).
4 ibid.

5 ibid.
6 Sacks, Jonathan, 'Beyond the Terror', *The Guardian*, 1 January 2002.

Chapter 6: War Crimes and Slavery

1 Harvey, Robert, *A Few Bloody Noses* (John Murray, 2002).
2 Bercovitch, Sacvan, *The Puritan Origins of the American Self* (Yale University Press, 1975).
3 Madsen, Deborah, *American Exceptionalism* (Edinburgh University Press, 1998).
4 Colley, Linda, *Britons, Forging the Nations, 1707–1837* (Yale University Press, 1992).
5 Morgan, Edmund S., *American Slavery American Freedom, the Ordeal of Colonial Virginia* (W. W. Norton, 1975).
6 ibid.
7 Woodson, Carter G., *The History of the Negro Church* (Associated Publishers, 1921).
8 Maxwell, John Francis, *Slavery and the Catholic Church* (Barry Rose Publishers, 1975).
9 Douglas, Ann, Introduction to Stowe, Harriet, Beecher, *Uncle Tom's Cabin* (Penguin, 1986).
10 Du Bois, W. E. B., *The Souls of Black Folk* (A. C. McClurg and Co., 1903).
11 Bercovitch, op. cit.

Chapter 7: Empire, Mission and War

1 Tuchman, Barbara, *Bible and Sword* (New York University Press, 1956).
2 Edwards, David, *Christian England* vol. 3 (Collins, 1984).
3 Quoted in Pakenham, Thomas, *The Scramble for Africa* (Abacus, 1991).
4 ibid.
5 Edwards, op cit.
6 Draper, Alfred, *The Amritsar Massacre, Twilight of the Raj* (Ashford Buchan and Enright, 1981).
7 Tuchman, op. cit.
8 ibid.
9 Fromkin, David, *A Peace to End All Peace* (Phoenix Press, 1989).
10 Tuchman, op. cit.
11 Wilkinson, Alan, *The Church of England and the First World War* (SCM Press, 1978).
12 ibid.
13 ibid.
14 ibid.

15 *Guardian*, 10 June 1915.
16 Foakes-Jackson, F. J. (ed.), *The Faith and the War* (1916).
17 Fussell, Paul, *The Great War in Modern Memory* (Oxford University Press, 1975).
18 Gibbs, Philip, *Now It Can Be Told* (New York, 1920).
19 Fussell, op. cit.
20 ibid.
21 '*Dulce et decorum est...*': Owen's own translation of this line from Horace's *Odes (III)* reads 'It is sweet, and meet, to die for one's country'.
22 Wilkinson, op. cit.

Chapter 8: Sex and Savages

1 Colley, Linda, *Britons, Forging the Nations, 1707–1837* (Yale University Press, 1992).
2 Calvocoressi, Peter, *Who's Who in the Bible* (Penguin Dictionaries, 1987).
3 Brown, Dee, *Bury My Heart at Wounded Knee* (Vintage, 1970).
4 Horsman, Reginald, *Expansion and American Indian Policy (1783–1812)* (University of Oklahoma Press, 1967).
5 Harvey, Robert, *A Few Bloody Noses* (John Murray, 2001).
6 Horsman, op. cit.
7 ibid.
8 ibid.
9 Schama, Simon, *Landscape and Memory* (Harper Collins, 1995).
10 ibid.

Chapter 9: The Chosen Meet the Modern

1 Phillips, Kevin, *The Cousins' Wars, Religion, Politics and the Triumph of Anglo-America* (Basic Books, 1999).
2 See chapter seven.
3 Du Bois, W. E. B., *The Souls of Black Folk* (A. C. McClurg and Co., 1903).
4 Bradford, Sarah, *Harriet, The Moses of Her People* (1869).
5 Miller, Keith D., *The Voice of Deliverance* (University of Georgia Press, 1992).
6 ibid.
7 ibid.
8 Discussed in chapter one.
9 Discussed in chapter four.
10 Miller, op. cit.

11 Philpot, Terry (ed.), *Political Correctness and Social Work* (IEA, 1999).
12 *The Observer*, 10 September 2000.
13 Barnett, Correlli, *The Verdict of Peace* (Macmillan, 2001).
14 ibid.
15 Horne, Alistair, *Macmillan 1957–1986* (Macmillan, 1989).
16 ibid.
17 Knight, Margaret, *Morals Without Religion and Other Essays* (Dennis Dobson, 1955).
18 Larkin, Philip, *Collected Poems* (Faber and Faber, 1988).
19 For a fuller discussion of Deism see chapter one.

Chapter 10: Wider Still and Wider

1 Words by A. C. Benson, set to music by Sir Edward Elgar.
2 Desmond, Adrian, *Huxley, the Devil's Disciple* (Michael Joseph, 1994).
3 Correlli, Barnett, *The Audit of War* (Macmillan, 1986).
4 Wilkinson, Alan, *The Church of England and the First World War* (SCM Press, 1978). Also see chapter seven.
5 In his inaugural address quoted more fully in chapter one.

Bibliography

Anderson, Benedict, *Imagined Communities: Reflections on the Origin and Spread of Nationalism* (Verso, 1991)

Bagehot, Walter (1826–77), *The English Constitution*

Barnett, Correlli, *The Audit of War* (Macmillan, 1986)

Barnett, Correlli, *The Verdict of Peace* (Macmillan, 2001)

Barr, James, *Fundamentalism* (SCM Press, 1977)

Baylin, Bernard, *The Ideological Origins of the American Revolution* (Harvard University Press, 1967)

Bence-Jones, Mark, *The Catholic Families* (Constable, 1992)

Bercovitch, Sacvan, *The Puritan Origins of the American Self* (Yale University Press, 1975)

Bradford, Sarah, *Harriet, The Moses of Her People* (1869)

Bradley, Ian, *Celtic Christianity, Making Myths and Chasing Dreams* (Edinburgh University Press, 1999)

Brown, Dee, *Bury My heart at Wounded Knee* (Vintage, 1970)

Calvocoressi, Peter, *Who's Who in the Bible* (Penguin Dictionaries, 1987)

Churchill, Winston, *The Speeches* (Penguin, 1989)

Clark, Jonathan C. D., *The Language of Liberty 1660–1832; Political Discourse and Social Dynamics in the Anglo-American World* (Cambridge University Press, 1994)

Colley, Linda, *Britons, Forging the Nations, 1707–1837* (Yale University Press, 1992)

Cross, F. L. and Livingstone, E. A. (eds), *Oxford Dictionary of the Christian Church* (Oxford University Press, 1997)

Davie, Grace, *Religion in Britain since 1945, Believing Without Belonging* (Blackwell, 1994)

Davies, Norman, *The Isles* (Macmillan, 1999)

de Tocqueville, Alexis, *Democracy in America* (Mentor, 1956)

Desmond, Adrian, *Huxley, the Devil's Disciple* (Michael Joseph, 1994)

Draper, Alfred, *The Amritsar Massacre, Twilight of the Raj* (Ashford Buchan and Enright, 1981)

Du Bois, W. E. B., *The Souls of Black Folk* (A. C. McClurg and Co, 1903)

Duffy, Eamon, *The Stripping of the Altars, Traditional Religion in England 1400–1580* (Yale University Press, 1992)

Edwards, David, *Christian England* vol. 3 (Collins, 1984)

Edwards, Jonathan, *Sinners in the Hands of an Angry God* (US Library of Congress)

Eliot, T. S., *The Idea of a Christian Society and Other Writing* (Faber and Faber, 1982)

Ellis, Joseph J., *Founding Brothers, The Revolutionary Generation* (Alfred A. Knopf, 2001)

Englander, David (ed.), *Britain and America, Studies in Comparative History* (Yale University Press, 1997)

Foakes-Jackson, F. J. (ed.), *The Faith and The War* (1916)

Foster, R. F., *The Irish Story, Telling Tales and Making It Up in Ireland* (Allen Lane, 2001)

Foxe (or Fox), John, *Book of Martyrs, Actes and Monuments of these Latter and Perillous Dayes* (1563)

Fromkin, David, *A Peace to End All Peace* (Phoenix Press, 1989)

Fussell, Paul, *The Great War in Modern Memory* (Oxford University Press, 1975)

Gibbs, Philip, *Now It Can Be Told* (New York, 1920)

Harvey, Robert, *A Few Bloody Noses* (John Murray, 2001)

Hastings, Adrian, *The Construction of Nationhood, Ethnicity, Religion and Nationalism* (Cambridge University Press, 1997)

Hastings, Adrian (ed.), *Oxford Companion to Christian Thought* (Oxford University Press, 2000)

Hill, Bridget, *The Republican Virago, The Life and Times of Catharine Macaulay, Historian* (Clarendon Press, 1992)

Hill, Christopher, *The English Bible and the Seventeenth Century Revolution* (Allen Lane, 1993)

Hill, Christopher, *God's Englishman, Oliver Cromwell and the English Revolution* (Weidenfeld and Nicolson, 1970)

Hodgson, Peter C., *Theology in the Fiction of George Eliot* (SCM Press, 2001)

Hooker, Roger and Sargant, John (eds), *Belonging to Britain, Christian Perspectives on a Plural Society* (CCBI Publications, 1991)

Horne, Alistair, *Macmillan 1957–1986* (Macmillan, 1989)

Horsman, Reginald, *Expansion and American Indian Policy (1783–1812)* (University of Oklahoma Press, 1967)

Jacobs, Louis, *The Jewish Religion, a Companion* (Oxford University Press, 1995)

Jones, Edwin, *The English Nation, the Great Myth* (Sutton Publishing, 1998)

Kantorowicz, Ernst, *The King's Two Bodies: A Study in Mediaeval Political Theology* (Princeton, 1957)

Kent, John, *William Temple* (Cambridge University Press, 1992)

Knight, Margaret, *Morals Without Religion and Other Essays* (Dennis Dobson, 1955)

Koterski, Joseph, SJ, 'How Jefferson Honored Religion', *Crisis*, vol. 19 no. 3, March 2001

Larkin, Philip, *Collected Poems* (Faber and Faber, 1988)

Levine, M. L. and Rachlis, E. (eds), *The Complete Book of Bible Quotations* (Robert Hale, 1986)

Lipset, Seymour Martin, *American Exceptionalism, a Double-edged Sword* (W. W. Norton and Co., 1996)

Longley, Clifford, *The Worlock Archive* (Geoffrey Chapman, 2000)

Madsen, Deborah L., *American Exceptionalism* (Edinburgh University Press, 1998)

Maier, Pauline, *American Scripture, How America Declared its Independence from Britain* (Pimlico, 1997)

Maxwell, John Francis, *Slavery and the Catholic Church* (Barry Rose Publishers, 1975)

McCullough, David, *John Adams* (Simon and Schuster, 2001)

Miller, Keith D., *The Voice of Deliverance* (University of Georgia Press, 1992)

Modrzejewski, Joseph Mélèze, *The Jews of Egypt* (Princeton University Press, 1995)

Morgan, Edmund S., *American Slavery American Freedom, The Ordeal of Colonial Virginia* (W. W. Norton, 1975)

Osmond, Rosalie, *Changing Perspectives, Christian Culture and Morals in England Today* (Darton, Longman and Todd, 1993)

Pakenham, Thomas, *The Scramble for Africa* (Abacus, 1991)

Paxman, Jeremy, *The English, a Portrait of a People* (Penguin, 1998)

Peterson, Merrill D., *Adams and Jefferson, a Revolutionary Dialogue* (Oxford University Press, 1976)

Phillips, Kevin, *The Cousins' Wars, Religion, Politics and the Triumph of Anglo-America* (Basic Books, 1999)

Philpot, Terry (ed.), *Political Correctness and Social Work* (IEA, 1999)

Randall, Willard Sterne, *Jefferson, a Life* (William Holt and Co., 1993)

Rahner, Karl (ed.), *Encyclopaedia of Theology* (Burns and Oates, 1975)

Raphael, Ray, *The American Revolution, a People's History* (Profile Books, 2001)

Richard, Carl J., *The Founders and the Classics, Greece, Rome and the American Enlightenment* (Harvard University Press, 1994)

Rittner, Carol, Smith, Stephen, and Steinfeldt, Irena, *The Holocaust and the Christian World* (Kuperard, 2000)

Romer, John, *Testament: The Bible and History* (Michael O'Mara Books, 1988)

Roper, William, *The Life of Sir Thomas More* (1626)
Schama, Simon, *Landscape and Memory* (HarperCollins, 1995)
Scruton, Roger, *England, an Elegy* (Chatto and Windus, 2000)
Shashar, Michael, *Lord Jakobovits in Conversation* (Vallentine Mitchell, 2000)
Stowe, Harriet Beecher, *Uncle Tom's Cabin* (Penguin, 1986)
Temple, William, *Citizen and Churchman* (Eyre and Spottiswood, 1941)
Tuchman, Barbara, *Bible and Sword* (New York University Press, 1956)
Weber, Max, *On Methodology of Social Sciences* (The Free Press, 1949)
Weber, Max, *The Protestant Ethic and the Spirit of Capitalism* (1930)
White, Michael, *Isaac Newton, The Last Sorcerer* (Fourth Estate, 1998)
Wilkinson, Alan, *Christian Socialism, from Scott Holland to Tony Blair* (SCM Press, 1998)
Wilkinson, Alan, *The Church of England and the First World War* (SCM Press, 1978).
Woodson, Carter G., *The History of the Negro Church* (The Associated Publishers, 1921)

Believing in the Church, Doctrine Commission of the Church of England (SPCK, 1981)
The Book of Common Prayer (Everyman's Library, 1999)
Catholic Encyclopaedia (Robert Appleton Company, 1908)
The Jerusalem Bible (Darton, Longman and Todd, 1966)
Luther's Works (Fortress Press, 1971)
Missal in Latin and English (Burns, Oates and Washbourne, 1958)
New Bible Commentary Revised (InterVarsity Press, 1970)
The Revised English Bible (Oxford University Press, 1989)
Sharing One Hope? The Church of England and Christian Jewish Relations (Church House Publishing, 2001)

Index